P9-DEV-652

The College Board

Guide to 150 Popular College Majors

The College Board

Guide to 150 Popular College Majors

College Entrance Examination Board

New York

Copies of this book may be ordered from College Board Publications, Two College Way, Forrester Center, WV 25438, or through the College Board Online Store at www.collegeboard.org. The price is $16.

Editorial inquires concerning this book should be directed to Guidance Publishing, The College Board, 45 Columbus Avenue, New York, New York 10023-6992.

Copyright © 1992 by College Entrance Examiation Board. All rights reserved.

The College Board and the acorn logo are registered trademarks of the College Entrance Examination Board.

In all of its book publishing activities the College Board endeavors to present the works of authors who are well qualified to write with authority on the subject at hand, and to present accurate and timely information. However, the opinions, interpretations, and conclusions of the authors are their own and do not necessarily represent those of the College Board; nothing contained herin should be assumed to represent a official position of the College Board, or any of its members.

Library of Congress Catalog Number: 92-073632

ISBN: 0-87447-400-0

Printed in the United States of America

9 8 7 6 5

Contents

❏ **Biological and Life Sciences** **85**

❏ **Business and Management** **109**

❏ Communications   133

❏ Computer and Information Sciences   149

❏ Education   157

❏ Engineering   175

❏ Health Sciences and Services   197

❏ Home Economics   221

❏ Humanities   241

❏ Interdisciplinary, Area, and Ethnic Studies 275

❏ Mathematics 299

❏ Physical Sciences 309

❏ ## Social and Behavioral Sciences 325

❏ ## Theology 349

Preface

This book responds to a pressing need identified by students, counselors, and parents for a readable, reliable volume that informs high school students and their parents about the rich array of undergraduate majors to be found in the country's colleges and universities. The high school student, often asked to select a tentative college major even before knowing what the choices are, can read here broad yet detailed descriptions of 151 of the most widely offered baccalaureate-level majors. Prepared by experienced college professors to reflect the common features of the majors as they are taught at institutions across the country, the descriptions will encourage students to explore their options in relation to their own skills and inclinations well before they declare a major. The contributors, teachers all, approached the writing assignment with a seriousness corresponding to the importance of its purpose—to reveal to students accurately and clearly the academic opportunities in higher education. They also approached it with the enthusiasm and insights that come with in-depth knowledge and enjoyment of their field.

The College Majors Project, from which this book grew, owes its shape and success in part to the thoughtful participation of its faculty advisory committee, who not only shared their knowledge and wisdom with me but wrote the model descriptions that so tellingly guided the work of all subsequent contributors. The committee is listed separately on a following page. To them I extend my heartfelt thanks for their fine work, and, not least, good humored ways. My thanks too to editorial consultant Harlan Hanson for his careful scrutiny of the descriptions and insightful comments. All aided me in the development of the book and by so doing helped lay a firm foundation for the planned electronic dissemination of the information at the next stage in the College Majors Project.

Dozens of scholarly societies and professional associations were generous with information and advice. In recommending suitably qualified professors to write the individual descriptions that make up the body of the book, they assured it an authority it would not otherwise have. Thanks are due especially to these professors, whose names appear below, for drawing with such enthusiasm and care on their professional experience to describe majors in their fields for the untold thousands of students who, it is hoped, will find guidance in this book.

Sue Wetzel Gardner
Director, College Majors Project

Contributors

Lynne S. Abel
Associate Dean for Undergraduate
  Education
College of Arts and Sciences
Cornell University

Frank Acito
Professor and Chairperson of
  Marketing
School of Business
Indiana University

Jan Allen
Associate Professor
Department of Child and Family
  Studies
University of Tennessee, Knoxville

Lawrence Allen
Chairman, Department of Parks,
  Recreation and Tourism
  Management
Clemson University

Norma M. Allewell
Professor, Department of Molecular
  Biology and Biochemistry
Wesleyan University

Dan Anderson
Chairman, Department of Insurance
  and Risk Management
University of Wisconsin

Walter Askin
Professor of Art
California State University,
  Los Angeles

Susan Read Baker
Professor, Department of Romance
  Languages and Literatures
University of Florida

C. Peter Bankart
Psychology Department
Wabash College

William E. Barstow
Chairman, Botany Department
University of Georgia

Michael J. Bednar
Associate Dean
School of Architecture
University of Virginia

Sylvia Ardyn Boone
Associate Professor,
  History of Art
Yale University

Lilly Ann Boruszkowski
Department of Cinema and
  Photography
Southern Illinois University

Adam T. Bourgoyne, Jr.
Professor, Petroleum Engineering
  Department
Louisiana State University

Thomas A. Bowers
Associate Dean
School of Journalism and Mass
  Communication
University of North Carolina at
  Chapel Hill

Abraham J. Briloff
Emanuel Saxe Distinguished
  Professor of Accountancy
Baruch College

R. F. Brodsky
Adjunct Professor of Aerospace
  Engineering
University of Southern California

Austin E. Brooks
Professor, Department of Biology
Wabash College

Stephen F. Brown
Department of Theology
Boston College

Judy K. Brun
Professor and Chair
Department of Family and
  Consumer Sciences Education
Iowa State University of Science
  and Technology

Richard W. Bulliet
Middle East Institute
Columbia University

Bonnie Bullough
Professor of Nursing
School of Nursing
State University of New York
  University at Buffalo

Jon Butler
Chairman, American Studies
    Program
Yale University

Heidi Byrnes
Professor of German
Georgetown University

J. Thomas Cain
Associate Professor, Department
    of Electrical Engineering
University of Pittsburgh

Neil G. Carn
Professor, Department of Real
    Estate
Georgia State University

Wayne F. Cascio
Professor of Management
Graduate School of Business
    Administration
University of Colorado at Denver

James Chelius
Chair, Industrial Relations and
    Human Resources Department
Rutgers University

Irma H. Collins
Professor of Music
Murray State University

A. Stephen Dahms
Director, Molecular Biology
    Institute
San Diego State University and
    California State University
    Biotechnology Program

Jane Z. Daniels
Director of Counseling
Department of Freshman
    Engineering
Purdue University

Henry N. Deneault
Associate Vice President for
    Academic Affairs
Babson College

Daniel E. Diamond
Dean, The Undergraduate College
New York University Stern School
    of Business

Edwin Dickey
College of Education
University of South Carolina

David Dilcher
Department of Natural Science
Florida Museum of Natural
    History

John C. Doolittle
Director of Journalism Programs
American University

Wayne Dumas
Department of Curriculum and
    Instruction
University of Missouri

Bruce Duncan
Professor of German
Dartmouth College

Geraldene Felton
Dean, College of Nursing
University of Iowa

John A. Ferguson
Eliot and Klara Stockdal Johnson
    Professor of Organ and Church
    Music
St. Olaf College

Leroy S. Fletcher
Professor, Mechanical
    Engineering Department
Texas A&M University

Sally L. Fortenberry
Professor, Department of Design
    and Fashion
Texas Christian University

Danny T. Foster
Program Director, Athletic
    Training
University of Iowa

Sally Francis
Professor and Head
Department of Apparel, Interiors,
    Housing, and Merchandising
Oregon State University

Henry C. Fung
Professor, Microbiology
    Department
California State University, Long
    Beach

John S. Gibson
Director, International Relations
    Program
Tufts University

Graham P. Glass
Professor of Chemistry
Rice University

John T. Gorgone
Professor, Computer Information
    Systems Department
Bentley College

L. A. Peter Gosling
Department of Anthropology
University of Michigan

Richard E. Grace
Vice President for Student
    Services
Purdue University

Robert E. Green
Director of Undergraduate
    Programs
School of Management
Georgia Institute of Technology

David B. Greene
Director, Arts Studies Program
College of Humanities and Social
    Sciences
North Carolina State University

Timothy J. Greene
Head, Industrial Engineering and
    Management
Oklahoma State University

Richard E. Greenleaf
Center for Latin American Studies
Tulane University

Bruce E. Gronbeck
Professor, Communication
    Studies Department
University of Iowa

George J. Hagerty
Associate Professor of Political
    Science
Stonehill College

Dan F. Hahn
Department of Communications,
    Art and Sciences
Queens College

Rose C. Hamm
Director of the Honors
    Program
Associate Professor of
    Mathematics
College of Charleston

T. E. Hartung
Associate Vice Chancellor
Institute of Agriculture and
    Natural Resources
University of Nebraska-Lincoln

Willis D. Hawley
Director, Center for Education
    and Human Development
    Policy
Vanderbilt University

Elizabeth R. Hayes
Professor of Dance Emerita
University of Utah

Rader Hayes
Department of Consumer
    Sciences
University of Wisconsin, Madison

Edward A. Hiler
Deputy Chancellor for Academic
    and Research Programs
Texas A&M University System

A. David Hill
Department of Geography
University of Colorado

David H. Hirth
Professor, School of Natural
  Resources
University of Vermont

W. Robert Houston
Associate Dean for Academic
  Affairs
College of Education
University of Houston

John R. Jones
Professor of Limnology, School of
  Natural Resources
University of Missouri-
  Columbia

Rhett S. Jones
Professor of History and
  Afro-American Studies
Brown University

Steven E. Jungst
Professor and Chairman
Department of Forestry
Iowa State University of Science
  and Technology

Larry A. Kantner
Professor of Art and Education
University of Missouri-Columbia

Ann-Mary Kapusta
Associate Dean, School of
  Business Administration
Georgetown University

John Kenelly
Department of Mathematics
Clemson University

Lorrin Kennamer
Millikan Centennial Professor
Department of Curriculum and
  Instruction
University of Texas at Austin

W. E. Kennick
Professor of Philosophy
Amherst College

Wendy Kerschbaum
Director of Dental Hygiene
School of Dentistry
University of Michigan

Martha Kingsbury
Professor of Art History
University of Washington

James G. Knudsen
Professor Emeritus
Department of Chemical
  Engineering
Oregon State University

Nickolas Kurtaneck
Professor of Theology and
  Biblical Studies
Biola University and Talbot
  School of Theology

Deborah R. Labovitz
Professor and Chair
Department of Occupational
  Therapy
New York University

Anthony LaMagra
Director of Music
Manhattanville College

Leanne K. Lamke
Associate Professor
Department of Family and Child
  Development
Auburn University

Wayne P. Lammers
Assistant Professor of Japanese
Lewis and Clark College

D. Terence Langendoen
Department of Linguistics
University of Arizona

Ken Larner
C. H. Green Professor of
  Exploration Geophysics
Colorado School of Mines

Donald W. Larson
Professor, Department of
  Agricultural Economics and
  Rural Sociology
Ohio State University

Kenneth L. Larson
Professor of Agronomy
Iowa State University of Science
  and Technology

Eleanor V. Laudicina
Professor of Public
  Administration
Department of Public
  Administration
Kean College of New Jersey

Richard T. Lee
Professor of Philosophy
Trinity College

Howard LeVant
Associate Professor of Applied
  Photography
Rochester Institute of
  Technology

Alan Lightman
Professor of Science and
  Writing
Massachusetts Institute of
  Technology

Charles E. Lindley (deceased)
Dean Emeritus
College of Agriculture and Home
  Economics
Mississippi State University

Peter L. Lutz
McGinty Eminent Scholar Chair
  in Marine Biology
Florida Atlantic University

John T. Lyle
Professor, Department of
  Landscape Architecture
California State Polytechnic
  University, Pomona

Stuart Y. McDougal
Professor, Program in
  Comparative Literature
University of Michigan

John McWilliams
Chairman
Department of American Literature
Middlebury College

Michael Marlais
Associate Professor
Department of Art
Colby College

Myron Marty
Dean, College of Arts and
  Sciences
Drake University

Charles J. Metelka
Director, Hospitality and Tourism
  Graduate Program
University of Wisconsin-Stout

Donald E. Mikkola
Department of Metallurgical and
  Materials Engineering
Michigan Technological
  University

Murray H. Milford
Associate Head for Academic
  Programs
Department of Soil and Crop
  Sciences
Texas A&M University

Philip L. Miller
Professor, School of Computer
  Science
Carnegie Mellon University

Dean Mills
Dean, School of Journalism
University of Missouri-Columbia

Watson E. Mills
Professor of New Testament
  Language and Literature
Mercer University

Margaret Morton
School of Art
Cooper Union

Caryn McTighe Musil
Senior Fellow
Association of American Colleges

James S. Naas
Speech Pathologist
Speech and Hearing Clinic
Brescia College

Paul Niebanck
Professor of Environmental
    Ethics and Planning
University of California at Santa
    Cruz

Arthur R. M. Nowell
Director, School of Oceanography
University of Washington

Carol E. Osborn
Assistant Professor
Medical Record Administration
    Division
Ohio State University

Richard D. Osborne
Chair, Graduate Music Studies
Butler University

R. N. Ottaway
Professor of Management
Fairleigh Dickinson University

Michael Padilla
Professor, Department of Science
    Education
University of Georgia

Hans C. Palmer
Professor of Economics
Pomona College

Eric Pankey
Director of The Writer's Program
Washington University

B. C. Pass
Professor and Chairman
Department of Entomology
University of Kentucky

David A. Peterson
Director, School of Gerontology
University of Southern California

Martha W. Pickett
Professor, Department of Nuclear
    Medicine Technology
University of Arkansas for
    Medical Sciences

Walter R. Pirie
Department of Statistics
Virginia Polytechnic Institute
    and State University

Robert E. Proctor
Professor of Italian
Connecticut College

Penny A. Ralston
Dean, College of Human
    Sciences
Florida State University

Benjamin Ravid
Jennie and Mayer Weisman
    Professor of Jewish History
Brandeis University

Sharon Redick
Chairperson, Home Economics
    Education
College of Human Ecology
Ohio State University

Kenneth W. Reisch
Professor of Horticulture and
    Associate Dean Emeritus
College of Agriculture
Ohio State University

Jonathan Reiskind
Associate Professor of
    Zoology
University of Florida

Judith E. Rink
Professor, Department of
    Physical Education
University of South Carolina

Gustav W. Rohrs
Chairman, Interior Design
    Department
Pratt Institute

Joseph P. Scartelli
Dean, College of Visual and
    Performing Arts
Radford University

Margaret C. Schmidt
Director, Education Service,
    Hospital Laboratories
Duke University Medical
    Center

John W. Seavey
Associate Professor
Department of Health
    Management and Policy
University of New Hampshire

Helen Segall
Chairperson, Department of
    Russian
Dickinson College

Darlene K. Sekerak
Director, Division of Physical
    Therapy
University of North Carolina at
    Chapel Hill

John J. Siegfried
Professor of Economics
Vanderbilt University

Jan Silverman
Associate Professor
Department of Theater
Temple University

Robert C. Small, Jr.
Dean, College of Education and
    Human Development
Radford University

J. Steven Smith
Associate Professor
Department of Criminal Justice
    and Criminology
Ball State University

Joseph Thomas Snow
Department of Romance and
    Classical Languages
Michigan State University

Marion G. Sobol
Professor, Management
    Information Sciences
Cox School of Business
Southern Methodist University

Bernard Spodek
Professor, College of
    Education
University of Illinois at Urbana-
    Champaign

John Spores
Department of Social Work
University of Montana

George R. Spratto
Associate Dean for Professional
    Programs
School of Pharmacy and
    Pharmacal Sciences
Purdue University

Arnold A. Strassenburg
Professor of Physics
State University of New York at
    Stony Brook

Anne Sweaney
Associate Professor
Department of Housing and
    Consumer Economics
University of Georgia

James G. Taaffe
Provost and Academic Vice
    President
University of Alabama

Charles R. Tolbert
Associate Professor
Astronomy Department
University of Virginia

Paul E. Torgersen
Professor, College of
    Engineering
Virginia Polytechnic Institute and
    State University

Gary L. Trennepohl
Pat and Bookman Peters
    Professor of Finance
Texas A&M University

Gregory J. Tripoli
Department of Meteorology
University of Wisconsin

Judy VanSlyke Turk
Dean, College of Journalism and
    Mass Communications
University of South Carolina

David A. VanHorn
Department of Civil
    Engineering
Lehigh University

Theodore C. Wagenaar
Department of Sociology
Miami University

John C. Wahlke
Professor Emeritus of Political
    Science
University of Arizona

J. Robert Warmbrod
Presidential Professor
Department of Agricultural
    Education
Ohio State University

Susan F. Weis
Professor of Home Economics
    Education
Pennsylvania State University

Kathleen White
Professor of Psychology
Boston University

Dan Whitney
Professor and Chair,
    Department of Anthropology
San Diego State University

James B. Wiggins
Professor and Chair
Department of Religion
Syracuse University

Harlan Wilson
Director, Environmental
    Studies Program
Oberlin College

Allen Winold
Professor of Music
Indiana University

Reinhard A. Wobus
Professor of Geology
Williams College

Thomas Wright
Professor, Department of Industry
    and Technology
Ball State University

Gene S. Yeager
Center for Latin American
    Studies
Tulane University

John Young
Distinguished University
    Professor Emeritus
Seton Hall University

Stuart H. Zweben
Associate Professor
Department of Computer and
    Information Sciences
Ohio State University

College Majors Project Committee

Lynne S. Abel
Associate Dean for Undergraduate
    Education
College of Arts and Sciences
Cornell University

Henry Deneault
Associate Vice President for
    Academic Affairs
Babson College

Richard E. Grace
Vice President for Student
    Services
Purdue University

David B. Greene
Director, Art Studies Program
College of Humanities and Social
    Sciences
North Carolina State University

Rose C. Hamm
Director of the Honors Program
Associate Professor of
    Mathematics
College of Charleston

Lorrin Kennamer
Millikan Centennial Professor
Department of Curriculum and
    Instruction
University of Texas at Austin

James G. Taaffe
Provost and Academic Vice
    President
University of Alabama

Introduction

What is a major?

A major is the subject you will study in greatest depth in college. You will take from one-quarter to two-thirds of your courses in that subject. At most colleges and universities, students must complete a required number of courses in their major in order to earn a bachelor of arts (B.A.) or a bachelor of science (B.S.) degree. There are hundreds of majors for you to choose from—in traditional disciplines such as physics or history, in new areas such as environmental studies or Asian studies, in career fields such as physical therapy and criminal justice. Your choices are wide; exploring them to decide what interests you most can be an exciting experience.

Keep two things in mind about the major you will eventually choose:

- It will give you a frame of reference that will help you make sense of the world.
- It will be only part of your undergraduate studies.

Let's take a look at how a major fits into the four years of undergraduate study.

Undergraduate study

No matter what college you attend, or what major you choose, you will take 25 to 50 percent of your courses in liberal arts subjects. This general education is intended to make you a well-rounded individual able to think, reason, reach conclusions based on relevant data, and communicate those conclusions effectively to others.

What are the liberal arts? Originally, the liberal arts were grammar, rhetoric, logic, arithmetic, music, geometry and astronomy—the subjects studied at medieval universities. Now, the term refers to courses in the humanities (literature, history of the arts, and philosophy), history, foreign languages, social sciences, mathematics, and natural sciences. Studying these disciplines helps you develop general knowledge and reasoning ability, rather than specific skills.

The social sciences—anthropology, psychology, economics, government, linguistics, sociology—examine human nature and society. The natural sciences—astronomy, biology, chemistry, geology, physics—measure and observe natural phenomena. The arts—art, dance, film, music, theater—explore the various forms people use to express their observations, values, and feelings. By taking courses in disciplines within the liberal arts, students learn about diverse ways of thinking about and understanding the world.

Most colleges expect you to take liberal arts requirements in your freshman and sophomore years. The experience lets you test interests you think you may have. It also gives you a chance to discover, develop, and explore new interests. It gives you time to become sure about the field you want to major in, or to change your mind!

How and when to decide on a major

More than half of all college freshmen are "undecided" about their major. And that's OK because college is designed to give you time to explore before you settle on a major. But, there are some reasons to *begin* to think about a major now, while you're in high school, even if you don't make a decision. Let's look at some strategies for thinking about this decision.

How to decide

There are several kinds of decisions we have to make in the course of our lives. A few have a long-lasting impact, for example, whether or whom to marry, whether or when to have children, whether to work for an organization or independently, which political and social values are most significant to us, what rewards are most important in our careers. No doubt you can add to this list.

Then, there are the decisions we make every day. Some are trivial (what should I wear?). Some seem trivial when we make them (should I stay up all night to write this paper?) but add up to something significant over time.

Choosing a major falls into a third category of decisions: It is important enough to take seriously, but it is not irrevocable and does not determine your way of living. It is a choice you can make tentatively and test several times over. You may be able to change your major as late as your senior year and still graduate on schedule. You may decide to choose two majors (a double major). Eventually, you will have to make a choice and fulfill its requirements, but that won't necessarily lock you out of an unrelated graduate program or career in the future.

So, why worry about this choice at all? Because you will be more fulfilled (and consequently better educated) studying a subject that truly engages you, a subject in which you feel something important is at stake—either to you or to the world. And, you want to choose a major in which you can succeed.

Your major will not define you, but choosing one that interests and challenges you will lead to rewarding study. Some students know instinctively what major suits them. Others choose a particular field because of one inspiring professor, who opens their eyes to the excitement of that major. But if you are like most students, you may have to do some careful thinking about yourself to determine what will suit you. Ask yourself:

> What are my interests?
> What are my hobbies?
> What are my favorite high school courses? Which ones do I excel at?
> What do I see myself doing in a future career?
> What do I hate doing?
> What do I most enjoy doing?
> What are my strengths? weaknesses?
> What are my intellectual interests?

Answers to these questions will probably lead to other, harder questions. Does your enjoyment of English classes point to a major in English, or perhaps one in creative writing, American literature, or linguistics? How can you translate an interest in racial or other social problems into a major? If you are good at biology, which biology major should you explore? The self-exploration needed to answer these questions may well be one of the more important parts of your college education. Don't be surprised if you continue refining your answers to these questions—you will discover a lot about yourself during your college years!

When to decide

It's perfectly all right to be undecided about your major when you start college. Most four-year colleges do not require students to formally declare (choose) a major until the end of their sophomore or beginning of their junior year. It won't even be a disaster if you find in your senior year that you should have studied something else. You may be able to change your major and still graduate on time, or after an additional semester or year of course work.

The undergraduate curriculum gives you time to take elective courses in whatever interests you, in addition to required courses. You can use electives to sample various majors. You can also talk to students in various majors and to professors to find out more about the course work of their subjects. You will probably take courses you never knew existed, which may point you in new and rewarding directions.

More good news: You won't have to make all these decisions by yourself. Early in your freshman year, you will be assigned an academic adviser. One of the adviser's chief responsibilities is to help you choose courses that will fulfill college graduation requirements and move you toward your personal goal. If you change your mind, the adviser can recommend courses that will help you achieve your new goal. To get advice that answers your needs, it is important to be honest, open, and clear about your goals with your adviser.

It may take you several years to decide on a major, so the earlier you start thinking about the key elements in that decision, the better prepared you will be. Browsing through this book is a good first step!

The relation of major to choice of college

No college, not even the largest university, offers every major; some offer relatively few. Obviously, you want to attend a college that has some of the majors you are considering. You can keep many options open by attending a university or college that offers a wide range of majors.

Some large universities are divided into "colleges" and students apply for admission to a specific college—of architecture, engineering, liberal arts, business. If you are applying to an institution with separate admissions requirements for different colleges, you will need to decide on your major by the time you apply. If you change your mind later, it may be difficult to transfer from one college to another, but it is often possible.

When you are choosing colleges, explore the strengths of the specific majors that interest you *as well as* the overall quality of the school. Read the college catalogs to see how many courses are offered in the major you want. Do the courses sound interesting? Varied? How often are they offered? Who teaches them? When visiting colleges, arrange to sit in on a class in a major that interests you.

The relation of major to future careers

At this point, you may or may not know what you want to do after you graduate. While many majors aren't directly linked with specific careers, they can certainly help you zero in on a future career choice.

Some majors are directly related to careers. The dental hygiene major prepares students to become dental hygienists. The same holds for architecture, civil engineering, physical therapy, nursing, accounting, and a number of other majors. These majors require students to take more courses in the major (gaining depth) and fewer general courses (breadth) than do majors in the liberal arts. Some of these majors prepare students for licensing exams at the end of college that enable graduates to practice the profession they have trained for.

Liberal arts majors, on the other hand, provide more general intellectual training not directly related to specific careers. That broad base of knowledge can be applied to such diverse fields as business, education, journalism, politics, public administration—anything really. To become an expert in a field, liberal arts majors can go on to a wide range of graduate schools.

Many colleges offer combined liberal arts and career majors. These majors often take five years to complete, but students emerge with a liberal arts degree *and* professional training in a field such as engineering, business, medicine, forestry, or other fields. (Colleges with these programs are listed in the *Index of Majors and Graduate Degrees*, published annually by the College Board.)

All areas of the work force need people who can think critically, communicate effectively, and continue to learn. Perhaps the best preparation for any career is to work hard at your chosen major, and to take challenging electives and liberal arts courses. The relationship between your college major and what you eventually choose as your life's work is much less direct than counselors, your parents, and you may think. Your character, personality, and how responsibly, creatively, enthusiastically, loyally, and critically you approach your work probably count as much as or more than your major in determining your future career path.

Prelaw, premed, and other preprofessional programs

For the most part, law, medical, dental, and business schools will accept students from any major. Professional programs do have requirements, but these requirements can be fulfilled by virtually any major.

For entrance into medical or dental school, students must complete five year-long science and math courses and English composition. At many colleges, premed students are assigned to a special adviser who can help them choose appropriate science courses. Law schools have no particular requirements. A challenging program of study in an area of great interest to you is excellent preparation for law school. Graduate business schools usually require five or six semester-long courses in basic economics, calculus, and statistics. Beyond that, business schools prefer a broad and challenging curriculum, with no one major preferred over another.

In general, the best preparation for professional school is rigorous courses in a liberal arts curriculum, with an emphasis on developing strong analytic skills.

What if I make a mistake?

Here are some interesting facts about a recent class of liberal arts and sciences graduates at a large university:

- 20 percent of the students who entered intending to major in a humanities subject switched their major

- 40 percent of the students who declared a social science major did not stay with it
- 45 percent of the students intending to major in science, math, or computer science chose a different major.

College is a place where you can change your mind.

If you sense you are on the wrong track with your chosen major, but are uncertain, consider completing a second major, or a minor. You take fewer subjects in your minor than in your major, but enough to demonstrate serious interest in the subject and considerable knowledge of it.

If you are majoring in a program that prepares you for a specific career and find that you dislike that major, consult your adviser as soon as possible. Your adviser should be able to help you change majors to avoid pursuing an undesirable career path.

If you enter college undecided about a major and then find that your college does not offer the specific major you want, consider transferring to a college that does. Since most colleges expect students to complete various liberal arts courses in their first two years, you may be able to transfer most or all of your credits to a new college in your sophomore or junior year.

Conclusion

No matter what your major, keep in mind that intellectual flexibility is the skill that enables you to work productively when the knowledge you have mastered is challenged or replaced by new ideas. Study within the major must hone the mind. It must provide opportunities for learning how to ask questions and to create and use sound evidence in clear arguments to answer those questions. It must help you understand how your chosen field contributes to the general knowledge and functioning of the world. And it should help you enjoy life more fully.

How to Use this Book

Purpose

This book is designed to help you explore the majors that interest you, to discover and learn something about ones you've never heard of, and to begin to zero in on what major might be best for you.

Contributors

The descriptions were written by professors teaching in the field. Their essays reflect *not* how the major is taught at a particular institution, but how it is taught at the many institutions, across the country, that offer it. Naturally, biology is taught somewhat differently at every college, depending upon the instructors' interests, laboratory facilities, even regional concerns (a college in the desert may offer a course on desert ecosystems). However, all biology programs have much in common. That's what's described here: the basic facts you need about these bachelor's degree programs.

Organization and approach

The 151 majors described in this book are grouped into 17 broad categories. You may want to skim the descriptions of several majors in the categories that interest you. The brief paragraph at the beginning of each description lets you get the flavor of a major quickly.

The introductions to the 17 categories provide overviews of each field and describe differences between the various majors—for example, how each business major differs from the others. You may enjoy reading some introductions simply as general background. After all, you will be taking courses in a wide range of subjects in college, and the information in the introductions may spur your interest in topics that you can pursue in elective courses.

If you haven't a *clue* what you want to study, read the brief description of a variety of majors. This smorgasbord of information may help you channel your thinking. You may discover that several social science majors intrigue you, or that engineering isn't what you thought it was.

The descriptions

Each description has nine parts. First you'll find a brief description of the major. This gives you the gist of what you learn in a field.

Interests, skills, and qualities associated with success in the major

Here you'll find brief lists of the interests, skills, academic strengths, and personal qualities that are associated with success in and satisfaction with each major. These are but an indication of a few qualities that might enable you to thrive in a major. Your strong interest in a particular major might be more important than any quality listed here in enabling you to succeed in the field.

Recommended high school preparation
The course units recommended here represent years of study in a four-year high school. These are recommendations only: your high school might not have some of the courses mentioned here. You'll discover that a well-rounded high school curriculum, with courses in language, science, math, and social studies, is important in every field. The term "precollege mathematics" refers to algebra, calculus, geometry, and trigonometry. Laboratory science refers to sciences (biology, chemistry, physics, earth science) that include labs. Two to four years of foreign language study is recommended for many majors: in general, you should take *one* foreign language for a minimum of two years rather than, for example, a year of French and a year of Spanish.

Typical courses in the major
This section lists some actual college courses you could take, and lets you see the range of topics covered in each major. Some of the words you'll see here may be unfamiliar, but don't worry. Once you're in college, you will quickly learn about concepts and topics you have never heard of before.

What the major is like
This tells you what you'll actually study in a major. The descriptions represent how majors are taught *in general*, not how they're taught at a particular institution. Differences in emphasis, requirements, and philosophies between different colleges are described so that you can better assess the curriculum at the colleges you are exploring. You will learn what degrees are awarded in each field (Bachelor of Science, Bachelor of Fine Arts) and what each degree represents. Alternative names for majors are mentioned here.

Specializations
It may be possible to specialize or concentrate in a certain area within a major: for example, creative writing majors may specialize in fiction writing. The specializations listed here are not available at all colleges.

Other majors to consider
This section lists majors related through subject matter or approach. Take the time to explore a variety of majors in order to find the one you can study happily. The majors in bold type are described in this book. (To find out which colleges offer the majors that interest you, consult the *Index of Majors and Graduate Degrees*. This annual publication of the College Board lists 580 majors and the colleges that offer them at the associate, bachelor's, and various graduate levels.)

Careers related to the major
This section may list actual jobs or career areas (business, journalism) that the major may lead to. In addition to finding out what your employment opportunities are after undergraduate study, you can also identify careers that are open to you after appropriate graduate or professional study.

Indexes

The Careers index lists approximately 150 jobs or careers, and some of the majors that prepare you for that career. Most majors described in this book can lead to a wide variety of careers. However, some majors provide a more direct path to particular careers than others.

Virtually every major described in this book can lead to the following:

Teaching (college or other levels)
Sales
Law, medicine, and other professions
Government work
Business

Therefore, the majors indexed under these headings are only those that often lead to these career areas.

The Related Majors index gives you an idea of the range of other majors that are related to a specific major listed in the index. You'll get a sense of the varied ways you can explore a particular interest through your college major.

Students Talk about Choosing a Major

DERRICK JONES

I am going to be president of the United States!

Like countless youngsters in grade school, I was convinced that my career path led only to the White House. I assumed that a college education was sufficient for the executive post. Later I discovered that becoming president was a little more involved than I had originally thought, yet getting the college education was still part of the plan.

My middle school and high school years were filled with activities, organizations, teams, and jobs. I viewed college as another job, so I tried to fill my resume as much as possible. It was not completely clear what I was going to do in college; I only thought about getting in.

I had a prelaw phase—I worked for attorneys for three years during high school and was convinced that the Supreme Court was at my fingertips. Later I went through a government phase, certain that political science was the only major for me. Working in the U.S. Senate as a page gave me a better understanding of the political world, but I still did not have the full picture.

Toward the end of my senior year I was under more stress than ever before. All my applications had been submitted. Every day at mail time, I was a cardiac arrest candidate. On the glorious day of April 24 (I will never forget the date), Tufts University opened its golden gates to me via an acceptance letter.

A month after high school graduation, the euphoria of getting into college had subsided and the new anxiety of what I was going to study for four years became a daily concern. I talked with people already in college and with people who had finished college. I had no idea that there were hundreds of college majors. Most of the people I spoke with told me to study what I enjoyed but to make sure it was "practical." At age 18, I wasn't sure what I most enjoyed *or* what was practical.

When I entered Tufts, I discovered it had a strong liberal arts philosophy and that students were encouraged to expose themselves to many different fields of study before selecting a major. In my sophomore year, I realized I liked a little bit of everything except the physical sciences and math. After consulting my adviser and a favorite professor, I decided English would be my field.

I mapped out a plan of study for the following two years which included six months of study in Spain to complete the Tufts language requirement. After five months abroad, I realized that in another month, I would not have attained my goal of fluency. I found a more advanced program in another part of Spain that would be compatible with Tufts' academic standards, and I enrolled for another six months. The new program was very challenging and piqued my interest in Spanish language and literature. I have decided that a Spanish major is most suitable for me. Some think this decision, coming in the second semester of my junior year, to be late. I don't agree. There is still time for me to focus on the Spanish degree and graduate on time.

In retrospect, I realize that the liberal arts experience is very important. Concurrently, equipping yourself for the competitive job market is equally important if you do not have immediate graduate school plans. My Spanish major has allowed me the flexibility of a liberal arts experience and has given me a marketable skill.

RACHEL SETZLER

What do you want to be when you grow up? That's an easy question to answer in grade school, but as we grow older it becomes harder to decide what career to pursue. Most people want careers that are fulfilling and in which they can be successful, but most important, they are looking for a vocation that is interesting and perhaps even challenging.

When I was in junior high school, I visited a cousin who trained dolphins, whales, and seals at the Miami Seaquarium. Because I had a family member on staff at the park, I was fortunate enough to get a behind-the-scenes look at the care and training of the animals. I decided that very day that I wanted to become a marine biologist.

When it was time to apply to colleges, I felt lucky that I knew what I wanted to do. During the intense process of choosing a college, I was glad I did not have the additional pressure of choosing a major. My classmates and I felt that at this point in our lives we should have our futures all figured out, and I was happy to have a head start, loving marine biology as much as I did.

I finally enrolled in a college that has a very strong marine program. Oddly enough, once I began the program, I was not satisfied. I found myself getting bored with my biology classes and getting more out of chemistry. This wasn't supposed to happen. I was in love with marine biology—I knew I was. Why was I so interested in my chemistry classes? I knew it was time to sit down and analyze my options.

The first step was to find out what I was really exposing myself to in the marine biology program. I discovered that in order to major in marine biology, I had to enroll in many general biology classes, geology, and physics. It was clear that I was bored with the program because only one or two of the required courses had anything to do with marine life.

I began to consider other majors. I had always enjoyed my classes in chemistry and seemed to have a knack for it. Why not try that? However, a chemistry major didn't seem exactly right. I read about the biochemistry major in the college catalog. Required classes included several chemistry classes, physics, math, and best of all, my choice of biology classes, including marine biology. It seemed too good to be true that this major offered training in all the areas that interest me.

The next and most important step was to talk to my adviser. Being a chemistry professor, he had a lot of insight to offer. He told me that biochemistry is a very broad major, but because of the flexibility of its course content, it can be very focused. Biochemistry provides an excellent background for students going to graduate school to study anything from medicine to marine biology. On the other hand, someone who is looking for a career immediately after college can also do something with a biochemistry major because it is so comprehensive. In general, my decision to major in biochemistry was a wise, practical one because of the extensive flexibility it will give me in the future.

Deciding what discipline to study is tough for all students. It is important, however, to realize that it is not a decision that needs to be made right away, or one that cannot change. Your college major merely serves as a guide to your course of study. It can lead to many opportunities in and out of its particular field.

JUSTIN CHANG

I grew up in Taipei, Taiwan, where medicine is regarded as a very noble and prestigious profession. No one in my family has ever been a doctor, but I have wanted to be one ever since I was little.

I am now a sophomore at the University of California at Berkeley, and my plans haven't changed—I intend to go to medical school after graduation. UC Berkeley does not offer a specific premedicine major; therefore, I had to choose a major that would help me fulfill all the prerequisites for medical school.

There are two ways to prepare for medical school. One way is to major in a science-related subject that includes all courses required for medical school. The other way is to major in something other than science but to take math, biology, general chemistry, organic chemistry, and physics. Since I have always enjoyed such courses as biology and chemistry, I chose integrative biology as my major. I also chose this major, with its emphasis on human biology, because I plan to become a general practitioner after medical school and it will give me a general survey of the different parts of the body.

I was encouraged by my freshman-year roommate, who was a philosophy major, to take two introductory philosophy courses. After taking ancient and modern philosophy, I decided to minor in philosophy because it will help me become familiar with different philosophers and their arguments. Philosophy might also help me think in a more logical and innovative way when answering the science questions I'm studying in my other classes. A minor can be used to strengthen one's major—for example, an entomology minor with a biology major focuses a student's particular interest on insects rather than the entire realm of biology. Or a minor can be used to develop a student's interest in two or more different fields of study. A minor in philosophy will help me create a more balanced work load and schedule. I will be able to take a break from science to study philosophy.

Medical school admission is very competitive, and I will need all the help I can get to be accepted. Since I am already majoring in science, my minor in philosophy, a humanities subject, will show medical schools that I am not just another narrowly focused science student, but one who is diverse and interested in many subjects.

SHANNON DERRICKS

Throughout my life I have been around sports—whether participating, cheering on my father or brother, or just watching some sporting event on television. Sports have always been a major factor in my life.

In my freshman year of high school I became a manager for several of my school's athletic teams. That's how I was introduced to athletic training. I did not know exactly what the duties and responsibilities of an athletic trainer were, but watching our high school's trainers had piqued my interest.

At the end of my freshman year, I talked with the person in charge of my high school's athletic training program to see if I could become a trainer. I was invited to work with the other trainers during spring football practice, and I went to a summer athletic training camp at a local university. During my sophomore, junior, and senior years in high school I continued to be an athletic trainer, gaining many hours of hands-on experience in the prevention and care of injuries in many different sports.

As my knowledge grew, so did my interest—especially in the rehabilitation of athletes' injuries. I found great satisfaction in watching an injured player get better and finally return to full participation status through a sound rehabilitation program. I continued to attend summer athletic training camps, and to learn more about injury prevention, care, and rehabilitation.

During my junior year of high school I realized athletic training was not just an extracurricular activity for me but something I could spend my life pursuing. I had always loved sports, and I loved to work with athletes. Also, I was very interested in a career in the medical field. So athletic training was a natural combination of the activities I loved and the interests I had.

I began to look at athletic training programs at several colleges. I was looking for a Division I university with good athletic training and physical therapy courses. I was also looking for an athletic training program that allowed females to train athletes engaged in a wide variety of sports. This became one of the major factors that influenced my decision to attend West Virginia University, since I found that many universities limit the sports for which a female can be a trainer. I found everything I was looking for at West Virginia University, where I have just completed my freshman year. I am a prospective student athletic trainer and am currently studying sports physiology and athletic training with the hope of going to graduate school in physical therapy.

GRACIELA MARTINEZ

By the end of my sophomore year at Stanford, I had taken many introductory courses, some of them the best classes I would take as an undergraduate. It was through this diversified course work that I was able to discover my academic interests and needs, for example, that I learned best in smaller classes that encouraged greater participation. Small classes also provided more personalized help with course materials and writing assignments. However, some of the classes that I was interested in were large lecture sections. To maintain a balance, I enrolled in at least one seminar or small class per academic quarter.

Class size, though one important consideration in my course selection, was not the only one. My need to further explore my cultural heritage led me to enroll in several Latin-American literature courses. These courses subsequently led me to major in Spanish. Most of the literature courses in the Spanish department were limited to 10 to 15 students.

My personal and academic interests, however, were not limited to Latin-American literature. Gender inequality, racism, poverty, and educational opportunities for minorities were and still are very important issues in my life. Many of the courses dealing with these issues were offered through the political science department. Thus, I ultimately decided to major in political science and Spanish.

My "majors" decision was mainly a result of personal needs and academic interests. I did not know at the time what I wanted to be when I grew up. All I knew were my personal interests and needs.

ABIGAIL HERRLY

It was my senior year in high school, and my best friend was explaining her reasons for applying to engineering schools. "Engineers have an average starting salary of twenty-seven thousand dollars," she said, as if that was enough explanation for anybody.

Twenty-seven thousand dollars—that figure remained fixed in my brain as an ideal. I was gradually learning that applying to college and choosing a major wasn't about what you were going to learn, it was about what you were going to do and how much you were going to make.

"Although actually, it's not really how much you make," another friend informed me. "These days, benefits are as good as cash in the bank. Health insurance and so on. I think I'm going to go into business. Financial services, or maybe personnel."

Financial services or personnel? I didn't even know what that meant. How could friends of mine, at seventeen, be planning to go into careers I had never heard of?

College was not desirable for its own sake. It was a ticket to success, and success meant a high starting salary, good benefits, upward mobility. In short, security. College was not a place of learning but a preprofessional training ground. I even had a friend who was going to Hamburger U (I kid you not) to learn to be a McDonald's manager.

I began to feel a little frightened. Clearly, I had wasted my time in high school. While my friends had been finding out about the job market and starting salaries and benefits and the right color suit to wear to an interview, I had been taking dance classes and writing poetry. Nothing very marketable there. What, oh what, could I possibly do with the rest of my life, and what could I study that would get me there?

I told my mother I was going to be an engineer.

"Why on earth would you do a thing like that? You hate math."

"I know, but engineers have an average starting salary of twenty-seven thousand dollars. Besides, I like science-fiction stories, and a lot of the best science-fiction writers were engineers before they became writers. If I were an engineer, I could write really good science fiction when I retired."

"You mean to tell me you'd spend forty years doing something you hated so that when you retired you could write technically correct science fiction? Why don't you skip the middle man and be a writer?"

"Don't be silly. There's no job market. Did you know that writers have an average yearly salary of five thousand dollars?"

"Study dancing, then. You love to dance."

"Sure I love to dance, but nobody dances for a living. I've got to start thinking about careers."

"Abby, you're seventeen years old. All you have to think about right now is going to college and studying something you enjoy. Think about getting a job when you graduate."

I shook my head over my mother's ignorance, but she did help me realize something important—I had to study something I could at least tolerate; I'd be miserable otherwise. There had to be some way I could study something I liked in college and still be able to get a job when I graduated.

I decided to major in English. I loved dancing even more than I loved writing, but dancing as a career was out of the question. With a degree in English, I reasoned, I could teach or go into publishing or something like that. And, in the meantime, I could study something I enjoyed.

I did enjoy it. I felt almost guilty when some of my Cornell friends talked about the biology, business, and engineering courses they hated that were necessary steps toward doing what they eventually wanted to do. My courses were a delight. I was able to study literature and take creative writing, and I kept up with dance classes as well. As my sophomore year drew near its close, however, I began to get nervous. I'd been learning a lot and having a great time, but what was I going to do with my life? It wasn't too late to declare a major in something useful—math or psychology or economics. A degree in English wasn't really marketable no matter what I'd told myself. Wasn't it time to get serious and think about a career?

All through my first two years of college I'd taken dance classes and participated in performances, knowing I'd probably have to give up my favorite hobby once I graduated. I envisioned myself working in an office—that's what everyone eventually does, after all—and I knew I wouldn't have time for dancing. That summer, I took a job teaching dance at an arts camp, figuring I might as well spend a few months doing what I loved more than anything else. It was a marvelous, exciting summer, and when I came back to Cornell I started to wonder glumly what life without dancing would be like. I cursed every dance teacher I'd ever had for instilling in me a love and a passion that I knew would never really go away, but which I couldn't in all practicality pursue as a career. My parents were spending sixteen thousand dollars a year to finance an Ivy League education. Was I then going to troop off to New York to wait on tables and go to auditions? Anyway, I was more than half committed to studying English. How could I just turn around and major in dance?

How could you not, another voice asked quietly.

Am I considering what I think I'm considering?

Well, why not?

Because it's outrageously impractical. Because there's no upward mobility, no company hierarchy, no starting salary at all. Because there are no benefits, not even a pension, and it's risky and scary and difficult, and you may break your body, your mind, and your heart and still not make it at all.

Even so, said the quiet voice, you have to do it.

And to my own and everyone else's surprise, I did. I decided to study dance, and I'm not sorry yet, though I'm facing graduation this spring and have no job network at all. I may go for an MFA in dance next fall; I may throw myself at the mercy of New York City. I may fail. But for the first time in my life, I'm not afraid of being afraid. The biggest fear in my life was not being secure, not being successful, not being safe. To make the decision to go into dance, I had to leap down the throat of that fear, and I found that the feeling of fear is the true horror, not the thing feared. If I took a secure corporate job because I feared not being secure, I would not be taking steps to dissipate that fear. Indeed, that fear would become the cornerstone of my life, and everything else would be built upon it. I prefer to make love the cornerstone of my life: love for an art that makes me feel truly alive and truly myself; an art that, in all its riskiness and capriciousness as a career, demands that its followers make an absolute commitment to their creativity and to themselves. The result is not guaranteed; it is the journey that counts, not the goal. My own journey will not look like something out of Donald Trump's path to achieve success, but even though I can't see down my path for more than a few feet, I'm not worried.

MICHAEL DEGGS

When I was younger I loved to take things apart just to see what made them work. When you open up a computer, it's not obvious exactly what makes it work. It's even harder to put your finger on exactly what it is that it does: watches tell time, stoves heat things, and computers...?

The high school I went to in Germany had just gotten into computers, and I got caught up in the frenzy. It fascinated me to see a powerful computer doing exactly what I programmed it to do. Perhaps if I had put as much energy into finding a college, I might be further along in my studies. Instead, I opted to join the army to save money and get some on-the-job experience.

During my two-year enlistment in the army, I was able to take advantage of a special incentive, through which I saved $15,200 toward my college education. I also enrolled in classes that gave me more exposure to the world of computers, applying what I learned by writing much-needed programs for my unit. I found myself spending much of my free time at the post's computer lab teaching myself how to use the variety of software packages they had in their library.

I was sadly disillusioned to discover that $15,200 would last only a little over one year at the university I wanted to attend. I decided to enroll at a local community college to fulfill the core requirements and transfer to the university later on. The community college was not only less expensive, but it also had a more flexible class schedule, which would free my days so I could earn the rest of the money I needed.

During my job search, I noticed that employers were not very interested in the specialized training I had acquired in the military as a telecommunications-center operator. To my surprise, they were eager to have me use my self-taught computer skills to assist their managers on special projects! I accepted a position at a major financial institution, where I excelled in developing creative solutions to problems involving computers.

Soon I was doing so well at my job that my education was taking a back seat to travel and off-site meetings. That was soon rectified by a phenomenon known as the "glass ceiling." In less than two years, I had been promoted all the way to systems analyst, but I did not even have a bachelor's degree. I learned that without that degree, the ladder to success has a glass ceiling at a certain level that can prevent one from climbing further. When the bank down-sized, forcing me to compete with staff that already had "credentials" for the remaining jobs, I found myself out of a job.

I then began investigating colleges in earnest and discovered that the University of Miami had both the degree program I wanted and a creative financial aid package to help me meet the costs of attending classes full time. I am working toward a degree in Computer Information Systems offered by the School of Business. It differs from a computer science degree in that it is geared toward business applications of emerging technologies rather than the development of technology itself.

When I finish my bachelor's degree, I plan to get a master's in the same field. My friends in the corporate world tell me it's fast becoming the new "credential" for those looking to reach the highest rungs on the ladder to success. I am preparing for it now. I would hate to get out there and find another "glass ceiling"!

ELIZABETH ANN KOBERG

When I first started thinking about how I wanted to spend the rest of my life, I thought about how I could make a good income. I had always enjoyed being around children and felt that I had a fair amount of patience, so I decided that I would become a child psychologist.

My parents were not delighted when I announced this. My dad soon enlightened my ideal world by reminding me that day after day I would deal with children who had very complicated and unsolvable problems. He mentioned that if I worked as a counselor in a school, I would have the opportunity to work with children who were not as disturbed as those that I would deal with as a clinical psychologist. The more I thought about this, the more appealing the school idea became.

I began to inquire about the requirements for becoming an elementary school counselor. In the state of Texas, to be a counselor in a public school, you are required to have a teaching certificate, three years of teaching experience, and a master's degree in counseling. I decided to pursue an elementary education major with reading certification and theater arts specializations.

I have thoroughly enjoyed my first two years at the University of Texas at Austin. I have finished almost all of my basic courses, including math, Spanish, and physical science. My first year, I took two education classes—social influences on education and child psychology.

They were both very interesting, and I never felt like I was forced to study them—I wanted to! For most education classes, some outside fieldwork is required. Thus far, I have been involved in a mentor program and have been a child-life volunteer at a children's hospital. These activities give a student "hands-on" experience with at-risk and handicapped children.

This spring I will take literacy acquisition, motivation and learning, and dramatic activities for the classroom. Next year will be devoted to observation of a classroom and actual student teaching in an elementary classroom. This will take two semesters and is a requirement for my degree.

My classmates are very helpful and friendly. I have discovered that almost all of them are very similar to me. I don't see the competition in education that I see in other fields.

As for working as a counselor, I will have to see where I am five years from now. I enjoy helping young people learn to read so much that I might choose teaching as my occupation. I can be such a positive influence on these children, and there is so much that I want to offer them and explore with them. The elementary classroom is where all reasoning and critical thinking begins. After all, could you have finished this paragraph if it had not been for the dedicated teachers that you had when you were in elementary school?

As the months and years go by, income seems very insignificant. When I think about what I plan to achieve in my lifetime, I think instead of the fulfillment and gratitude that will come from helping and encouraging young people. One of my favorite quotes from Ralph Waldo Emerson encourages me every day: "To know even one life has breathed easier because you have lived—this is to have succeeded."

MICHAEL ESQUIBEL

One of the most important decisions I had to make in college is what major to pursue. Initially, the decision about a college major appeared rather simple. When I first began to consider my options seriously, I discovered a series of questions confronted me whose answers would have long-term effects on my life. Within three years, I would have to begin making critical decisions concerning employment or graduate school.

While I considered various majors, I talked with a variety of people including my family, college staff, and upper-classmen. The majority suggested I pursue a major that not only interested me, but drew on my academic strengths. My interest has always been in history, especially American history and the presidents. I realize that I have a weakness in math. By taking a wide range of courses, I was able to confirm both my strengths and weaknesses.

I began taking courses in political science and sociology. I found both areas appealed to me. My dilemma came when attempting to fulfill the requirements for both majors and the general requirement courses needed to graduate. Ultimately, I decided to major in political science and minor in sociology.

Now, as I make more decisions concerning my future, I see that a college major supplies critical courses that are used as building blocks for greater things to come. An advantage of a major in political science is that I am not limited in what I am able to do with it. I am not restricted to work in government. I am prepared for employment in any major corporation. In terms of furthering my education, I am able to enter almost any field of study, including law, business school and most graduate schools.

The best overall advice I can give for choosing a college major is to (1) look at all the majors available; (2) take a variety of courses to see what you like before you make a decision; (3) find a major that not only interests you but also uses your strengths; and (4) think about what you want to do when you graduate. It is extremely important to find out how your proposed major will help you in the future.

TREVON DYREL GROSS

When I entered college, I thought my easiest decision would be the choice of a major. After all, I had previously worked as a computer technician and consultant for four years and had enjoyed it. In addition, the University of Virginia's School of Commerce, our undergraduate business college, was ranked as one of the most elite in the country.

I had planned my entire future within the first days of my collegiate experience. I would take my degree in Management of Information Systems (MIS) and work for a Fortune 500 company. Like many other members of this capitalistic society, I could see large dollar signs in my future. My first semester, I took the prerequisites that would prepare me to enter the commerce school in my third year.

While this dream was in its embryonic stages, I went to speak to one of my religious studies professors about a grade I'd received on an exam. Learning that I was planning to be an MIS major, he challenged me to think about why I had chosen my major and whether it would be something with which I could happily occupy myself for at least the next ten years.

After much thinking, I had to answer no. Sure, I thrived on the challenge of working out solutions to complex problems on a computer in the five programming languages I knew. But I didn't think the intricacies of computers would hold my attention for an extended period of time. Working with computers was a great summer job, but I would not be satisfied with it for a career.

This was the crux of my problem. Should I major in something that would bring me great personal gain but very transient happiness, or should I forgo the fancy house with a two-car garage, and major in something that would bring lifelong happiness?

I am now a religious studies major with a minor in classics. I am very interested in the critical analysis of Biblical literature. Moreover, this degree makes use of my skills: a love for writing and reading and an acquired ability in systematic and critical thinking. Now that I am pursuing a field that deeply interests me, I have set even higher goals. One includes earning a PH.D. in Hebrew Bible and Semitics. Afterward, I hope to secure a professorship in a college or university.

Why waste time and money doing something that in the long run will not satisfy you? Find something with which you can be happy. Pursue a career that helps you grow and takes advantage of all your abilities.

MARQUIS T. WILLIAMS

Choosing a college major is not always easy even to those of us who were "born" knowing what major we would pursue in college. There was no doubt I would become a doctor or go into a medical profession. It was not until my junior year in high school that I started having doubts about this.

Like most kids, I went through the stages of wanting to become a doctor, a lawyer, a policeman, etc. However, I enjoyed the sciences the most and I had wanted to become a doctor ever since I was in fifth grade. My parents also encouraged me to become a doctor.

In high school, I realized that there were more options than becoming a doctor or lawyer. I found other things that I really liked and I became confused about my future. But because my parents really wanted me to be a doctor, I continued on that route so that they would be satisfied. Actually, my mother at one time convinced me not to go into the medical profession because it would be too stressful, but later she changed her mind and decided that medicine was still for me as long as I was not a surgeon.

I entered Yale as a premedical major on the biology track. By this time, my love for medicine had faded, but I stuck with it because I wanted to make Mom happy. However, after my first semester of science courses, I began to dislike the sciences and medicine. Finally, like many other premed students I made my change. I explored different majors and found one that I really enjoyed—economics. I decided to major in economics and use it for a future in business.

When I told Mom that I no longer wanted anything to do with medicine, I think it broke her heart. I felt like a big disappointment to her. At first she tried to sway my decision, but I stood firm. She finally realized that I had to do what I wanted to do. After that became clear, she told me that whatever my decision, she would give me her support. She told me that she would be happy with what made me happy. That made me happy because I wanted to make my own decisions without conflict from her.

Things worked out pretty well for me. After initial pressure on me to become a doctor, my family eventually came to respect my decision to study economics. Also, I was lucky to realize early in college that I wanted to get off the premedical track—it's harder to change gears your junior or senior year. Going into my junior year, I will be majoring in economics, but even that may change!

As I see it, the most important things in choosing a major are: (1) to choose something that you are happy with; (2) not to let anyone else make decisions for you; and (3) to be open-minded about and to explore the different majors available. You might just find a perfect one that you had not even imagined.

JOANN SOLOMON

When I was growing up, the attitude toward womens' education and careers was much different than it is today. Many women, if they attended college at all, entered the traditional female occupations of teaching and nursing, but wife and mother were the roles they ultimately expected to play in life. I did very well in school, and was fortunate to have many excellent teachers. I took French from the fifth grade on, and Spanish throughout high school. I was an avid reader, and English and literature were my favorite subjects. My fascination with the beauty and intricacy of language led me, the first in my family to enter college, to be a foreign language major.

After one semester of college, I dropped out to get married. In two years I had two children, the second of whom was not healthy. As I entered the maze of the medical world with her, I was very frightened. I soon found that the more I learned, the more in control I felt. The more I knew, the more power I had and the better I could take part in her treatment and care. This experience kindled a whole new area of interest in me.

Unfortunately, my marriage lasted only eight years, and I found myself alone with no skills with which to support myself or my children. I quickly learned that one never knows what life will bring and that self-sufficiency is both desirable and necessary for both sexes.

I entered a local community college planning to take prerequisite courses to qualify for entrance into its associate degree nursing program. Once I entered, however, I became so enamored with learning that I took a full liberal arts program rather than focusing solely on nursing. My studies gave me an excellent background in psychology and sociology, which I can bring to nursing, but, more important, through them I gained confidence in my ability as a student and as an independent person. I graduated in three years with a 4.0 average.

After remarriage, another child, and ten years away from school, I am now attending a public university as a nursing major. It seems ironic that I have again chosen a stereotypically "female" major, but time and experience have shown me that this field is right for me. The stereotype should be fading, because more and more men are entering nursing!

At eighteen I would never have chosen nursing as a major, but at thirty-nine I am sure it is what I want. The choices we make regarding majors when we enter college are not necessarily the ones we are satisfied with as we gain more knowledge and experience. Time has a way of shifting our pathways and even the best laid plans are subject to change. My case just goes to show that some people take longer to get it right.

Agriculture

KENNETH LARSON
Iowa State University

Agriculture is a broad and diverse discipline that leads to many rewarding and satisfying careers. The field ranges from computer science to forestry, genetics to food technology, business to biochemistry, public service and administration to animal and plant sciences. Its challenging curricula include programs in agronomy, horticulture, entomology, plant pathology, dairy and poultry sciences, fisheries and wildlife, and preveterinary medicine.

Everyone uses the products of the science-based food and agricultural industry. As societal requirements for food, feed, and fiber of high quality increase and as resources for producing them decrease, the need for cost-efficient production in a safe environment will grow.

In the forefront of this industry that stresses biotechnology, genetic engineering, human nutrition, and related sciences are bright young men and women who have pursued studies in food and agricultural sciences and natural resources. For many years, agriculture focused on the science of producing crops and raising livestock. With its many emerging subdisciplines, however, it has taken on new meaning. The development of highly scientific and specialized production, marketing, and processing techniques has moved it into a position of prominence. Today's agriculture requires the cooperation of educated and skilled producers, researchers, teachers, and other professionals with people in business and industry who grow, market, process and use agricultural products or provide agricultural services.

Students interested in agriculture will learn about the wealth of opportunity for study and eventual work in the descriptions of agriculture majors that follow. There are subdisciplines within agriculture that may interest them as well:

Agricultural biochemists explore animal medicine, plant and animal nutrition, genetics, photosynthesis, animal growth, and nitrogen fixation. Graduates in this major are qualified for entry-level research or management positions with pesticide, herbicide, and pharmaceutical industries.

Agricultural engineers design, test, and manufacture agricultural and industrial equipment and machinery, structures for soil and water conservation control, farm buildings, confinement units for animal production, systems for electric power applications, and systems for food and crop processing. Graduates in this major (which is described in the engineering section), are employed by agricultural-related industries and by state and federal agencies.

Agricultural journalists combine agricultural experience and interests with professional education in journalism. They write and report stories on modern agriculture for the mass media. Graduates are in demand for

23

editorial, advertising, and public relations positions by newspapers, magazines, radio, television, federal and state information agencies, and private concerns.

Agricultural microbiologists study agriculture and the life sciences and work in research, development, and quality control laboratories within the dairy, food processing, pharmaceutical, and fermentation industries. Many agricultural biotechnology companies need agricultural microbiologists. Graduates in this major occasionally seek advanced training in medical technology, animal or human medicine, or other graduate study.

Geneticists study the molecular nature of genes and DNA and the transmission of genes from one generation to the next. They develop new techniques of genetic engineering to promote efficient crop and animal production, to provide methods for diagnosing and treating human disease, and for producing the proteins of higher organisms in bacterial "factories." Geneticists are often employed in university, industrial, and government laboratories. Graduates have an excellent background for advanced study in genetics, human medicine, veterinary medicine, plant and animal breeding, biochemistry, and other biological sciences.

Plant pathologists understand plant diseases and they develop measures to control them effectively. Graduates are employed primarily in research and development and in production agriculture and sales. They are sought by government agencies, such as extension services and the Environmental Protection Agency, and by agrichemical companies, farm service organizations, food processors, seed producers, and commercial nurseries.

Rural sociologists are interested in public service and administration in agriculture. Graduates are prepared for public service and community affairs positions in rural areas. They administer government and other public agricultural programs and they work in public relations or customer services for businesses concerned with the rural sector.

Seed scientists fill management positions in the seed industry. Studies in seed science integrate crop science, physiology, pathology, and engineering in order to resolve problems with the seeds used in horticulture and agronomy. Graduates work as managers in seed production, seed processing, marketing, plant supervision, technical sales, and quality control.

Animal ecologists study the relations between animals and the biological and physical environment. Graduates are employed to solve practical problems relating to pollution; to the impact of power plants, pipelines, and dams on the environment; and to the sound use of natural resources. Companies seeking the services of animal ecologists are environmental consulting firms, power companies, government conservation agencies, and colleges and universities.

Many colleges and universities offer other majors in agricultural and food sciences and natural resources. United States employment data indicate expanding career opportunities in science, engineering, and related professions for graduates in agriculture, natural resources, and veterinary medicine. The role of these graduates will be critical in enhancing the competitive advantage of United States technology in today's global economy and markets. To fill these needs, graduates could take jobs as an animal scientist, biochemist, biometrician, entomologist, environmental engineer, food scientist, food technologist, forest scientist, geneticist, microbiologist, nutritionist, physiologist, safety engineer, soil scientist, technician, toxicologist, veterinarian, water engineer, and weed scientist.

Many organizations seek managers and financial specialists with food and agricultural expertise to work in food processing, manufacturing, and distribution. The food industry is big business and represents approximately 20 percent of the gross national product. It needs accountants, appraisers, business managers, credit analysts, economists, financial analysts, food service managers, retail managers, and wholesale managers.

Graduates with food and agricultural expertise, business and communication skills, and specific preparation in sales techniques are needed in both domestic and international markets. Examples of positions to fill marketing, merchandising, and sales needs are commodity broker, food broker, grain merchandiser, livestock buyer, market analyst, marketing manager, sales representative, technical service representative, and timber buyer.

Education, communication, and information specialists will be employed to fill the growing demand for information systems and computer-assisted instruction. Professional opportunities are expected to expand for food and agricultural public relations specialists and advertising representatives. Examples of positions in the education, communication, and information arena are advertising specialist, broadcaster, computer systems analyst, cooperative extension agent and specialist, editor, illustrator, information systems analyst, public relations specialist, reporter, and vocational agriculture instructor.

Graduates with a social service background will find opportunities in agricultural and natural resources as personnel and labor relations specialists, recreation workers, naturalists, regional planners, and community development specialists. Other examples are career counselor, food inspector, nutrition counselor, regulatory agent, youth program director, and 4-H youth specialist.

Approximately three million agricultural production specialists are employed as farmers and ranchers. Since the trend is now toward larger production units, there have been fewer jobs for production specialists. Therefore producers must acquire both business and technical expertise through a college education. Examples of positions in this sector are farmer, feedlot manager, fish manager, forest manager, game rancher, fruit and vegetable grower, nursery product grower, professional farm manager, rancher, tree manager, and turf producer.

Students who wish to pursue careers in the food and agricultural sciences and natural resources can expect to take the following courses in college: communication, biological and physical sciences, mathematics, business and economics, humanities and social science, and computer science. Foreign cultures, geography, and languages are also beneficial for students interested in international programs.

Agribusiness

An agribusiness major prepares students to apply business and economic principles to firms that produce, process, distribute, and sell food and other agricultural products. The student also learns how to apply these principles to the management of natural resources.

Interests, skills, and qualities associated with success in the major

Interests. Taking initiative, leadership, decision making, problem solving, analyzing data, global interdependence, working with people.

Skills and qualities. Planning, organizing, making business decisions, leadership, teamwork, creative and critical thinking, working with people, written and verbal skills, adapting to change.

Recommended high school preparation

English 4, precollege mathematics 3, biology 1, chemistry 1, social studies 2, foreign language 2, and visual arts 1.

Typical courses in the major

Accounting	Business Law
Economics	Finance
Human Resources Management	International Trade
Marketing	Management
Public Policy Analysis	Production Decision Analysis

What the major is like

The agribusiness major (sometimes called agribusiness and applied economics) prepares students to make economically sound and environmentally acceptable decisions by applying economic and business principles to both domestic and international markets, the consumption of food and other agricultural products, and the management of natural resources.

Many agribusinesses are family-operated companies, small private corporations, or cooperatives with needs and regulations that differ from those of large corporations. An understanding of the principles of accounting, economics, finance, labor marketing, management, and public policy is necessary to analyze and cope with business and environmental risk, identify and meet changes in consumer demand for food products and services, improve profitability, and recognize the effect of economic development on the environment.

Agribusiness majors take supporting course work in the arts, data analysis, humanities, international studies, life/natural sciences, mathematics, social sciences, technical agriculture, and written and oral communication. Agribusiness majors also learn to use computers to prepare reports, analyze data, and manage records. Students need to become familiar with data base management, graphics, spread sheets, statistical software, and word processing.

Many agribusinesses provide internships that give students practical business experience.

Specializations

Agribusiness finance, consumption, economic development, international agriculture, public policy, resource economics.

Other majors to consider

Agricultural education
Agronomy
Animal sciences
Business administration
Entomology
Fisheries and wildlife
Food sciences
Forestry
Horticultural science
Range management
Soil sciences

Careers related to the major

Over 90 percent of the jobs for agribusiness graduates are with firms in business and industry. The multibillion dollar agribusiness industry has a growing demand for managers and specialists trained in accounting, credit analysis, marketing, and international trade. Agribusinesses are involved in world trade, food supply, food processing, credit and finance, and land resource management. As farms and ranches become larger, more specialized, and more sophisticated operations, firms that supply inputs to farmers and ranchers and that buy, process, transport, and sell agricultural products are becoming more important. Graduates may find entry-level jobs as an agricultural statistician, commodity merchandiser, credit analyst, grain operations trainee, loan representative, management trainee, market analyst, natural resource manager, production supervisor, public relations representative, quality assurance supervisor, or sales representative.

For more information

American Agricultural Economics Association
80 Heady Hall
Iowa State University
Ames, IA 50011-1070
(515)294-8700

Agricultural education

The agricultural education major combines the art and science of teaching with technical knowledge in agriculture. It prepares students to teach agriculture in high schools and middle schools, to become 4-H and agricultural extension agents, and to work as educational specialists and trainers in agricultural businesses, industries, and organizations.

Interests, skills, and qualities associated with success in the major	**Interests.** Working with people, working with plants, working with animals. **Skills and qualities.** Communication, science (especially natural sciences and chemistry).
Recommended high school preparation	English 4, precollege mathematics 2, biology 1, chemistry 1, physics 1, social studies 1, history 1, and foreign language 2. 2 to 4 years of agricultural education are also recommended.
Typical courses in the major	Teaching Processes Philosophy of Education Media and Communication Educational Psychology Extension Education Learning Processes Multicultural Experiences Human Development Program Planning Agriculture Education Student Teaching

What the major is like

Agricultural education majors usually complete core courses in teaching and learning processes, human development, and psychology. Then students take specialized courses to prepare for a career in teaching, agricultural extension, or agribusiness.

Experience in real settings is usually a part of the course requirements. This allows students to understand education from the teacher's point of view. Additional courses in general and agricultural education include youth activities, adult education laboratory teaching, program planning, and audiovisual and computer technology. Students also complete courses in specific agricultural areas to gain the technical knowledge that will be required on the job. Most programs culminate by working for 10 to 15 weeks in a school classroom, in a county extension office, or in an agricultural business or organization. This enables students to apply what they have learned, to practice the art and science of teaching, and to "try on" the role of teacher.

Although teaching requirements vary from state to state, agricultural education programs are similar. Typically agricultural education majors receive Bachelor of Science degrees.

Specializations

Public school teaching, extension service.

Other majors to consider

Education
Trade and industrial education

Careers related to the major

The agricultural education major prepares students to teach in public schools. It can also lead to careers as a human resources trainer, extension agent, county extension agent with 4-H, or county extension agent involved with agricultural issues.

For more information

Your state's land-grant university and agricultural colleges can provide more information about the agricultural education major.

Agronomy

Agronomy majors learn about three basic natural elements—crops, soils, and climates—and their interdependence in producing food, feed, fiber, and fuel. Agronomists study theory and practices for improving crop production while conserving natural resources and maintaining environmental quality.

Interests, skills, and qualities associated with success in the major

Interests. Nature and the outdoors, environmental quality (soil, water, and air), conservation of natural resources, biological and physical sciences, problem solving, plant growth and experimentation, weather, climate, geologic formations.

Skills and qualities. Oral and written communication skills, group dynamics, leadership, organizational (interpersonal) skills, analytic reasoning, creative thinking.

Recommended high school preparation

English 3, algebra 1–2, geometry 1, biology 1, chemistry 1, physics 1, social studies .5, American government .5, U.S. history 1, speech 1, and computer science .5.

Typical courses in the major

Botany	Entomology
Genetics	Inorganic Chemistry
Organic Chemistry	Biochemistry
Seed Science and Technology	Physics
Pest Management	Geology
Meteorology	Plant Breeding
Economics	Plant Pathology
Soil Fertility	Statistics
Weed Science	Crop Production
Crop Management	Crop Physiology

What the major is like

Agronomy (sometimes called crop science, plant science, or soil science) uses plant and soil sciences to produce abundant, high-quality food, feed, and fiber. Crop and plant sciences relate primarily to the genetics, breeding, physiology, and management of field and turf crops. Soil science concentrates on soil physics, soil chemistry, soil origin, soil microbiology, soil fertility, and soil management. It also covers other soil uses, such as foundations for buildings and road construction, waterways, and waste disposal systems. Majors also learn to understand the components of weather and climate.

Agronomy students generally begin by studying soil science, crop production, botany or biology, geology, chemistry, English, and statistics. In addition, they study physical and social sciences, communications, economics, and mathematics. All agronomy students are encouraged to take at least one course in plant pathology, entomology, weed science, and soil fertility/plant nutrition.

As students learn more about agronomy, they develop specific interests in crop science, soil science, or climatology. They may specialize in farm management, fertilizer and agricultural chemicals, pest management, seed production and technology, soil conservation, turfgrass management, or biotechnology. Students may take double majors or minor in agribusiness, agricultural journalism, animal science, environmental sciences, or extension education.

Field trips or industrial tours often supplement classroom and lab courses, and travel courses (domestic and international) are encouraged at some institutions. Agronomy students also benefit from seminars by visiting professors and other professionals on current agronomy issues, problems, and solutions. Furthermore, most campuses encourage students to participate in extracurricular activities to develop leadership and interpersonal skills and to enhance self-confidence. Students participate on crop and soil judging teams and compete in local, regional, and national contests.

Most colleges and universities offer internships and other work opportunities with industry and government agencies. Students earn academic credit for these experiences, and it is applied toward graduation requirements.

Agronomists provide consumers with low-cost food and help producers increase profitability and efficiency. This unique dual contribution has created a mounting demand for professional agronomists, both in the United States and abroad.

Specializations

Crop and soil sciences, climatology, environmental sciences, farm management, fertilizers and agricultural chemicals, molecular biology, pest management, seed production and technology, soil conservation, turfgrass management.

Other majors to consider

Biochemistry
Biology
Botany
Entomology
Genetics, human and animal
Horticultural science
Microbiology
Plant pathology
Range management

Careers related to the major

Because agronomists provide consumers with low-cost food while helping producers increase profitability and efficiency, there is growing demand for their services, both in the United States and abroad. The agronomy major may lead to careers as an agricultural attache, agricultural climatologist, agricultural lawyer, agrichemical technologist, arborist, commodity broker, crop chemist, crop and soil specialist, grain elevator manager, environmental specialist, food and drug inspector, farm or ranch manager, food processor, geneticist, golf course manager, grain buyer, grain inspector, greenhouse manager, land appraiser, marketing director, park ranger, plant breeder, public relations representative, research technician, sales manager, seed analyst, soil and water conservationist, and turfgrass specialist.

For more information   American Society of Agronomy
677 South Segoe Road
Madison, WI 53711
(608)273-8080

Animal sciences

Students in the animal sciences learn how to manage livestock and poultry. They study the role of animals in the economy, how animal products influence eating habits and are part of the global food supply, and how animals help serve people's recreation needs.

Interests, skills, and qualities associated with success in the major

Interests. Working with plants, working with animals, working with people.

Skills and qualities. Speaking and writing effectively.

Recommended high school preparation

English 4, precollege mathematics 4, biology 3, chemistry 1, physics 1, social studies 2, history 2, foreign language 2, and computer science 2.

Typical courses in the major

Chemistry
Livestock Nutrition
Animal Genetics
Farm Animal Behavior
Meat Science
Swine Production
Mathematics
Physiology
Animal Diseases

Biology
Domestic Animal Biology
Animal Reproduction
Poultry Biology
Dairy Herd Management
Beef Cattle
Nutrition
Animal Production

What the major is like

An animal science major covers the fundamentals of breeding, nutrition, physiology, marketing, management, and processing of livestock and poultry. Students can specialize in a species—for example, sheep, swine, horses, dairy and beef cattle, or poultry—or in a subject, such as nutrition, management, or physiology.

To give students a sound general education, at least 40 percent of the animal sciences curriculum is made up of courses in the humanities, fine arts, social sciences, natural sciences, and mathematics. These are usually taken during the first two years. Students then focus on animal science courses during their third and fourth years. These are taught in a lecture-laboratory format with the lab demonstrating the principles discussed in the lecture. Students are also encouraged and helped to learn through summer work and internships.

Students are expected to be computer literate upon graduation. Microcomputers are usually available and many courses have computer-assisted instruction.

An animal science degree prepares students to work in production agriculture, government service (state and federal), and agribusiness. Students may also continue into graduate or professional schools.

Specializations

Animal science (meat animals and horses), dairy science, poultry science.

Other majors to consider

Biochemistry
Biology
Chemistry
Plant sciences
Preveterinary

Careers related to the major

The animal sciences major may lead to jobs as a 4-H youth agent with the state cooperative extension service, sales representative for major feed, chemical, or other companies, farm or ranch manager, agent for government or private farm credit agencies, soil conservationist, livestock buyer, field representative for a livestock organization, processing plant manager, research assistant, food marketing specialist, quality control analyst, or a representative for agricultural publications.

For more information

American Society of Animal Science
309 West Clark Street
Champaign, IL 61820
(217)356-3182

American Dairy Science Association
309 West Clark Street
Champaign, IL 61820
(217)356-3182

American Poultry Science Association
309 West Clark Street
Champaign, IL 61820
(217)356-3182

Entomology

Entomology majors study the biology, ecology, classification, distribution, physiology, economic importance, and management of insects and their relatives.

Interests, skills, and qualities associated with success in the major

Interests. Science, techniques of scientific research, the environment, the health and well-being of people.

Skills and qualities. Curiosity, rational thinking, objective thinking, performing laboratory tasks carefully.

Recommended high school preparation	English 4, precollege mathematics 3–4, biology 1–2, chemistry 1–2, physics 1–2, social studies 1, history 1–2, foreign language 4, communications .5–1, and computer science 1–2.

Typical courses in the major

General Entomology	External Insect Morphology
Apiculture	Forest Entomology
Insect Taxonomy	Insect Behavior
Insect Physiology	Insect Pests of Field Crops
Aquatic Insects	Integrated Pest Management
Medical Entomology	Livestock Entomology
Parasitology	Insect and Host Interactions

What the major is like

Entomology is a basic and an applied science dealing with the study of insects and their relatives. It is a separate field because of the enormous impact that insects have on humans. In many institutions, entomology is a division of the college of agriculture with close ties to the biology department.

Some entomologists study field crop insects to help farmers produce crops more efficiently and with greater environmental safety. Others work in forest or ornamental plant industries to protect trees from such pests as the gypsy moth or the beetles that transmit Dutch elm disease. Still others work in livestock production or for agencies charged with solving public health pest problems. Entomologists also conduct basic research in ecology, physiology, toxicology, genetics, and biotechnology; insects can serve as test organisms for the examination of biological principles common to all animal life.

Entomology majors use the basic tools of science: biology, mathematics, chemistry, and physics. Before taking courses in the major, students learn about plant and animal biology, chemistry (including organic chemistry), physics, and mathematics through elementary calculus. Majors progress from a general entomology course to advanced courses in insect morphology, taxonomy, physiology, ecology, and behavior.

Elective courses may include plant physiology, plant pathology, nematology, microbiology, parasitology, animal science, computer science, agricultural engineering, agronomy, sociology, and economics. Advanced courses include biotechnology, biochemistry, and molecular and cell biology. Some universities offer introductory acarology and pesticide chemistry/insecticide toxicology as undergraduate courses.

Summer internships, part-time and summer employment, and entomology clubs and seminars are usually available. Independent study projects along with research papers stimulate original thinking and provide experience in creative research. They also offer an opportunity for one-on-one interaction between the student and faculty.

Specializations

Systematics (classification), ecology, behavioral physiology, insect toxicology, integrated pest management, medical and veterinary entomology.

Other majors to consider

Animal sciences
Biochemistry
Computer science
Microbiology
Parasitology
Plant pathology

| Careers related to the major | Graduates in entomology will find career opportunities in agriculture, academe, private industry, and in state, federal, and international agencies. |

Careers related to the major

Graduates in entomology will find career opportunities in agriculture, academe, private industry, and in state, federal, and international agencies.

For more information

The Entomological Society of America
9301 Annapolis Road
Lanham, MD 20706
(301)731-4535

The pamphlet "Discover Entomology" is available from the Entomological Society of America.

Fisheries and wildlife

Fisheries and wildlife students take courses in the natural sciences and in management to help maintain and manipulate our land, water, and animal and plant resources for the best ecological, commercial, recreational, and scientific uses.

Interests, skills, and qualities associated with success in the major

Interests. Nature and the outdoors, science, research.

Skills and qualities. Solving problems, communicating effectively, working with others.

Recommended high school preparation

English 4, precollege mathematics 3, laboratory science 3–4, history or social studies 3, and computer science .5.

Typical courses in the major

Zoology	Botany
Ichthyology	Ornithology
Mammalogy	Limnology
Ecology	Fisheries Management

What the major is like

Fisheries and wildlife majors study the environmental requirements of fish or wildlife species, populations, and communities. They also study sound practices to manipulate the environment and learn to regulate human activity by controlling animal harvest, pollution, and the recreational use of specific areas. Students also learn principles of conservation as well, focusing on sound efforts to maintain and manipulate natural resources.

About 35 to 40 percent of a fisheries and wildlife major's course work consists of general education courses in communications, quantitative sciences (calculus, computer studies, and statistics), social sciences, and humanities. These courses generally are taken during the freshman and sophomore years.

Fisheries and wildlife majors take a broad range of courses in physical sciences (10 to 15 hours in chemistry/biochemistry, physics, and earth science) and biological sciences (about 30 hours in zoology, botany, conservation, genetics, population dynamics, physiology, and ecology). They also take courses in policy, administration, and law to obtain a background in resource policy, land-use planning, and the legal and social aspects of natural resource management.

Moreover, students take advanced courses in fisheries and wildlife science (ichthyology, limnology, ornithology, mammalogy) and fisheries and wildlife management (fish husbandry and habitat management). These courses typically are taken during the junior and senior years and account for about 15 hours of the degree program. Students often specialize in either fisheries or wildlife.

Students can broaden their general education background and add specialized courses important to their career goals by taking elective credits. Majors commonly add courses in natural resource sciences (such as waterfowl biology and forestry) or in recreation and tourism. Students interested in careers in scientific research often choose to take additional courses in chemistry, computer studies, statistics, and mathematics. Students interested in careers involving the maintenance and restoration of animal populations and habitat often take management and conservation courses.

Some programs offer areas of specialization: Fish culture, for example, involves the breeding of fish and shellfish for release into natural systems for food. Water resources sciences—limnology (fresh water), water quality, and toxicology—examine the aquatic environment to determine its functions and its suitability for plants and animals.

Those majors who wish to pursue careers in research with a university, a private consulting firm, or the federal government often must obtain a graduate degree. Researchers working for federal agencies, such as the Fish and Wildlife Service, may work in laboratories or wildlife refuges. Most fisheries and wildlife professionals are certified by the American Fisheries Society of the Wildlife Society.

Specializations	Conservation, fish culture, toxicology.
Other majors to consider	**Animal sciences** **Biology** Environmental health engineering **Forestry** **Oceanography** **Parks and recreation management** **Wildlife management**
Careers related to the major	Fisheries and wildlife graduates may find jobs as a fisheries management biologist, wildlife management biologist, research scientist, research technician, park naturalist, fish culturist, water quality specialist, toxicologist, laboratory technician, zoo worker, high school teacher, or college professor.
For more information	National Wildlife Federation 1400 Sixteenth Street NW Washington, DC 20036-2266 (202)797-6800 The Wildlife Society 5410 Grosvenor Lane Bethesda, MD 20814 (301)897-9770

The American Fisheries Society
5410 Grosvenor Lane
Bethesda, MD 20814
(301)897-9770

American Institute of Biological Science
Education Department
730 Eleventh Street NW
Washington, DC 20001-4521
(202)628-1500

National Association of Conservation Districts
509 Capital Court NE
Washington, DC 20002
(202)547-6223

Food sciences

The food science major uses biological, physical, and social sciences to transform raw materials into safe, nutritious, and economical foods. Advanced concepts of microbiology, chemistry, engineering, and business are applied to the world's largest industry—the food industry.

Interests, skills, and qualities associated with success in the major

Interests. Biological and physical science, public well-being, teamwork, observing details, solving complex problems.

Skills and qualities. Good laboratory technique, manipulating instruments, understanding human behavior, working with people, organizing people.

Recommended high school preparation

English 4, precollege mathematics 3–4, biology 1, chemistry 1, physics 1, social studies 2, history 2, computer science 1–2, and nutrition 1–2.

Typical courses in the major

Principles of Food Processing	Economics
Chemistry	Human Resources Management
Statistics	Nutrition
Physics	Food Microbiology
Finance	Food Chemistry
Marketing	Food Analysis

What the major is like

The food sciences program provides an understanding of the nature, properties, and characteristics of food. Food science practitioners provide the essential nutritional needs for people of all ages and lifestyles worldwide. Students normally start with a two-year program generally consisting of 25 percent food sciences, 10 percent bioscience nutrition, 10 percent chemistry, 10 percent mathematics/statistics, 10 percent communications, 10 percent humanities, 5 percent physics, and 20 percent electives. Study is then directed toward understanding and applying technology to the processing, preservation, sanitation, storage, and marketing of foods. There may be special emphasis on food microbiology, food chemistry, food engineering, food marketing, consumer education, nutrition, business, or economics.

Students become skilled at using food sciences instruments and processing equipment. They also receive extensive laboratory training. Moreover, industry and government internships provide work experience.

An exciting and challenging part of this major is applying new services and technology. Food sciences majors may pursue a variety of professional positions in commercial establishments, educational institutions, consulting firms, and government agencies.

Specializations

Food chemistry, sensory evaluation, food microbiology, food sanitation, quality assurance, food engineering, food plant management.

Other majors to consider

Agricultural engineering
Biochemistry
Chemical engineering
Chemistry
Marketing
Microbiology

Careers related to the major

The food sciences major may lead to careers as a food technologist, process engineer, quality control analyst, food inspector, food sanitarian, consumer services representative, food plant manager, food merchandiser, technical sales representative, technical service representative, packaging technologist, food chemist, or food microbiologist. With graduate training, one may work as a food scientist, research scientist, or extension food technologist.

For more information

The Institute of Food Technologists
221 North LaSalle Street
Chicago, IL 60601
(312)782-8424

Forestry

Forestry is the science, art, and practice of managing and using the natural resources on forestlands. The major combines social, physical, and biological sciences to ensure informed management of forests and associated resources.

Interests, skills, and qualities associated with success in the major

Interests. Nature and the outdoors, working with people, planning activities, solving problems.

Skills and qualities. Communicating effectively, working with quantitative and qualitative problems, presenting ideas to others.

| **Recommended high school preparation** | English 4, precollege mathematics 3, biology 1, chemistry 1, physics 1, and social studies 2. |

Typical courses in the major

Forest Administration	Forest Ecology
Forest Economics	Forest Measurements
Forest Management	Forest Policy
Silviculture	Wood Anatomy
Pest Management	

What the major is like

Foresters are frequently involved in managing timber, water, recreation, forage, and wildlife habitat. They also play an important role in improving the environment. In addition to managing the forest's many resources, some forestry professionals are involved in wood science and technology—that is, they study the physical and chemical properties of wood as an industrial raw material. These specialists are concerned with all aspects of the manufacture and sale of wood products, such as oriented strand board and wafer board, and with new techniques for manufacturing other composite products. Their jobs may involve developing new wood products or monitoring the manufacture of existing products.

Undergraduate programs begin with general course work in English, mathematics, chemistry, physics, speech, and statistics. Basic forestry is usually studied in the freshman year. Because forestry is a diversified field, students have to choose one of several specialized areas. Introductory forestry courses and field studies conducted by forestry faculty provide information about these options. Once students have acquired this background, they begin course work in their chosen area. The decision on the specialty may come as early as the freshman year or as late as the end of the sophomore year.

Laboratory sessions concentrate on statistical analysis of data collected in the field, on biological relationships between different species of trees, and on interrelationships of trees and other living organisms in the forest. A portion of the courses are conducted in the field, so that students can experience firsthand the intricacies of the forest and its associated natural resources.

Nonforestry courses that will better prepare students for their careers include computer applications, business management, industrial engineering, and technical report writing. Students are encouraged to use their summers to work in forestry-related jobs. Many programs offer credit for these summer experiences, most of which are paying jobs with private industry; with county, state, or federal government agencies; or with other resource management agencies. Such work experience improves students' understanding of forestry and their prospects for permanent employment after graduation.

Specializations

Forest resource management, forest products, forest engineering, urban forestry, forest recreation, international forestry.

Other majors to consider

Botany
Civil engineering
Environmental science
Fisheries and wildlife
Landscape architecture
Wildlife management

Careers related to the major

The forestry major may lead to jobs as a forester, park ranger with the National Park Service, industrial forester, city forester, or wood product developer. With graduate work, students may find jobs in extension teaching or research.

For more information

Society of American Foresters
5400 Grosvenor Lane
Bethesda, MD 20814-2198
(301)897-8720

Horticultural science

The study of horticulture provides students with the opportunity to develop expertise in the production, marketing, and use of plants. Horticulturists work with fruits, vegetables, flowers, and the landscape in a variety of careers.

Interests, skills, and qualities associated with success in the major

Interests. Science, working with plants, business, working with people, solving problems, improving the environment.

Skills and qualities. Biological and physical sciences, written and oral communication, organization, creativity, quantitative thinking, computer competency, working with people.

Recommended high school preparation

English 4, precollege mathematics 3, biology 1, chemistry 1, physics 1, social studies 2, history 1, foreign language 2, visual arts 1, and computer science 1.

Typical courses in the major

Plant Propagation
Postharvest Plant Physiology
Plant Breeding
Floral and Planting Design
Greenhouse Management

Plant Nutrition
Genetic Engineering
Plant Identification and Use
Landscape Maintenance

What the major is like

Horticultural science has a strong foundation in the biological and physical sciences. Students usually major in one of these subdisciplines:

Floriculture is the production, marketing, processing, and use of potted plants, cut flowers, and garden annuals and perennials. It includes greenhouse management, plant breeding, floral design, and interior plantscaping.

Landscape/ornamental horticulture is the production, marketing, installation, and maintenance of landscape plants. It includes nursery and garden center management, landscape planting design, arboriculture (tree care), and public garden management.

Landscape architecture is the profession that relates to planning and redesigning the landscape.

Landscape horticulture involves designing, planting, and maintaining landscape plantings.

Olericulture/vegetable science is the production, marketing, and processing of vegetables. It includes plant breeding and greenhouse management.

Turf management is the production, marketing, installation, and maintenance of turfgrasses. It includes golf course and athletic field management. (This may be offered in agronomy departments.)

University horticultural programs emphasize basic science, business, and the environment. Problem solving and quantitative reasoning skills are stressed because horticulture, an applied science, seeks answers to problems concerning food, ornamental plants, and environmental quality.

Undergraduate students learn many skills essential to professional careers, such as the principles and practices of plant propagation (including tissue culture) and production; genetic engineering/plant breeding; weed, insect, and disease control (including integrated crop/pest management); arboriculture and landscape plant maintenance; management of controlled environments in greenhouses and conservatories; turf and golf course management; plant nutrition; design of floral products, landscape plantings, and interior plantscapes; and computer use and systems management. In addition they learn about plant identification and culture.

Because many horticultural graduates may achieve managerial positions in industry and the public sector, curricula include horticultural business management and economics. Emphasis is also placed on sustaining horticultural production systems by the combined principles of biological sciences, ecology, and horticultural technology. The increased concern for the environment and demand for garden and technical information also offer career opportunities in journalism and education.

Advanced degree programs are primarily science based and emphasize biotechnology and the application of molecular biology to the solution of horticulture and environmental problems. Genetics, microbiology, biochemistry, and physiology are often studied at an advanced level.

Specializations

Fruit and vegetable production systems management, floriculture/greenhouse systems management, nursery management, landscape design and management, turf management, plant/crop protection, horticulture education, parks management.

Other majors to consider

Agronomy
Biology
Botany
Conservation and regulation
Forestry
Landscape architecture
Plant pathology

Careers related to the major

The horticultural science major may lead to management positions with garden centers, retail florists, roadside markets, landscape firms, and golf courses. Graduates may find jobs as sales representatives with horticultural equipment firms, plant suppliers, and chemical supply companies. The degree can be preparation for working in arboretums and public gardens and for careers as a park naturalist, a city forester, or a plant inspector. Graduates with an interest in technology may want to work with tissue cultures or genetic engineering. With advanced degrees, students may work as researchers, extension agents, or college teachers.

For more information

American Association of Nurserymen
1250 I Street NW
Suite 500
Washington, DC 20005
(202)789-2900

Society of American Florists
1601 Duke Street
Alexandria, VA 22314
(703)836-8700

Soil sciences

Majors in soil sciences apply principles of biology, chemistry, mathematics, geology, and physics to a dynamic natural system—the soil. The curriculum focuses on the development, nature, and properties of soils, and on how they are used, conserved, and managed.

Interests, skills, and qualities associated with success in the major

Interests. Nature and the outdoors, conservation of natural resources, the environment, science.

Skills and qualities. Quantitative reasoning, keen observation of natural phenomena, oral and written communication, applying scientific knowledge to complex systems.

Recommended high school preparation

English 4, precollege mathematics 4, biology 1, chemistry 1, physics 1, history or social studies 2, foreign language 2, and computer science 1.

Typical courses in the major

Chemistry
Physics
Biology
Calculus
Soil Genesis
Statistics
Ecology

Soil Morphology
Soil Physics
Geology
Soil Chemistry
Soil Conservation
Plant Physiology

What the major is like

Soils constitute a significant component of the environment and are among the world's most important and fundamental natural resources. Soil sciences involve the chemistry, classification, conservation, fertility, genesis, microbiology, mineralogy, and physical properties of soils. Soil properties are usually related to a specified use, such as plant growth, structural support, waste disposal, land reclamation, or other environmental considerations. Soil scientists have prime responsibility for determining the distribution of soils on the landscape, assessing their characteristics, and predicting their suitability and limitations for different purposes. They also assist users in adopting practices that will conserve or reclaim soils.

Majors learn to describe soils in the field, make separations among them on the landscape, predict uses, recognize limitations, and make recommendations for erosion control, reclamation practices, water movement, and soil improvement.

Curricula in the soil sciences, usually offered only in land-grant universities, may be options within agronomy, earth sciences, plant and soil sciences, or natural resources majors. In every case a solid foundation in chemistry, biology, physics, and mathematics is required along with courses in the humanities and social sciences. Courses in geology, geography, economics, plant sciences, statistics, nutrition, and genetics are recommended or required. Students will take at least 16 semester credit hours, or their equivalent, in soil science. In addition to an introductory course, soil morphology, soil conservation, soil chemistry, soil fertility, soil genesis, soil management, soil microbiology, and soil physics may be available. Summer internships with field soil scientists are encouraged, if not required.

Specializations

Soil conservation, soil-crop management, land reclamation, soil surveying, waste disposal.

Other majors to consider

Agronomy
Biology
Chemistry
Earth sciences
Environmental science
Geology

Careers related to the major

Soil science graduates may find job opportunities as field soil scientists with the Soil Conservation Service, the Forest Service, private industry, or regulatory bodies. There are opportunities with consulting firms that help local and state governments deal with land reclamation and waste disposal, and that conduct environmental impact studies. With graduate work, students may find jobs doing industrial impact studies or in industrial research in areas such as soil chemistry, soil microbiology, or soil management.

For more information

Soil Science Society of America
677 South Segoe Road
Madison, WI 53711-1086
(608)274-1212

Soil and Water Conservation Society
7515 Northeast Arkeny Road
Arkeny, IA 50021-9764
(515)289-2331

The Soil and Water Conservation Society publishes a pamphlet called "Want to Be a Conservationist?"

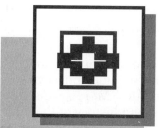

Architecture and Design

MICHAEL J. BEDNAR
University of Virginia

People sometimes think about how to make a house or an apartment a better place to live. They wonder how and why skyscrapers are built. They may walk into a store whose atmosphere makes them interested in the clothing sold there. They become curious about why old buildings look so different from new ones. They enjoy the serene beauty of a park. They wish that traffic congestion were no longer a problem.

The student who has seriously thought about the built environment may want to major in architecture or a related major such as interior design, landscape architecture, or city planning. These study areas concentrate on the appearance, function, and construction of everything from houses to parks, office towers to streets, chairs to rooms. The common concern is for spatial design that forms an integrated built environment, a world of quality places in which to live, work, and relax.

Architecture has been a human endeavor since people first emerged from caves and built their own shelters. For many centuries persons who designed and constructed buildings were master builders or craftsmen. During the Renaissance, in the fifteenth and sixteenth centuries, architecture evolved as a profession practiced by painters, sculptors, and engineers. Formal education to prepare individuals to become architects developed in the United States at the end of the nineteenth century. In the twentieth century, architecture became more specialized as some professionals chose to focus on specific elements of a building or its setting rather than on the structure itself. Interior designers make areas into rooms that are shaped and furnished for human activities. Landscape architects design communities, campuses, streets, parks, and gardens. City planners organize the total urban context and manage its development. Architects primarily design buildings, but they often coordinate all planning and design as well. Because there is so much overlap among these fields, broad-based professional knowledge and cooperation are important.

Although students in architecture, interior design, landscape architecture, and city planning may focus on aspects of the environment that differ in scope and scale, their common bond is a commitment to shaping the world creatively. The course work encourages students to see the world as an arena for design—the artistic and skillful planning of spaces and places. They develop sensitivity to visual appearance and its effects on human beings. They learn to communicate their intentions through sketches, renderings, technical drawings, and models prepared by hand or by computer. Architects, interior designers, landscape architects, and city planners are both artists and humanists. Their goal is to enhance the environment by designing buildings, interiors, parks, and cities.

To do this, they must take courses in the liberal arts, environmental design, and their chosen major. The basic program includes physical sciences, social sciences, humanities, and mathematics. More specialized courses focus on graphic skills, analytic methods, and history of the built environment. Advanced courses involve professional training to develop the skills and expertise needed to pursue a given area as a career. Courses are both theoretical and applied. The majority are studio based to allow students to acquire skills and apply their knowledge to the design of theoretical projects.

Undergraduate study in these majors can be either the basic education for a career or a liberal education that prepares students for graduate study.

Four undergraduate majors are described in this section: architecture, interior design, landscape architecture, and city planning. The following other majors are strongly related to these.

1. *Architectural history*: study of historic structures, sites, and communities
2. *Architectural preservation*: training to preserve or restore historic structures and places
3. *Environmental design*: generalist training in all aspects of designing the environment
4. *Architectural engineering*: training in the analysis and design of the technological components of environments

All these fields have a common concern with the environment that people build for their use and habitation. Here are just a few of the kinds of questions raised by that concern: Why are so many nice old buildings being torn down? Why does that new highway ruin the view of the mountains? Why does a house cost so much to heat? Why isn't the blackboard visible in this classroom? Why are they cutting the trees to add more power lines along Main Street? These are typical questions that people ask daily about the places where they live and work. The concerns about the built environment continue to grow in number and seriousness as more people try to live in less space on a limited planet. The role of architects, interior designers, landscape architects, and city planners in addressing these issues will continue to grow. Professionals in these fields will have many opportunities to become involved, to make a difference, to shape the world, to make beautiful places.

In the built environment there are no observers, only participants. And all participants have to live somewhere, work somewhere, shop somewhere. That somewhere can be inhospitable, ugly, dysfunctional, and degrading. Or it can be joyful, beautiful, meaningful, and supportive. The difference is up to architects, interior designers, landscape architects, and city planners. For students who want to take a direct hand in shaping the world, one of these majors could be the right choice.

Architecture

Architecture students concentrate on the design of buildings and other elements of the built environment. They work in design studios that develop skills and foster creative expression. Architecture students also study the history of the built environment (rooms, buildings, landscapes, cities), the technology required to create it, and related graphic communication.

Interests, skills, and qualities associated with success in the major

Interests. The formation of the physical environment; the history of buildings, cities, and landscapes; applied creative expression.

Skills and qualities. Communicating by sketching and drafting; solving spatial problems; sensitivity to visual forms, proportions, and colors.

Recommended high school preparation

English 4, precollege mathematics 4, physics 1, social studies 1, history 1, foreign language 2, and visual arts 1.

Typical courses in the major

Architectural Design
Architectural Construction
Design Graphics
Engineering Mechanics
Environmental Analysis

Architectural History
Building Technology
Perspective Drawing
Fundamentals of Design

What the major is like

The undergraduate major in architecture combines liberal arts subjects and preprofessional courses. Although the institution determines which curricular area is emphasized, in general architects must understand the culture in which they work (humanities), the physical world (physical sciences), and human relations (social sciences). They must also know the history of art and architecture.

Following this balanced general preparation, students begin the study of architecture with courses in graphic and visual skills. Accompanying courses in the history and theory of architecture reveal how the built environment was formed and describe the role of allied disciplines.

Every architecture curriculum emphasizes the design studio sequence. Each semester students take a studio course in which they develop skills in designing hypothetical buildings and environments. Beginning studios involve the design of objects, furniture, architectural elements, and rooms in which to live and work.

Intermediate studios stress the design of small buildings such as museums, libraries, and schools. In the final year, students design larger buildings in urban areas. Work in design studios is supported by courses in building technology, computer graphics, and design theory.

Design studio procedures are similar. The instructor assigns a project, outlines expectations, and provides resources. The instructor then works with each student to develop a design for the project with interim group reviews of the work. At the end of the project each student presents a solution through drawings (in various media) and models to the faculty for a critique of its strengths and weaknesses before beginning the next project. Studio work can include field trips, documentation, photography, interviews, research, graphic analysis, model making, and computer graphics.

Professional education to become a licensed architect requires five or six years of study. The four-year undergraduate major in architecture is a significant part of this professional education but it does not qualify the student to become a professional architect. Additional one-, two-, or three-year study leading to a Bachelor's of Architecture or Master's of Architecture is required. A period of internship and examination follows before a person becomes a licensed architect.

Specializations

Housing design, construction, computer graphics, historic preservation, architectural engineering.

Other majors to consider

Art history
City, community, and regional planning
Environmental design
Interior design
Landscape architecture

Careers related to the major

An undergraduate degree in architecture is a liberal arts education grounded in a specific professional discipline. It is useful preparation for every career in the building arts: architecture, construction, real estate, urban development, city planning, housing, and interior design. It may also lead to careers in industrial design, graphic arts, advertising, and photography.

Professional education to become a licensed architect requires five or six years of study. The undergraduate major in architecture leading to a four-year bachelor's degree is a significant part of this professional education but does not qualify the student to become a professional architect. Additional one-, two-, or three-year study leading to a bachelor's or master's in architecture is required. A period of internship and examination follows before a person becomes a licensed architect.

For more information

Association of Collegiate Schools of Architecture
1735 New York Avenue NW
Washington, DC 20006
(202)785-2324

City, community, and regional planning

Planning is a way to deal systematically and creatively with important issues at the city, community, and regional levels. Students commit themselves, through planning, to the future and to social and environmental improvement.

Interests, skills, and qualities associated with success in the major	**Interests.** Solving problems, working with people, helping groups, communities, and organizations improve people's lives. **Skills and qualities.** Working with numbers, listening, interpreting and communicating what you've observed or heard.
Recommended high school preparation	English 4, precollege mathematics 2, biology 1, social studies 2, history 1, foreign language 2, visual arts 1, and computer science 1.

Typical courses in the major

Planning Theories	Planning Law
Planning Practice	History of Cities
Regional Studies	Urban and Landscape Design
Environmental Issues	Social and Economic Issues
Technology of Urban Life	Community Development
Economic Development	

What the major is like

Planners learn to approach creatively the many problems facing cities, regions, and communities. They try to understand modern life critically—that is, by looking at how things arrived at their current state and analyzing how they might be improved. Planners continually ask what can be done, here and now, to set the stage for improvement. Students of planning study economics, history, political science, and other subjects that will enable them to solve social and environmental problems.

Because planning overlaps many other fields, students may major in planning and another subject, or minor in a related field. In the major, students often work in groups, helping one another to grasp thorny issues and figure out ways to address them. Planners address such questions as these: Can communities experiment successfully with recycling, resource conservation, and wildlife protection? Are a community's land-use and transportation systems appropriate to conditions anticipated in the next century? How can a city upgrade the standard of living of its low-income citizens? How much land should a growing suburban area preserve for recreational use? How can conflicts be resolved between developers and architectural preservation groups? How can volunteer groups, corporations, and governments work together to solve problems?

Students also work individually, under faculty supervision, learning a range of tools and techniques—from computer modeling to group decision making, from statistical programming to brainstorming and values clarification, from scheduling and managing devices to models planning.

Planning majors learn to analyze a situation, to imagine a better one, and to determine how to bridge the gap. The ultimate goal is to learn to work together to help build a better world.

Specializations

Environmental management, housing and community development, social welfare, urban design, policy analysis, community health, infrastructure and urban systems, land-use planning.

Other majors to consider

Architecture
Business administration
Civil engineering
Communications
Economics
Environmental studies
Geography
Health services management

Landscape architecture
Management
Political science and government
Public administration
Social work
Sociology

Careers related to the major

An undergraduate degree in planning can lead to a professional job with local and county government agencies, special district and state agencies, and private firms that do general planning or specialize in an area such as environmental regulation, land development, or policy analysis. The major is also excellent preparation for graduate or professional degrees in law, social work, architecture, urban design, public affairs, public administration, or planning itself.

For more information

American Planning Association
1776 Massachusetts Avenue NW
Washington, DC 20036
(202)872-0611

Interior design

Interior design majors study all aspects of the built environment: scale, proportion, arrangement, light, acoustics, temperature, textures, colors, and materials. They learn how to develop surroundings that are satisfying, creative, and appropriate to human needs.

Interests, skills, and qualities associated with success in the major

Interests. Architecture, design (interior, industrial, graphic), building construction, interaction of colors, nature of materials and textures.

Skills and qualities. Design, organization, working with people, drawing, communicating ideas.

Recommended high school preparation

English 4, precollege mathematics 4, physics 1, social studies 2, history or social studies 3, music 1, visual arts 2, computer science 1, architectural drawing 1, and wood and metal shop 1. If available, history should include social, aesthetic, and literary history as well as politics, diplomacy, and war.

Typical courses in the major

Design
Building Construction
History of Design
Furniture Design
Project Management

Drawing
Mechanical Systems
Lighting Design
Environmental Theory
Computer-aided Design

What the major is like

The interior design profession has changed fundamentally in recent years. Because interior designers take many different approaches, interior design education has branched out in diverse ways and will probably continue to do so until the licensing of interior designers is generally accepted, thereby establishing both consistency in the profession and standards in training.

The profession's original approach to design education assumes a "decorative" perspective and emphasizes furniture and the embellishment of surfaces within a given space. Recently, however, interior design has taken an architectural direction, shifting its focus toward spatial design and control of the environment.

Thus, interior designers study all aspects of the built environment: scale, proportion, arrangement, light sources, acoustics, temperature, textures, colors, and materials. By interpreting the impact of these elements on the user, they can manipulate them to produce creative and appropriate spaces.

Interior design programs usually consist of a series of design courses that begin in the freshman year and culminate in the senior thesis. Generally the courses use a hands-on, problem-solving approach: the professor presents a problem and the student works on a solution, all the while discussing and evaluating progress with the professor. In the early semesters, the problems are modest and few, but they gradually become more complex, varied, and numerous.

Interior designers must understand the physical, intellectual, and emotional impact of an environment on the individual user as well as its general social, ethical, economic, and political impact. The aim is to control, orchestrate, and enhance user satisfaction. Graduates are ready to enter the field as competent, responsible professionals who are at home with the aesthetic, technical, and administrative challenges of the field.

Specializations

Lighting design, furniture design, exhibition design, stage set design, acoustics, fabric design.

Other majors to consider

Architecture
Graphic design
Industrial design

Careers related to the major

The interior design major may lead to careers as an interior designer with an architectural firm or other corporation that designs interiors. It may lead to a position as a representative of a company that designs fabrics or furniture. Graduates may find jobs designing manufactured items such as windows, doors, bathroom and lighting fixtures, etc. They may pursue jobs restoring or preserving homes. Exhibition design and facilities management tap the skills of interior design majors. Some graduates move into design criticism or journalism. With appropriate graduate training, majors may become architects or landscape architects.

For more information

American Society of Interior Designers
608 Massachusetts Avenue NE
Washington, DC 20002
(202)546-3480

Interior Designers for Legislation in New York
200 Lexington Avenue
Suite 226
New York, NY 10016
(212)688-0521

Foundation for Interior Design Education Research
60 Monroe Center NW
Grand Rapids, MI 49503
(616)458-0400

See also *Interior Design* magazine and *Interiors* magazine.

Landscape architecture

Majors in landscape architecture gain knowledge, skills, and techniques for planning, designing, and managing the land. To reshape and conserve landscapes, they creatively apply information and principles drawn from both the arts and the sciences.

Interests, skills, and qualities associated with success in the major

Interests. Visual arts, ecology, nature, environmental issues.

Skills and qualities. Drawing and graphic expression, problem solving, written communication.

Recommended high school preparation

English 4, precollege mathematics 4, biology 1, chemistry 1, physics 1, social studies 2, history 2, foreign language 2, music 1, visual arts 2, and computer science 1.

Typical courses in the major

Basic Design
Landscape Planning
Landscape Design
Landscape Architecture History

Graphic Communication
Applied Ecology
Landscape Construction
Plant Materials

What the major is like

Landscape architects plan, design, and manage the land in ways that are useful, beautiful, and harmonious with nature. Students of landscape architecture work with the land: drawing, painting, and mapping it; describing it; studying and analyzing it; imagining what it might become in the future. They learn about the complex ecology of natural landscapes and the even more complex human ecology of urban landscapes.

In a typical university program students first learn drawing and computer graphic skills and the basic principles and vocabulary of design. They also study ecological systems and learn to identify and work with a broad range of indigenous plants. Related courses emphasize how social and political institutions are involved with the land and other courses present the theory and history of landscape architecture.

At more advanced levels, students build on this foundation to shape increasingly complex landscapes and to develop the detailed drawings, specifications, and other means of implementing their plans. In a typical studio course at the junior or senior level, students may design a park, a public garden, or a plaza; they may plan a site for a residential development or a sports complex; or they may develop a management plan for a natural reserve. In construction courses they learn how to produce the detailed drawings for any of these projects. Such assignments are carried out with ongoing instruction and guidance by faculty members.

Over 50 universities in the United States offer the landscape architecture major. Some offer a bachelor's degree in landscape architecture; others offer the Bachelor of Landscape Architecture (B.L.A.). The bachelor's is usually a four-year degree, and the B.L.A. usually takes five years. In most institutions landscape architecture programs are found in schools of design, along with architecture and planning. Programs, however, may also be offered by schools of agriculture, natural resources, or fine arts. Regardless of degree title or university organization, the curriculum generally follows a similar pattern and sequence. Students are given a foundation in the culture, knowledge, and skills of landscape architecture and are prepared for entry-level positions in professional organizations. The Landscape Architecture Accreditation Board evaluates accredited programs every five years for their effectiveness.

Many universities also offer the Master of Landscape Architecture (M.L.A.), which provides study in certain aspects of the profession. Students with bachelor's degrees from related fields can also enter an M.L.A. program for graduate professional education.

Specializations

Students do not specialize at the undergraduate level.

Other majors to consider

Anthropology
Architecture
City, community, and regional planning
Civil engineering
Ecology
Environmental design
Environmental studies
Graphic design
Ornamental horticulture

Careers related to the major

Most graduates of landscape architecture programs work in private consulting firms as designers, planners, or managers. Landscape architects are usually on the staffs of city planning, recreation, and parks departments at the local level and land management agencies such as the National Park Service, National Forest Service, and Bureau of Land Management at the federal level. An education in landscape architecture also provides a foundation for other careers related to shaping the environment.

For more information

American Society of Landscape Architecture
4401 Connecticut Avenue NW
Fifth Floor
Washington, DC 20008-2302
(202)686-2752

The brochure "Shaping Our Land" is available from the American Society of Landscape Architects.

The Arts

DAVID B. GREENE

North Carolina State University

As the word *major* implies, a major part of a college education is study in a particular field. If you major in one of the arts, you will study the history of that art and learn how to analyze and interpret it. You will gain technical skills in studio and performance courses. You will find out what people who are not artists say about art. You will explore the connections between art and the rest of life. You will begin to understand what makes an area of the arts special. In short, you will arrive at a first level of expertise in the field.

The word *major* also implies that your college course work includes a wider range of subjects than those in your area of concentration. This other part of higher education goes by various names—"general education" or "core curriculum" or "distribution" courses and electives. These courses outside the major make up what is called liberal education, because it prepares students to take an open-minded approach to learning. The knowledge, concepts, and skills learned in these courses are valuable even though they do not directly contribute to training for a profession or a career. They lead you into the natural and social sciences so that you may become acquainted with, and better able to function in, your physical and social environments. They let you explore the humanities (history, philosophy, language, and literature) so that you may begin to understand the human past, evaluate the present, and work toward a humane future. Because the arts touch every aspect of life, arts students must study many subjects. This strengthens students' ability to make a contribution in the world of art.

The major, in contrast to liberal education, is often thought of as professional training. And indeed it does give information, methods, procedures, and techniques needed in a career. A professional program in theater, for example, aims to offer students such good training in acting or other aspects of stagecraft that they can meet the standards of the field and seek theatrical employment with some confidence.

But an arts major itself also provides a liberal education. As you learn about a certain art, you learn to think, to turn a tangle of facts and feelings into a question. You learn several ways to follow through on a question— to make comparisons and to find an important difference between two similar ideas or objects, to sort out what is central from what isn't. You discover for yourself what every liberally educated person knows—that the deeper one goes into a particular area, the closer one gets to other areas. Painters begin to understand what psychologists know about perception. Composers move toward what computer scientists know about intelligence. Dancers discover some of what physicists know about space. These discoveries are as important as the professional training afforded by arts majors.

Some of the majors described in this section are closely related. Students interested in music will find six music-related majors. Each takes rudimentary knowledge of music in very different directions. Do you want to compose, learn theory, manage music companies, teach, perform, perfect one instrument, several? These are just some of the branches you can explore through various music majors.

The visual arts tap your interest in manipulating materials, composing (visually!), thinking about art in our past and that of other cultures. They teach you how to assess painting, drawing, sculpture, film, typography, and other forms of physical art. Whether your interest is wide ranging (various media) or narrow (only one type of art), you will learn to assess your motives and that of other artists, learn to use various techniques and materials, explore color, think two-dimensionally and three-dimensionally, and expand your technical ability and creativity.

Dance and drama are connected through their emphasis on training the body to be a vehicle of creative expression. Dance majors undergo rigorous physical training in order to convey meaning through choreographed movement. Dramatic arts students who are focusing on acting study voice control, group interaction, and movement. But drama also includes the study of every aspect of theater production—stage design, production, directing, and the history of theater. And dance can lead you down many interesting paths—to choreography, teaching, and mastery of different types of dance.

Majoring in one of the arts will teach you how to pursue an interest or activity you enjoy with discipline and dedication. This is an excellent educational foundation for whatever you pursue after college.

Art education

The major in art education provides students with the knowledge and skills to develop their artistic talents and with the information and experience to become effective art teachers. Students explore the value of art both to the individual and to various cultures throughout history.

Interests, skills, and qualities associated with success in the major

Interests. Visual arts, creating art, teaching.

Skills and qualities. Working with others, solving problems creatively, manipulating materials creatively, responding to other people's art with sensitivity.

Recommended high school preparation

English 4, precollege mathematics 3, biology 1, chemistry 1, social studies 1, history 2, foreign language 2, visual arts 4, computer science 1, and humanities 1.

Typical courses in the major

Design and Color Theory
Art Appreciation
Art of the Western World
Foundations of Art Education
Teaching Art

Studio Art
Art History
Teaching Aesthetics
Art for Young Children
Teaching Art Criticism

What the major is like

The major in art education is a professional degree program that includes certification to teach. (Each state has its own requirements.) The program leads to a Bachelor of Science in Education (which includes teaching certification) or a Bachelor of Arts or Bachelor of Fine Arts with certification. The major may be found in a range of departments (art, curriculum and instruction) or divisions (fine arts, education).

Whatever its location within the university, the art education program normally offers five choices of general focus: elementary, middle, secondary, all-level, and noncertificate (for students not planning to teach in public schools). All provide a liberal and professional education that fosters creative and aesthetic development.

Programs have varying emphases, but all offer a range of beginning courses in art and design and introduce the techniques of at least one studio area of concentration, which students pursue in upper-level courses. Aesthetics and criticism, a part of new trends in art education, are often incorporated in existing courses.

The amount of course work in instruction and curriculum development in art education varies among programs; the common goal is the proper sequencing of the art experience so that subject matter, materials, teaching strategies, and assessment are appropriate to each grade level. An important facet of all programs is the internship, which includes student teaching. Many institutions are now increasing the involvement of their students with local public schools in fifth-year, or induction year, programs.

Specializations   Studio art, aesthetics, museum education, art history, art criticism.

Other majors to consider

Advertising
Anthropology
Archaeology
Architecture
Art history
Art therapy
Arts management
Fashion design
Film arts
Graphic design
Humanities
Interior design
Museum studies
Photography
Studio art

Careers related to the major   The majority of art education majors go on to careers in elementary or secondary schools as art teachers, curriculum specialists, supervisors, or art administrators. Art education credentials are also helpful, if not necessary, for careers in museum education, community art centers, and arts and crafts centers. Students who want to teach at the college or university level need advanced degrees.

For more information   National Art Education Association
1916 Association Drive
Reston, VA 22091
(703)860-8000

National Association of Schools of Art and Design
11250 Roger Bacon Drive
Suite 21
Reston, VA 22090
(703)437-0700

Art history

Art history majors study works of art—how they came about and what they mean. Students examine artworks as they appear now and also consider appearance and function in their original contexts. Through their visual analysis and extensive reading and writing, students explore the traditions of appearance and technique that guided the creation of art in different cultures.

Interests, skills, and qualities associated with success in the major	**Interests.** Visual arts, past civilizations, the connections between different aspects of a civilization, artists, art techniques. **Skills and qualities.** Observing carefully, reading critically and carefully, remembering visual images.
Recommended high school preparation	English 4, precollege mathematics 2, biology 1, chemistry 1, physics 1, social studies 2, history 2, foreign language 2–4, music 1, and visual arts 2.

Typical courses in the major

Survey of Ancient Art   Renaissance Art
Art Since World War II   Baroque Art
Rembrandt   Michaelangelo
American Art   Japanese Prints
Chinese Painting   Architecture of Medieval Europe
European Landscape Tradition

What the major is like

Fundamental to art history are the description and identification of art objects that exist today. Students learn to distinguish artworks by style, materials, workmanship, and other characteristics in order to attribute them to particular artists or cultures or periods. Conversely, the art's style, materials, workmanship, and other characteristics provide means of learning about the artists and cultures where the art originated. Judgments about quality or artistic worth also depend partly on description and identification.

Art history also considers how individual works of art and groups of artworks can manage to express anything or to say or symbolize anything. In attempting to understand art as a system of meanings and values, art historians sometimes consider psychological factors, philosophical and aesthetic questions, or linguistic issues in addition to historical contexts.

Because the character of art varies so widely among historic cultures and because we understand art to be an especially vivid and accessible expression of these cultures, it has become customary to study art in association with particular periods and places. When studying how art reveals the material culture or the rituals of a civilization, art history students examine the artifacts and the various ritual and social practices of that civilization (similar to studies in archaeology and anthropology). They discover that often the art's original value and full meaning were results of its connection with religious, political, or social practices of the culture. Art history courses often include some account of the religions, government, economic structures, literature, and intellectual history of the cultures that produced the art. Students read about art patrons, critics, and viewers, as well as about artists.

Art history majors usually take broad introductory art history courses in their freshman and sophomore years along with liberal arts courses in science, English, math, and history. In their junior and senior years, they take courses that concentrate on a period (Baroque art), types of art (Japanese prints), or an artist (Michaelangelo). Many art history majors take selected courses in related areas of history, anthropology, or literature, for example. Also, many study two or more years of a foreign language in order to further their understanding of different cultures. Many art history students find it rewarding to take courses in studio art, where their understanding of techniques and processes of art is much enhanced.

Specializations

Students may specialize in the art of a time or place, such as classical art and archaeology, medieval art, Asian art, or European painting.

Other majors to consider	Anthropology
	Classics
	Comparative literature
	History
	Philosophy
	Studio art

Careers related to the major

Art history majors graduate with a liberal arts degree that has trained them in observation, analysis, and communication. This training is the basis for many jobs in business and government. With appropriate graduate training they may become college or high school teachers, educators, curators, or archivists in museums, or they may work with art through galleries, publishers, or government and corporate art collections.

For more information

College Art Association
275 Seventh Avenue
New York, NY 10001
(212)691-1051

Learning to Look. Joshua Taylor. Chicago: University of Chicago Press, 1957.

What Is Art History? Mark Roskill. New York: Harper & Row, 1976.

Arts management

Students learn to analyze and address the issues concerning the health of theaters, dance companies, museums, and other arts organizations through twin study of business and one or more fine or performing arts.

Interests, skills, and qualities associated with success in the major

Interests. Visual and performance arts, leadership, working with people.

Skills and qualities. Oral and written communication, organizational ability, creative thinking, critical thinking.

Recommended high school preparation

English 4, precollege mathematics 3, laboratory science 3, history or social studies 2, foreign language 2, and visual arts 4.

Typical courses in the major

Accounting	Advertising
Economics	Marketing
Public Relations	Statistics

What the major is like

A program in arts management aims to prepare students to serve as effective, responsible administrators in some aspect of the arts. The specific art (or arts) involved depends upon the interests of the student.

At least 25 to 30 percent of a student's total course work will be taken in an arts area. Common concentrations are music, theater, dance, or the fine arts. A strong business component is also required, typically another 25 to 30 percent. The rest of the student's undergraduate courses are normally in general studies of humanities, mathematics, social and laboratory sciences, and arts areas other than the major concentration.

Business courses tend to be taken in the first three years. During the third and fourth years special courses in arts administration or arts management are typically available. These courses focus on the organization and administration of arts agencies as well as the promotion of the arts. Such matters as planning, managing labor relations, fund-raising, and communications are also covered.

The music concentration involves basic music theory and music history as well as applied music and ensemble experiences. Minimal keyboard skills are necessary, and attendance at certain music functions—as well as other arts productions—is required.

In the theater concentration, courses in acting, stage scenery, makeup, costume design, play analysis, and lighting are common. Acting in plays or doing technical work in productions is expected.

The dance students take courses in ballet, modern, and theater dance as well as in dance history and choreography. Practical dance experience is required.

Fine arts courses devote much time to drawing, design, painting, and other media. Art history courses are valuable, especially those in the various periods, genres, and schools.

In the upper division, introductory courses are taken in arts management, and seminars are frequently offered where various topics in arts management are discussed. An internship with an arts organization in the senior year normally completes this major.

Specializations

Public relations, marketing, promotion of music, dance, or theater, human resources management.

Other majors to consider

Business administration
Dance
Dramatic arts/theater
Film arts
Management
Music business management
Music education
Public relations

Careers related to the major

The degree in arts management may lead to jobs as a theater manager, public relations representative, symphony orchestra manager, dance company manager, admissions director (at an arts-related institution), and other administrative positions with arts organizations.

For more information

National Network for Artist Placement
935 West Avenue 37
Los Angeles, CA 90065
(213)388-1989

Dance

Dance majors learn to develop their bodies as articulate instruments for dance expression; to understand contributions that dance has made to the arts; and to create their own dances. They take daily classes in technique that emphasize modern dance and ballet. Students have opportunities to perform, choreograph, and teach.

Interests, skills, and qualities associated with success in the major

Interests. Dance, other arts, the physicality of movement.

Skills and qualities. Physical stamina, a strong body, flexibility, sense of rhythm and musicality, creative daring.

Recommended high school preparation

English 4, precollege mathematics 2, biology 1, history 2, music 1, visual arts 1, and dance 2. Dance should be taken in high school or through private study with qualified teachers.

Typical courses in the major

Dance Technique	Composition
Dance Improvisation	Kinesiology for Dancers
Dance History and Philosophy	Dance Costuming and Lighting
Dance Notation	Dance for Children
Teaching Methods	Dance Repertory
Choreography	

What the major is like

The dance majors differ greatly from one institution to another. For many years dance was considered a physical education activity, rather than an art form, and the program prepared students to teach dance as physical education. Today dance programs may be administered within physical education, music, or theater departments, or they may exist as independent departments within colleges of fine arts.

Students should carefully examine the dance curriculum at the colleges they wish to attend. When dance is part of the physical education department, the B.S. or the B.A. may be awarded. The B.A. usually requires a greater number of liberal arts credits than does the B.S. When dance exists within fine arts, either a B.A. or a B.F.A. (Bachelor of Fine Arts) may be awarded. The two degrees differ in that the B.A. program usually emphasizes teaching and academic classes, and the B.F.A. program stresses performance and choreography.

A good dance program provides daily hour-and-a-half classes in technique. Most of these daily technique classes focus on modern dance and ballet, but they are augmented by classes in other kinds of dance, such as ethnic, folk, social, jazz, tap, or character dance. In-depth training in dance technique is essential, but a breadth of experience is also important. Technique classes help dancers develop a kinesthetic sensitivity to movement, so that they may use movement expressively and creatively.

Kinesiology, based on an understanding of anatomy, demonstrates how movement is accomplished and injury avoided. This knowledge helps dancers attain correct technical skills.

Classes in rhythmic analysis, percussion accompaniment, and music resources sharpen students' sensitivity to rhythm and help them find or create appropriate accompaniment for their choreography. Classes in dance notation teach students to analyze movement and record it, as well as to read movement scores.

Dance philosophy may teach principles of aesthetics that can be applied to choreography; dance history develops an awareness of, and an appreciation for, dance as an innate and universal form of human expression.

Dance majors should expect to choreograph throughout their college careers, simple dance studies and improvisations at first, and eventually at least one fully staged dance. Students learn to design costumes, to light dances, and to help produce concerts. They also learn to work cooperatively with others, to direct, to evaluate choreography (including their own), and to accept and benefit from criticism.

And they perform! Some performances are informal presentations for teachers and classmates; others are theater productions before the public. Performed dances may be student or faculty choreographed, or they may be repertory pieces by professional choreographers.

Students should take advantage of classes in teaching methods when possible. Although professional dancers may not plan to teach, almost all dancers eventually do so. It is important to learn to be a good teacher and to discover the joy of sharing a love of dance with others.

Specializations

Most dance departments do not encourage specialization at the undergraduate level because a broad background in dance is needed for almost any specialization. In states that offer teaching certification for dance, students may pursue an education specialization. At the graduate level, specializations in performance, choreography, teaching, dance kinesiology, dance history, dance ethnology, dance therapy, and special education are available.

Other majors to consider

Art education
Art history
Dramatic arts/theater
Elementary education
Fine arts
Music
Physical education
Physical therapy

Careers related to the major

Careers open to those with undergraduate degrees in dance include teaching dance in public schools (with dance certification), in YWCAs, YWHAs, private schools, and dance studios; dancing and choreographing for regional professional companies; and dancing in musical theater productions. For dancers with advanced degrees, the career field is further opened to include college teaching; dance research in areas such as history and kinesiology; dance therapy and work with special populations; arts administration; dance notation; and professional performance and choreography.

For more information

National Association of Schools of Dance
11250 Roger Bacon Drive, Number 21
Reston, VA 22090
(703)437-0700

Dance Directory. Reston, Virginia: National Dance Association of the American Alliance for Health, Physical Education, Recreation and Dance (Telephone: 703-476-3436).

Dramatic arts/theater

Theater is both a collaborative art and a practical skill. In the dramatic arts/theater major, students gain breadth of knowledge about past and present culture, art, literature, politics, psychology, and philosophy. They also learn the skills needed to become actors, directors, playwrights, designers, technicians, and managers.

Interests, skills, and qualities associated with success in the major

Interests. Self-expression, communication of ideas and feelings, literature and language, art and music, human personality and motivation.

Skills and qualities. Careful observation, critical reading, listening, solving problems creatively, physical daring, emotional openness.

Recommended high school preparation

English 4, precollege mathematics 1, biology 1, chemistry 1, physics 1, social studies 2–3, history or social studies 2–3, foreign language 2–3, music 2–3, visual arts 2–3, and computer science 1.

Typical courses in the major

Introduction to Dramatic Art
Acting
Stage Movement
Lighting Design
Directing
Playwriting
Theater Management

Theater History
Voice and Speech
Scenery Design
Costume Design
Musical Theater
Stage Management

What the major is like

Because the dramatic arts/theater major varies greatly among different institutions, the prospective student should explore individual programs thoroughly. Most programs offer instruction in both academic and practical areas; the difference lies in emphasis.

Students should note the degree offered by each college or university and determine if it's the degree that best meets their needs. A Bachelor of Arts (B.A.) in theater is a liberal arts degree awarded in a program in which students study the humanities through the study of theater and get some hands-on work in stage production (acting, design, directing, stage management, technical theater). A Bachelor of Fine Arts (B.F.A.) is a professional degree awarded in a program in which the student is trained specifically for a career in theater, as an actor, a designer, a director, a technician, etc. The B.F.A. has an academic component, but it is considerably less than that offered in the B.A. program.

The breadth and quality of the program may be affected by its size; a large faculty offers a greater variety of courses as well as more levels of work in acting, directing, design, and history. The presence of a graduate theater program at an institution may have both advantages and disadvantages: the faculty connected with a graduate program tend to be more high-powered, and production work standards tend to be more professional. On the other hand, the graduate program may receive more emphasis than the undergraduate program does, and the graduate and undergraduate faculties and facilities may be separate. A smaller college with no graduate drama program sometimes offers more production opportunities and faculty contacts to undergraduates.

Theater majors can choose courses in the following:

Dramatic art: The actor-audience relationship, dramatic style and structure, theater spaces, theories of criticism, and the functions of theater artists, technicians, and managers.

Theater history/literature: Classical Western theater, Renaissance and Elizabethan theater, and eighteenth-, nineteenth-, and twentieth-century theater.

Acting: Various levels of training, focusing on studio work. Introductory courses show students how actors train, how they deal with fundamentals of relaxation, trust, sensory awareness, group interaction, reaction and response, actions, and objectives. Improvisations and group exercises and some simple scene or monologue work are usually included. Advanced acting courses are usually concerned with scene work of increasing scope and complexity, including various classical as well as contemporary styles. Students work to free themselves emotionally, to commit to actions, and to create characters honestly, fully, and specifically. Students may read the books of the masters on the art of acting. Larger theater programs generally offer more levels of studio work than do smaller ones.

Speech and voice: (Sometimes included in acting classes.) Speech teaches proper articulation, phrasing, and dialect. Voice deals with freeing the natural voice and developing breath control and a fuller, richer vocal sound.

Stage movement: (Sometimes taught as dance.) Develops relaxation, suppleness, and daring that make the body an expressive instrument.

Design: Includes introductory courses in scenic design, lighting, costuming, and technical theater. Usually the theoretical side of each course is coordinated with a laboratory session in which students work with tools and equipment in a hands-on experience. The size of the individual theater program usually determines the number of instruction levels available in each area.

Directing: Includes the analysis of a script's style, form, and throughline of action with the objective of translating the written script into a fully staged production. Students learn to develop a unified point of vision in concrete terms.

Courses in musical theater, playwriting, stage combat, stage managing, scene painting, theater management, and more, are offered in some programs.

Specializations

Dramatic literature, theater history and criticism, acting, directing, design (scenic, lighting, costume), playwriting, stage management, theater management.

Other majors to consider

Architecture
Art history
Business administration
Creative writing
Dance
Education

History
Music
Musical theater
Philosophy
Political science and government
Psychology

Careers related to the major

The dramatic arts major may lead to jobs as an actor, director, designer, playwright, stage manager, or technical director. For the latter, postgraduate training to the M.F.A. level is desirable but not mandatory. Some human services positions make use of dramatic techniques in dealing with interpersonal structures and problems in the workplace. There are jobs in theaters for grant writers or public relations experts. Students may use drama in teaching at the elementary and secondary school level, or teaching special education classes. Advanced degrees are necessary to teach at a college or university.

For more information

University Resident Theater Association
1560 Broadway
Room 903
New York, NY 10036
(212)221-1130

Film arts

Students majoring in film arts study cinema history, screenwriting, and the aesthetic and technical aspects of cinema production, including directing, cinematography, and editing. They also examine the economic, technical, social, cultural, and ideological aspects of film as a medium for communication and personal expression.

Interests, skills, and qualities associated with success in the major

Interests. Film, literature, psychology, theater, music, art, history, biography, current events.

Skills and qualities. Creativity, ability to express oneself verbally and visually, self-discipline, understanding of human psychology, organization, attention to detail, flexibility, working with people.

Recommended high school preparation

English 4, precollege mathematics 3, laboratory science 2, history or social studies 3–4, foreign language 2–4, and visual arts 3–4.

Typical courses in the major

Film Production	Film Editing
Animation	Film Analysis
Authors and Genres	Film History
Film Theory	Documentary Film
Experimental Film	Special Topics
Visual Perception	Social Aspects of Media

What the major is like	Most film programs offer curricula that balance production, screenwriting, and film studies (history, theory, and criticism) with the option to concentrate in one of these three areas. Students are often required to produce a final project in their area of concentration.

In their first years of study, students gain a foundation in cinema history, screenwriting, and the aesthetic and technical aspects of cinema production. They also examine the economic, technical, social, cultural, and ideological aspects of film as a medium for communication and personal expression. Typically, students concentrate in their junior and senior years in one area of film arts.

The curriculum in film production begins with introductory courses in video or Super-8, stressing pictorial composition, lighting, exposure, camera techniques, editing, and visual communication. In the junior and senior years, advanced production courses acquaint the student with 16-mm synchronous sound camera and editing equipment. Filmmaking assignments may include individual as well as group projects.

The goals of a cinematography/film production program are to give the student a concrete foundation and practical experience in all aspects of cinematic production, including idea development, screenwriting, budgeting, producing, production management, directing, cinematography, sound recording/mixing, and editing.

A specialization in screenwriting emphasizes writing for the narrative dramatic genre. The student learns the structure, format, and technical requirements of screenwriting as well as how to develop characters and plot. Careful reading of screenplays and close textual analysis of films are essential. Attention is also devoted to the business aspects of marketing a screenplay.

The student in film studies concentrates on the history, theory, analysis, and criticism of film. Courses include in-depth histories (early silent cinema, Vietnam War films), genres (Westerns, musicals, melodramas), and author-directors (Hitchcock, Renoir, Fellini) in American and international cinema. Major theories will be introduced, from the classics (Eisenstein, Arnheim, Bazin) to contemporary semiotic, feminist, and psychoanalytic theories.

The undergraduate major in film typically leads to either a Bachelor of Arts or a Bachelor of Fine Arts. The program may be housed in a college of communications, theater, or fine arts.

Specializations

Film production, animation, screenwriting, film studies.

Other majors to consider

Art history
Creative writing
Dramatic arts/theater
Fine arts
Photography
Radio/television broadcasting

Careers related to the major

Jobs in the creative and business aspects of film are extremely competitive. Professional possibilities include entry-level production positions such as production assistant and production office worker and apprentice positions in editing, cinematography, art direction, wardrobe, and props. Talented writers may be offered a writing assignment on speculation.

Specialized training in animation, computer imaging, special effects, and sound mixing can lead to entry-level positions with companies specializing in such areas. An undergraduate degree also prepares the student for graduate studies in film.

For more information

American Film Institute Center for Advanced Film Studies
2021 Northwestern Avenue
Los Angeles, CA 90027
(213)856-7600

"The American Film Institute Guide to College Courses in Film and Television" is available from the American Film Institute.

Fine arts

Fine arts majors learn about the creation of art historically, in contemporary society, and through their own efforts in studio classes. They are taught to analyze and understand compositional structure as well as historical significance. They develop skills by working in various media.

Interests, skills, and qualities associated with success in the major

Interests. Making things with your hands, other cultures, history, paintings, sculpture, film, self-expression, different times and places.

Skills and qualities. Speaking and writing well, learning foreign languages, working with your hands, concentrating on visual images.

Recommended high school preparation

English 3–4, precollege mathematics 2, biology 1, history or social studies 3–4, foreign language 4, music 1–2, visual arts 1, art history 1, and religion and philosophy 2. Students should gain a foundation in studio drawing through their visual arts course.

Typical courses in the major

Foundations in Studio Practice	Drawing
Sculpture	Painting
Ancient Art	Indian Art
Chinese Art	Japanese Art
Photography	Ceramics
Design	Survey of Art History
African Art	Pre-Columbian Art
American Art	Baroque Art
The Renaissance	

What the major is like

In many liberal arts colleges, and in some universities as well, the program in fine arts involves theoretical, historical, and practical study of the activity we have come to call art, with a concentration ordinarily offered—or even required—in either art history or studio art. In either field, art students will spend some time considering exactly what art is.

It is a common misconception that a student must be creative to major in art. The liberal arts student who concentrates in art history is not a specialist in creativity but rather is interested in studying the history of creativity in the visual arts. Nor does a student need to possess a magical creative instinct to enjoy the studio concentration. Students who do best in studio courses work hard and are willing to spend long hours learning how to make things out of various materials.

The art history student deals with varying conceptions of art in different times and in different societies. Until recently the focus has been on European art, but the art of other cultures is coming to the fore in liberal education and in the next few years students can expect to be exposed to an impressive, worldwide array of art in their courses.

The study of art history requires much reading and also memorization. Students are expected to remember major works of art as well as to recognize unfamiliar works in the style of important artists previously studied. Similarly, they are expected to recognize and understand the nature of artistic production in many societies and at many times.

Students concentrating in studio art (that is, in the actual making of works of art) work in many different media—printing, print making, photography, painting, sculpture, ceramics, or even environmental projects. Many studio programs require a firm grounding in the basics of figure drawing and a solid education in the craft of making objects in any media attempted. Most programs require studio art students to take a variety of art history courses as well, for few liberal arts colleges see themselves as professional art institutes. At the same time, it is possible for students to concentrate in art history while taking only basic studio work. Indeed, many institutions require only one studio course in such a program.

Art history classes usually involve lectures illustrated by slides; students therefore need to learn to take notes from a slide presentation in a darkened room. Studio sessions are often much longer than the usual 40 to 50 minute classes, because more time is needed to get projects under way and moved ahead. Such projects often require large blocks of time outside class for their completion.

All fine arts students in a liberal arts setting are expected to understand the history, philosophy, literature, and general culture of the societies they study. Art students are most successful when they are concerned with learning for its own sake, whether it is the pleasure of knowing the past or of expressing themselves in the present.

Specializations Studio art, art history.

Other majors to consider **American studies**
Classics
Dramatic arts/theater
English
History
International studies
Music
Philosophy

Careers related to the major Like any other liberal arts graduate, the art student is prepared well for many professions but explicitly for none. Careers in government, business, education—indeed, any job requiring a general education background, are all strong possibilities. Employment as an art educator or a curator in museums or government agencies requires at least a master's degree. A doctorate is necessary to be a professor of art history; a master of fine arts is needed to teach studio art at the college level. Architecture is another option that requires further, specialized education. Most liberal arts students continue their studio work in graduate school if they seek careers as artists.

For more information

College Art Association
275 Seventh Avenue
New York, NY 10001
(212)691-1051

Graphic design

In the graphic design major students learn to communicate information visually using words and images. They also study how people perceive and interpret information.

Interests, skills, and qualities associated with success in the major

Interests. Visual arts; the relationship between intuition, intellect, creativity, and critical thinking; working with people.

Skills and qualities. Drawing, photography, meeting deadlines.

Recommended high school preparation

English 4, precollege mathematics 4, biology 1, chemistry 1, physics 1, social studies 2, history 2, foreign language 2, music 1, visual arts 4, and computer science 1. Social studies should include psychology if available.

Typical courses in the major

Information Design
Typography
Photodesign
Publication Design
Letterform Drawing
Reproduction Processes

Environmental Design
Identity Design
Computer-aided Design
Poster Design
Graphic Design History
Communication Theory

What the major is like

The graphic design major requires the student to understand aesthetic issues, to research and analyze how people perceive information and other issues related to visual communication, and to develop two- and three-dimensional visual constructs that use words and images. The major taps students' intellectual, analytic, and artistic abilities. Creativity in drawing, color, sculpture, and photography is combined with study of the history and development of communication, exposure to photomechanical and reproduction processes, and insight into personal and social issues posed by the profession.

Students typically begin the major with a foundation program that introduces them to the underlying conceptual, perceptual, and spatial principles of all the visual arts. Courses are given in drawing, designing in two and three dimensions, and color. Projects encourage the investigative process while exposing students to tools, methods, and materials. Foundation studies also include courses in art history, humanities, and social sciences.

Specific course work in graphic design usually begins in the sophomore year with an introduction to the history and practice of graphic design, typography, and photography. By working on studio projects, students develop an understanding of visual metaphor and the relationship between word and image. Additional studies in areas such as the philosophy of communication provide an intellectual base for projects that explore the relation of word to image.

In advanced courses students typically apply what they have learned and create charts, graphs, books, brochures, invitations, posters, symbols, signs, and exhibition designs. Students become familiar with the technical aspects of graphic reproduction when they take field trips to printing and paper firms and become involved in projects that use photomechanical and printing processes.

Seniors generally have opportunities for independent projects and internships in graphic design studios. Some senior classes may undertake a project for nonprofit clients. Through these experiences, students not only increase their technical understanding, but gain greater awareness of the historical and social context of the profession.

Specializations

Book design, magazine design, symbol design, identity programs, information design (charts/graphs), poster design, computer graphics, packaging design, film titles, typeface design, architectural signage, exhibition design, environmental graphics.

Other majors to consider

Architecture
Film animation
Film arts
Industrial design
Painting
Photography
Printmaking
Video

Careers related to the major

Graphic design training leads to careers with design groups or studios, publishers, museums, and other nonprofit institutions, government agencies, corporations, architects, multimedia studios, computer graphics firms, and exhibition design firms. Graduates may also work as consultants, freelance designers, and design educators.

For more information

American Institute of Graphic Arts
1059 Third Avenue
New York, NY 10021
(212)752-0813
(800)548-1634

Music

Music majors learn to listen creatively and perform intelligently. The music major involves work in three areas: music history, music theory, and performance.

Interests, skills, and qualities associated with success in the major

Interests. Many kinds of music, musicians, the development of musical forms.

Skills and qualities. Listening carefully, keyboard ability, singing intervals at sight, hearing music from studying a score, using computers.

Recommended high school preparation

English 4, precollege mathematics 2, laboratory science 2, social studies 1, history 2, foreign language 3, music 4, and computer science 1. One year of visual arts, dance, or theater is recommended.

Typical courses in the major

Analysis and Writing
Form and Analysis
Performance
Composition

Music History
Counterpoint
Conducting
Particular Composers and Periods

What the major is like

The music major involves work in three areas: music history, music theory, and performance. Although the exact amount in each area varies with the institution and the student's own interests, the total number of one-semester courses in each area is usually between 12 and 20.

Almost all music programs require at least four music history courses in which students study the features of musical styles and genres of different periods as well as the styles of the most important composers. Students may do advanced work in the music of one period or composer, in the process of change from one period to the next, or the connection between music and its social context. More and more colleges are offering work in music other than that produced in Europe and America—for example, traditional Chinese music, the music of the West African coast, and European folk music.

Music theory courses presuppose that the student can work quickly with the rudiments of music (rhythmic and pitch notation, key signatures, and scales). In a minimum of four theory courses, the student learns the principles of four-part music and practices these principles in weekly writing exercises.

These courses also teach methods of analyzing music in detail and in depth. Students may extend their theory work into counterpoint, do advanced work in analysis or in the history of music theory, or begin work in composition. Increasingly for students who have facility in writing computer programs, composition programs offer opportunities to synthesize music electronically.

The music major almost always involves work in basic musicianship—basic piano, sight-singing, score reading, keyboard harmony, and melodic and harmonic dictation. Many programs offer individual voice and instrumental lessons and classes in conducting. All offer the opportunity for, and many require, performance in ensembles. Some colleges offer a music performance degree, which involves much more work in performances (for example, a major in voice, violin, trumpet, or percussion). These programs often lead to the Bachelor of Music degree rather than to a liberal arts degree with a music major.

Because colleges sponsor recitals and concerts by faculty and guest artists, students frequently meet and talk extensively with professional performers and also participate in the management of these concerts. Many colleges offer music majors the opportunity to present their own recitals when they are seniors.

Specializations

Music theory, composition, conducting, music history, performance.

Other majors to consider	**Music business management**
	Music education
	Music performance
	Music therapy
	Religious music

Careers related to the major

The music major does not generally lead directly to careers in music, although it prepares the student for graduate work in music history, theory, composition, or performance. Like other liberal arts majors, it helps students to think critically and imaginatively, to pose new problems and suggest solutions, and to relate ideas in original ways. It may lead to careers as a teacher, performer, composer, computer software developer, music instrument manufacturer, music critic or journalist, music librarian, music therapist, or art administrator.

For more information

National Association of Schools of Music
11250 Roger Bacon Drive
Suite 21
Reston, VA 22090
(703)437-0700

Music business management

Majors in music business management typically study the functional areas of business (accounting, marketing, finance, and resource management), as well as music performance, history, and theory.

Interests, skills, and qualities associated with success in the major

Interests. Music, leadership, organizing people, business, solving problems, negotiating.

Skills and qualities. Oral and written communication, patience, leadership, organization, creative thinking, using computers.

Recommended high school preparation

English 4, precollege mathematics 2, biology 1, physics 1, social studies 1, history 2, foreign language 3, music 4, visual arts 1, and public speaking 1. One year of computer science is also recommended.

Typical courses in the major

Economics
Marketing
Human Resource Management
Arts Patronage
Music Theory
Music Performance

Accounting
Financial Management
Computer Processing
Arts Organization Management
Music History

What the major is like

The purpose of programs in music business management is to prepare people to enter the business world able to address issues in music and the arts such as patronage, copyright laws, and musicians' union regulations, and with knowledge of fund-raising, grant-proposal writing, and advertising techniques. To do this, programs provide students with a broad understanding of both music and business and with the opportunity to diversify their studies.

The major may be offered in courses of study leading to the Bachelor of Music or Bachelor of Arts degrees, or in combined programs with the departments of music and economics or management. Students can expect to become widely acquainted with the history and theory of music and to participate in various musical performances on campus. At the same time, they will take courses that provide core knowledge of methods, concepts, and principles of management and business practices. Additionally, most institutions expect that all students in this major will take between 30 and 40 percent of their total course work in humanities, mathematics, and the sciences to ensure a solid foundation for personal growth.

Many colleges and universities offer students of music business management opportunities for internships where they earn academic credit while getting hands-on experience in business or management. These internships, commonly in cooperation with recording studios, music publishing houses, arts organizations, symphony orchestras, or television studios, provide a unique way for the student to explore the professional field under the guidance of college and university mentors.

Many degree programs in this field have enough flexibility to allow students to choose areas of specialization. For example, a student interested in a career with international possibilities is often able to study a foreign language and to take area studies courses focusing on a particular culture or country.

Specializations

Musical theater, studio production, copyright laws, international business, marketing, musical theory, history, or performance.

Other majors to consider

Arts management
Computer science
Economics
Management science
Music
Music education
Music performance
Musical theater

Careers related to the major

The continually expanding popularity of music of all kinds has created a vast array of career opportunities for individuals with skills in both music and business. Whether on the local, national, or international scene, there are challenging, rewarding, and even lucrative positions for capable, qualified music business managers. The major may lead to careers as an orchestra manager, artist representative, music facilities manager, music personnel manager, concert booking agent, or recording studio manager. There are also job opportunities in publishing, promotion, retailing and distribution, and arts administration.

For more information

National Association of Schools of Music
11250 Roger Bacon Drive
Suite 21
Reston, VA 22090
(703)437-0700

Music education

Music education prepares students to become music teachers in public schools. Students learn the basics of music and the fundamentals of teaching in order to share music with people of all ages and abilities.

Interests, skills, and qualities associated with success in the major

Interests. Listening to music, performing, working with young people, leadership.

Skills and qualities. Musical ability, including a sense of rhythm and pitch; discriminating listening; vocal or instrumental performance, keyboard facility; oral and written communication.

Recommended high school preparation

English 4, precollege mathematics 3, laboratory science 1–3, social studies 2, history 2–3, foreign language 2, music 4, visual arts 1, and computer science 1. One year of drama, speech, or dance is also recommended.

Typical courses in the major

Music Theory	Aural Skills
Music Analysis	Applied Music
Conducting	Arranging
Ensemble	Music History
Wind Instruments	Percussion
Stringed Instruments	Voice
Instrumental/Vocal Methods	Educational Psychology

What the major is like

Students majoring in music education learn the basics of music, its history, and how it is communicated through notation and performance. They also learn to share this art through principles of teaching and learning found in professional education courses.

The program is broad and complex, and the diversity of courses and skills to be mastered means that a student must begin the major in the freshman year. Some institutions—depending on state requirements for teacher certification—offer as many as three options in this major: (1) comprehensive, preparing students to teach both vocal and instrumental music from kindergarten through high school; (2) instrumental, preparing students to teach instrumental music only; and (3) vocal, preparing students to teach vocal music only. The comprehensive option is a five-year program. The instrumental and vocal options require four years each.

Music education majors study voice or instruments privately. They learn to read, write, and analyze music at advanced levels; perform in vocal and instrumental ensembles, in recitals with others, and in solo recital their senior year; arrange music, conduct, and compose during their college career. They observe classes in schools and prepare lesson plans. They teach microlessons, private instrument lessons, and general music classes from kindergarten through high school, use computer-assisted instruction, design individualized music lessons, and are creatively involved in electronic/computer music making.

A music education student, although specializing in music, also studies the liberal arts. All students take courses in English, mathematics, science, social science, fine arts, and humanities. Some students even complete a second major in areas such as languages, business, theater, mathematics, computers, or accounting. All students have opportunities to attend recitals by faculty and guest artists and to participate in education workshops and conferences.

The most common degrees offered in music education are the Bachelor of Music Education (B.M.E.), Bachelor of Music in Education, Bachelor of Arts in music education, and Bachelor of Science in music education. In B.M.E. and Bachelor of Music in education programs, approximately half the course work is in music studies and half is in general and professional education. The B.A. in music education and the Bachelor of Music in education usually require two to four semesters of a foreign language.

The music education major provides broad career preparation in that it crosses all disciplines; involves students in learning how to work with normal, gifted, and disabled persons; and introduces students to a variety of lifelong learning opportunities.

Specializations

Specializations are not available at the undergraduate level.

Other majors to consider

Arts management
Computer science
Electrical engineering
Music
Music business management
Music therapy
Religious music

Careers related to the major

Career options are varied for music education graduates. With teaching certificates, graduates are eligible for employment in any school setting. They may pursue a career in church music, solo performance, or music drama.

The Music Educators National Conference (listed below) has a pamphlet, available on request, listing job possibilities, salary expectations, and required schooling. Some of these positions are: music teacher; music therapist; music librarian; instrumentalist with the armed forces, pop/rock bands, orchestras, instrument clinics; vocalist with a church choir, in radio/TV, or an opera chorus; organist, choir director, or soloist with a church or temple; composer/arranger/copyist; and conductor. In the music industry there are jobs as publisher, software designer, or technician. Television and radio stations need music editors, sound mixers, music engineers, disc jockeys, and program directors.

For more information

Music Educators National Conference
1902 Association Drive
Reston, VA 22091

National Association of Schools of Music
11250 Roger Bacon Drive
Suite 21
Reston, VA 22090
(703)437-0700

Music performance

Students, who upon entering college are expected to have a high level of performance skill and musical understanding, reach even higher levels of technical proficiency and musical sensitivity as music performance majors. In addition, they become well-rounded musicians through the study of core music theory and history courses.

Interests, skills, and qualities associated with success in the major

Interests. Communicating through music performance, the theoretical and historical aspects of musical structure and style, the relation of music to society.

Skills and qualities. Natural aptitude for music, technical skill, strong background in piano (including two to three years of private piano study immediately preceding the freshman year).

Recommended high school preparation

English 4, precollege mathematics 3, laboratory science 2, social studies 2, and humanities. High school courses in ensemble and performance are recommended but are not specifically required. Prospective students are encouraged to take courses emphasizing ear training and sight-singing. Courses in music theory and literature may be helpful, but students should be aware of the great diversity of methods and materials in university courses in areas such as written harmony and analysis.

Typical courses in the major

Written Music Theory
Aural Music Theory
Sight-singing
Keyboard Harmony
Conducting
Music Theory

Private Lessons
Piano
Choral Ensemble
Composition
Pedagogy

What the major is like

The music performance major involves work in three principal areas: performance, core courses in music history and theory, and related music courses.

Music performance courses and ensembles consist of private lessons in the student's principal performance medium, private or classroom lessons in secondary piano, chamber music ensembles, and large choral and instrumental ensembles.

Core courses in music theory include analysis, writing, sight-singing, ear training, and keyboard harmony, offered as either separate or integrated courses. Music literature and history courses are usually organized by chronology or genre.

Related courses are typically in repertoire, pedagogy and music education, conducting, composition, jazz studies, and the like.

A substantial portion of the credit hours for the degree are in study relating to performance. Private lessons enable students to solve their technical problems and explore their interests in expression and repertoire. In addition to weekly private lessons, students participate in master classes, studio recitals, and solo recitals. Also, instrumentalists participate in chamber music coaching and performances; vocalists in opera coaching, workshops, and performances; and all students in rehearsals and performances of large ensembles (band, orchestra, chorus).

Specializations

Voice, piano, organ, guitar, individual orchestra or band instruments, jazz studies, early music, church music, instrumental pedagogy, vocal pedagogy, conducting.

Other majors to consider

Music education
Music history and appreciation
Music theory and composition
Music therapy

Careers related to the major

After graduation, performance majors are ready to compete for positions with orchestras, ensembles, and other music organizations and are prepared to teach privately in their performance areas. Music performance degrees alone are not sufficient credentials for public school teaching positions. Some institutions, however, combine music performance degrees with music education degrees in five-year bachelor's programs; others make it possible for students to fulfill requirements for teacher certification while working on a master's degree. Advanced (master's and doctoral) degrees in music not only improve performance skills and musical understanding, but they also provide the necessary credentials for college teaching positions.

For more information

National Association of Schools of Music
11250 Roger Bacon Drive, Suite 21
Reston, VA 22090
(703)437-0700

Music therapy

In the music therapy major students apply specifically designed music experiences and activities to the treatment of individuals and groups in all age categories who have psychological, emotional, physical, social, intellectual, or medical disorders.

Interests, skills, and qualities associated with success in the major

Interests. Music, the arts, behavioral and life sciences, helping others.

Skills and qualities. Competency in music performance and theory, preferably through formal training; oral and written communication; working with people.

Recommended high school preparation

English 4, precollege mathematics 2, biology 2, chemistry 1, physics 1, social studies 1, psychology 1, history 2, foreign language 2, music 4, visual arts 2, and computer science 1.

Typical courses in the major	Music Theory	Music History
	Music Literature	Conducting
	Child Psychology	Abnormal Psychology
	Anatomy and Physiology	Music in Therapy
	Psychology of Music	Clinical Practicum

What the major is like

Throughout the ages, music has been recognized for its curative effects. In the study of modern music therapy, students learn to apply the art of music, with all its effects, to the science of therapeutic treatment. A career in music therapy demands maturity and creativity. Strong musical skills and a desire to work with, and to help, others are musts.

This major is housed in departments (or schools and colleges) of music that have been approved by the National Association for Music Therapy or the American Association for Music Therapy. In large part, these associations prescribe the curriculum, which comprises four areas: music, behavioral and life sciences, music therapy, and general education.

The music component of the program, as for most music majors, requires music theory, music history and literature, applied music study and performance, and conducting. In addition to this traditional study, training in music therapy also requires the study of piano, guitar, and voice. Functional skills on these instruments include performing children's folk and popular songs by ear (without accompaniment) and in more than one key. These music skills—both functional and basic—are the tools of the trade, for without question, the stronger the musician, the better the music therapist.

The behavioral and life science component of the program includes extensive work in psychology, sociology/anthropology, biology, and anatomy/physiology. The study of both normal and abnormal human function provides students with the informational background of the disorders they will work with.

The music therapy portion of the degree draws on the above areas to train students to assess a client, develop an individualized music therapy program or strategy, implement the program, and evaluate its results. Students study the effects of music on behavior and on human function in order to apply music to improve a client's current condition.

A unique aspect of this major is the considerable amount of clinical fieldwork required throughout the program, thus providing many hands-on experiences and culminating in an internship after the completion of all course work. After graduation, students take an examination in music to certify that they have attained minimal competencies for professional practice.

Specializations

Psychology, music education, music performance, special education.

Other majors to consider

Art therapy
Dance therapy
Music education
Occupational therapy
Psychology
Social work
Special education
Speech correction

Careers related to the major	Graduates may find jobs as a music therapist in psychiatric, medical, state, and Veterans Administration hospitals, and in schools, clinics, and private practice. Graduate degrees in music therapy can lead to supervisory positions in a clinical setting and in university-level teaching.

Music therapists usually work as part of a treatment team that includes physicians, psychologists, teachers, social workers, and other therapists. Many music therapists establish private practices. |
| **For more information** | National Association for Music Therapy
8455 Colesville Road
Suite 930
Silver Spring, MD 20910
(301)589-3300

American Association for Music Therapy
P.O. Box 80012
Valley Forge, PA 19484
(215)265-4006 |

Photography

Photography is for students who have an interest in communicating ideas and concepts visually. Students gain a broad background in the technical aspects of photography and an even broader understanding of the social, political, and interpersonal aspects of society. The major covers the use of photography for commercial, educational, informational, scientific, and technical work as well as for personal expression.

Interests, skills, and qualities associated with success in the major	**Interests.** Expressing yourself in a visual medium; creating images from your ideas and those of others; helping people see and understand subjects to which they might not otherwise have access.

Skills and qualities. Visualizing images from ideas and the written or spoken word; good sense of color, composition, and style; communicating with others. |
| **Recommended high school preparation** | English 4, precollege mathematics 3–4, biology 1, chemistry 1, physics 1, social studies 2, history 2–3, visual arts 3–4, and computer science 2. Photography, business, and theater classes are recommended if available. |
| **Typical courses in the major** | Color Theory and Printing   Materials and Processes
Studio Lighting   Photojournalism
Fine Arts   Image Permanence
Museum Practices   Photography Business
Black-and-white Photography   Editing
Photography and Art History   Design
Color Photography |

What the major is like

Photography is an area of sharply distinct specializations, yet a few common threads are woven among virtually all the specialities. For all photographers share a desire—or even a passion—for communicating information and ideas on film. Commercial photographers, for instance, illustrate information about products and services available to the public; photojournalists document current and special events; technical and medical photographers show procedures and details that might be invisible to the unaided eye; and fine artists express their own emotions and ideas.

All successful photographers have something to say. Therefore, a photography program, while teaching the necessary technical skills, generally provides students the opportunity to expand their intellectual viewpoints. Technicians who have nothing to say, after all, are as useless as thinkers who cannot express their thoughts.

In their courses, students of photography study the fundamentals of design, form, color, and composition. An inquiry into the nature of light and an examination of how it is translated in the photographic medium is basic to the study of photography, as is the analysis of how three-dimensional space is converted into two-dimensional form. Printmaking, lighting and laboratory technique, film handling and processing, in both black and white and color, are basic to the curriculum. Photographic history as well as contemporary issues in photography are studied and discussed—the student evaluates his or her own work and that of others in this context. Students may take courses in other arts, such as drawing, sculpture, and painting, in order to add these media to their work. Students whose interest lies in documentary photography or photojournalism may take classes in journalism, English, and anthropology. Throughout the study of the medium, a balance between the technical and the creative aspects of the art is sought.

Most programs specialize in one or two areas of photography; fine arts and journalism are the most common. (Such courses may be offered in conjunction with broader art or journalism programs.) Commercial advertising and portraiture are often taught in separate, specialty programs in larger photography departments. A few universities have courses in technical and biomedical photography, processing management, or science photography; some offer entire degree programs in these special fields.

Specializations

Commercial photography, architectural photography, biomedical photographic illustration, electronic imaging, fashion photography, photographic science, photography as fine art, photojournalism, portraiture, processing and photo management, technical and industrial photography.

Other majors to consider

Arts management
Computer graphics
Film arts
Graphic design
Video

Careers related to the major

Photojournalists usually work for publications such as newspapers, magazines, and photo agencies. Technical and science photographers are hired by industrial companies or medical facilities. Most college-educated commercial and portrait photographers are independent entrepreneurs.

Many graduates become technical and sales representatives for photo-oriented corporations. Some find careers as sales representatives for other photographers. The introduction and rapid assimilation of the electronic media have opened the door to a variety of additional career opportunities. A person who may once have done only photography may now be involved in the graphic layout of an assignment, the retouching or enhancement of an image, or the process of preparing an image for reproduction through computer technology.

For more information

Biological Photographic Association
115 Stoneridge Drive
Chapel Hill, NC 27514
(919)967-8247

Association for Education in Journalism and Mass Communications
1621 College Street
University of South Carolina
Columbia, SC 29208-0251

Society for Photographic Education
P.O. Box 1651
FDR Station
New York, NY 10150

College Art Association
275 Seventh Avenue
New York, NY 10001
(212)691-1051

Professional Photographers of America
1090 Executive Way
Des Plaines, IL 60018

Religious music

Students of religious music develop their skills and interests as musicians and learn to use music in religious celebrations while focusing on the role and history of music in worship.

Interests, skills, and qualities associated with success in the major

Interests. Music, music history, the fine arts, the place of music in religious celebrations, matters of faith, working with people.

Skills and qualities. Ability to listen carefully, including some ability to hear and sing intervals, chords, and melodic patterns; keyboard ability (piano or organ); vocal or choral experience.

Recommended high school preparation

English 4, precollege mathematics 2, laboratory science 2, social studies 1, history 2, foreign language 3, music 4, visual arts 1, and computer science 1.

Typical courses in the major	Performance (Voice, Piano)	Music Theory
	Musicianship	Music History
	Conducting	Composition
	Choir-training Techniques	Ensemble (Choral, Instrumental)
	Church Music	

What the major is like

The major in religious music is much like other music majors but with an added emphasis on the use of music in religious services today. Students study basic musicianship. Music theory courses review the rudiments of music (rhythmic and pitch notation, key signatures, triads and scales) and explore the concepts of harmonic activity as well as structural nature. (Many colleges now include the use of computers and synthesizers in music theory.) Students can expect courses in the history and literature of music, including experience with music other than that of Europe and America, such as African music, traditional Asian music, folk music, and popular music.

Because most majors in religious music have a vocational goal of musical leadership in a congregation, programs comprise performance and ensemble participation, conducting, choir training, and choral literature.

Most colleges offer the study of religion and the history of music in worship through such courses as Biblical studies (especially the Psalms), music in worship, and liturgics.

Since musicians serving congregations often function as performers, most colleges encourage solo junior and senior recital opportunities in addition to concerts and recitals by ensembles, faculty, and visiting artists. The solo recitals allow students to experience music making and to relate their classroom study to actual performance and composition.

Specializations

Organ performance, vocal performance, conducting.

Other majors to consider

Music education
Music performance
Religion
Theological studies

Careers related to the major

Although there has never been an abundance of positions for full-time musicians in churches and synagogues, there are and will continue to be positions in this field, especially in major metropolitan areas. Many of the better opportunities come to those who have done graduate study. Some students find that combining the music degree with religious education or counseling provides a wider variety of positions. Some go on to seminary, using their musical skills while serving as ordained clergy. The major may lead to positions as an organist, music director, music teacher, or cantor.

For more information

National Association of Schools of Music
11250 Roger Bacon Drive, Suite 21
Reston, VA 22090
(703)437-0700

Studio art

Studio art majors create works of art by exploring a variety of techniques and materials. They focus on learning to master new media, discovering unique solutions to visual problems, exploring fresh ways to create satisfying images, and evaluating what is worth doing.

Interests, skills, and qualities associated with success in the major

Interests. Visual arts, manipulating materials, observing and responding to visual phenomena in nature and works of art, communicating and experimenting with forms, colors, images, and symbols.

Skills and qualities. Working independently, creating fresh and lively images, finding visual metaphors for nonvisual ideas, seeing art history as the basis for creative work, solving visual problems, evaluating what you and others create.

Recommended high school preparation

English 4, precollege mathematics 2, laboratory science 2, social studies 1, history 2, foreign language 2, visual arts 4, computer science 1, and wood and metal shop 2. One year of music, dance, or theater is recommended.

Typical courses in the major

Drawing
Sculpture
Printmaking
Product Design
Computer Graphics
Crafts (ceramics, fiber, metal)
Architecture
Art Theory

Painting
Life Composition
Graphic Design
Fashion Design
Photography
Intermedia
Art History

What the major is like

Studio art majors are involved in creative activities from their first course in drawing, painting, sculpting, or designing. They also assess the quality of what they and others produce and try to gain knowledge of the relationship of these works to society's needs. They come to understand the ideas, values, motives, and vocabulary of artists, develop a broad appreciation of how art was created in other times, and its uses within various cultures. The instructors are practicing, exhibiting artists and designers who work in their own studios and generate ideas with which students experiment.

Programs are designed not only to promote the ability to create high-level work but also to encourage students to make a commitment to an area of special interest. Many studio art students focus as much as one-third of their work in the major on courses in their emerging interests, such as sculpting, drawing, or painting. In gaining a knowledge of what artists from a variety of cultures and historical periods have produced, students develop an extensive visual vocabulary. (Most programs in art history and art appreciation begin with surveys of art history as platforms for the selection of more advanced and specialized courses.) Students are encouraged to keep up with current art magazines and with exhibitions in galleries and museums. They are also encouraged to work with, and build on, the ideas of the artists they have studied.

In colleges at which art is taught in the context of a broad general education, the Bachelor of Arts is the most frequently offered degree. The Bachelor of Fine Arts is awarded after completion of a program that focuses on a specialization in art, and includes general education courses as enrichment. Either degree prepares the student for continuing work toward a Master of Arts or Master of Fine Arts. The major also provides the preparation essential for a fulfilling career as a practicing artist or commercial designer.

Specializations

Painting, sculpture, graphic arts, photography, intermedia, graphic design, fashion design, product design, computer graphics, architecture, ceramics, metals, fiber arts.

Other majors to consider

Art education
Art history
Art therapy
Computer graphics
Computer science
Museum studies
Theater design

Careers related to the major

The art major may lead to careers as an artist, teacher at all levels from elementary school to graduate school, commercial artist, art critic, museum curator, restorer/conservator, graphic designer, art book editor, art agent, or art administrator.

For more information

College Art Association
275 Seventh Avenue
Fifth Floor
New York, NY 10001
(212)691-1051

National Art Education Association
1916 Association Drive
Reston, VA 22091
(703)860-8000

Biological and Life Sciences

WILLIAM E. BARSTOW
University of Georgia

On April 2, 1953, a revolution in biology began. On that day James D. Watson and Francis H. C. Crick, working at the Cavendish Laboratory in Cambridge, England, mailed to the British journal *Nature* a one-page manuscript that began: "We wish to suggest a structure for the salt of deoxyribonucleic acid (DNA). This structure has novel features which are of considerable biological interest." What an understatement! Nothing in biology has been the same since.

Found in every living organism from the simplest bacterial cell to the tallest redwood tree, DNA is the genetic molecular code that is passed from generation to generation. What is the DNA code for? It is for the sequence of amino acids that make up proteins. Scientists can now manipulate the DNA of some organisms to form distinctive proteins. For example, some bacterial cells are manufacturing human growth hormone protein, and some bacteria, incredibly, are synthesizing human insulin. The list grows longer every day.

In the 1960s the genetic code was cracked, and the specific DNA code for each amino acid is now known. In 1972 Paul Berg, at Stanford University, removed DNA from one bacterial cell strain, inserted it into another, and changed the genetic makeup of the recipient cells. The cells were transformed! During the 1980s researchers learned how to cut, modify, manipulate, recombine, and control the expression of DNA. In the 1990s they are at the threshold of a new biology. Incredible progress is being made in molecular biology and genetics, particularly in understanding the workings of the gene and its application in genetic engineering. By the year 2000 biologists expect to have figured out the DNA sequence for the complete set of human genes. If so, the DNA code of all the genes of *Homo sapiens* will then be known.

Enormous leaps are being made in understanding biology at every level—from molecules to organisms to ecological systems. Computers are being used in hundreds of ways to store and manipulate data. Just as research in the 1960s and 1970s led to solving so many cell mysteries, the present efforts against AIDS are leading to almost daily discoveries in how the immune system works.

From that fateful April day in 1953 to today, the flow of biological discovery has swelled from a trickle to a torrent. It is an exciting time to be involved in the life sciences.

What do biologists do? Most people working in the life sciences seek to understand and manipulate the characteristics of plants, animals, and microorganisms. Some traditional disciplines are classified by the organisms studied. *Botanists* study plants, *microbiologists* study microorganisms such as bacteria, *mycologists* study fungi, *zoologists* study animals. Others may generalize: *ecologists* study the relationship of organisms to their environment; *geneticists* study how DNA has evolved and how it is transmitted, manipulated, and expressed; *pathologists* study plant and animal diseases; *systematists* and *taxonomists* name, classify, and establish evolutionary relationships among species.

There are numerous specialties. *Biochemists* study the structure and interaction of the many kinds of molecules found in living organisms; *cell biologists* study cell structure and function; *developmental biologists* study the embryology and differentiation of organisms; *anatomists* and *morphologists* study the form and structure of tissues; *molecular biologists* study the interaction of DNA and RNA and other molecules produced by living organisms; *paleobotanists* and *paleozoologists* study evolution through the fossils of extinct plants or animals.

Some biologists are classified and named by the groups of organisms they investigate: marine biologists, parasitologists, tropical biologists, wildlife biologists. Pharmacologists or toxicologists test the effect of additives, drugs, medicines, pesticides, and toxins on organisms.

Many life science professionals are agricultural scientists who specialize in the sciences of cultivating the soil, producing crops, and raising livestock. These professions include agronomists (field crop production); plant pathologists (plant diseases); agrigeneticists (genetic improvement by DNA manipulating, tissue culturing, cloning, embryo transplanting, and selective breeding); horticulturists (landscaping, ornamental and food crop production, and greenhouse, plant nursery, orchard, and turf management); and foresters (developing, cultivating, and managing growing timber). There are, of course, many subspecialties within these broad areas. (Some of these areas are discussed in the agriculture section.)

Many biologists teach as well as conduct basic research in the life sciences. According to the Bureau of Labor Statistics, more than 37 percent of the life scientists in the United States work for educational institutions.

Many people study biology as a foundation for other pursuits. For example, training in the life sciences is absolutely essential for those who want to enter the medical profession (physicians, dentists, veterinarians, nurses, laboratory technicians, exercise physiologists, sports medicine specialists, physical therapists, nutritionists). A good background in biology is also important for naturalists, science writers, illustrators, nature photographers, museum specialists, and marketers of biomedical products.

What are the major research areas in biology today? During the past two decades biological research has become an interactive science of biology, chemistry, physics, and engineering. This means that future life scientists must be well prepared not only in biology but in these other disciplines, as well as in computers.

In 1989 the National Academy of Sciences Committee on Research Opportunities in Biology published *Opportunities in Biology*, a book about research opportunities in the new biology of the 1990s. It included the following areas:

1. *Structural biology.* An important research area concerns the structure, function, and behavior of macromolecules such as proteins, nucleic acids, carbohydrates, and lipids.

2. *Genes and cells.* Research in cellular structure, function, and communication explores how parts of cells interact and what effects those interactions have.

3. *Development.* Advances in understanding how biological molecules work are leading to understanding how an organism develops from a single cell to a complex individual.

4. *The nervous system and behavior.* One of the most challenging and complex of all biological frontiers—a field of enormous potential for future research—is an understanding of the ways in which the nerve cells of the brain direct behavior.

5. *The immune system and infectious diseases.* Research is revealing the details of major structures involved in the immune system, and increasing understanding of the immune response. Ultimately, these studies will lead to practical benefits, including more successful organ transplants, better control of immune responses, and improved treatment of AIDS patients.

6. *Evolution.* Research in evolution provides the key for understanding the marvelous diversity of life on earth. Since the 1980s the use of molecular analyses and genetic techniques has made it possible to analyze the genetic differences among species with much greater precision. This study is just beginning, but major long-range opportunities are available through the use of new techniques for cloning and mapping large DNA molecules.

7. *Systematics.* The field of systematics charts the diversity of life on earth. Approximately 1.4 million species of plants, animals, and microorganisms have been described to date, but the number of species of organisms that exist on earth is not known. The rapid pace of destruction, especially in the tropics, makes it necessary for biologists to speed up their efforts to understand the nature of evolution of species and communities.

8. *Ecology.* Because ecosystems represent the most complex levels of biological integration, ecology draws theories and practical methods from all the other parts of biology. Ecological principles have been used to form the new discipline of *conservation biology*, in which modern studies of systematics, evolution, and ecology are applied to the problem of species and community survival.

9. *Plant biology and agriculture.* Molecular biology and recombinant DNA technology are rapidly expanding fundamental knowledge about plants. These tools are being applied to real-world, practical problems, with the result that genetically engineered plants have already been produced that resist herbicides, certain viral infections, and some insects. The study of interactions between plants and their pathogens has been enhanced by new techniques in cell culture, chemical analysis, and molecular biology.

It is an exciting time to be a student of the life sciences and to share in the new biology.

The majors whose descriptions follow (with the exception of science education) do not lead to professional degrees, but they prepare students for professional programs in veterinary medicine, dentistry, medicine, pharmacy, and so forth. They are also preparation for advanced degrees in the biological and life sciences—that is, master of science and doctor of philosophy.

Biochemistry

Biochemistry majors use the physical and biological sciences to explore the nature of living organisms. They study the structure and behavior of complex molecules and how they interact to form cells, tissues, and entire organisms. Students also gain a fundamental grasp of metabolism, energy flow, and the regulation of various life processes.

Interests, skills, and qualities associated with success in the major

Interests. Nature, problem solving, research.

Skills and qualities. Using information from many areas of science, manual dexterity, good laboratory practice, handling and interpreting data, critical thinking, setting and completing goals, adjusting to change.

Recommended high school preparation

English 4, algebra 1, geometry 1, trigonometry 1, biology 1, chemistry 1, physics 1, and social studies 2–3. Advanced science courses, exposure to computers, and precalculus or introductory calculus are also desirable.

Typical courses in the major

Physics
Organic Chemistry
Biochemistry
Genetics/Molecular Genetics
Plant Biochemistry
Physiology
Advanced Inorganic Chemistry
Immunology/Immunochemistry
Physical Chemistry
Virology
Organic Qualitative Analysis

Calculus
Analytic Chemistry
Developmental Biochemistry
Physical Biochemistry
Microbiology
Biophysics
Neurobiology
Cell Biology
Instrumental Methods
Bacterial and Viral Genetics

What the major is like

Biochemistry deals with the chemistry of living organisms. Students relate the physical principles of chemistry to the functions of living systems. Because the sciences of biology and medicine have been studying the molecule more and more to understand biological phenomena, the boundaries between biochemistry and allied sciences are not as clear as they once were. Chemists, psychologists, biologists, physicists, physicians, sociologists, criminologists, and even paleontologists also study biochemical problems. Therefore the major requires the student to be knowledgeable outside the field of biochemistry.

As in biotechnology, computers are used to store, retrieve, and manipulate data. The use of computers in DNA and protein sequence analysis is integrated into the undergraduate curriculum by most institutions.

The core undergraduate program is strong in all elements of chemistry (physical, organic, inorganic, and analytic) and contains fundamentals of biology. Students can vary the amount of time spent exploring physical and mathematical sciences. In general, the formal study of biochemistry follows a solid foundation in chemistry and physics and usually begins in the junior year.

Biochemistry is an experimental science. Laboratory experience with biochemical techniques and instruments is gained mainly in biochemistry laboratories but also in laboratories in cell biology, physical chemistry, recombinant DNA technology, biotechnology, etc. Required undergraduate research projects may be carried out under the direction of a professor, a graduate student, or another member of the research team. The projects may be semester long or may become part of a four-year undergraduate degree program. Undergraduates may also write scientific papers or give presentations at meetings. Research experience during either the academic year or the summer can lead to a graduate degree program or an entry-level position in biochemistry in a corporate or academic research laboratory.

Specializations

Students ordinarily do not specialize at the undergraduate level.

Other majors to consider

Biology
Biotechnology
Chemistry
Microbiology
Molecular and cell biology

Careers related to the major

A bachelor's degree in biochemistry provides a good foundation for a graduate degree in biochemistry, molecular biology, or an allied molecular life science. It is also a logical choice for entry into medical, dental, or veterinary school or into allied health and agricultural careers in such areas as biotechnology, toxicology, biomedical engineering, clinical chemistry, plant pathology, and animal sciences.

Some bachelor's degree holders enter the job market directly. Those who wish to work at the bench (in the laboratory) find jobs in universities or government, research institutes, or industrial laboratories.

With appropriate education courses, the broad-based scientific background of a biochemistry major makes the person ideally suited to teach science at the primary or secondary school level.

For more information

American Society for Biochemistry and Molecular Biology
9650 Rockville Pike
Bethesda, MD 20814
(301)530-7145

Biology

In biology the animals, plants, and microorganisms that constitute the living world are studied at the levels of molecule, cell, organism, and population. Courses emphasize an understanding of structure and function, and of hereditary and evolutionary relations.

Interests, skills, and qualities associated with success in the major

Interests. Quality of life, laboratory work, fieldwork.

Skills and qualities. Problem solving, quantitative reasoning, critical observation, innovative thinking, effective communication, manual dexterity.

Recommended high school preparation

English 4, precollege mathematics 4, biology 1, chemistry 1, physics 1, social studies 2, and computer science 1.

Typical courses in the major

General Biology
Invertebrate Biology
Cell Biology
Biochemistry
Genetics
Comparative Anatomy

Ecology
Plant Biology
Evolution
Human Anatomy and Physiology
Microbiology
Embryology

What the major is like

The biology major prepares students to understand how living organisms solve the problems they face in particular environments. Most biology programs stress the contribution of ecological principles and hereditary factors to the evolution of plants, animals, and microbes, producing a high variety of life forms. A lecture format is common in most biology courses, and most require a laboratory. In advanced biology courses students read and discuss significant research literature.

Introductory freshman courses present the major concepts, processes, and vocabulary of the discipline, describing the major subdivisions in a broad, general manner. Cell biology and physiology courses examine how the structure of cells relates to their functional activities, like acquiring and using, dividing and differentiating, and regulating their own processes. Laboratories emphasize microscopic observation of cells and data-gathering experiments using different kinds of cells.

Genetics identifies the molecular, cellular, and organismal aspects of heredity in animals and plants. Many genetics courses also consider the hereditary mechanisms of microorganisms. Topics include human hereditary disorders and DNA technology. Laboratories usually require independent student work on fruit flies, molds, bacteria, and viruses.

In ecology, students study the relation of plants and animals to their environment. Topics include aquatic and terrestrial ecosystems, population dynamics, community structure, food webs, energy flow, nutrient cycles, and environmental pollution. Laboratory fieldwork is followed by data analysis using varied computational and statistical methods.

Biology courses that focus on plants (seed plants, algae, fungi), invertebrate animals (entomology, protozoology), and vertebrate animals (ornithology, ichthyology) rely on careful observation of the structure and reproduction of such groups of organisms. The lecture often points out how function is related to the structural features of the organism, emphasizing the diversity of the organisms within a group in the context of evolution. In the laboratories students make use of microscopy, dissect fresh and preserved material, and sometimes apply culture techniques.

Microbiology concentrates on the structure, function, genetics, and ecology of bacteria and viruses. The impact of microbes on people brings up issues of disease, industrial uses of microbes, and food. In the laboratories, a student will usually isolate and study microorganisms.

Molecular biology and biochemistry are concerned with the chemicals that play important structural and regulatory roles in living systems.

Comparative anatomy and embryology make heavy use of microscopy and dissection techniques in order to understand how embryos develop in representative adult vertebrates.

Developmental biology studies the molecular, cellular, and organismal events that allow a single cell to form an adult organism.

In addition to taking the courses mentioned, biology majors often conduct independent research. Many departments require seniors to take a seminar in which current biology literature is read, analyzed, and discussed.

Specializations

Environmental science, neurobiology, microbiology, botany, zoology, aquatic biology.

Other majors to consider

Agronomy
Biochemistry
Biophysics
Botany
Food sciences
Forestry
Horticultural science
Marine biology
Psychology
Zoology

Careers related to the major

The biology major may lead to careers in biotechnology-based businesses as sales representatives or laboratory technicians, park naturalists, science journalists, middle school or high school teaching. With postgraduate degrees: medicine, dentistry, veterinary medicine, optometry, physical therapy, hospital administration, public health administration, college teaching, biological research in private industry or government laboratories, and law.

For more information

American Institute of Biological Sciences
730 Eleventh Street NW
Washington, DC 20001-4584
(202)628-1500

The pamphlet "Careers in Biology" is available from the American Institute of Biological Sciences.

Biophysics

Students majoring in biophysics use biology, physics, chemistry, and mathematics to explore the properties of biological molecules and groups of molecules. Recent advances in molecular biology, computing, and instrumentation make it possible for biophysicists to study the inner workings of biological systems with unprecedented precision and to learn how proteins fold, how genes are switched on and off, how organisms respond to light, how cells move, how the nervous system works, and more.

Interests, skills, and qualities associated with success in the major

Interests. Natural history (astronomy, birdwatching, butterfly or rock collecting), puzzles, solving problems, crossword puzzles, computer games, crafts, reading, writing, electronics, building models.

Skills and qualities. Curiosity, quantitative thinking, communicating effectively, manual dexterity, mathematics, physics, chemistry, biology.

Recommended high school preparation

English 3–4, algebra 2, calculus 1, geometry 1, trigonometry .5, biology 1, chemistry 1, physics 1, history 2, foreign language 2, visual arts 1, and computer science 1.

Typical courses in the major

Cell and Molecular Biology
Biochemistry
Organic Chemistry
Mechanics
Electricity and Magnetism
Statistics
Linear Algebra

Genetics
Chemistry
Physical Chemistry
Calculus
Numerical Analysis
Computer Programming

What the major is like

Biophysics asks how three-dimensional structure determines biological function. It involves the study of entire organisms, of single cells, and of the biomolecules that make up cells. Some questions biophysicists explore are: Why do molecules take certain shapes, and how do they change their structure under changing conditions? How do proteins bind with DNA, and how does this affect genes? How do cell membranes work? How does light affect living organisms? How does our nervous system work?

While over 50 colleges and universities offer an undergraduate major in biophysics, students can prepare themselves at other institutions for careers or advanced training in the field by completing a major in biology, biochemistry, or molecular biology with supplementary courses in chemistry, physics, and mathematics; they can also complete a major in mathematics, physics, or chemistry with supplementary courses in biology. Many students find that majoring in a physical science or mathematics is the best preparation for more advanced work in biophysics.

Because biophysics is highly interdisciplinary, it is important to obtain a solid foundation in not only biology and physics but also chemistry and mathematics. Biophysics majors generally take at least four semesters of courses in each of these subjects as well as advanced courses in one or more areas of particular interest. A strong biophysics program might consist of the following courses:

Biology: introductory biology; cell biology; molecular biology and/or genetics

Chemistry: general chemistry; organic chemistry; physical chemistry (thermodynamics, statistical mechanics, kinetics, and quantum mechanics)

Physics: mechanics; electricity and magnetism; atomic and molecular physics

Mathematics: calculus; differential equations; linear algebra; numerical analysis and statistics; computer programming.

It is often possible to deemphasize one or more of these areas by postponing more advanced course work until later in one's career.

Early hands-on research and laboratory experience are invaluable. Many courses have laboratory sessions; however, students often find that the most rewarding experiences come from working in a laboratory in a university, hospital, research institute, or industry in the summer or in a faculty member's laboratory during the academic year. Several government and private foundations support programs that make this kind of experience possible.

Most careers in any science require not only technical mastery but also good interpersonal and communication skills, and courses in the humanities and social sciences are extremely useful in developing these skills. Knowledge of such foreign languages as French and German often proves useful in communicating with scientists from other countries.

Specializations

Molecular biophysics, neurobiology and neurophysiology, physiology, photobiology, enzymology, mathematical and computer modeling.

Other majors to consider

Biochemistry
Biology
Chemistry
Computer science
Engineering
Mathematics
Molecular and cell biology
Physics

Careers related to the major

Many careers are immediately open to biophysics majors because of the breadth of the training they receive. Biophysicists work in universities and medical centers, national laboratories, public and private research centers, and in corporations that manufacture health products, pharmaceuticals, and scientific instruments. Many biophysicists earn master's or doctoral degrees before entering the work force.

For more information

Biophysical Society
9650 Rockville Pike
Bethesda, MD 20814
(301)530-7114

The pamphlet "Careers in Biophysics" is available from the Biophysical Society.

Biotechnology

Biotechnology is an interdisciplinary field involving the molecular life sciences and engineering. Students learn techniques for using living matter to develop new products.

Interests, skills, and qualities associated with success in the major

Interests. Science, treating and preventing disease.

Skills and qualities. Creative thinking, effective communication, manual dexterity, endurance, tackling problems from many angles, teamwork, setting and achieving goals.

Recommended high school preparation

English 4, algebra 2, geometry 1, trigonometry 1, biology 1, chemistry 1, physics 1, and social studies 3. Advanced science courses, exposure to computers, and the study of precalculus or introductory calculus are also desirable.

Typical courses in the major

Physics
Organic Chemistry
Biochemistry
Physical Chemistry
Plant/Animal Physiology
Organic Qualitative Analysis
Engineering Design
Separation Sciences
Downstream Processing
Industrial Microbiology
Reactor Design and Theory

Calculus
Analytic Chemistry
Genetics/Molecular Genetics
Immunology
Plant/Animal Tissue Culture
Plant/Animal Breeding
Thermodynamics
Bioseparations
Chemical Engineering
Statistics

What the major is like

Biotechnology is a field of scientific research that meshes the study of engineering and molecular life sciences. Biotechnology is used to create new products and services in agriculture (plant growth hormones, food additives), health care (vaccines, improved drugs and vitamins), the environment (detoxification of chemicals), and other areas.

The molecular life sciences are among the most diversified of all the sciences. Increasingly, scientists seek to understand living organisms at their molecular level. Recent dramatic increases in molecular-biological understanding are due to the use of tools from the physical sciences, for example, chemistry, physics, and mathematics. Biotechnology helps advance our study of living things even more by adding the perspective of engineering.

Some of the technologies used to explore organisms are genetic engineering (altering gene characteristics for a specific purpose), bioprocessing (large-scale separating and purifying techniques), immunobiochemistry, protein engineering, and biocatalysis. Basic research in biotechnology is usually done in the laboratory. To prepare a product or application on a large scale, for the market place, engineering skills become critical. Thus, the biotechnology major needs all the tools of the biochemist, the molecular biologist, the immunologist, and the engineer.

No single format leads to a biotechnology degree that prepares a student for a career in this field. A number of institutions offer programs specifically geared to training biotechnologists, however, and many other institutions offer alternative approaches to learning biotechnology from traditional disciplines and majors. Some academicians and industrial observers believe that students can best prepare for biotechnology by training in a more traditional discipline such as biochemistry, microbiology, or immunology while learning the tools of biotechnology. A major in biotechnology, whether through a formal degree program by that name or through a traditional molecular life science program, with extra experience in engineering and its industrial perspective, must be recognized as one of the most versatile life science majors.

As in biochemistry and molecular biology, the use of computers in storing, retrieving, and manipulating data on protein and DNA structure and function has become routine in biotechnology, and familiarity with computers is essential for undergraduate biotechnologists. Laboratory experience with biochemical techniques and instruments is important. Normally acquired in biochemistry laboratories, the techniques may be learned in laboratories in cell biology, physical chemistry, immunology, recombinant DNA technology, biotechnology, biomedical instrumentation, radioisotope handling, and bioprocess engineering.

At many institutions, undergraduates study in the biotechnology research laboratory of a professor under the professor or another member of the research team. Typically, this study lasts for a semester or two, although students may choose to integrate a two-year research experience into a four-year undergraduate degree program. Undergraduate students frequently write scientific papers and give presentations at meetings. Undergraduate students may participate in research activities for academic credit. Such research experience, during the academic year or in the summer, can be a significant stepping stone to a graduate program or an entry-level position in a corporate or academic biotechnology laboratory. Some institutions require corporate work experience or an internship program. About a third of biotechnology corporations have cooperative programs with a university or a college.

Specializations

Animal biotechnology, microbial biotechnology, genetic engineering, process engineering, biomedical instrumentation, plant/agricultural biotechnology, cell culture technology, separation sciences, biocomputing.

Other majors to consider

Biochemistry
Biology
Chemical engineering
Chemistry
Microbiology
Molecular and cell biology

Careers related to the major

The biotechnology major may lead to careers in research, quality control, clinical research, information systems, regulatory affairs, biotechnology patents, manufacturing/production, and marketing/sales. There is a wide array of opportunities for specialists knowledgeable in biotechnology, including lawyers (patent and regulatory), computer scientists, physicians, toxicologists, veterinarians, professional managers at all corporate levels, and regulatory agency personnel.

For more information

Industrial Biotechnology Association
1625 K Street NW, Suite 1100
Washington, DC 20006
(202)857-0244

American Chemical Society
1155 Sixteenth Street NW
Washington, DC 20036
(202)872-4600

American Society for Microbiology
1325 Massachusetts Avenue NW
Washington, DC 20005-4171
(202)737-3600

Association of Biotechnology Companies
1666 Connecticut Avenue NW, Suite 330
Washington, DC 20009-1039
(202)234-3330

Botany

Majors in botany, a branch of biology, study all aspects of plant biology to become familiar with the cellular and molecular functioning of life.

Interests, skills, and qualities associated with success in the major

Interests. Nature, problem solving, analytic reasoning.

Skills and qualities. Applying information, focusing on a question, analyzing data, drawing logical conclusions.

Recommended high school preparation

English 4, precollege mathematics 1, biology 1–2, chemistry 1–2, physics 1, social studies 1, history 1, foreign language 2, visual arts 1, and computer science 1.

Typical courses in the major

Introductory Botany
Cell and Molecular Biology
Plant Development
Plant Anatomy
Biosystematics

Introductory Biology
Genetics
Plant Physiology
Survey of the Plant Kingdom
Ecology

What the major is like

The study of botany is increasingly important to human well-being. The current biological revolution has provided the technology to splice genes, alter the fate of cells, and manipulate plants to suit our needs. In the face of the world's environmental concerns and dependence on plant life, this technology must now be used to solve plant-related problems. The need for botanists in all areas of applied biology will continue to grow as increasing population presses on our ability to grow sufficient food and yet maintain forest buffers to stabilize world climates.

The major is offered either as the undergraduate program of a botany department or as a biology degree with a focus on courses related to plants. The course in cellular and molecular biology combines biochemical understanding of life with knowledge of cell functions. Biochemical pathways of reactions that maintain and promote life through each of the cell's parts are studied. This relates directly to molecular aspects of genetics, which deal with sexual reproduction of organisms on molecular, cellular, and whole-organismal levels.

The unique nature of plants is studied in plant development and anatomy and in plant physiology: how cells are organized; how organs are formed and function; and how processes of growth, development, and reproduction are coordinated within a whole plant. Plant ecology focuses on the integration of individual plants into communities with other organisms and on their response to their environment. This includes, for example, the study of plants as they coexist with animals as sources of food or in relation to pollination as part of their reproductive biology.

The interrelations of plants and other plants and animals have resulted in the radiation of diverse types of plants known in the world today. The study of plant biodiversity and plant systematics, once considered old-fashioned biology, has recently been revitalized. Plant explorers are now collecting information and trying to understand the plant diversity of remote areas of the world before the plants are destroyed. As a result, plants new to science—which may be important sources of food, building materials, fibers, and medicine or may act as experimental organisms—are being discovered regularly in remote areas.

As the biological revolution gains momentum, and as we push the limits of the natural world's ability to buffer the impact of human existence, botany becomes even more important to human survival.

Specializations

Molecular biology, ecology, mycology, paleobotany/plant evolution, plant anatomy, plant geography, genetics, plant/animal coevolution, phycology, plant physiology, biosystematics.

Other majors to consider

Agricultural sciences
Biochemistry
Biology
Forestry
Horticultural science
Plant pathology
Plant sciences
Zoology

Careers related to the major

A bachelor's degree in botany prepares graduates to work as assistants in laboratories, to enter biology-related businesses or conservation programs, or to continue in graduate school toward teacher certification or a doctorate. Examples of some jobs students may pursue are technical posts in all areas of biology, forestry, and horticulture; sales of biology products; science education in museums, independent schools, and public programs; environmental consulting; natural resource management.

For more information

Christopher H. Haufler
Botanical Society of America
University of Kansas - Botany Department
Hayworth Hall
Lawrence, KS 66045-2106
(913)864-3255

Marine biology

In the marine biology major students learn about the diversity of life in the ocean, how ocean species relate to each other as food and prey, and how different species depend on and use the physical and chemical structures of the ocean.

Interests, skills, and qualities associated with success in the major

Interests. Life in the ocean, how organisms use the sea as a habitat.

Skills and qualities. Quantitative thinking, physics, chemistry, biology.

Recommended high school preparation

English 4, precollege mathematics 4, biology 2, chemistry 1, physics 1, history or social studies 2, and computer science 2.

Typical courses in the major

Invertebrate Zoology	Comparative Vertebrate Anatomy
Survey of the Algae	Chemical Oceanography
Physical Oceanography	Oceanographic Techniques
Coastal Law	Ocean Law
Marine Pollution	Ocean Ecosystems

What the major is like

The ocean has a special fascination. Covering two-thirds of the earth's surface, it contains a great abundance and wide diversity of life forms, ranging from the bizarre to the beautiful. How ocean species relate to each other, as food and prey, as sources of nutrients, or even as animal and chemical structures of the ocean are all topics of deep interest to marine biologists.

Students majoring in marine biology will not only receive broad exposure to the extraordinary complexity of this major ecosystem, but also insight into some of the most important environmental problems facing our future. For example, they will explore the consequences of global climate changes, which threaten to produce a warming of the ocean and a rise in sea level, and the consequences of increasing ocean pollution.

Marine biology majors study the ocean as a system and learn about the interaction and interdependency of the physics, chemistry, and biology of the ocean. They learn about the form, structure, development, evolution, physiology, biochemistry, and genetics of marine systems, including fisheries. Through such study they come to appreciate the many competing interests and concerns that center around people's use of the ocean.

Students will learn about the spatial and regional distributions of important species (e.g., coastal versus open ocean, cold versus warm water, deep versus shallow water), and will learn how species are linked and dependent on the physics and chemistry of the ocean. They may study why certain species are endangered and what can be done to help them. Some may pursue special interests, such as the commercial aspects of ocean science, or perhaps the economic potential of marine organisms as sources of food, chemicals, and energy.

Typically, majors in marine biology will concentrate for the first two years on basic sciences such as biology, chemistry, physics, and mathematics, and on such liberal arts as English, the humanities, and computer science. A survey of marine environments with fields trips may be offered in the freshman year. The sophomore year may examine marine biology in more depth, with emphasis on adaptations to the marine environment with laboratory exercises concerning the morphology, ecology, physiology, and behavior of marine organisms.

The junior and senior years include courses specifically designed for the specialized area of marine biology. Courses may include an examination of coastal law, marine pollution, economic resources of the ocean, and in-depth studies of oceanic ecosystems. Often a senior thesis is required; students conduct an independent research project under faculty supervision and summarize it with a formal written report.

Some universities require that students combine marine biology with another major, such as biology, chemistry, geology, or physics.

Specializations	Biological oceanography, pollution, environmental management, conservation, mariculture, marine biotechnology, biomedical studies.
Other majors to consider	**Biochemistry** **Biology** **Chemistry** Physiology, human and animal
Careers related to the major	Marine biology graduates find jobs with government, state, and federal environmental programs, particularly those dealing with coastal management, conservation, and recreational and commercial fisheries. Commercial positions are available in mariculture (cultivation of marine organisms). Students may become environmental consultants or, with appropriate professional education, specialists in marine and environmental law. With appropriate certification, graduates can teach in public schools.
For more information	Marine Technology Society 1828 L Street NW, Suite 906 Washington, DC 20036-5104 (202)775-5966

Microbiology

Majors in microbiology use the basic knowledge acquired from other biological sciences, chemistry/biochemistry, and physics to study microscopic organisms such as bacteria, yeasts, molds, viruses, rickettsia, and protozoa.

Interests, skills, and qualities associated with success in the major

Interests. Biological sciences, health and medicine, ecology, food production.

Skills and qualities. Working with detail, analytic thinking, patience, inquisitiveness, manual dexterity, sciences.

Recommended high school preparation

English 4, algebra 2, geometry 1, trigonometry 1, biology 1, chemistry 1, physics 1, history or social studies 2, foreign language 2, and computer science .5.

Typical courses in the major

Chemistry
Organic Chemistry
Biology
Calculus
Microbiology
Microbial Genetics
Applied Microbiology

Quantitative Chemistry
Biochemistry
Physics
Computer Science
Immunology
Microbiology Physiology

What the major is like

Microbiology is the interdisciplinary study of microscopic organisms—life forms that outnumber human beings and that are found everywhere in the environment. Majors in this discipline are well informed about microbes and their many capabilities and are among the most employable science majors. General microbiology provides an overview of microorganisms—their diversity, structure, function, growth, reproduction, genetics, physiology, preservation, and control. Immunology studies the means by which humans and other organisms defend themselves against foreign substances and other agents as well as the injuries that can result from these encounters. Microbial genetics informs students about mutation, gene mapping and structure, means of transferring genetic information, and applications of genetic modifications. Microbial physiology presents, in greater depth, information on microbe structure and function, metabolism, and controls.

Depending on the institution, this program may be offered in the department of microbiology, biological sciences, biology, or molecular biology. The degree granted most often is a Bachelor of Science in microbiology or a B.S. in biology with a concentration in microbiology. Some departments grant a Bachelor of Arts instead.

Specializations

Medical microbiology, immunology, microbial genetics, virology, marine microbiology, microbial physiology, molecular biology, biotechnology, hematology, mycology, public health microbiology, industrial microbiology, food microbiology.

Other majors to consider

Biochemistry
Biotechnology
Civil engineering
Ecology
Entomology
Marine biology
Molecular and cell biology

Careers related to the major

The microbiology major can lead to careers in the health professions, the food and beverage industry, water and wastewater management, pharmaceuticals, scientific sales, production of home/personal care products, the oil and aerospace industries, aquaculture, agriculture, chemical and energy industries, sterilization industries, biomedical devices and diagnosis, microbiology equipment design and sales, government, education, law, space microbiology, basic and applied research, biotechnology/molecular biology, and genetic engineering. Appropriate graduate study is needed for some of these pursuits.

For more information

American Society for Microbiology
Office of Education and Professional Recognition
1325 Massachusetts Avenue NW
Washington, DC 20005
(202)737-3600

The ASM publishes the "American Society for Microbiology List of Colleges and Universities Granting Degrees in Microbiology."

Molecular and cell biology

Molecular and cell biology is the study of the molecular foundation of living organisms, especially how DNA is used to define an organism, how genes are regulated, and how human beings are related to other organisms. Molecular biology, like biochemistry, underlies many aspects of genetic engineering, protein engineering, and other new approaches to improving upon nature.

Interests, skills, and qualities associated with success in the major

Interests. Organisms and their development; how things work; the molecular basis of plant, animal, and human disease; disease prevention.

Skills and qualities. Laboratory skills, manual dexterity, using information from many areas of science, analyzing data, persistence, working with computers.

Recommended high school preparation

English 4, algebra 1, geometry 1, precalculus 1, trigonometry 1, biology 1, chemistry 1, physics 1, history 2, and computer science 1.

Typical courses in the major

Physics	Calculus
Organic Chemistry	Biochemistry
Microbiology	Cell Biology
Genetics	Analytic Chemistry
Physical Chemistry	Microbial Genetics
Human Genetics	Bacterial/Viral Genetics
Recombinant DNA Techniques	Physical Biochemistry
Separation Sciences	Bacterial Genetics
Developmental Biology	Molecular Immunology
Molecular Neurobiology	Virology

What the major is like

There is some disagreement about whether there really is a science called molecular and cell biology. It is a relatively new field, which some persons say started in 1973 with the revolutionary technology known as recombinant DNA. Others argue that the chemists who analyzed the molecular content of DNA and determined the molecular defect in sickle-cell anemia in the 1940s were among the first molecular biologists. The *Journal of Molecular Biology* started publication in 1959, well before the discovery of recombinant DNA and restriction enzymes, the "magic scalpels" used by scientists to cut and piece together DNA.

To appreciate these differences of opinion, students must understand where the tools of molecular and cell biology came from. Modern biochemical research of gene structure and function—in particular, research into the molecular aspects of the storage, transmission, and expression of genetic information—has led to the development of highly sophisticated techniques; these are often clustered in the field of biochemical genetics or molecular genetics. Between biochemistry on the one hand and biochemical genetics on the other lies an ill-defined area that is most often referred to as molecular biology.

Molecular and cell biology takes a technological approach, using biochemical, genetic, and immunologic tools, to problems of the molecular basis of biological phenomena.

The goal of a student whose major is molecular biology is to understand molecules—why they do what they do and how they can be manipulated. Because of the emphasis on the molecular aspects of nature's most intimate secrets, students receive a good foundation in chemistry, physics, and mathematics. Generally, students do not take a course titled "Molecular and Cell Biology" until they have had courses in organic chemistry, genetics, and biochemistry.

At institutions that do not offer molecular and cell biology, students can prepare to work in the field by studying biochemistry or biology, and focusing on molecular genetics, the physical sciences, and computers.

Students will examine the nature of the information stored in DNA and reflected in the sequence of amino acids in proteins; these investigations lend themselves to the use of computers. Storing, retrieving, and manipulating data by means of computers is a routine endeavor for graduate students of biochemistry or molecular biology. The use of computers in DNA and protein sequence analysis will soon be integrated into the undergraduate curricula at most institutions.

The major in molecular and cell biology is a laboratory-based program. Beyond the course-based laboratory experiences, many institutions offer students the opportunity to work in research laboratories, usually on a small research project under the direction of a professor or a graduate student. These additional laboratory experiences in the academic year or summer are often critical to developing new perspectives and give students a chance to put knowledge gained in course work into action.

Specializations

Microbial plant and animal molecular biology, biotechnology.

Other majors to consider

Biochemistry
Biology
Biotechnology
Chemistry
Microbiology

Careers related to the major

Many graduates of molecular biology programs enter the job market directly. They take positions in university, government, or corporate laboratories. In addition, pharmaceutical and biotechnology firms involved with genetic engineering have a constant demand for well-trained individuals who have a strong analytic perspective and can work as members of research teams.

A degree in molecular biology is an excellent stepping stone to a graduate degree in biochemistry or an allied molecular life science. It is also a logical degree choice for entry into medical, dental, or veterinary medicine at a time when health sciences are moving into the molecular arena at a very fast pace. Molecular biology can prepare students for graduate study in such allied fields as biotechnology, toxicology, plant pathology, animal science, and clinical diagnostics.

For more information

American Society for Biochemistry and Molecular Biology
9650 Rockville Pike
Bethesda, MD 20814
(301)530-7145

American Society for Microbiology
1325 Massachusetts Avenue NW
Washington, DC 20005-4171
(202)737-3600

American Society for Cell Biology
9650 Rockville Pike
Bethesda, MD 20814
(301)530-7153

Science education

A science education major is prepared to teach science in grades 7 through 12. Students typically major in one science and take additional course work in two other sciences. They also learn techniques for teaching science.

Interests, skills, and qualities associated with success in the major

Interests. Working with young people, helping others, the learning process, solving practical problems, understanding complex processes, learning how things work.

Skills and qualities. Logical thinking, analytic reasoning, working with numbers.

Recommended high school preparation

English 4, precollege mathematics 4, biology 1, chemistry 1, physical science 1, physics 1, social studies 3, history 2, foreign language 2, and computer science 1.

Typical courses in the major

Educational Psychology
Science Teaching Methods
Biology
Physics
Student Teaching

Philosophy of Teaching
Curriculum Development
Chemistry
Earth Science

What the major is like	Science education, which prepares students to teach science in middle and secondary schools, is a major at most institutions that have teacher-training programs and majors in the sciences. Sometimes science education is offered by science departments. Students major in biology, chemistry, physics, or another science, take introductory courses in two other sciences, and take courses in principles and practices of education. Education courses are usually taken in the senior year. In some institutions students major in science education within a college, school, or department of education; in these programs the education courses may be integrated throughout the college career instead of coming at the end.

In some states, students take the necessary education courses and student teaching during a fifth year of study that follows the bachelor's degree.

Science course work is the same for potential science teachers and for science majors. In addition to the science the student focuses on, some introductory course work in two other sciences is necessary because teachers are often responsible for teaching more than one subject—for example, biology and chemistry—particularly in small schools.

Requirements for science teachers include a thorough knowledge of available curriculum materials and strategies for teaching particular science concepts (for example, through hands-on laboratory experience). Students also learn to understand the learning process, create effective teaching units, design fair tests for evaluation, and manage a science laboratory for maximum learning. All these subjects are taught in curriculum, methods, and educational psychology courses.

Science education majors must also learn to interact with students and to manage large groups of them for effective learning. These skills are usually acquired during a 10-week full-time student teaching practicum in a science classroom at a cooperating school. In addition to this, in most programs students observe and help in classrooms throughout their undergraduate studies.

Specializations

Middle school teaching.

Other majors to consider

Astronomy
Biology
Chemistry
Earth sciences
Geology
Physics
Secondary education

Careers related to the major

With a bachelor's degree in science education, one can teach science in a high school or middle school. Most teachers continue to take courses and may complete a master's degree. With graduate training, one can become a supervisor of science teachers in a school system, a principal, a curriculum coordinator in a school system, or a college or junior college teacher of science education.

For more information

National Science Teachers Association
1742 Connecticut Avenue NW
Washington, DC 20009

National Education Association
1201 Sixteenth Street NW
Washington, DC 20036

Wildlife management

Majors in wildlife management receive a solid background in basic biology, followed by study of natural resources and wildlife management. They study conservation of animal populations and their habitats, paying special attention to species that are hunted regularly and species that are threatened or endangered.

Interests, skills, and qualities associated with success in the major

Interests. Nature, conservation of natural resources, hunting, bird watching.

Skills and qualities. Science, mathematics, quantitative reasoning.

Recommended high school preparation

English 4, algebra 2, geometry 1, precalculus .5, trigonometry .5, biology 1, chemistry 1, physics 1, and history or social studies 2.

Typical courses in the major

Wildlife Management
Ecology
Wildlife Behavior
Ornithology
Uplands Ecology/Management
Natural Resource Policy

Field Methods
Mammalogy
Anatomy and Physiology
Wetlands Ecology/Management
Plant Taxonomy
Statistics

What the major is like

Wildlife management requires a knowledge of both biology and resource management. Students pursuing this major should therefore have strong scientific and mathematical aptitudes. Though most of their college courses are in the area of biology, students also acquire a foundation in chemistry, mathematics (through elementary calculus), and statistics.

In addition to biology, wildlife students study anatomy and physiology. Vertebrate zoology courses, such as ornithology and mammalogy, are also important. It is essential, however, that a wildlife biologist be able to identify plants as well as birds and mammals, so at least one plant taxonomy course is generally required. Most of the other courses in a wildlife management program are field oriented and deal with ecology.

Wildlife management involves animals living in natural environments. Students in this major therefore need to be prepared to manipulate animal populations and their habitats. As human populations continue to grow throughout the world, animal populations are inevitably affected by loss or alteration of habitat, reduction in food supply, presence of pollutants, and other human-related factors. Of particular concern are species that are hunted on a regular basis and species that are threatened or endangered, but many other species merit attention as well.

Because most wildlife courses include field work, students gain experience in identifying birds and mammals, estimating their populations, and analyzing various aspects of their habitats. Field trips also give students firsthand knowledge of the habitat preferences of the animals they study in the classroom. At many universities summer courses give students an opportunity to work full-time on field projects.

Specializations

In general, students do not specialize at the undergraduate level.

Other majors to consider	**Botany** Environmental science **Fisheries and wildlife** **Forestry** **Zoology**
Careers related to the major	The wildlife management major may lead to jobs as a wildlife biologist/manager, environmental educator, environmental consultant, park naturalist, or research wildlife biologist.
For more information	The Wildlife Society 5410 Grosvenor Lane Bethesda, MD 20814 (301)897-9770

Zoology

Majors in zoology, a branch of biology, study living organisms in the animal kingdom, exploring their form and function, chemistry and structure, growth, reproduction, maintenance, and interactions with each other and their world. The transmission of characteristics from one generation to the next (genetics) and organismal change through time (evolution) are of central importance.

Interests, skills, and qualities associated with success in the major	**Interests.** Natural history, wildlife, the outdoors, bird-watching, how things work, living things, fossils, working with animals. **Skills and qualities.** Synthesizing information, thinking objectively, analyzing information, working with numbers.
Recommended high school preparation	English 4, precollege mathematics 3–4, biology 1–2, chemistry 1, earth science 1, physics 1, social studies 2, history 1, foreign language 3, visual arts .5, and computer science .5.

Typical courses in the major

General Zoology
Invertebrate Biology
Ecology
Physiology
Comparative Anatomy
Animal Physiology
Genetics
Physics
Botany
Virology
Chemistry

Vertebrate Biology
Developmental Biology
Evolution
Animal Behavior
Histology
Neurobiology
Calculus
Statistics
Microbiology
Cell Science

What the major is like

In zoology, students explore how animals are formed and how their various parts function separately and together. They study how each organism acquires energy and material for growth and reproduction. In addition, they examine interactions of the individual with the world around it, both with other members of its own kind and all other living and nonliving things. Finally, zoology considers how each kind of animal has evolved to be the way it is.

The study of living systems requires learning diverse fields, from mathematics and statistics to physics and chemistry. After gaining a foundation in general zoology and chemistry (usually in the first two years), students take courses in genetics, developmental biology, ecology, animal physiology, neurobiology, and evolutionary biology.

Zoology trains students to examine the natural world carefully through observation and experimentation. Laboratory and field exercises train students in the techniques and methods of collecting and analyzing data. These include light and electron microscopy, chemical analysis, videotaping, computer modeling, and more.

Zoological concepts and phenomena cannot be divorced from other areas of human knowledge. Because of the interaction of science and history, a course in the history of science is highly recommended.

Students should do individual research in the junior or senior year and get to know instructors and find out how they, as zoologists, see the world. Throughout college, students can explore potential careers by participating in extracurricular activities (e.g., volunteering to work in a veterinarian's office or laboratory, as a research assistant to a faculty member or graduate student, or as a science tutor in a local high school). In this way, zoology majors can get a feeling for the kind of work they'd like to do.

Specializations

Genetics, animal behavior, ecology, neurobiology, cell biology, developmental biology.

Other majors to consider

Agricultural sciences
Animal sciences
Anthropology
Biochemistry
Biology
Botany
Entomology
Environmental science
Geography
Marine biology
Microbiology
Nursing
Premedicine
Preveterinary
Psychology
Wildlife management

Careers related to the major

A bachelor's degree in zoology may lead to a job as a research assistant or a teacher in a secondary school. The major is excellent preparation for professional study leading to careers in medicine, veterinary science, dentistry. It can lead to jobs in other health professions, such as optometry, nursing, medical technology, genetic counseling. It can also lead to careers in agriculture and environmental research. A doctorate is generally required in order to work as a zoologist.

For more information

American Society of Zoologists
Box 2739
California Lutheran University
Thousand Oaks, CA 91360
(805)492-3585

American Institute of Biological Sciences
730 Eleventh Street NW
Washington, DC 20001-4564
(202)628-1500

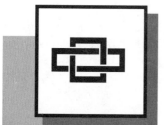

Business and Management

DANIEL E. DIAMOND
New York University

You have undoubtedly heard and used the terms *business* and *management* many times. They are common words that describe a broad range of activities and functions. Business, to paraphrase a famous statement by the British economist Alfred Marshall, is all those activities by which individuals earn their living. Management involves the direction of an enterprise—large or small—to achieve a successful result, which is usually stated in the amount of profits earned. In a university, the terms *business* and *management* are often used interchangeably in identifying these educational areas.

The origin of schools of business

Business schools are relative newcomers to the world of higher education. As the nineteenth century drew to a close, American society was becoming increasingly urban and interdependent. The country had emerged as a major industrial power. A national railroad system efficiently linked the nation from coast to coast. U.S. steel production exceeded that of Great Britain, France, and Germany combined. As a consequence of the Spanish-American War, the United States had international military and economic commitments. Large national corporations increasingly dominated the business landscape. These factors led the University of Pennsylvania to establish The Wharton School of Finance and Commerce in 1881 in response to a gift by Joseph Wharton. Other major universities soon followed.

The role of the American Assembly of Collegiate Schools of Business

The growth of collegiate business education created a need for adequate standards. Accordingly, in 1916 the American Assembly of Collegiate Schools of Business (AACSB) was formed. AACSB is the official accrediting agency for collegiate business education . Of the approximately 1,300 universities and colleges that now offer business and management majors, approximately 300 are nationally accredited by the AACSB. However, many nonaccredited institutions are members of the AACSB, participate in its meetings, workshops, and seminars, and generally adhere to its curriculum standards. Other things being equal, you should look for a school that is AACSB accredited.

Until the late 1940s most baccalaureate business programs focused on a particular profession or industry—for example, accounting, insurance, retailing, hotel and restaurant management, or real estate. For the most part, they prepared students for their first jobs. Furthermore, business students were required to take only a limited number of arts and science courses.

Accelerated growth and reform

In the post-World War II period there was an explosion in business school enrollments as thousands of veterans avoided liberal arts colleges to seek a more structured route to the labor market. Business schools became increasingly important on college campuses, and the large number of graduates gave them increasing visibility.

Working closely with the AACSB, the nation's business schools made a number of reforms. Admissions standards were raised. Faculty were required to have doctorates and to do significant research in their respective fields. The curriculum was enhanced: freshman and sophomore years were devoted to arts and science subjects, and business subjects became upper-level courses. Wherever possible, business majors were built on an arts and science platform in a related discipline—for example, finance was tied to mathematics and economics; marketing and management to behavioral science. Specialization was deemphasized in favor of a more generalized approach. The goal was to teach skills and knowledge that would apply throughout life rather than to prepare for the first job.

These profound changes substantially improved business education. Business enrollments from the early 1960s to the late 1980s increased by more than three-and-a-half fold. As a percentage of all graduates, business majors increased their share from under 13 percent to over 24 percent, thereby making business the most popular discipline on college campuses. Business schools now attract the best high school students as measured by grade-point average and Scholastic Aptitude Test scores.

Important changes have also occurred in the composition of the student body. In the early 1960s, women made up less than 8 percent of business graduates; they rose to over 46 percent by the late 1980s. In the 1960s most women in business school were marketing majors; now they are represented in all business disciplines. In some colleges and universities women account for 30 to 50 percent of the student body.

A new period of curriculum change

Despite the current healthy state of collegiate business schools, major educational and curriculum changes are under way. The deterioration of America's competitive advantage in many international markets, a disappointing rate of growth in national productivity, a slowdown in the rate of improvement in the U.S. standard of living, and breaches of legal and ethical behavior by business leaders have again raised questions about collegiate business education. As a consequence, most major business schools are reviewing and restructuring their curricula. Changes under way include:

1. Strengthening the liberal arts base of business education. Students need a more balanced and broad-based education. Future business leaders must be well-rounded individuals.
2. Greater exposure to and familiarity with other languages and cultures. The U.S. ability to compete internationally depends in part on the ability of its business professionals to communicate and feel confident in foreign countries.

3. Emphasis on providing a more complete view of the management process. Core courses must be integrated to give students interrelated views of basic subject areas.

4. Better understanding of the environment—political, ecological, technological, and ethical—in which business decisions are made.

5. Further improvement of written and oral communication skills.

6. More "real-world" applications and experiences built into the curriculum.

7. The return of operations management to a central place in the program of study. This area deals with the efficiency and quality of the production process, an area in which U.S. businesses are lacking compared to their international competitors.

8. Redirection of the faculty toward quality teaching, giving instruction the same emphasis and importance now given to research.

These changes are expected to yield great benefits comparable to those achieved by the reforms of the 1960s.

Program structure

If you decide to attend a college of business or management, you can expect to have a highly structured program of study. Your freshman and sophomore years will be devoted principally to arts and science courses. While you will have some electives, you will be required to take courses in calculus for the social sciences, psychology and/or sociology, economics, computers, writing workshops, oral and written communications, accounting, and statistics.

In your junior year, you will begin your professional education by taking a set of core courses in basic areas such as finance, management and organizational behavior, marketing, and operations management. The balance of the junior and senior years will be devoted to your major, electives, and a capstone course in business policy that requires you to apply all of the subjects you have studied in order to solve actual business problems.

Characteristics of a successful business student

The most successful business students are comfortable with numbers and the manipulation of data, enjoy working with a computer, and have good communications skills, both written and oral. They can work alone or as members of a team addressing a specific problem. Often they have exhibited leadership abilities at their high school or in their community. They typically have a clear view of the objectives they wish to achieve in life and see business education as one of the principal means of achieving them.

Outcomes

Most business school graduates go to work immediately after graduation. Only 10 to 15 percent go directly to graduate school, usually law school. While a sizable percentage eventually earn a master's degree in business administration (MBA), they do so after working two or more years in a professional capacity. About 30 percent attend graduate school as full-time students and the balance as part-time students.

As a business or management major, you will take a mix of liberal arts and professional subjects. This balanced curriculum will give you the tools, analytical skills, and knowledge for your first position following graduation, as well as lay the foundation for career advancement and lifetime employment.

Accounting

A major in accounting teaches students to record, analyze, control, interpret, and communicate information about money flows and balances. Students can apply this knowledge in all areas of business, government, and nonprofit enterprises.

Interests, skills, and qualities associated with success in the major

Interests. Working with numbers, competition, economics, computers, mathematics, entrepreneurship, social and political activism, moral and ethical responsibility.

Skills and qualities. Mathematical or arithmetic skills, written and oral communication, working with people, leadership.

Recommended high school preparation

English 4, algebra 2, geometry 1, trigonometry 1, laboratory science 2, social studies 2, foreign language 2, and computer science 2. One year of music or visual arts is recommended.

Typical courses in the major

Introductory Accounting
Intermediate Accounting
Federal Income Taxation
Financial Statement Analysis

Advanced Accounting
Cost Accounting
Auditing

What the major is like

A major in accounting is an open sesame to careers in economics that involve recording, analyzing, controlling, interpreting, and communicating information about money flows and balances. Important decisions are made on the basis of information generated by accountants in the realms of business and government as well as in educational, religious, charitable, and scientific institutions. Because the economic environment has become globalized, accounting responsibilities transcend geographic and political boundaries. At the same time accounting supplies useful skills to individuals when budgeting, paying taxes, and planning their personal finances.

Accounting may be studied in most colleges and universities. If the institution includes a school of business or management, the major is housed there. Otherwise, accounting programs may be offered as part of a program in the liberal arts or sciences, usually in the economics or social science department. Students earn a Bachelor of Business Administration degree from a school of business or a Bachelor of Arts or Bachelor of Science from a college of arts and sciences.

Students of accounting will be required to pursue extensive course work in economics and finance, business law, business organization and management, marketing, and computer information sciences. In addition, students must pursue a broad education in the liberal arts and the sciences: effectiveness in business and related professions requires a solid background in history, writing, foreign languages, and communications, in addition to the interpersonal skills needed for teamwork.

Course work in accounting educates students in the special language of accountancy and in the procedures for recording, summarizing, interpreting, and communicating financial information. Students learn to measure costs, compile cost data, and determine how accounting data affect efficiency and profitability within organizations. Having completed their introductory accounting courses, students move on to study financial statements and how financial analysts, credit grantors, governmental agencies, and others rely on them when making decisions.

The major prepares students for careers in public or managerial accounting. Public accountants work with auditing firms to produce credible financial reports; managerial accountants work with top management to develop and monitor a firm's financial health. Managerial accountants often need special knowledge about taxes, budgeting, and investing.

Specializations

There are no specializations at the undergraduate level.

Other majors to consider

Business administration
Economics
Finance
Information sciences and systems
International business management
Management
Marketing
Mathematics
Real estate
Statistics

Careers related to the major

The accounting major may lead to jobs as a certified public accountant (CPA) with a public accounting firm; accountant in a bank or other financial institution; accountant in a commercial, industrial, or nonprofit enterprise; government accountant; or accountant with a law firm.

For more information

American Institute of Certified Public Accountants
1211 Avenue of the Americas
New York, NY 10036
(212)575-6200

Business administration

Business administration majors learn the fundamental principles, concepts, and applications of accounting, finance, and management, while gaining a foundation in the liberal arts.

Interests, skills, and qualities associated with success in the major

Interests. Leadership, organizing people, taking initiative, starting and running a business, working with numbers, solving problems, competing, taking risks, working with people.

Skills and qualities. Oral and written communication, organizational skills, teamwork, understanding and analyzing numerical data, creative and critical thinking.

Recommended high school preparation	English 4, algebra 2, geometry 1, trigonometry 1, laboratory science 2, social studies 2, and foreign language 2.

Typical courses in the major

Accounting
Financial Management
Organizational Behavior
Production Management
Business Law
Statistics

Economics
Marketing
Business Policy
Operations Management
Management Information Systems

What the major is like

In the business administration major, students gain a broad foundation in the liberal arts and are exposed to the basics of business. They then specialize in a specific area of business such as accounting, business finance, management, marketing, statistics, management information systems, production and operations management, and management policy and strategy. The major prepares students to serve as effective and responsible managers in business, government, and nonprofit sectors.

To develop a sound foundation in all areas, business administration students typically take between 40 and 60 percent of their courses in the humanities, fine arts, mathematics, and social sciences, mostly during the first two years of study. Students generally begin their business studies as first-semester sophomores with required business and management courses that introduce the basic tools and functions of business.

Although many business classes follow the lecture format, they use the case study approach extensively to develop problem-solving skills and the ability to think analytically, defend ideas logically, and challenge the propositions of others. Students analyze actual business problems, develop viable courses of action, and present and defend their recommendations to their professors and classmates. Discussions of cases in class are challenging and provide excellent experience with business problems and situations that managers face.

Business majors use the computer to gain proficiency with spreadsheet programs, data base packages, and other programs for conducting statistical analysis, preparing financial projections, and carrying out marketing research.

Some colleges and universities offer internships, in which business majors may earn academic credit while getting firsthand business experience.

Specializations

Accounting, finance, international business, marketing, management information systems, human resources management, production and operations management, organizational behavior.

Other majors to consider

Agribusiness
Computer science
Health services management
Hotel/motel and restaurant management
International relations
Labor/industrial relations
Management science
Operations research (quantitative methods)
Public administration
Statistics

Careers related to the major

As the relationships among the world's business, social, and government institutions grow more complex, there is greater need for competent professional managers. The management major may lead to careers as an entry-level manager, accountant, auditor, human resources specialist, assistant product manager, market researcher, public relations representative, systems analyst, labor relations specialist, securities salesperson, or financial analyst.

For more information

American Management Association
135 West 50 Street
New York, NY 10020
(212)586-8100

Finance

Finance majors study financial and accounting information, economic models, and analytic techniques that can be applied to financial problems. They learn to determine prices of assets such as stocks, bonds, and businesses and to manage assets to maximize their economic value.

Interests, skills, and qualities associated with success in the major

Interests. Business, the stock market, the economy, budgets.

Skills and qualities. Logical thinking, analytic thinking, quantitative thinking, organizational skills, solving problems with computers, working with people, making oral and written presentations.

Recommended high school preparation

English 4, precollege mathematics 4, biology 2–3, physics 1–2, social studies 2, history 2, foreign language 2–4, and computer science 1–2. Social studies should include economics if available. One to two years of accounting or bookkeeping is recommended.

Typical courses in the major

Corporate Finance	Financial Institutions
Investments	Economics
Bank Management	Portfolio Analysis
Real Estate	Accounting
Options and Futures	Insurance

What the major is like

During their first two college years, finance majors, like all business students, fulfill general education requirements that include courses in mathematics, humanities, natural sciences, and social sciences. Economics and accounting are usually taken during the sophomore year because most institutions require students to complete one or two semesters in those subjects before beginning classes in finance. In their junior year majors take introductory courses in finance and other functional areas of business—accounting, management, marketing, and management information systems.

The first finance course focuses on corporate financial analysis as well as valuation principles for financial assets such as stocks and bonds. Emphasis is on the tools of financial analysis, including the evaluation of financial statements and the time value of money calculations. Subsequent classes cover investments and portfolio management, corporate finance, banking and financial institutions, and international finance. Because of the critical relation of economics and accounting to finance, most finance programs require at least 12 to 15 semester hours of course work in both economics and accounting.

Many finance courses require the use of personal computers in problem solving, thus improving students' facility with spreadsheet programs, statistical and financial analysis, financial forecasting, and preparation of financial reports. Electives may be in statistics, economics, accounting, computer applications, and communications.

Finance graduates are immediately productive because their training emphasizes analytic techniques, computer applications, and practical problem solving. Though demand in the financial services industry has cooled since the boom period in the 1980s, excellent opportunities exist for finance majors.

Specializations

Financial management, investment management, banking, real estate, insurance.

Other majors to consider

Accounting
Actuarial sciences
Agricultural economics
Business administration
Economics
International business management
Management science
Public administration
Real estate
Statistics

Careers related to the major

Major banks employ finance graduates as bank officers in a variety of areas from corporate lending to bank trust operations. Large corporations hire graduates as financial managers, financial planners, financial controllers, or in international financial operations. Brokerage and investment banking firms offer opportunities as account executives or financial consultants for clients. Insurance companies and real estate developers offer entry-level opportunities for graduates. Large accounting firms hire finance graduates to work as financial consultants for their major clients. Some finance majors elect to go into business for themselves as financial advisers and planners for wealthy individuals.

For more information

Financial Management Association
College of Business Administration
University of South Florida
Tampa, FL 33620
(813)974-2084

The Financial Management Association publishes a brochure called "Careers in Finance."

Human resources management

Majors in human resources management are concerned with issues that affect men and women at work. Students study recruitment, performance appraisal, pay and benefits, labor relations, health and safety at work, and other topics in order to support union and nonunion, domestic and multinational organizations.

Interests, skills, and qualities associated with success in the major

Interests. Solving problems, working with numbers, working with people of different ages and backgrounds, leadership.

Skills and qualities. Logical thinking, communicating clearly, understanding and analyzing numerical data, critical thinking, teamwork.

Recommended high school preparation

English 3–4, precollege mathematics 2, laboratory science 2, social studies 2, history 2, foreign language 2–4, and computer science 1.

Typical courses in the major

Business
Training and Development
Labor and Industrial Relations

Personnel Recruitment
Compensation and Benefits
Statistics

What the major is like

The major in human resources management prepares specialists who provide staff support (advice, direction, research capability) to managers and employees both in business and in nonprofit organizations. Given the expected shortages of entry-level workers during the 1990s, plus the large numbers of women, older workers, minorities, and immigrants who will be joining the work force during this decade, human resources specialists will be in considerable demand by all kinds of organizations.

Because of the range of persons and situations they will encounter in their work, human resources management majors should have a sound foundation in the humanities, fine arts, mathematics, and social sciences, including philosophy, psychology, and sociology. During the first two years, students generally take 40 to 60 percent of their course work in these areas. The remaining courses are related to business—economics, introduction to business, and introduction to management.

During the junior and senior years, students mix business administration and human resources management. Business administration courses are marketing, finance, accounting, statistics, information systems, and organizational behavior. Human resources management courses include the following:

Legal and social environments of business: Students study laws dealing with civil rights, pay, benefits, and worker health and safety, plus court rulings that govern employment relationships. Majors in human resources management must be knowledgeable in these areas so that they can advise managers and employees of their rights and obligations in employment relationships.

Recruitment and selection: Students learn how to find and attract potential employees and use job-related methods to decide which employees to hire. Students learn about employment interviews, psychological tests, reference checking, and various screening devices to separate better candidates from less qualified ones.

Training and development: Students study methods and procedures for designing, implementing, and evaluating programs designed to enhance knowledge, skills, and abilities of managers as well as lower-level workers.

Compensation and benefits: The focus is on designing and implementing pay and benefit systems in unionized and nonunionized firms. Students learn about social security, unemployment and workers' compensation programs, pensions, life and health insurance, and various employee incentive programs.

Labor and industrial relations: Students study the history of labor-management relations in the United States, plus the legal framework that governs current relations between labor and management. They learn about collective bargaining, strikes, grievances, arbitration, and current problems that face both labor and management in unionized and nonunionized companies.

International human resources management: Given the increase in U.S. companies doing business overseas and foreign firms doing business in the United States, students need to understand the important differences between domestic and multinational human resources management. Topics that are important in domestic operations are examined in the international context.

Many businesses offer internships to students in human resources management, which enable them to earn academic credit while gaining firsthand experience. Master's and doctoral programs in human resources management offer further specialization in such fields as organizational behavior, employment testing, compensation, and labor and industrial relations.

Specializations　　Compensation, labor/industrial relations, personnel psychology.

Other majors to consider

Economics
Industrial and organizational psychology
Psychology
Sociology

Careers related to the major　　The human resources major leads to jobs as a personnel generalist, or as a human resources specialist in areas such as benefits, pay systems, labor negotiations, labor/industrial relations, employment interviewer, and recruitment.

For more information　　Society for Human Resource Management
606 North Washington Street
Alexandria, VA 22314
(703)548-3440

The brochure "Careers in Human Resources Management"
is available from the Society for Human Resource Management.

Insurance and risk management

Majors in insurance and risk management analyze and solve problems involving loss of personal and corporate assets. Programs integrate knowledge from finance, quantitative analysis, and management and include study of the legal, social, and institutional environment in which losses may occur.

Interests, skills, and qualities associated with success in the major

Interests. Leadership, taking initiative, working with numbers, solving problems, competing.

Skills and qualities. Oral and written communication, organization skills, understanding and analyzing numerical data, creative and critical thinking.

Recommended high school preparation

English 3–4, precollege mathematics 3–4, laboratory science 2, social studies 1, and computer science 1.

Typical courses in the major

Risk Management
Liability Risk Management
Government Insurance
Financial Planning

Property Risk Management
Employee Benefits Management
Life and Health Insurance
Insurance Company Operations

What the major is like

The major in insurance and risk management prepares students to assess and treat the risks taken by profit-seeking and nonprofit organizations. Typically, in the first two years of college students concentrate on the liberal arts. A core of business studies, providing an understanding of complete business enterprises, follows—or overlaps with—the liberal arts courses. The specialized courses of this major are typically taken in the third and fourth years.

This specialized program usually traces two parallel paths: one focuses on possible losses both to actual property and through legal liability. The other focuses on the losses associated with employees—poor health, retirement needs, and unexpected death. Methods to minimize the negative impact of these events, as well as tools to analyze those methods, are the substance of the major courses.

Because risk managers and insurance underwriters must be able to assess the potential losses to which organizations are exposed, the development of thorough, critical thinking is especially significant to this major.

Specializations

Specialization is not available at the undergraduate level.

Other majors to consider

Accounting
Actuarial sciences
Engineering
Finance
Human resources management

Careers related to the major

The insurance and risk management major may lead to careers as a risk manager, insurance broker, insurance representative, employee benefits manager, insurance underwriter, insurance claims adjustor, and insurance regulator.

For more information

The Insurance Institutes of America
720 Providence Road
Malvern, PA 19355-0770
(215)644-2100

The American Risk and Insurance Association
Department of Management
School of Business Administration
California State University - Sacramento
6000 J Street, BUS 2017
Sacramento, CA 95819-6088

International business management

Majors in international business management learn basic business management techniques and practices and also study how business is conducted in other countries and between different countries. They examine financial systems, government policies, cultural differences, production, management styles, and other issues that affect how business is conducted abroad.

Interests, skills, and qualities associated with success in the major

Interests. Other cultures, politics, different peoples and environments.

Skills and qualities. Problem solving, learning languages, organizing and managing people.

Recommended high school preparation

English 4, algebra 1, calculus 1, geometry 1, trigonometry 1, laboratory science 2, social studies 2, history 1, foreign language 4, and computer science 1.

Typical courses in the major

Economics	Accounting
Finance	Marketing
Management	Statistics
International Business	International Finance
International Management	International Marketing

What the major is like

The international business major provides a foundation in basic knowledge of accounting, marketing, finance, and management. It also includes courses that enable students to analyze information about businesses in other countries and to think globally when making business decisions. The business environment differs from country to country, and it is increasingly important that business managers have an understanding of these differences.

In general, students take basic business courses and then move on to courses with an international focus. These may examine how money and capital (equipment and other goods) move within and between countries; how technology is transferred between various countries; what management skills are practiced abroad. Students learn to analyze the international economic scene, study competition and interdependence, and evaluate cultural differences. They may study how to sell U.S. goods abroad, or how to evaluate the strength of investments in different countries.

Key to the study of international business is an understanding of politics and government, so students should take electives in these areas. Most programs require students to master a foreign language. Study abroad for an academic year, a semester, or a summer enhances students' course work. Sometimes these opportunities include visits to foreign companies and meetings with business managers.

The major prepares students to meet the business challenges of the 1990s, which demand imaginative and responsible leaders in business here and abroad. Students gain professional expertise that will enable them to operate in an international business environment, while also gaining a greater understanding of their own and other cultures.

Specializations	Accounting, economics, finance, management, marketing.
Other majors to consider	**Asian studies** **European studies** **International relations** **Latin American studies** **Management science** **Middle Eastern studies** Russian and Slavic studies
Careers related to the major	The international business major prepares students for careers in international divisions of American foreign companies; in import-export businesses; with the State Department, the military, and government agencies concerned with international trade or development; in international businesses; and in commercial and investment banking on an international scale.
For more information	**Opportunities in International Business Careers.** Jeffrey Arpin. Lincolnwood, IL: VGM Career Horizons, 1989. $10.95.

Labor/industrial relations

Labor and industrial relations majors study the relationship between workers and employers. The economic foundation and the psychological and sociological dimensions of the employment relationship are examined. Particular attention is given to government policies, labor unions, and human resources management.

Interests, skills, and qualities associated with success in the major	**Interests.** The employment relationship, human behavior, problem solving.

Skills and qualities. Working with people, fitting individual and group needs into the structure and goals of a larger organization. |
| **Recommended high school preparation** | English 4, algebra 1.5, calculus 1, geometry 1, trigonometry .5, biology 1, chemistry 1, physics 1, social studies 2, history 2, and foreign language 4. |
| **Typical courses in the major** | Human Resources Management   Labor Economics
Industrial Psychology   Labor History
Collective Bargaining   Employment/labor Law
Public Policy |

What the major is like

The major in labor and industrial relations uses study of fields such as economics, psychology, and sociology to understand relationships between workers and their employers. Government policies, labor unions, and human resources management are emphasized. Majors learn how governments attempt to influence the employment relationship through regulation of areas such as safety and health, wages and hours, and international trade. Students specializing in human resources management apply principles from the basic social science disciplines to understand how to attract, retain, and motivate employees. When employees group themselves together into labor unions and bargain collectively with employers, the employment relationship takes on many unique and important features that warrant separate study.

In many universities the major is offered through the business school and is similar to the major in personnel/human resources management. Several universities have a separate school of labor and industrial relations, and some colleges offer the major within arts and sciences.

The multidisciplinary nature of this major gives the student a wide perspective, providing excellent preparation for employment or for postgraduate education in, for example, law or business.

Specializations

Specialization is not common at the undergraduate level.

Other majors to consider

Economics
Human resources management
Industrial and organizational psychology

Careers related to the major

The study of labor and industrial relations prepares students for positions in industry, labor unions, or government. Typical duties in private industry—by far the most substantial source of jobs for majors—include recruitment, training, and compensation. With some experience, individuals in this field can become responsible for relations with labor unions and interaction with government agencies. A few graduates work for labor unions, typically as union organizers or office administrators. Government agencies are a source of jobs in their role as regulators of the private employment relationship, and government organizations hire employees and therefore require professionals to manage that function.

For more information

Employee and Labor Relations. John Fossum, editor. Washington, D.C.: Bureau of National Affairs Books, 1990.

Human Resources Management: Evolving Roles. Lee Dyer, editor. Washington, D.C.: Bureau of National Affairs Books, 1989.

Management

The management major is designed for the generalist who wants a broad business background. Students take courses in business areas, such as accounting, marketing, finance, and business law, and courses that prepare them to function as managers in any organization.

Interests, skills, and qualities associated with success in the major

Interests. Working with people, listening, persuading, leading, starting new systems.

Skills and qualities. Thinking analytically, solving puzzles, working with people, presenting information to others, organizing, thinking quickly.

Recommended high school preparation

English 4, precollege mathematics 3, biology 1, chemistry 1, physics 1, social studies 2, sociology 1, history 2, foreign language 2, music 1, visual arts 1, and computer science 2.

Typical courses in the major

Accounting	Managerial Economics
Financial Management	Marketing
Business Strategy	Production Management
Operations Management	Computer Science
Organizational Behavior	Human Resources Management
International Management	Business Law
Supervisory Skills	Entrepreneurial Studies
Statistics	

What the major is like

The objective of the management major is to prepare students to lead others in a work organization, regardless of the organization's purpose and location. Because that is the goal, most management courses seek to increase students' powers of critical thinking and persuasion. Classes rely on lectures, case studies from the business world, vigorous debate, and classroom presentations. Managers are often brought in to share their experiences using the methods the students are learning. The growing number of older students in college is an advantage, as they bring to management classes their maturity and life experience.

Business programs usually admit students after they have completed two years of liberal arts study, which often includes courses in business ethics and international politics. (The grade-point average for admission to the business program is usually higher than that required for other programs.) Once students are in the business program, they begin the fundamental courses all business majors take. Following these foundation courses in accounting, marketing, and finance, students take specialized courses in management such as organizational behavior, human resources management, supervisory skills, and international management. As the students progress, they take electives that suit their particular interests.

Business strategy, or business policy, is usually the capstone course for all management majors. A senior year course, it pulls together the information and skill from all the courses to study an organization's internal operation and its interaction with the environment.

Most management programs offer internships, usually for a term, to expose students directly to possible careers and to enable students to relate classroom learning to the workplace. Most internships award academic credit and require students to submit material to be graded.

Management, perhaps more than any other business major, is culture-specific: an organization's policies and practices reflect the nature of the culture in which it is located. Many business programs offer a term abroad, enabling the management major to apply management skills in a cross-cultural setting. For a manager in an international setting—and American business is becoming increasingly global—understanding the cultural values and morals of other countries is critical.

Specializations

International business, small business management, management of technology, public administration, management information systems, human resources management, hotel and restaurant management, entrepreneurial studies.

Other majors to consider

Agribusiness
Computer science
Engineering
Health services management
Hotel/motel and restaurant management
Industrial and organizational psychology
Information sciences and systems
International relations
Labor/industrial relations
Management science
Operations research (quantitative methods)
Public administration
Sociology

Careers related to the major

The management major may lead to the following jobs: entry-level manager, human resources recruiter, human resource specialist, product manager, office manager, career manager, public relations representative, systems analyst, labor relations specialist, sales representative, corporate communications specialist, trainer.

For more information

American Assembly of Collegiate Schools of Business
605 Old Ballas Road
Suite 220
St. Louis, MO 63141-7077
(314)872-8481

Management information systems

The management information systems major unites computer science and business knowledge. Students learn to act as intermediaries between persons with information needs and the computer programmers who provide the solutions to the problems.

Interests, skills, and qualities associated with success in the major

Interests. Computer languages, computer programming, problem solving, logic, taking initiative, organizing groups.

Skills and qualities. Communication, working in groups, creativity, solving oral and written problems, understanding human behavior.

Recommended high school preparation

English 2–3, algebra 1–2, geometry 1, trigonometry 1, laboratory science 1, social studies 2, history 1, foreign language 1–2, communications 1, and computer science 1–2. Social studies should include psychology if available.

Typical courses in the major

COBOL Programming
System Design
Telecommunications Design
Telecommunications Policy
Systems Analysis
Data Base Analysis and Design
Decision Support Systems
Artificial Intelligence

What the major is like

In the management information systems (MIS) major, students study business, computer programming, and how to use existing computer software. One of the most rapidly growing fields, MIS is usually offered in a university's school of business administration. Students take all the core courses of the business administration program in addition to specialized MIS courses.

In most business schools at least two of the courses required of business majors are computer oriented. One is management information systems, a survey course describing all the areas of systems analysis. The second may be a course in a programming language such as BASIC or Pascal, or one covering several software packages such as spreadsheets, data bases, word processing, and a graphics or expert system package.

Majors in MIS ordinarily take the computer-oriented business courses before taking six to eight courses that make up the rest of the major. These normally include some or all of the following.

COBOL: Students learn this computer language, which is especially useful for treating business problems. Most companies have programs in this language that may need updating. Other languages, such as C and Ramis, may be offered as new tools are developed.

Systems analysis and design: Topics are interviewing to determine the need for a system; analyzing costs and benefits; designing a new system; implementing the new system; testing the new system.

Data base design and administration: Topics are defining data needs; designing and managing data bases; using common data base programs.

Telecommunication design and policy: Topics are voice, video, and data communications; methods of transmitting data; wiring and equipment; costs; speed of transmission. Design of local area networks and network management are normally included.

Expert systems and artificial intelligence: Topics are design of these systems and use of existing programs in these areas.

The basic task of the information systems specialist is to act as an intermediary between the persons in an organization who have information needs, such as record keeping, sales, production, or planning, and the computer programmers who write the solutions to these problems. The information analyst knows the business functions (accounting, marketing, finance, operations, strategic planning) as well as computer programming and the computer programs available for solving particular problems. The MIS specialist interviews the potential user, finds out the goals of the organization, determines the information needs and tools required to support these goals, and helps to design computerized systems to support these goals. Then the analyst may review the solutions and user needs with the programmers. Finally the analyst may participate in the programming, implementation, and testing of these newly designed systems.

Many institutions offer local internships to give students hands-on experience.

Specializations

Specialization is not available.

Other majors to consider

Computer science

Careers related to the major

The major may lead to jobs as a systems analyst, computer programmer, information systems manager, or information systems consultant. It may also lead to work in computer marketing and sales.

For more information

Data Processing Management Association
505 Busse Highway
Park Ridge, IL 60068
(312)693-5070

Association for Computing Machinery
1515 Broadway, 17th Floor
New York, NY 10036
(212)869-7440

"Computer Careers" is available from Data Processing Management Association.

Management science

Majors in management science use mathematics, computers, and statistical and economic analysis to solve managerial and business problems.

Interests, skills, and qualities associated with success in the major	**Interests.** Mathematics, solving business and management problems, computer languages, computer programming.

Skills and qualities. Quantitative thinking, computer programming, working with computers, creativity, oral and written communication, group leadership, persuasiveness. |
| **Recommended high school preparation** | English 4, precollege mathematics 4, chemistry 1, physics 1, social studies 3, foreign language 2, and computer science 1. |
| **Typical courses in the major** | Management Science Mathematical Statistics
Decision Analysis Management Theory
Accounting Economics
Econometrics Financial Management
Organization Behavior Management Information Systems
Strategic Management |
| **What the major is like** | The management science major is designed for students with an interest in applying mathematical, statistical, and economic analysis to the solution of managerial problems. Graduates typically find employment as staff analysts in industry and government, as systems analysts, or in other positions for which a high degree of analytic ability is required.

The major is organized on much the same basis as are management and business administration programs. The first two years are typically devoted to English, mathematics, humanities, natural sciences, and social sciences, including fundamentals of economics. Students usually take accounting courses and an initial course in management information systems during the first two years. The junior and senior years are devoted to studies in the core business areas (accounting, finance, management), advanced management science courses, and the development of a specialization.

A distinguishing feature of the management science major is its strong emphasis on mathematics. The required studies include basic differential and integral calculus, applications including calculus of functions of several variables, Lagrangian multipliers, and series approximations and convergence tests. Another distinguishing feature is its strong reliance on computer facility and programming capability in the analysis and solution of business and management problems.

Courses include lectures, discussion, and analysis of case studies. Some courses may be taught in a computer laboratory. Management science majors also take a required course in business policy/strategic management, usually taught by the case method. Students are presented with real-world problems and are expected to use knowledge, skill, and understanding from previous studies in their analysis. They then defend their recommendations before their colleagues and professor. |
| **Specializations** | Economics, marketing, psychology, computer science, accounting, finance, organizational behavior, production/operations management, management information systems. |
| **Other majors to consider** | **Business administration**
Industrial engineering
Management
Operations research (quantitative methods)
Systems engineering |

Careers related to the major	Management science majors can find entry-level jobs as systems analysts, systems engineers, consultants with national consulting firms, internal staff consultants in large organizations, and computer consultants. With additional training in the specific area they can become programmers, market research analysts, or financial analysts.

The management science major is also excellent preparation for graduate study in a wide variety of business-related areas. |
| **For more information** | The Institute of Management Sciences
290 Westminster Street
Providence, RI 02903
(401)274-2525

Operations Research Society of America
1314 Guilford Avenue
Baltimore, MD 21202
(301)528-4146

The Institute of Management Sciences publishes the brochure "Key Steps to Your Future." "Student Communications" is available from Operations Research Society of America. |

Marketing

Marketing, a specialization within business studies, is concerned with getting products and services from producers to consumers. Marketing majors learn to make decisions about product design and quality, pricing, advertising, selling, and distribution.

Interests, skills, and qualities associated with success in the major	**Interests.** Running a business, economic issues, social issues, working on new products, problem solving, analyzing data, understanding how people buy, use, and sell products and services.

Skills and qualities. Completing tasks on time, communicating clearly and persuasively, working with numbers, creativity, understanding human behavior. |
| **Recommended high school preparation** | English 4, algebra 1, calculus 1, geometry 1, trigonometry .5, laboratory science 2–3, social studies 1–2, history 2–3, foreign language 2–4, and computer science 1. |
| **Typical courses in the major** | Principles of Marketing   Marketing Management
Marketing Research   Advertising Principles
Retailing   Buyer Behavior
Industrial Marketing   Marketing Strategy |
| **What the major is like** | Marketing involves activities that identify and devise ways to satisfy consumer wants and needs with an organization's products and services. |

Majors in the field learn that marketing is much more than advertising and selling; it involves analyzing consumer opinions, attitudes, and tastes, both in the United States and abroad. The principles of marketing help organizations determine what products and services people want, forecast the demand for them, and stimulate consumer interest in them.

Students learn the role of marketing in the economy and the basic functions of marketing professionals. They study the four basic elements: (1) the products and services consumers want, (2) the prices buyers are willing to pay, (3) the role of intermediaries such as wholesalers and retailers, through whom products and services flow from producers to buyers, and (4) the technique of communicating with prospective customers through advertising, personal selling, and publicity.

In the study of marketing, students learn how goods and services are provided to businesses and individual consumers. Business-to-business marketing is concerned with products like computers, copying machines, steel, or chemicals that are sold to other businesses. Consumer marketing is concerned with goods such as appliances, automobiles, packaged goods (food, soaps, paper products, and other everyday items) and services like insurance and banking.

Courses in marketing principles and marketing management teach students to develop and implement plans to market products and services successfully. Other courses specialize in a single aspect of marketing management. Marketing research, usually required of all marketing majors, uses surveys, experiments, test markets, and other research techniques to obtain the information needed for effective marketing decisions. Advertising management concerns the design, testing, execution, and monitoring of advertising campaigns. (Marketing majors are usually not involved in the creative efforts needed to actually design and produce advertisements.) Courses in selling and sales management focus on the psychology of effective selling and the management of salespeople (recruiting, selecting, organizing, training, and motivating). Courses in marketing channels study institutions (retailers, wholesalers, industrial distributors) that work as intermediaries between manufacturers and buyers.

Marketing is usually offered in schools of management or business. Majors take the courses required of all business students, and approximately half the course work is in the liberal arts. Business programs usually require one marketing course for all students, and the marketing major takes four to six additional marketing courses.

Specializations

Advertising management, marketing research, personal selling, product management, retailing, sales management, transportation and logistics.

Other majors to consider

Advertising
Communications
Economics
Fashion merchandising
Journalism
Psychology
Public administration
Public relations
Sociology
Statistics

| **Careers related to the major** | There are career opportunities for marketing graduates in personal selling, retailing, advertising, and marketing research. Jobs in personal selling offer independence, potential for high compensation, and opportunities for advancement. Retailing careers generally take one of two paths: merchandising (which involves selecting and buying products for resale, setting prices, and coordinating promotions and advertising) and retail management (which involves the supervision of store personnel, management of the store facilities, and responsibility for the store's financial performance). Advertising careers exist in client organizations that use advertising, such as manufacturers, retail stores, and other companies; in advertising agencies, which specialize in creating and placing the ads; and in media, such as newspapers, magazines, and radio and television stations. Market researchers may work in independent firms that specialize in research about consumers and markets or with in-house market research staffs in many large companies. Each year most positions available to graduates majoring in marketing are in personal selling and retailing, whereas relatively fewer positions are available in the other careers. |
| | The major may lead to a job as a market research analyst, advertising media buyer, retail buyer, retail store manager, sales representative, sales manager, market analyst, or public relations representative. With an M.B.A., graduates may find jobs as product managers, advertising account executives, or marketing consultants. |

For more information

The American Marketing Association
250 South Wacker Drive
Suite 200
Chicago, IL 60606
(312)648-0536

Real estate

The real estate major enables students to gain an understanding of and proficiency in the business and social principles that affect how real property—buildings and land—is developed, operated, and traded.

Interests, skills, and qualities associated with success in the major

Interests. Business, people and social conditions, the economy, public affairs.

Skills and qualities. Oral and written communication, making decisions, working independently, organizing and managing others, critical thinking, analytic thinking, using mathematics.

Recommended high school preparation

English 4, precollege mathematics 4, biology 1, social studies 3, history 3, foreign language 2, visual arts 1, computer science 1, and business 1.

Typical courses in the major	Economics	Accounting
	Finance	Marketing
	Management	Statistics
	Real Estate Law	Real Estate Investment Analysis
	Real Estate Finance	Real Estate Market Analysis
	Appraisal	Property Management and Leasing
	Mortgage Lending	Urban Development Regulations

What the major is like

Most real estate degree programs are part of a business program. The degree offered is usually a Bachelor of Business Administration or a Bachelor of Science or Bachelor of Arts in business. A real estate major typically does not begin taking real estate courses until the junior year. The freshman and sophomore years are devoted to a liberal arts curriculum and introductory business courses such as accounting, economics, and statistics.

In the junior year, students take a course that introduces them to principles of real estate. This covers the language of real estate, ethics, brokerage, appraisal, contracts, and property management. This course serves as a prerequisite to higher-level courses, in which students learn about laws affecting real estate ownership, transfer, and land-use control; methods and considerations that affect the financing of real estate purchases and sales; appraisal; the effect of tax laws on investment; management of real estate such as office buildings and apartment buildings; and marketing techniques.

Because housing is one of the most common and largest parts of the real estate business, many people think selling houses is the basic business of real estate. In fact, most college-trained real estate professionals are employed as financial analysts or in other business aspects of the field. Their knowledge is needed by large corporations, financial institutions, and funds management organizations that need to manage their real estate assets professionally. Corporate real estate operations, professional real estate asset management, and related operations of facilities planning are rapidly being integrated as specializations in the field of real estate. In addition, real estate majors are being trained in development and redevelopment activities, including ways of salvaging problem properties.

Real estate classes typically follow a lecture-discussion format and use case studies and computer programs as tools for solving problems. Some real estate programs also focus on the physical elements (sites, buildings, etc.) and have studio courses to teach physical planning and construction.

A student holding a business degree with a major in real estate may seek employment in many fields of business or go into a specialized real estate business. Although many majors work in the established sectors of the real estate industry, others become entrepreneurial and establish their own business or manage their own investments. Graduates must pass a state real estate licensing exam in order to work as a sales agent or broker. Although the courses in college programs cover most topics needed for state licensing, students may need to take supplemental courses covering specific state laws, ethics, or peculiar licensing requirements before taking the licensing exam.

Specializations

Real estate investment management, real estate asset management, real estate finance and mortgage lending, appraisal, market analysis, brokerage and sales, securities management and sales, real estate development.

Other majors to consider

Accounting
Architecture
City/community/regional planning
Civil engineering
Economics
Finance
Landscape architecture
Management
Marketing
Public administration
Urban studies

Careers related to the major

A bachelor's degree in real estate will prepare a student for an entry-level position in the following areas: mortgage lender, loan processor, appraiser, tax assessing officer, real estate financial analyst, property manager, real estate securities analyst or sales agent, real estate broker or sales agent, real estate market and feasibility analyst, construction manager, corporate real estate manager, real estate asset manager for a public agency or nonprofit organization.

For more information

National Association of Realtors
430 North Michigan Avenue
Chicago, IL 60611

Urban Land Institute
1090 Vermont Avenue NW
Washington, DC 20005

Communications

DEAN MILLS

University of Missouri

The global village that Marshall McLuhan predicted in the 1960s has become a reality. Broadcast satellites, cable television transmitters, global computer networks, and other mass media technology have bound us together into a single communications community.

Broadly speaking, the field of communications includes all those people who in some way work to hold that symbolic village together by using their skills in communication: the anchor on the network news, the designer of a four-color ad layout for *Spin* magazine, the video editor who splices together the music and images of an MTV video, the vice president for public relations advising a corporate chief executive.

Would you be happy in a career in communications? Probably so, if you have an interest in the ways people communicate—or miscommunicate. The tools of communication vary. It may be the written or spoken word or the visual images of video, still photography, graphics. But whichever tools are preferred (and several are used in any communications job), you should have a deep interest in how human beings communicate, how to improve communication among them, and how communication affects them.

Should you pursue a career in communications? That, of course, only you can answer—perhaps after sampling some courses in the field during the first year or two in college. Usually, but not always, people who do well in the communications field show an early interest in such subjects as English, photography, speech, or social studies. Often they are attracted to extracurricular activities like the school newspaper or yearbook, debate, drama, or student government. Sometimes, though, people do not gravitate to the field until their college years. Two things about communications are certain:

1. The field includes so many different careers that students with widely different skills and interests can find successful careers in communications.
2. A rigorous college program in the communications area can help students prepare for careers in business, the professions, and government that have no direct relation to the mass media. Like other broadly based liberal arts disciplines, most programs in communications are preparation for several different careers in our constantly changing global village. The student will become a better writer and speaker; learn how to research a subject, analyze it, and present it in ways that others can understand; and, in most programs, acquire crucial knowledge for anyone living in the global village—the structure and effects of the modern mass media.

There are some misconceptions about what it takes to make it in communications. Journalists are not usually the pushy, insensitive, headline-chasing stereotypes seen in movies and on television. Most of them are thoughtful, sometimes even shy, people who care deeply about the information and open debate that are essential to free societies. A pretty face and voice are not needed in television news; for every anchor there are dozens of writers, producers, and others who work together to put a news show on the air. A creative genius isn't required in advertising; in addition to copywriters and art directors, the business relies on researchers, media planners, account managers, and others. Public relations executives do not get by on backslapping and three-martini lunches; they use detailed research and planning and excellent writing and speaking skills to accomplish their goals.

Let's shatter one other stereotype: Communications jobs are not all glamour. As in any highly competitive field, there are hundreds of hours of hard work to match every minute in the spotlight. Indeed, most jobs in communications do not get the airtime, the byline, or the other marks of fame that many associate with the field.

But two stereotypes about the communications field are justified. Careers in the field often are exciting—because, in one way or another, they usually involve the mass media. And the competition is tough to get into many communications jobs, precisely because they hold great interest for many people.

A communication(s) lexicon

A brief lesson in the terminology of the field may help you sort through college catalogs and brochures. In part because communications is such a broad field and in part because it is a relatively young academic discipline, terms can be confusing. The same, or nearly the same, field can have different labels. Worse, not even people in the field always agree on which labels to use. Here are some of the terms you'll run across:

Communication: Generally, the *process* of human interaction, whether verbal (speech, writing) or nonverbal (hand gestures, photographs, or the moving images of film or video).

Communications: The s makes a difference. Communications is usually used to refer to acts and methods of communicating through *institutions.* So we usually use communications, with the s, when we emphasize the media of communications or the people who work in those media. (Media is the Latin plural for medium. Radio is a medium. Television is a medium. Radio and television are two of the mass media.)

Mass communication(s): The means or institutions through which professional communicators prepare and distribute information and entertainment to tens of thousands of people. (A personal telephone call is an individual, not a mass, medium because even though it may travel around the globe, it involves only two, or at most a few, persons.)

Mass media: The means by which modern mass communication occurs: radio, television, newspapers, magazines, books, recording (sound and video), cable, film, direct broadcast satellite services. What about computer bulletin boards or 900 number services? Maybe, although they don't yet affect millions of people as the older media do.

Because communications is such a broad field, preparation in the field can lead to an almost infinite number of jobs. Conversely, a number of different educational routes can lead to careers in communications.

The journalism and mass communication approach

Since the founding of the world's first school of journalism at the University of Missouri in 1908, major universities throughout the country have developed curricula to prepare people specifically for work in mass communication.

Students who know that they want to pursue careers in the mass media can get solid preparation by majoring in journalism or mass communication at one of the roughly 90 programs accredited by the Accrediting Council on Education in Journalism and Mass Communication.

Accredited programs combine a broad liberal arts education with specific course work in such areas as advertising, broadcast, newspaper, or magazine journalism, or public relations. At least 75 percent of course work is in the liberal arts and sciences. That is to ensure that graduates study psychology, sociology, political science, literature, history, economics, and other subjects that will give them a broad understanding of modern society. The remainder of the course work is devoted to both conceptual and skills courses in a mass communication field. In these courses students learn to cover a news event, to plan an advertising campaign, public relations strategies, or to produce a television newscast.

The size and focus of accredited programs vary widely. Some offer specializations (often called sequences) in all areas of the mass media. Some specialize in only one or two. There is a wide range, too, in the amount of hands-on experience available to students. In some major programs, students can work on daily newspapers, at student advertising agencies, and at radio and television stations. In other programs, students pick up such experience in internships, usually during the summer, at professional media or advertising agencies.

The advantage of a journalism or mass communication major is that it assures both a solid college education and enough practical exposure to mass communication to help graduates get their first jobs. More than 80 percent of people taking their first newspaper jobs in the United States today, for example, have majored in journalism or mass communication.

The communication or speech communication approach

A major in communication can offer a general or specific preparation for careers in the field, depending on the university or college. Sometimes called communication arts, speech communication, or even communication science, historically these majors grew out of speech departments at major universities. Because of the importance of good speech in radio and television, many speech departments offered courses in the broadcast area.

Today, these departments vary widely in approach. Some emphasize conceptual courses such as rhetoric, the content and styles of written and spoken language, small-group communication, organizational communication, and the like. Proponents of this approach to communication education argue that it gives students an extensive theoretical understanding of the field that will prepare them for careers in the mass media, business, government, and other areas.

Some communication departments, on the other hand, offer extensive course work in all the elements of broadcast production, including the technological side of radio or television. Such programs produce graduates with more detailed knowledge of the technical aspects of broadcasting. Students in such programs have relatively less time to devote to the liberal arts and sciences.

The nonspecialized approach

Some students prepare for careers in the communications field by majoring in one of the liberal arts or sciences—history, political science, psychology, English, biology, chemistry. This route usually makes it more difficult to acquire the practical experience and the knowledge of mass media that are helpful in getting that first job in the field. But the handicap can be overcome if the student is resourceful enough to gain experience and contacts through work on student media and internships.

Some believe that the best possible preparation for a career in communications is an undergraduate degree in noncommunications fields followed by a professional master's degree emphasizing communications skills.

Communications in the twenty-first century

If you want a career in the communications field, you'd better get used to the idea of change. If there is one certainty about the field, it is that change will be a constant. New communications technologies, new combinations of media, and changing public tastes assure that almost any communications job you can think of will be a different job within a few years. Newspapers likely will be delivered electronically, through a combination computer-printer that will spew out as many pages as you want about any news event you want to know about. Giant interactive television media centers will provide virtually any movie, news clips, lecture, or concert from centralized entertainment/news banks. Or, both information and entertainment will be available from a portable device the size of a magazine that can be folded and carried. Movies, music, electronic newspapers, computer data, or any other form of text or image will be selected by punching a few buttons.

It is quite possible, therefore, that the job you will have doesn't even exist yet. But the necessary aptitudes and skills are known. You will need to be curious, to be flexible and ready to adapt to changing circumstances. You will need to be comfortable in dealing with people from other cultures, whether from your own country or across the globe. You will need to be able to think, speak, and write well. In other words, you will need to be ready for the global village.

Advertising

Advertising majors learn how advertising campaigns are produced, how advertising is coordinated with marketing, and how advertising strategies develop from research. They learn to write advertising copy for broadcasting and print and to select media for advertising campaigns.

Interests, skills, and qualities associated with success in the major

Interests. Writing, art and design, analysis, knowing something about lots of things.

Skills and qualities. Analytic reasoning, quantitative reasoning, writing clearly and concisely, public speaking, art and design, leadership.

Recommended high school preparation

English 4, precollege mathematics 3, biology 1, chemistry 1, physics 1, social studies 1, history 1, and foreign language 2.

Typical courses in the major

Principles of Advertising	Copywriting
Media Planning	Campaigns
Management	Research
Media Sales	Advertising and Society
Marketing	Mass Media Law

What the major is like

Advertising programs are usually given in schools of journalism and mass communication and are therefore influenced by the strong emphasis on the liberal arts found at such institutions. Advertising is a liberal arts major.

At accredited schools of journalism and mass communication, advertising students must do 75 percent of their course work outside the major. Thus, a typical advertising major consists of four or five advertising courses; a few courses in news writing, mass media law, and ethics; and many courses in such liberal arts as foreign language, history, physical and natural sciences, literature, and philosophy. Since advertising and marketing are so closely related, advertising students are strongly advised or required to take at least one course in marketing, usually taught in a school of business.

The first course in the advertising major, usually called principles of advertising, is a survey that exposes students to the history and regulation of advertising as well as its social and economic effects. Also covered are such topics as copy writing, media planning, and research.

Courses in writing copy introduce students to the analysis and strategic thinking that precede the creation of advertisements for radio, television, newspapers, magazines, direct mail, and billboards. Students have to write the copy and explain and defend their advertisements.

Media-planning courses explain the process of selecting appropriate advertising media and using those media in the most effective way. Media courses involve quantitative analysis, much of which is done using computer programs.

Research courses introduce students to the methods of advertising research, including surveys, focus groups, and experiments. Good analytic reasoning and statistical skills are important here.

Campaign and management courses integrate copy writing, media planning, research, and marketing. Students typically work in groups, preparing and presenting complete advertising campaigns for actual or hypothetical clients.

Advertising sales courses introduce students to the process and techniques used by advertising media to sell advertising to clients (broadcasting stations and newspapers, for example). Excellent interpersonal skills are essential to be successful in sales.

Advertising art and design do not get much attention in most college mass-communication programs. Students with artistic talent who seriously intend to pursue a career in advertising art should consider schools that specialize in commercial art.

Advertising courses are a mix of the theoretical and the practical. Students are introduced to concepts and principles, which must then apply to actual or hypothetical advertising situations. Many advertising courses include group projects because much advertising work is a group effort. Most courses also require students to make oral presentations because that too is an essential part of advertising work. All advertising courses stress good, clear, concise writing.

Practical experience is not part of formal advertising programs, but it is essential for students aspiring to careers in advertising. Students will find it difficult to get full-time jobs after graduation if they have not had some experience. An excellent way to get that experience is an internship—a summer job with an advertising agency, newspaper, or broadcasting station. Part-time jobs with campus publications might also be helpful.

Specializations

None.

Other majors to consider

Business administration
Commercial art
Communications
English
Graphic design
Journalism
Marketing

Careers related to the major

The advertising major may lead to jobs as an advertising copywriter, advertising media planner and/or buyer, advertising agency account executive, media sales representative, or advertising manager (for a company or brand). After graduate study, one may work as an advertising research specialist. Advertising has become an extremely popular college major. The number of graduates far exceeds the number of job openings in advertising, so competition for jobs is very keen.

For more information

American Association of Advertising Agencies
666 Third Avenue
New York, NY 10017
(212)682-2500

Where Shall I Go to Study Advertising?. Billy I. Ross, editor. Annual publication of Advertising Education Publications, 3429 55th Street, Lubbock, TX 79413.

The American Association of Advertising Agencies publishes the brochure "Go For It: A Guide to Careers in Advertising."

Communications

Communications majors study the history of political and religious oratory; write critiques of speeches, television programs, and films; explore the sociology of interpersonal relations, group dynamics, and messages; study the impact of organizations and the media on individuals and society; examine ways of thinking about human symbol systems (semiotics); and inquire into the ethics of communication.

Interests, skills, and qualities associated with success in the major

Interests. Politics, presentations, advertising, television, film, analyzing oral and electronic messages.

Skills and qualities. Oral and written communication, critical listening, logical analysis, leadership.

Recommended high school preparation

English 4, laboratory science 2, social studies 2, history 1, foreign language 4, visual arts 1–2, speech 1, and computer science 1.

Typical courses in the major

Interpersonal Communication
Organizational Communication
Advertising
Media Criticism
Interviewing
Radio/TV/Film Production
Public Relations

Public Speaking
Argumentation
Mass Media in Society
Group Communication
Persuasion
Broadcast Journalism

What the major is like

The study of communications is as old as the writings of Plato and Aristotle on rhetoric and politics. Today, social and electronic communications are explored historically, critically, theoretically, ethically, and sociologically by student investigators of interpersonal, group, organizational, public, and mass communication.

The major blends practical training and liberal arts education. To fulfill liberal arts recommendations, majors in communication commonly select history courses (Great Speeches in the Western World); broad theory courses on interpersonal, group, and public communication; media criticism courses (analyses of speeches, television programs, films); social science courses that review discoveries about how personal relations begin, grow, and decline, how political campaigns operate, the logical and psychological aspects of arguing, and the impact of television on society; and public policy courses, which examine the ethics of persuasion and First

Amendment guarantees of free speech. Some programs stress only inter-personal, group, organizational, and public communication; others also offer courses in radio, television, film, and journalism.

Three kinds of classes are common in the communication major. Performance and production courses are usually small; 12 to 15 students present oral or media work for evaluation. Large introductory lecture courses are supplemented by small weekly discussion sections; students attending the lectures may be assessed by objective tests. Junior and senior courses are typically in the form of lecture/discussion. Students may read and discuss communication theories, television programs, videotapes of presidential speeches, or First Amendment court cases. In these classes they are graded on their mastery of the readings, their contributions to class discussions, and their ability to analyze what they read and see.

Performance and production classes offer practical training. Specific communications skills—preparing and delivering messages, critically listening to messages of others—are taught in courses in public speaking, interpersonal communication, interviewing, group communication, persuasion, and argumentation. Production programs teach students to run a radio console, studio television and portable video equipment, and, perhaps, 16MM film cameras. Media production programs train students in the skills of preproducton (planning and writing), production (shooting), and postproduction (editing). Some institutions have modern studios and others send students to work in the field for their media projects. Sometimes journalism courses are included in departments of communication.

Internships are a popular feature of many communication programs: students spend a few hours per week or an entire term getting on-the-job training in a radio station, an advertising firm, an insurance agency, a cable TV company, a county or regional public service unit, or a customer relations department. Students who know a foreign language may spend a term abroad studying the politics, theater, mass media, or cinema of another culture.

Specializations

Advertising, radio, television, film, journalism, public relations, station management, interpersonal communication, corporate communication.

Other majors to consider

Advertising
Arts management
Creative writing
Educational media technology
English
Film arts
Journalism
Radio/television broadcasting
Sociology
Telecommunications

Careers related to the major

The communications major can lead to careers as a television producer or director, political staff member, on-air or on-camera talent, press secretary, traffic manager or continuity writer in radio, speech writer, reporter, communication researcher. The major is excellent preparation for jobs in other fields. Many graduates become advertising account executives, public relations specialists, publishers, office managers, teachers, government officials, lawyers, insurance representatives, clergymen, politicians, personnel trainers.

For more information

Speech Communication Association
5105 Blacklick Road, Suite #F
Annandale, VA 22003
(703)750-0533

Journalism

Journalism majors study the liberal arts and sciences to acquire the depth and breadth of knowledge they need in order to understand the world better and communicate information about it to others. They also learn the special skills needed by reporters, editors, broadcasters, and photojournalists.

Interests, skills, and qualities associated with success in the major

Interests. Human psychology and behavior, reading widely, photography, world events.

Skills and qualities. Writing, learning quickly about a wide range of topics.

Recommended high school preparation

English 4, precollege mathematics 3, biology 1, chemistry 1, social studies 2, history 2, foreign language 4, visual arts 1, journalism 1, and computer science 1.

Typical courses in the major

Newswriting and Reporting
Copy Editing
Magazine Writing
Feature Writing
Journalism Ethics
Law of the Mass Media
Minorities and the Media

Public Affairs Reporting
Photojournalism
Broadcast News
Newspaper Management
History of U.S. Mass Media
Women and the Media
International Communication

What the major is like

Journalism students learn how to communicate using the written or spoken word and using visual communication skills such as graphic design, video, and still photography. They learn how to find information, usually by interviewing news sources. They learn the different writing styles used to convey news through different media—newspapers, radio, and television. (With their insistence on professional standards, journalism programs often offer the most rigorous training in writing of any major.) At most institutions students can specialize in various forms of journalism; newspaper, magazine, broadcast, and photojournalism are four popular choices.

Journalism majors typically take 75 percent of their college course work in the liberal arts and sciences in order to have a broad understanding of history, geography, political science, economics, literature, and the natural sciences. In courses in the major, they will learn about both the theory and practice of journalism. Courses may cover the history and law of journalism in foreign countries, and the special contributions of women and minorities to the field.

Students also develop specialized skills. Those interested in newspaper journalism take courses in reporting, writing, and editing. Students interested in photojournalism take courses in reporting and photography. A broadcast news major learns how to report on and produce news for radio or television broadcasts. In advanced courses, students may learn the particular skills of the investigative reporter or the science writer. They may learn how to design newspaper or magazine pages with computers.

Hands-on experience is acquired in reporting for a student newspaper, magazine, or radio station. Some institutions also offer experience in cable or broadcast television, and most journalism programs arrange for internships in the professional media.

Journalism majors may be offered in departments, schools, or colleges of journalism, communications, communication arts, or communication studies. Although there are hundreds of journalism programs in the United States, fewer than 100 are accredited by the Accrediting Council on Education in Journalism and Mass Communication.

Specializations

Newspaper journalism, magazine journalism, broadcast journalism, photojournalism.

Other majors to consider

Advertising
Communications
Public relations
Radio/television broadcasting

Careers related to the major

The journalism major prepares students for careers as a newspaper reporter or editor, magazine writer or editor, radio or television reporter, television or radio station manager, public relations representative, public information analyst, or photojournalist. Although many employers do not require a journalism degree of applicants for journalism jobs, about 80 percent of those entering the field major in journalism.

For more information

Accrediting Council on Education in Journalism and
Mass Communication
University of Kansas, School of Journalism
Stauffer-Flint Hall
Lawrence, KS 66045
(913)864-3973

Public relations

The public relations major examines how to manage an organization's or an individual's communication and relationship with others. Students learn not only what to communicate but also why and how to communicate it. They also master technical and managerial skills, such as writing and producing printed and visual materials, and study strategic planning and problem solving.

Interests, skills, and qualities associated with success in the major

Interests. Solving problems, mediating between opposing groups, writing, public speaking, giving advice.

Skills and qualities. Communicating clearly, planning events, organizing people, thinking creatively and critically.

Recommended high school preparation

English 4, precollege mathematics 2–3, biology 1, chemistry 1, physics 1, social studies 2, history 2, foreign language 3–4, music 1, visual arts 1, and journalism 3–4. One half-year of computer science is also recommended.

Typical courses in the major

Mass Media Writing
Public Relations Research
Public Relations Writing
Principles of Public Relations
Public Relations Campaigns

Graphic Design
Public Relations Internship
Video Production
Public Relations Law and Ethics

What the major is like

As individuals, businesses, and institutions increasingly rely on effective communication to build good relationships with others on whom their success depends, there is a growing need for professionally trained public relations practitioners.

Public relations courses address three aspects of professional work. One group of courses—writing, graphic design, and video production—focuses on skills required to effectively communicate a client's message: the how of communication.

The second group of courses—social sciences, humanities, natural sciences, mathematics, foreign language, business, and fine arts—provides understanding of the social and cultural environment, the "what" that public relations practitioners communicate.

The third group of courses, designed to provide knowledge of why organizations and other clients communicate with their various publics, includes such subjects as public opinion, research methods, strategic planning, problem solving, and ethics.

Most public relations programs are offered by schools or departments of journalism or mass communication. Sometimes the major is in a department of speech or communication, where it may be called organizational communication. Wherever the major is housed, students take about 25 percent of their courses (usually 10 or 11 semester courses) in public relations, primarily in writing and other communication skills and in methods to plan, develop, and implement public relations campaigns. The rest of the courses are usually in the liberal arts and sciences.

Students majoring in public relations are encouraged to complete a minor, or to concentrate much of their elective course work in business, especially if they are interested in public relations work for a corporation or a public relations firm that represents corporate clients. Business courses may include accounting, finance, and marketing.

A highlight of the major is an internship, which may be required, during the regular academic year or in the summer. On-the-job experience gives students the opportunity to apply in the real world the principles and techniques learned in the classroom.

Many public relations courses are taught in a laboratory format; students complete in-class writing, editing, or production assignments. Others use the case study approach, in which students critique an organization's real or hypothetical public relations performance to develop skills in problem-solving and critical analysis. In-class discussion and debate give students the opportunity to express and defend their viewpoints about what was done and why. Most public relations students plan, develop, implement, and evaluate a public relations campaign for an organization, working individually or in the groups they're likely to encounter in real-life public relations.

Specializations

Corporate public relations, consumer relations, employee relations, public affairs, nonprofit public relations, financial or investor relations, publicity and media relations, international public relations.

Other majors to consider

Advertising
Business administration
Communications
English
Health services management
Journalism
Marketing
Political science and government
Psychology
Public administration

Careers related to the major

Public relations graduates are prepared for professional careers as staff writers and editors, corporate video producers, media relations specialists, special events planners, investor or financial relations specialists, speechwriters, strategic planners, consumer relations specialists, public relations agency account executives, employee relations or publications specialists, management counselors, public opinion researchers, fund-raising or development specialists, marketing promotion managers.

For more information

Public Relations Society of America
33 Irving Place
New York, NY 10003
(212)995-2230

Radio/television broadcasting

Majors in radio and television broadcasting study the relationship between the mass media and society and develop skills in such specialties as reporting, performance, production, sales, and management.

Interests, skills, and qualities associated with success in the major

Interests. Writing; speaking; editing words, pictures, or sound; operating a camera; sound recording.

Skills and qualities. Interviewing people, working under tight deadlines, writing and speaking clearly, operating technical equipment, persuasion, working with others.

Recommended high school preparation

English 2, precollege mathematics 2, laboratory science 2, social studies 2, history 1, foreign language 2, and computer science 1.

Typical courses in the major	Introduction to Mass Media	Writing for Mass Media
	History of the Mass Media	Broadcast Law and Regulation
	Broadcast Production	Broadcast Program Building
	Broadcast Performance	Broadcast Operation
	Broadcast Sales	Broadcast Newswriting
	News Editing	New Communication Technology
	Broadcast Management	

What the major is like

Broadcasting courses are generally taught in departments or schools of communication, journalism, telecommunication, and radio/television/film. Wherever its official home, the major in broadcasting provides students with both an understanding of how the electronic media function in society and the skills needed to work in the broadcast media. This knowledge and training is the foundation for careers in news, promotion, program production, writing, audience research, management, and sales.

Students normally take 50 percent of their course work in the liberal arts. These courses in history, literature, computer science, social sciences, and natural sciences are usually taken in the first two years. Students begin their specific broadcast curriculum with an introductory examination of the mass media, a course that provides an overview of the social, political, economic, and historical factors that affect all media in our society. A course in media ethics concentrates on fairness and accuracy in reporting. Other courses deal with such subfields as broadcast news, program production, and sales.

In addition to lecture classes, students take laboratory courses in which they can apply what they are learning. The labs include creative work in a production studio, interviews with people outside class, and preparation of information for a production. Students also receive training in specialized communication equipment used in production studios, such as audio and video recorders, editing equipment, and word-processing computers.

Most programs allow students to take at least one internship for which they earn academic credit while working in the broadcast industry. In addition, many colleges and universities that have campus radio, television, or cable television facilities invite students to join their staffs.

Specializations

Broadcast news, broadcast program production, broadcast sales/management, communication technology.

Other majors to consider

Advertising
Communications
Film arts
Journalism
Marketing

Careers related to the major

The broadcasting major prepares one for jobs as a radio or television writer or reporter, station manager, announcer, or producer. The broadcast industry is in a rapid state of change. New technologies such as cable television, satellite delivery systems, fiber optics, and others are revolutionizing how audiences receive messages. These new systems will require staffs with training in the shaping of messages meaningful to their listeners and viewers. The well-trained graduate who can communicate effectively will be in demand by a wide range of employers.

For more information

Broadcast Education Association
1771 N Street NW
Washington, DC 20036
(202)429-5355

Association for Education in Journalism and
Mass Communication
1621 College Street
University of South Carolina
Columbia, SC 29208-0251
(803)777-2005

Radio-Television News Directors Association
1000 Connecticut Avenue
Suite 615
Washington, DC 20036
(202)659-6510

Speech

Majors in speech learn to produce and receive a variety of oral communications, from formal presidential speeches to informal small-group conversations. Through courses in speech making and rhetorical criticism, students learn the skills needed for competence in a variety of professions.

Interests, skills, and qualities associated with success in the major

Interests. Public speaking, human behavior.

Skills and qualities. Working with people.

Recommended high school preparation

English 4, precollege mathematics 2, laboratory science 2, social studies 2–3, history 2–3, and visual arts 1–2.

Typical courses in the major

Public Speaking	Speech Composition
Listening	Group Communication
Ancient Rhetoric	Rhetorical Criticism
Rhetorical Theory	Nonverbal Communication
Political Communication	Persuasive Speaking
Audience Analysis	Interpersonal Communication
Contemporary Rhetoric	Role of Rhetoric in Society
Media Analysis and Criticism	Cross-cultural Communication
Organizational Communication	

What the major is like

The major in speech, whether offered through a department of speech or under another title, such as communication arts, rhetoric, or speech communication, focuses on the responsible and effective uses of public and private speech.

In speech production courses, students analyze audiences, prepare and present speeches of various kinds (informative, interpretive, persuasive), and study other forms of oral presentation, such as interpreting literature, newscasting, and, in some programs, acting. In speech consumption, the other half of the major, they judge public speech performances—from speeches by their fellow students to televised presentations by newscasters and politicians.

Nearly every speech department offers courses in private communicative behavior, such as interpersonal and marital communication. These various approaches to public and private speech are unified in advanced theoretical courses like communication theory, nonverbal behavior, and international communication.

A sideline of many departments of speech, as a part of the academic program or simply as an extracurricular activity, is intercollegiate competition in forensics (debate, speeches, and oral interpretation of literature). This activity is especially treasured by students who plan to go into law, politics, or teaching, realms in which the oral clash of ideas is particularly important.

Many students take the speech major in tandem with some other field. For instance, students who plan to become psychological counselors major in both psychology and speech, and future lawyers combine speech with political science or business.

Specializations

Organizational communication, health communication, broadcasting, journalism, political communication, business communication.

Other majors to consider

Communications
Graphic design
Journalism

Careers related to the major

Graduates with a speech major will find job opportunities in advertising, public relations, speech writing, public information, corporate communications, and journalism.

For more information

Speech Communication Association
5105 Backlick Road, #F
Annandale, VA 22003
(703)750-0533

Computer and Information Sciences

STUART H. ZWEBEN
Ohio State University

It has been said that never in the history of the world has a technology had the rapid and pervasive impact on our lives that computer technology has had in the past few decades. Computer and information sciences is a young discipline, which began in the 1940s. Computers are now an integral part of most fields, and their capabilities continue to increase at an amazing rate. A major in computer and information sciences prepares the graduate to contribute to the future development of this exciting and dynamic field. The demand for persons who are skilled in the computing field is strong and is expected to continue to exceed the supply of qualified persons.

People often think of the computing field in terms of its division into hardware and software. Hardware refers to the physical components of a computer system, such as processing units and storage devices. Software refers to the nonphysical components, such as algorithms (procedures) and data elements (characteristics of the information being processed—for example, its internal structure). The study of computer and information sciences includes the design, development, and analysis of hardware devices as well as the organization and processing of instructions and data (information) to perform computations by the use of these devices. More generally, the discipline of computing has been described as "the systematic study of algorithmic processes that describe and transform information: their theory, analysis, design, efficiency, implementation, and application" (P. J. Denning, "Computing as a discipline" in *Communications of the ACM*, January 1989). Theoretical studies, experimental methods, and engineering design are all important to the discipline.

Historically, the computing programs at most colleges and universities evolved from mathematics, electrical engineering, or a combination of the two. The location of the program therefore varies. Most often, the program is in either engineering or arts and sciences, and at some institutions it is within the business school. There may be more than one computing program at a given institution. Sometimes the programs are taught by the same faculty and share many of the same courses, while at other institutions different faculty and separate courses are involved in the various programs. Occasionally, there is within the institution a separate school or division for the computing programs.

The titles of computing programs also vary considerably from institution to institution. Generally the program is called computer science, although many other titles are used such as computer and information sci-

149

ence and computer science and engineering (the latter term is actually a combination of computer science and computer engineering). Most of the programs with these titles prepare their graduates both for entry into the computing profession and for graduate study in the field. Computing programs that are in business schools generally have titles like information systems. They place more emphasis on management and business and less emphasis on the technical aspect than do computer science programs.

Often, people associate a computing program with computer programming, but there is much more to the discipline than programming. Likewise, there is much more to a computing program than knowledge of elementary computer terminology, characteristics, and components and exposure to general-purpose applications such as word processing and spreadsheets. A computing professional must be able to properly describe and analyze the specifications of a problem and must also be able to design, implement, and evaluate solutions to the problem in order to meet functional, performance, and cost objectives. The core of a typical computing program should therefore include the theoretical foundations of computing, the design and analysis of algorithms, the concepts of programming languages, the design and implementation of data structures, the elements and architecture of computer systems, and the design and development of software. Depth of coverage in some of these areas should be required. A good grounding in mathematics, including calculus, discrete mathematics, and probability and statistics, is also important.

The computing professional usually works as part of a team, and must therefore interact with other members of the team and sometimes with the people who will ultimately use the product or system. Good oral and written communication skills are essential, and a computing program should help students develop and apply these skills. It should also develop students' appreciation for the social implications of computing.

The computing field is broad, and other topics often found in a computing curriculum include artificial intelligence, computer networking and communication, data base systems, parallel computation, distributed computation, computer-human interaction, computer graphics, operating systems, and numerical and symbolic computation. Artificial intelligence involves understanding and modeling human intelligence in computational terms and incorporating principles of intelligence into computing systems. Computer networking deals with the principles of intercomputer communication. Data base systems study the organization and retrieval of large bodies of information. Parallel computation is concerned with methods of dividing complex computation so that different parts of it can be performed simultaneously. Distributed computation deals with problems associated with computations whose elements reside on different devices. Human-computer interaction makes it easier for computer system users to work with the system. Computer graphics studies computational techniques for facilitating graphic display of information, including animation. Operating systems are the central, internal software systems that control the function of the overall computer system. Numerical and symbolic computation deal with problems that involve the finite representation of numerical data and the processing of symbolic data.

Several of the topics mentioned above have strong ties to other disciplines. For example, close relationships exist between the areas of artificial intelligence and computer-human interaction and the area of cognitive psychology. Computer graphics has close ties to fine arts and industrial

design, and numerical and symbolic computation has a strong relationship with mathematics.

If a student's goal is simply to use the computer as a tool in some other discipline, it is frequently better to major in that discipline and to supplement the major with appropriate computing courses. In fact, since computers are used in most fields, a concentration or a minor in computing is often useful. The minor should provide a level of expertise that allows the student to use computers effectively and to design rudimentary applications software for use in the major discipline.

Since 1985 undergraduate programs in computer science whose objective is to prepare their graduates for entry into the computing profession have been able to apply for accreditation by the Computer Science Accreditation Commission of the Computing Sciences Accreditation Board (CSAC/CSAB). Because computer science accreditation is still fairly new, there may be several good programs that are not yet accredited. An increasing number of computer science programs are expected to apply for and achieve accreditation during the 1990s. Programs accredited by CSAC/CSAB have satisfied criteria that assess the program's faculty, curriculum, laboratory and computing resources, students, and institutional support. As of 1992, there is no accreditation of programs in information systems.

Computer science

Computer science majors learn how computers work and how to program computers to perform tasks and provide services. They study both hardware (the physical components of computer systems) and software (procedures for making computers work).

Interests, skills, and qualities associated with success in the major

Interests. Human thinking patterns, electronics, robotics, math, music.

Skills and qualities. Problem solving, logic, abstract reasoning, oral and written communication, working in groups.

Recommended high school preparation

English 4, algebra 1, geometry 1, trigonometry .5, biology 1, chemistry 1, physics 1, social studies 1, history 2, foreign language 1, music 1, visual arts 1, and computer science 1.

Typical courses in the major

Mathematical Foundations
Operational Systems
Programming
Algorithms
Software Engineering
Operating Systems
Artificial Intelligence
Compilers
Computer Architecture
Computability

What the major is like

The major in computer science begins with a liberal education and study of the necessary mathematical tools, which include calculus, discrete math, and modern algebra. Students will learn about the design, development, and analysis of hardware; they will study the organization and processing of instructions and data to perform computations by hardware devices.

Because virtually all computer scientists program computers, programming is also an early topic of study. Students learn techniques for writing correct, understandable, and maintainable programs. Students first learn a high-level programming language such as Pascal, C, or Scheme. FORTRAN, BASIC, and COBOL, once very important in the study of computer programming, are used less today. These languages are tools used to instruct the computer to accomplish various tasks.

In computer architecture the student learns how computers work. Although detailed study of logic circuitry, processors, memory, and peripheral devices is the domain of electrical engineering, every computer science major is schooled in the basics of hardware.

In operating system courses, students learn how the resources of a computer are automatically managed to provide services to the user. A course in compilers teaches how to program and implement languages. Software engineering focuses on the techniques and problems of large software systems—systems that are measured in millions of lines of source code and years of programmer time.

Students will study artifical intelligence in software that exhibits intelligent behavior. These programs play games, solve puzzles, recognize speech, and recognize and act on visual images. Artificial intelligence is closely connected to robotics and cognitive psychology.

Students will learn that there are many problems for which there is no solution, and that there are problems for which the solutions take so long to compute that you are better off not bothering. Courses in algorithms and computability give computer scientists tools for analyzing problems and designing good programs.

The computer science major will use personal workstations that are a hundred times more powerful than the mainframes of just a generation ago. Massively parallel computers, networks, supercomputers, graphics, and animation tools are objects of study. Artificial life, interactive fiction, and synthesized reality are on the horizon.

Specializations

Hardware (computing systems), programming systems, robotics, computer graphics, computer theory, artificial intelligence, software engineering, graphics, theory.

Other majors to consider

Computer engineering
Electrical engineering
Information sciences and systems
Mathematics
Philosophy
Psychology

Careers related to the major

A degree in computer science leads to many positions in industry, government, and small companies. Computer scientists are much needed in organizations devoted to education, business, science, or technology. Graduates can find jobs as programmers, computer designers, computer scientists, software and hardware developers, sales representatives, technical specialists.

For more information

Association for Computing Machinery
1515 Broadway
New York, NY 10036
(212)869-7440

Information sciences and systems

Students majoring in information sciences and systems receive broad exposure to computer and programming concepts. The major prepares students to bring people and computers together to solve problems in businesses and other organizations.

Interests, skills, and qualities associated with success in the major

Interests. Solving problems, working with details, taking initiative, games, puzzles, working with numbers, organizing information, music, working with people.

Skills and qualities. Oral and written communication, working in groups, understanding and analyzing numerical data, creative and critical thinking, logical thinking, working with changing technology.

Recommended high school preparation

English 4, precollege mathematics 4, laboratory science 2–4, social studies 2, and foreign language 2.

Typical courses in the major

Computer Concepts
Data File Structures
Data Communications
Decisions Support Systems
Artificial Intelligence

Programming Languages
Systems Design
Data Base Management Systems
Systems Analysis

What the major is like

Majors in information sciences and systems learn to analyze, conceptualize, design, and implement computer solutions to organizational problems in business, government, and nonprofit organizations. The programs prepare students to bring people and computers together to solve problems.

Although the major is found in different departments or schools, its most common home is a college of business. Departments offering the programs may be called computer information systems, computer technology, accounting and information systems, quantitative analysis, or information management. At many institutions the program is offered in liberal arts and sciences, within departments of computer science or mathematics, or in a separate school of computer and information systems.

Depending on its location, the major may lead to a bachelor's degree in computer information systems or a Bachelor of Business Administration, B.B.A., with a major in computer information systems.

Students majoring in information sciences and systems devote approximately half their course work to general education—mathematics, science, oral and written communication, social sciences, humanities, and electives—most of it during the first two years. Beginning in the sophomore year, students learn the basic functions and tools of business; 20 to 25 percent of this course work is in accounting, economics, finance, management, marketing, and business law.

Although computer studies begin in the freshman year, most computer courses are taken in the junior and senior years; 25 to 30 percent of the total undergraduate program is in information sciences and systems. Core requirements are spread evenly over the following areas.

Computer and programming concepts: Fundamental concepts and terminology of computer hardware, computer operating systems, and computer programming.

Data and file structures: Fundamental concepts and techniques of the logical and physical structures of both data and files.

Data base management: The logical design of data base systems and the physical implementation of them.

Data communications: Basic concepts, terminology, design, and applications of data communications and networks.

Systems analysis and design: Tools and techniques of analyzing and developing computer-based systems.

In computer laboratories students learn a variety of computer languages and computer systems and are usually required to gain programming proficiency in at least one high-level computer language. Electives and advanced courses in the field may be offered in data communications, data base management systems, expert systems, systems analysis and design, and computer-aided systems engineering.

Specializations

Applications programming, systems analysis and design, data communication, data base management systems, expert systems.

Other majors to consider

Accounting
Business administration
Computer science
Management information systems
Management science
Operations research (quantitative methods)
Systems analysis

Careers related to the major

The information sciences and systems major can lead to careers as an applications programmer, programmer/analyst, systems analyst, data base administrator, data communication/telecommunication analyst, information systems designer, or information systems manager.

For more information

Association for Computing Machinery
1515 Broadway
New York, NY 10036
(212)869-7440
(212)944-1318 (fax)

Association for Systems Management
1433 West Bagley Road
Berea, OH 44017
(216)243-6900

Data Processing Management Association
505 Busses Highway
Park Ridge, IL 60068-3191
(708)825-8124

Society for Information Management
401 North Michigan Avenue
Chicago, IL 60611-4267
(312)644-6610

Education

W. ROBERT HOUSTON

University of Houston

When teachers were asked why they were teaching, the reason most often given was the opportunity to make a difference, not only in the lives of individual students but also in the future of the nation. If you enjoy working with people, particularly young people, and feel rewarded when they succeed, then you are likely to enjoy teaching. Some people teach because of the flexibility the profession provides—summers free, with hours and holidays the same as those for school-age children. Others choose to teach because of the availability of jobs in various parts of the world. Most enjoy the subject they teach and are dedicated to student learning.

Although you have attended school most of your life, you may know very little about what teachers actually do, how they are educated, and how to learn about the benefits and realities of teaching. It is somewhat like viewing an iceberg from the deck of a ship; only 10 percent of the iceberg is above water and visible. Education majors explore issues about teaching and learning that are important to them and to the nation but may not be recognized by the average person outside the field.

More than 1,200 colleges and universities in the United States offer programs that prepare teachers, and they vary widely in scope and quality. Although one may be geographically more convenient than others, it would be wise to explore those known for their high quality or specific areas of interest to you.

Some colleges of education are very large, with more than 100 faculty members; others have only one or two faculty members, often part time. Not all colleges prepare teachers in all fields. All institutions that prepare teachers are accredited by the state in which they are located, and in addition, over 500 are nationally accredited by the National Council for the Accreditation of Teacher Education.

Some universities have specific colleges or schools of education, others have departments of education within another college such as the college of arts, literature, and sciences. Schools, departments, and colleges of education are responsible for the professional educational course work, and colleges of arts and sciences teach the academic content.

Preparation program

Prospective teachers complete programs based on two sets of requirements—their institution's bachelor's degree requirements and state certification requirements. Your adviser helps you prepare a degree and certification plan to meet those twin demands.

Teacher preparation programs typically include three phases. First, general or liberal education courses make up about half the requirements

157

(the equivalent of nearly two years in a four-year program, or 48 to 60 semester hours) and are usually completed in the freshman and sophomore years. They include English and the humanities, social sciences, mathematics, and the natural sciences.

In the second phase, prospective teachers major in a teaching specialization (48 to 60 semester hours). If you plan to teach in elementary schools, your major includes a wide range of courses related to the content taught in elementary schools (reading, mathematics, art, and social studies). Elementary teachers are usually majors in the education department, school, or college.

If you plan to teach in secondary schools, you concentrate on one or two subjects. In most institutions you major in the subject you plan to teach and complete a minimum of 24 semester hours in another. (School personnel directors prefer secondary school teachers who are certified to teach more than one subject.) At some colleges, prospective mathematics teachers, for example, major in mathematics, and their adviser is in the mathematics department. In other institutions a secondary education student is in the department of education. In this case, prospective mathematics teachers major in secondary education, and their adviser is in the education department. They take mathematics courses, however, in the mathematics department.

The third phase of your program includes professional education courses, completed in a department, school, or college of education. These are usually begun in the junior year. In most states prospective teachers are required to pass a basic skills test before admission to teacher education courses. Professional course work—an average of 24 semester hours in secondary education to 36 hours in elementary education—includes educational psychology, cultural foundations of education, and teaching methods. From 45 to 200 clock hours observing and working in schools are also required. During the last semester, students intern full time, student teaching under the direction of a classroom teacher in the school and a university supervisor. This experience provides ample opportunity to practice teaching and to hone skills. Before certification most states require candidates to pass an achievement test in the field they are preparing to teach. At the end of your program, you receive a bachelor's degree and state teacher certification.

Each state sets its own certification standards. Although there are more similarities than differences, state requirements vary. When teachers move to another state, they apply to the state education department for evaluation of their credentials. Certificates are generally of three kinds: Elementary school certificates qualify teachers to teach from kindergarten or grade 1 through grade 8. Secondary school certificates are granted for specific subject areas, such as mathematics or industrial arts, and are usually valid for grades 6 through 12. Four fields typically have all-level certification (valid for kindergarten through grade 12): music, art, physical education, and speech therapy and audiology. Some states permit specialization in areas such as special education, nursery schools, bilingual classes, and gifted and talented classes.

Postgraduate certification
Prospective teachers may also separate degree requirements from certification. After completing a bachelor's degree, they enroll in education

courses as part of a postgraduate program. Although it takes longer, this route to teaching is particularly useful for persons who decide to obtain teaching certification after graduating from college or who attend one of the few colleges that do not offer education programs.

This alternative is often attractive to adults who have worked in business and industry and decide to teach as a second career. More and more adults in their late twenties or even their late fifties are entering teacher education programs.

Opportunities in teaching

One of the questions students ask as they explore teaching as a career is, "will I get a job when I finish?" The availability of teaching positions depends on a number of factors. State requirements can result in teacher shortages; for example, when a state decides to limit the number of pupils enrolled in primary grade classrooms, to require three rather than two years of mathematics for high school graduation, or to permit schools to have prekindergartens, the number of new teachers employed increases. Shifts in the demographic characteristics of a school district or the nation as a whole can result in shortages; for example, the growing number of non-English-speaking immigrants increases the need for bilingual and English as a Second Language teachers. Federal laws such as Pub. L. No. 94-142 for exceptional children and the Civil Rights Act of 1964 for racial integration affected not only the number but the assignments of teachers.

Because of their liberal arts preparation, teachers can also find numerous nonteaching jobs. The availability and attractiveness of such jobs affect the number of teachers available for the classroom. A great number of teachers are needed in states and areas where population is increasing. In 1990 these areas included the Sunbelt states, western United States, and Alaska. Conversely, the lowest demand for teachers was in the Great Lakes region, the Northeast, and the Middle Atlantic states.

The greatest teacher shortages in 1990 were in special education, bilingual education, and speech pathology and audiology, followed by mathematics, physical sciences, and computer sciences. The least demand was for teachers of physical education, art, social science, and health. Even in these fields however, there were job openings, particularly in rural areas and in center-city schools.

Teachers often teach in the school district in which they completed student teaching; school officials have had an opportunity to see them teach and to know them as individuals. For this reason most teachers teach within 25 miles of where they attended college. Those willing to relocate, particularly to regions of the country with teacher shortages, may be in high demand.

The opportunities for teachers are almost limitless. Education is big business. In the United States over 40 million students attend 83,000 public schools and another 5 million attend 25,000 private schools, and they are taught by nearly 2.5 million teachers. Most cities throughout the world have private American schools that employ experienced American teachers. The United States Department of Defense has an overseas school system for children of its service personnel that employs thousands of teachers. Many trained teachers are employed outside schools. Thousands provide training in basic skills for adults in the armed forces or to immigrants through local social agencies. Corporations employ

more than a quarter million teachers as instructors of job-related skills for their employees.

Exploring teaching

High school students have several options to learn about teaching. Many high schools have clubs for future teachers in which members have chances to tutor younger children, visit nearby colleges, and meet prospective teachers. Teachers belong to professional associations that have useful information about teaching. Local and state professional associations are often affiliated with national organizations such as the National Education Association, the American Federation of Teachers, the National Council of Teachers of English, the National Council of Teachers of Mathematics, and the Council for Exceptional Children. It is helpful to discuss teaching and teacher preparation with a favorite teacher and with fellow students.

Early childhood education

Students majoring in early childhood education prepare to teach infants and children through age eight. Students learn a variety of appropriate teaching methods and strategies.

Interests, skills, and qualities associated with success in the major

Interests. Childhood development, working with children, communicating with children and their parents.

Skills and qualities. Flexibility, creativity, endurance, music or artistic ability.

Recommended high school preparation

English 4, precollege mathematics 3, laboratory science 2, social studies 2, and foreign language 2.

Typical courses in the major

Philosophy of Education
Child Development
Methods of Teaching
Play Theories
Special Education
History of Education
Field Experiences
Classroom Organization

Family and Community
Curriculum Development
Teaching Mathematics
Evaluating Young Children
Communication Arts
Teaching Social Studies
Student Teaching

What the major is like

The early childhood education major is designed to prepare students to be certified as teachers of infants and young children. In many states, in addition to completing an approved program of study, the candidate must pass tests of both basic academic skills and professional knowledge. Most programs require a broad general education background, some specialization in a general education area, and a core of professional courses that includes education foundations, curriculum knowledge, teaching methods in the general subject areas appropriate for the education of young children, and opportunities to observe, participate, and student teach in a variety of settings and at a variety of age/grade levels.

Since early childhood teachers are teachers of general education, they are expected to be well grounded in broad areas of knowledge. Majors in the field are expected to meet general education requirements similar to those in colleges of liberal arts and sciences. These include areas such as communications skills, humanities, mathematics, biological and physical sciences, social sciences, history, and health and physical education. Increasingly students are expected to complete a minor, or specialization, in one of the general education areas. If they choose this route, general education courses will constitute between two-thirds and three-fourths of the undergraduate program.

In professional education courses students study the history and philosophy of education and child growth and development, focusing on general or early childhood education in particular. The nature of early childhood curriculum and classroom organization is also explored to allow prospective teachers to learn how to plan, organize, implement, and evaluate a program that is appropriate for young children. In addition, courses providing students with techniques of teaching language arts, reading, mathematics, science, social studies, art, and music are required. These may be taught as separate courses or integrated in some way. Because handicapped and nonhandicapped children are increasingly being educated in the same setting, classes on ways of teaching handicapped children in the regular classroom are usually available.

The professional education component includes field experiences that allow students to observe and participate in programs for young children in various settings such as public elementary schools, child care centers, and Head Start programs at the preschool, kindergarten, and primary grade levels.

The program culminates in a student teaching or internship experience, in which students take on increasing responsibility for a class of children. In early childhood programs, several student teaching experiences at different levels may be required. Through student teaching, students are able to integrate the technical knowledge that comes from working with children to arrive at the professional knowledge upon which good teaching is based.

Some states do not offer the early childhood teaching certificate. Instead they might provide a kindergarten endorsement on an elementary teaching certificate. In these states, early childhood education may be a minor offered to elementary students. It may include courses in kindergarten curriculum and methods. There might be an additional field experience or student teaching placement provided for students seeking this endorsement.

Specializations

Specialization is not available at the undergraduate level.

Other majors to consider

Child development, care and guidance
Elementary education
Psychology
Social work
Special education

Careers related to the major

The early childhood education major may lead to jobs as an early childhood teacher, child care administrator, and family service coordinator.

For more information

National Association for the Education of Young Children
1834 Connecticut Avenue NW
Washington, DC 20009-5786
(800)424-2460

Elementary education

Majors in elementary education prepare to teach children in grades K (kindergarten) through 8. Students gain a foundation in liberal arts subjects, learn a variety of methods for understanding how and why children develop socially and intellectually, and get professional experience that includes research in teaching and learning.

Interests, skills, and qualities associated with success in the major	**Interests.** Working with children, the importance of education. **Skills and qualities.** Communication, creativity, problem solving, flexibility, ability to organize, energy, enthusiasm.
Recommended high school preparation	English 4, precollege mathematics 3, biology 1, chemistry 1, physics 1, history 2, foreign language 2, and computer science 1.

Typical courses in the major

Philosophy of Education
Methods in Teaching
Teaching Language Arts
Teaching Mathematics
Special Education
Curriculum Development
Field Experiences
History of Education

Child Development
Teaching Science
Teaching Social Studies
Children's Literature
Classroom Management
Educational Measurement
Student Teaching

What the major is like

The elementary education major prepares students for state certification to teach children in grades K (kindergarten) through 8. (Each state has different rules, and special preparation may be required to teach K-3 or grades 6 through 8.) In addition to completing the elementary education major, many states require that students pass tests of subject matter, communication, and professional knowledge in order to be certified to teach. Almost all programs consist of a liberal arts foundation, a professional education core that includes course work in teaching methods, and a variety of teaching experiences in elementary schools.

To be prepared in all learning areas, majors typically take between 50 and 60 percent of their course work in the humanities, fine arts, social sciences, natural sciences, technology, and mathematics—most of these courses during the first two years.

In teaching method courses students learn various ways to teach children and develop the capacity to solve learning problems in reading, language arts, mathematics, science, and social studies. They also learn to plan lessons, evaluate learning, and manage the classroom.

Many states have begun to require a second major in a liberal arts discipline or an interdisciplinary field as a companion to the elementary education major. In other instances, elementary education majors take a second concentration in early childhood or special education.

Practical experiences in schools are typically interwoven with classroom studies throughout the major. As students observe, assist, and teach elementary children, what they learn in their classes becomes more meaningful and useful.

Student teaching is often the high point of the elementary education major. This experience, under the supervision of university and school instructors, helps the student move toward becoming a teacher.

Specializations

There are no specializations at the undergraduate level.

Other majors to consider

Communications
Early childhood education
Junior high education
Physical education
Psychology
Secondary education
Special education

Careers related to the major

The elementary education degree prepares graduates to teach in elementary schools. With appropriate graduate study, it can lead to careers as a school administrator, educational researcher, or school counselor.

For more information

National Association for the Education of Young Children
1834 Connecticut Avenue NW
Washington, DC 20009-5786
(800)424-2460

Parks and recreation management

The parks and recreation management major explores how individuals and communities pursue leisure and recreation. Students explore what recreation is, investigate what motivates people's recreation choices, and develop skills to manage a variety of leisure and recreation enterprises and organizations.

Interests, skills, and qualities associated with success in the major

Interests. Working with people.

Skills and qualities. Helping others, creativity, leadership, solving problems, communicating effectively.

Recommended high school preparation

English 4, precollege mathematics 2–3, laboratory science 3–4, history or social studies 3–4, foreign language 1–3, and computer science 1–2. 2-4 years of music and/or visual arts and 2-3 years of drama or speech are also recommended.

Typical courses in the major

Introduction to Recreation
Program and Event Planning
Financial Management
Design of Recreation Facilities
Commercial Recreation
Managing Recreation Personnel

History of Leisure
Philosophy of Leisure
Marketing Recreation Enterprises
Outdoor Recreation
Recreation for Special Populations

What the major is like

The parks and recreation management major encompasses many areas—from the operation of community leisure services to the study of therapeutic recreation.

Generally, a core curriculum, taken during the freshman and sophomore years, covers the history and philosophy of recreation, recreation leadership and management, recreation policy, and recreation programming. Students usually begin courses in their chosen concentration as second-semester sophomores or first-semester juniors. In these classes they specialize in one of the following areas.

Community leisure services refer to traditional public recreation; students prepare for careers in municipal or county recreation programs, youth service agencies, or military recreation. Studies include the following courses: facilities and parks maintenance and design, program planning and administration, comprehensive planning of vacation services, recreation and community development, marketing of vacation services, supervision and management of recreation personnel, public policy, legal aspects of recreation services, financial management.

Park, outdoor, or natural resource management is for students planning to work in outdoor recreation—for example, in public parks and forests. Topics include the following: interpretation of national and cultural resources, outdoor recreation planning, forestry and soil management, outdoor recreation management, wildlife and/or forest recreation resource policy, park maintenance, landscape and design, landscaping and law enforcement.

Travel, tourism, and commercial recreation focuses on the fast-growing private sectors of recreation—resorts, theme parks, transportation, travel, the recreation service and facility industry, and hospitality-related fields. Courses in this concentration vary but usually include the following: introduction to tourism, tour planning, personnel and fiscal management, resort management, marketing, event planning, business law, and tourism planning. Students who emphasize travel and tourism often take courses in international studies, international law, geography, and foreign languages.

Therapeutic recreation trains students to work in rehabilitative recreation, which involves serving hospitals, hospices, and nursing homes or helping special populations like burn victims, the terminally ill, or at-risk young people. This specialization may require courses in physiology, anatomy, psychology, and sociology in addition to several courses preparing students to develop therapeutic recreation programs for people with specific needs.

Most programs require internships, giving students firsthand experience in their concentration. Generally these field experiences are available to sophomores, juniors, and seniors.

Not all programs offer all the specializations described above, and students should get in touch with the parks and recreation management departments at universities that interest them to learn which areas are offered. Some institutions may call the program leisure studies, leisure services, or recreation. Students should talk with college staff to determine how well the institution can meet their needs.

Specializations

Community leisure services, park, outdoor or natural resource management, travel, tourism, commercial recreation, therapeutic recreation, urban recreation, campus recreation, church recreation, camp administration.

Other majors to consider

Biology
Business administration
Education
Hotel/motel and restaurant management
Marketing
Physical education
Physical therapy
Psychology
Sociology
Sports medicine
Wildlife management

Careers related to the major

There is a wide variety of career choices for graduates of parks and recreation management. They may find jobs as a community recreation planner or director; social director of a cruise ship, resort, camp, retirement community, or health club; convention planner; guest services coordinator or sales and marketing director at a hotel; park or forest ranger; naturalist or interpreter for a regional, state, or national park; facility manager for a public or private recreation facility; camp director; director or coordinator for nonprofit organization such as YMCA/YWCA, Boy Scouts, Girl Scouts, Special Olympics; recreation equipment salesperson; coordinator of military recreation; aquatics director; university or school campus activity coordinator; church youth coordinator or camp director.

Many executive positions in this field require a master's degree or several years of experience. A doctorate is usually required for positions in universities, where duties include teaching, research, and extension programs (working with recreation agencies).

For more information

National Recreation and Park Association
2775 South Quincy Street
Suite 300
Arlington, VA 22206
(703)820-4940

Physical education

Physical education majors study how the human body is affected by exercise and sports. They combine this with courses in a specialized area—for example, teacher preparation, athletic training, or sports management.

Interests, skills, and qualities associated with success in the major

Interests. Physical activity, sports, working with people, health-related issues, biological science.

Skills and qualities. Physical stamina, biological sciences, leadership.

Recommended high school preparation

English 4, precollege mathematics 3, biology 1, chemistry 1, physics 1, social studies 2, history 2, foreign language 2, music 1, and visual arts 1. Students should take 4 years of physical education and play on an athletic team 4 years.

Typical courses in the major

Motor Learning
Anatomy and Physiology
Exercise Physiology
Sport/activity Courses
Measurement and Evaluation
Psychology of Coaching

Motor Development
Biomechanics
Sports Psychology
Curriculum Development
Methods of Instruction
Student Teaching

What the major is like

Majors in physical education take general education courses during their first two years. At the same time they explore their career choices so they can choose their specialization within the major. For although teacher certification is offered as a concentration in almost all physical education programs, it is usually not the only option. Students frequently choose to concentrate in such areas as athletic training, sports management, health fitness, recreation therapy, or dance.

No matter what their specialization is, students take courses in the scientific foundations of physical education. These courses give students an understanding of how the human body is affected by exercise and sports and of how its performance can be improved. Students are usually required to pursue a broad spectrum of activities and sports, although little academic credit is given for this work.

Students interested in teacher certification take courses in child development, psychology, and curriculum and instruction, and they have opportunities to work with children in supervised field settings. The programs include special courses to meet state certification requirements and ordinarily culminate in student teaching.

Students interested in health-related fitness take more course work in the health sciences and exercise physiology. Many programs provide opportunities for these students to do practicums in health spas, hospitals, and rehabilitation centers.

Students who want to become athletic trainers get a strong foundation in the biological sciences, human anatomy, and physiology and take courses related to the prevention and care of athletic injuries. Programs in this concentration are accredited by the National Athletic Training Association and include considerable work with various athletic teams.

The concentration in recreation or prephysical therapy also requires substantial work in the biological sciences and in rehabilitation. (Recreation therapists can be certified with a bachelor's degree, but most states certify physical therapists at the master's level only. Undergraduates must submit excellent academic credentials to be strong candidates for admission to graduate programs in physical therapy.)

Students working in sports management take courses in business as well as in the administration of athletic programs. Requirements differ widely, depending on where the program is housed in the institution.

Dance is usually found either in physical education or in fine arts. Most programs emphasize either dance performance or dance education; those offering both specializations ask students to choose one or to combine them. Depending on their concentration, dance students take course work in the performing arts in education.

Specializations

Teacher certification, exercise science, health/fitness, sports management, recreation therapy, motor development, athletic training, coaching, dance, prephysical therapy.

Other majors to consider

Athletic training
Dance
Health education
Physical therapy
Sociology
Sports management
Sports medicine

Careers related to the major

The physical education major may lead to jobs as a physical education teacher, aerobic dance instructor, athletic trainer, fitness director (of a health spa, hospital recreation center), athletic administrator, recreation therapist (in a hospital or rehabilitation center), wellness director. With additional study, one may undertake exercise science research or become a physical therapist.

For more information

American Alliance for Health, Physical Education, Recreation and Dance
1900 Association Drive
Reston, VA 22091
(703)476-3400

Secondary education

The major in secondary education prepares students to teach in high schools and to meet the needs and abilities of teenagers. Students get a general education through liberal arts courses, gain depth of knowledge in the subject they intend to teach, and develop teaching skills through professional education courses.

Interests, skills, and qualities associated with success in the major

Interests. Serving others, teaching young people and helping them develop their academic interests and career choices.

Skills and qualities. Working with people, teaching, learning, understanding human behavior.

Recommended high school preparation

English 4, precollege mathematics 3, laboratory science 2–3, social studies 1.5, history 2, and foreign language 2. History courses should include American and world history.

Typical courses in the major

Educational Psychology	Principles of Learning
Classroom Management	Test Construction
Issues and Trends	Student Teaching
Instructional Methods	

What the major is like

The major in secondary education prepares students to teach in secondary schools and to meet the needs and abilities of teenagers. The major ensures that students are well educated in the general, or liberal, sense; prepared in depth in a major area of study (or in two majors or a major and a minor area); knowledgeable and skillful in teaching procedures; and aware of the importance of the school in society.

Although each state sets its own standards for teacher training, all programs in the secondary education major fall into one of two categories. In the first category, the program for the secondary teaching certificate is completed as a part of the work toward a bachelor's degree. Usually, a bachelor's in education with a major in secondary education is the degree earned. About half this program consists of courses in liberal studies, another 30 to 40 percent of courses are in a major subject or field of specialization, and 15 to 25 percent are in pedagogy (teaching methods) and professional education. In the second category, the program for the secondary teaching certificate is taken after all work is completed for a bachelor's degree. This postgraduate program may be taken to meet state teacher certification requirements only, in approximately 15 to 24 semester hours. Or, with additional hours it may lead to completion of a master's degree.

Secondary education majors do student teaching in an actual school setting for one semester as part of their preparation. Majors in the field are trained in the responsibilities of secondary school teaching. High school teachers design classroom presentations to meet the requirements of teenage students. They lecture, run demonstrations, and use films, slides, overhead projectors, and microcomputers. They assign lessons, give tests, and maintain classroom discipline. The effective teacher uses various teaching and learning procedures with individual students, large groups, and small groups. Science teachers supervise laboratory work, and vocational education teachers give students hands-on experience with instruments, tools, and machinery.

High school teachers plan lessons, grade papers, prepare report cards, oversee study halls, work with homerooms, supervise extracurricular activities, and meet with parents and school staff. They may help students deal with academic and personal problems. They may also advise students in choosing courses, colleges, and careers. Teachers participate in conferences and workshops to hone their teaching skills and to keep informed in their subject matter.

Specializations

There is no specialization within secondary education.

Other majors to consider

Chemistry
English
English education
History
Mathematics
Mathematics education
Physics
Science education
Social studies education

Careers related to the major

The secondary education major prepares students to teach in their chosen field in secondary schools. In addition, they may become (usually with graduate study) administrators, supervisors, or guidance counselors in public schools, or staff members in professional associations and government offices of education. Teachers may move into positions as school librarians or curriculum specialists. Special education teachers work with students who are mentally retarded, emotionally disturbed, hearing impaired, or learning disabled. Other teachers work with very bright or gifted students.

For more information

American Association of Colleges for Teacher Education
One Dupont Circle NW
Suite 610
Washington, DC 20036-1186
(202)293-2450

American Federation of Teachers
555 New Jersey Avenue NW
Washington, DC 20001
(202)879-4400

National Education Association - Student Programs
1201 16th Street NW
Washington, DC 20036
(202)833-4000

A brochure called "Teaching as a Career" is available from the American Federation of Teachers.

Special education

A major in special education prepares teachers to work with children and young people with special needs arising from physical, mental, or psychological disabilities.

Interests, skills, and qualities associated with success in the major

Interests. Helping others, particularly children challenged by disabilities; working with people.

Skills and qualities. Accepting differences in people, communicating effectively, teaching.

Recommended high school preparation

English 4, precollege mathematics 3, laboratory science 3, social studies 3, history 2, foreign language 2, music 1, visual arts 1, and computer science 2. Social studies should include sociology and psychology if available.

Typical courses in the major

Introduction to Education
Classroom Management
Teaching Methods/Materials
Disabilities in Children
Educational Assessment
Teaching Methods

Introduction to Psychology
Speech/Language Development
Developmental Psychology
Strategies for Mainstreaming
Educational Policy and Law
Student Teaching

What the major is like

Special education majors are prepared to educate students who have special needs because of physical, mental, or psychological disabilities. By federal and state law, every student with a disability, regardless of its nature and severity, is entitled to a free and an appropriate education. Special educators are trained to make this law a reality.

To enter the field, the candidate must complete a course of study that includes supervised classroom training and meets state certification standards. Information about certification is available from schools of education at colleges and universities and from the certification office of each state department of education.

Special education is marked by diversity, both in the persons served and in the settings where service is provided. Programs therefore include a general orientation to education and specialized course work addressing the full spectrum of disabling conditions. Although national policy mandates the education of students in the least restrictive setting—such as a regular classroom or a regular school—the intensity of some students' needs can require services in special facilities, in hospitals, or at home. Special education majors are therefore introduced to the full range of environments in which they might teach and are trained to collaborate with other professionals as well as with parents and other advocates for learners with special needs.

Freshman undergraduates intending to major in special education usually enroll in introductory courses in education or psychology along with general studies. As sophomores, students balance core courses in education, psychology, and child development with their remaining requirements in general studies. Juniors take specialized training related to various disabling conditions and are scheduled for classroom observations and supervised experiences in school and community settings. Seniors prepare for certification by taking advanced courses in special education, along with electives, and by fulfilling requirements in student teaching.

General studies constitute about 40 percent of the undergraduate program; 20 percent is devoted to education psychology and child growth and development; 40 percent concentrates on the knowledge and skills needed for the education of students with disabilities.

Specializations

Children with mild disabilities, children with moderate special needs, children with severe or profound disabilities, teaching the hearing impaired, instructing students with visual impairments, adaptive physical education, orientation and mobility, early childhood special education, vocational special education.

Other majors to consider

Early childhood education
Elementary education
Occupational therapy
Physical therapy
Psychology
Secondary education
Speech pathology/audiology

Careers related to the major

The special education major prepares graduates to teach special education in a school or institutional setting. With graduate study, students often pursue careers as administrators of special education. Advanced training may also lead to a career as a speech/language pathologist, audiologist, physical therapist, occupational therapist, school psychologist, school counselor, evaluation specialist, teacher trainer, college teacher, parent/community coordinator, rehabilitation counselor, vocational/special needs teacher, or adaptive physical education instructor.

For more information

American Association of Colleges for Teacher Education
One Dupont Circle NW
Suite 610
Washington, DC 20036-1186
(202)293-2450

National Association of State Directors of Special Education
1800 Diagonal Road
Alexandria, VA 22314-3320
(703)519-3800

The Council for Exceptional Children
1920 Association Drive
Reston, VA 22091-1589
(703)620-3660

Technology (industrial arts) education

Majors in technology education (industrial arts) are trained to teach the design, operation, and impact of technological systems to students in grades 6 through 12.

Interests, skills, and qualities associated with success in the major

Interests. Helping people learn about the design, operation, and impact of technological systems.

Skills and qualities. Working with people, written and oral communication, organization, analyzing and describing technological systems.

Recommended high school preparation

English 4, precollege mathematics 2, biology 1, chemistry 1, physics 1, social studies 1, history 1, visual arts 1, computer science 1, and technology education 2–4.

Typical courses in the major

Production Systems
Transportation Systems
Computers in Technology
Graphic Communications
Construction Processes
Curriculum Development

Communication Systems
Materials and Processes
Power and Energy Systems
Electronic Communications
Product Design
Student Teaching

What the major is like

The major in technology education involves the study of technology, its applications in industry, and its social and cultural impact. Students learn how and why people create and use technology and the consequences of its creation and use. In middle and secondary schools, technology education is a general education subject like mathematics, language arts, history, or science. It is not intended to prepare students for immediate employment, but rather helps develop their ability to contribute to society as citizens, wage earners, and consumers.

Majors in technology education typically devote 30 to 40 percent of their courses to general education (sciences and humanities). The remainder of their program prepares them to teach technology. This preparation is divided into knowing technology, doing technology, and teaching technology.

The "knowing technology" courses are laboratory centered and focus on the technological systems used to communicate information, produce products and structures, and transport people. Students learn how each system is designed and operated and how it affects the natural, social, political, and economic environment.

The "doing technology" courses extend this knowledge into significant practice. Students design and operate technological systems. These classes focus on the techniques and practices used in communication, production, and transportation systems.

The "teaching technology" courses develop the students' ability to determine course content, identify and use teaching methods, and evaluate instruction of technology education classes in grades 6 through 12. First-hand experience is gained through student teaching.

Specializations

None.

Other majors to consider

Agricultural education
Business education
Science education
Trade and industrial education

Careers related to the major

Graduates in technology education can enter directly into technology teaching at the middle school or junior or senior high level. With additional training the areas of guidance and school administration are also open. Many industries employ technology education teachers in supervision, sales, and training positions.

For more information

International Technology Education Association
1914 Association Drive
Reston, VA 22091
(703)860-2100

Engineering

RICHARD E. GRACE
and JANE Z. DANIELS

Purdue University

From reports in the newspaper and on TV, students undoubtedly are aware of the engineers who design artificial hearts and kidneys; the teams of engineers who design the propulsion systems, computer controls, and spacecraft that allowed a man to set foot on the moon; and the engineers who design planting techniques, genetic controls, and energy-efficient farm machinery to alleviate some of the world's hunger problems. These are only a few of the engineering accomplishments that bring a higher quality of life to many people.

"It's the most interesting and challenging work you can imagine, yet I get paid more than any other professional who has completed only a bachelor's degree." That's how one engineer describes the profession. Officially, engineering is described by the Accreditation Board for Engineering and Technology as "the profession in which a knowledge of the mathematical and natural sciences gained by study, experience, and practice is applied with judgment to develop ways to utilize, economically, the materials and forces of nature for the benefit of mankind."

For an understanding of the variety of engineering positions, the geometry of a simple cube is helpful. The vertical dimension of the cube in the illustration on the next page represents engineering disciplines (majors). The horizontal dimension shows the functions of engineering (design, manufacturing, consulting, etc.) The third dimension represents interest areas (for example, health care, transportation, energy). A single engineering job exists at any of the hundreds of places where three dimensions intersect on the cube. For example, the square where the electrical engineering major intersects with the design function and interest in health care may represent an engineer who is modifying a new pacemaker so that it can be produced less expensively.

Engineering *majors* are described individually in a later section of this book. The various functions of engineering describe what engineers do. The function that an engineer enjoys and excels in is closely related to his or her talents and personality. The main functions of engineering are described below.

Research

The scientist and the engineer work together closely in the research function. The scientist may focus on discovering new scientific truths or knowledge, and the engineer is interested in using research to solve a problem or satisfy a need. The two areas are sometimes described as "pure research" and "applied research." The relationship between re-

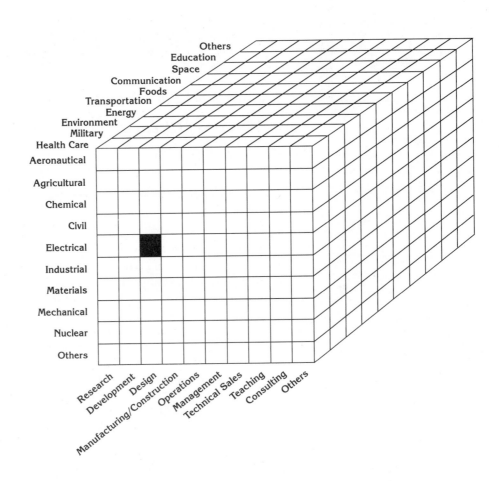

search and development is so close that the two functions are often combined and are known as R & D.

Development

More than 10 percent of all engineers are involved in development. These engineers apply the discoveries of the research scientist and the engineer for useful purposes. A newly discovered material may have certain characteristics of strength and heat resistance that suggest its use in rocketry, kilns, or vats to hold molten glass. A breakthrough in laser research might point the way to new surgical applications. The engineer involved in development creates pilot processes, models, or prototypes.

Design

Twenty percent of all engineers with bachelor's degrees are concerned with design. An engineer working in design takes a product, process, or concept from the research and development engineers and prepares it for production or construction. An engineer may take the prototype of a newly developed biodegradable trash bag, computer, or coating process and redesign it so that it can be produced or used at a reasonable cost. An engineer may take the model of a building, a tunnel, or a dam and design its construction so that workers and machinery will be used as efficiently as possible. Design is not only the most common function of engineers, it is their hallmark.

Manufacturing/construction

More than 10 percent of all engineers are involved in making a finished product. If that product is made in a factory, the engineer is usually called a product or manufacturing engineer. If the product is a large, somewhat permanent structure, like a building or bridge, the engineer is often called a construction engineer. It is the job of the manufacturing or construction engineer to take a plan and specifications from the design engineer and bring them to reality—the finished product. The manufacturing or construction engineer decides *how* the product will be made.

Operations

The operations engineer maintains a finished piece of equipment or a structure. This engineer may maintain the mechanical and electrical systems of a football stadium complete with a retractable roof, heating and cooling systems, and an elaborate multimedia scoreboard. The operations engineer may work to ensure the ongoing stability of an interstate highway system, or perhaps oversee the continuing operation of the launch facility for space shuttles. Operations engineers are essential to maintaining the usefulness of expensive machinery and structures. This function is sometimes referred to as plant engineering or maintenance engineering.

Management

An important function for many engineers is management. Almost half of all engineering graduates are performing managerial, supervisory, or administrative functions within 25 years after they graduate. Engineers in management may be supervising teams of other engineers, or they may be managing the equipment or financial assets of a company. These engineers are concerned with the long-range effects of policy decisions. The technical complexity of today's products and processes requires technically trained people to be involved in management. Management is the function in which people skills become equally important to technical skills. Many corporate leaders in the United States have a background in science or engineering.

Technical sales

As products become more complex and technical, many engineers are needed in the sales function. These engineers know the technical capabilities and limitations of their products and use that knowledge to improve the operations of their customers. A sales engineer may suggest new computer equipment to improve production in a factory or may demonstrate a new robotic device that could replace humans in a hazardous work area. Sales engineers are sometimes supported by technical specialists called application engineers and by field representatives called service engineers.

Other engineering functions

Two other important functions in engineering cut across the functions described above. Consulting engineers provide expertise to companies, government agencies, or individuals. Consulting may especially appeal to engineers who wish to be self-employed or to work part-time. A teaching career is rewarding for engineers who want to help others learn engineering concepts and problem solving. Typically, engineering faculty members lean toward the theoretical side of engineering and are more closely related to research and development functions.

Engineering as preparation for other professions

The combination of an engineering degree with graduate study in medicine, law, or business administration opens the door to many other career opportunities. Most patent lawyers, many presidents and chief executive officers of major corporations, and a growing number of physicians have received their undergraduate education in engineering.

The future for engineers

Employment opportunities for engineers have been excellent for a number of years and should continue to be strong. The College Placement Council reports that in recent years engineering majors have received about half the on-campus job offers, even though they have made up fewer than 10 percent of the graduates. The *Occupational Outlook Handbook*, published by the United States Department of Labor, shows that employment of engineers is expected to increase faster than will the average for all occupations throughout the 1990s. Most companies are less likely to lay off engineers than other workers. Many engineers work on long-term projects that continue even during recessions.

It is important for engineers to continue their education throughout their careers because their value depends on knowledge of the latest technology. Employers often offer seminars or classes on-site or through telecommunications with engineering schools. Some companies even pay for engineers to return to college full time for graduate studies.

Most employers of engineers realize that the best solution to tomorrow's problems can only be found by using the talents and creativity of individuals with a wide variety of personalities and experiences. Successful engineers are women and men coming from a variety of racial and ethnic groups who have diverse interests and personalities.

Aerospace/aeronautical engineering

The major in aerospace/aeronautical engineering is concerned with the design and development of high-speed transportation vehicles such as aircraft, spacecraft, missiles, launch vehicles, space habitats, boats, and cars, as well as the physics of the flow of air, water, and plasma around these vehicles.

Interests, skills, and qualities associated with success in the major

Interests. Model aircraft and rocketry, astronomy, piloting, space exploration, computer games, engine operation, computer programming, solving problems, working with people.

Skills and qualities. Imagination, leadership, initiative, mathematics, physical sciences, computer technology.

Recommended high school preparation

English 4, algebra 1, calculus .5, geometry .5, precalculus 1, trigonometry .5, biology 1, chemistry 1, physics 1, economics .5, history or social studies 2, foreign language 2, and computer science .5–1. An additional year of science is recommended. Foreign languages should include French, German, or Japanese.

Typical courses in the major

Statics	Dynamics
Structural Analysis	Linear Control Systems
Propulsion Systems	Vehicle Design
Aerodynamics/Fluid Mechanics	Stability and Control
Flight Mechanics	Wind Tunnel Testing
Orbital Mechanics	Spacecraft Systems
Orientation and Control	Telecommunications
Power and Thermal Control	

What the major is like

The major in aerospace/aeronautical engineering treats the analysis, synthesis, and design of aeronautical and astronautical vehicles. It is generally possible to specialize in either aeronautics (aircraft) or astronautics (spacecraft) at the undergraduate level by proper selection of elective courses. Related programs in aerospace technology normally apply engineering and management methods and technical skills in support of the diverse activities associated with air transportation. Some of the programs emphasize hands-on skills and detailed subsystem design. About 10 institutions currently have aerospace technology accreditation in the United States.

The academic program for engineers generally consists of two years of science and engineering basics, followed by two years of specialty courses, which—at some universities—allow options for various career emphases. The specialty courses typically cover propulsion, structures, thermodynamics, controls, avionics, and dynamics. Subsequent careers include research, design and development, management, test and field service, marketing/sales, manufacturing, software development, materials and processes, and teaching.

Academic programs in technology may be found in both two- and four-year programs and have varying educational and vocational aims. Schools of aviation concentrate on courses designed to produce graduates who can supervise various airline and airport operations, including retrofitting, repair, and maintenance of aircraft and operation of fixed bases. More technical courses produce mechanics, avionics technicians, and designers of many complex aircraft subsystems such as hydraulics, landing gears, internal power systems, environmental control systems, brakes, transmissions, and power plant support systems.

The two main branches of aerospace engineering are aircraft/missiles and spacecraft/space systems. Some universities provide a curriculum that covers both areas, usually with less emphasis on space. Others, however, offer only aeronautics or only astronautics. A limited number of schools of aviation serve the airline industry, and a number of aerospace technology schools serve both the airline and the aircraft industries.

Specializations

Aeronautics, astronautics.

Other majors to consider

Computer engineering
Electrical engineering
Engineering physics
Mathematics
Mechanical engineering
Physics
Systems engineering

Careers related to the major

Aerospace engineering majors usually enter the aerospace industry, which loosely includes the aerospace prime contractors and their major suppliers, the propulsion industry, academe, NASA, Department of Defense research and development, other allied government agencies, and the airlines. Within this framework there are careers in the following areas: R & D (research and development), marketing/planning, computer application technology. Engineers generally work in groups devoted to specific disciplines, such as systems engineering, structures, aerodynamics, controls, and human factors.

A master's degree is advisable for research and development work in industry; firms frequently offer financial aid to help their qualified engineers seek higher degrees. The doctorate is for those wishing to teach at universities or to do advanced research.

The undergraduate major in aerospace engineering has proved to be an excellent stepping stone to graduate education in medicine, law, and business.

For more information

The American Institute of Aeronautics and Astronautics
370 L'Enfant Promenade SW
Washington, DC 20024-2518
(202)646-7400

Educational Programs/NASA Headquarters
300 E Street SW
Washington, DC 20546
(202)358-1519

Agricultural engineering

In the agricultural engineering major, students learn to apply science and engineering principles to the challenges of producing agricultural products in the quantity and quality needed by today's consumers.

Interests, skills, and qualities associated with success in the major

Interests. How things work, solving problems, improving the quality of life, quantitative games, computers, leadership.

Skills and qualities. Problem solving, oral and written communication, computers, organizing projects and people, mathematics, biology, chemistry, physics.

Recommended high school preparation

English 4, algebra 2, calculus .5, geometry 1, trigonometry .5, laboratory science 3–4, history or social studies 2, foreign language 2, and computer science .5–1.

Typical courses in the major

Solid Mechanics
Thermodynamics
Energy Systems
Mathematics
Inorganic Chemistry
Biochemistry
Plant and Animal Physiology
Engineering Economics
Biological Materials Science
Food Engineering
Irrigation and Drainage

Fluid Mechanics
Heat Transfer
Biology
Organic Chemistry
Physical Chemistry
Microbiology
Electrical Circuits
Hydrology
Environmental Systems
Professional Ethics

What the major is like

Agricultural engineering is dedicated to the advancement of food production, fiber production, and other biological needs by the application of engineering to the environment, natural resources, and associated industries. In core courses, students learn to analyze the design of agricultural equipment, explore the nature of biological materials, and to study hydraulic systems, irrigation, machinery design, and erosion control.

Agricultural engineering degree programs emphasize engineering theory and analysis as well as design and include supporting laboratory work and project design. Students take mathematics, including calculus and differential equations; basic science courses, including biology, chemistry, physics, biochemistry, materials science, plant and animal physiology; and basic engineering. In addition, they take some humanities and social science courses. An emphasis on oral and written communication is recommended.

Students may specialize in several areas: food processing, where they focus on issues involving production, nutrition, packaging, food plant design, and preservation; water and soil resources, where they deal with irrigation, soil science, drainage and hydraulic structure design, and erosion control; biotechnology; or machine systems, which may include the automation of feed handling and processing necessary for large-scale farming. There may be other areas of concentration as well.

Since computers are used as a tool in the solution of many agricultural engineering problems, the curriculum normally includes computer programming and numerical analysis. The use of computers is essential to successful completion of the course work.

Cooperative education programs, which provide opportunities for full-time employment during alternating academic terms, are offered by many institutions. Students enter these programs after they have completed basic engineering course work.

The four-year bachelor's degree is necessary for entry-level employment as an agricultural engineer. Registration as a professional engineer is normally required for private practice. Many agricultural engineering graduates go on to earn advanced degrees; approximately 30 percent complete a master of science or master of engineering degree. Approximately 15 percent of students with master's degrees continue on for the Ph.D. or Doctor of Engineering. Some students continue their education in other fields, such as business, law, or medicine.

Specializations

Biotechnology engineering, bioenvironmental controls engineering, machine systems engineering, bioprocess systems engineering, water and soil resource engineering, food engineering.

Other majors to consider

Biochemistry
Biology
Chemical engineering
Civil engineering
Electrical engineering
Environmental health engineering
Mechanical engineering

Careers related to the major

Agricultural engineers hold positions in industry, business, government, and universities. They work for food and fiber processing companies, machinery companies, government agencies (dealing with protection of the environment and energy, soil, and water resources), and the electric and gas utility industry. Their work can include research, testing, design and development, manufacturing, marketing and sales, operations, teaching, and administration.

For more information

American Society of Agricultural Engineers
2950 Niles Road
St. Joseph, MI 49085-9659
(616)429-0300

Chemical engineering

Through study of mathematics, physical sciences, and life sciences, chemical engineering majors learn to develop means of converting basic raw materials into useful products for people.

Interests, skills, and qualities associated with success in the major	**Interests.** Science (especially chemistry), mathematics.
	Skills and qualities. Applying knowledge of science and mathematics to real-world problems.

Recommended high school preparation

English 4, algebra 1, calculus 1, geometry 1, trigonometry 1, biology 1, chemistry 1, physics 1, social studies 1, history 1, and computer science 1.

Typical courses in the major

General Chemistry
Organic Chemistry
Calculus
Physical Chemistry
Physics
Energy and Material Balances
Statics and Dynamics
Chemical Reactor Engineering

Statistics
Electrical Circuits
Differential Equations
Engineering Economics
Thermodynamics
Heat, Mass and Momentum Transfer
Industrial Plant Design
Computer Programming

What the major is like

Majors in chemical engineering are trained to play a key role in the design and development of chemical processes and products necessary for modern living, such as antibiotics, fertilizers and agricultural chemicals, wood products, polymers, synthetic fibers and fabrics, semiconductors, petroleum and petrochemicals, and synthetic fuels. Majors in the field also learn to design equipment for chemical plants. All of this must be accomplished economically and safely; chemical engineers are active in pollution control and in the safe disposal of hazardous wastes.

Chemical engineering programs are relatively standard throughout the United States, particularly if they are accredited by the Accreditation Board for Engineering and Technology. These programs are based in the natural sciences, especially chemistry. (Physics and biochemistry or biophysics may be included as electives.) A strong mathematics background is required because processes in chemical plants are subject to rigorous mathematical analyses.

One of the most important courses in the major, energy and material balances, studies the laws of conservation of energy and mass. Another important course is thermodynamics—the basis of determining the energy consumption, and hence efficiency, of chemical processes.

The capstone engineering course involves designing the production of a major chemical product in a petroleum refinery, a food processing plant, a biomedical polymer plant, an electronic device, or the like. Fundamental chemical engineering principles are applied with rigorous judgment, alternative designs are considered, and economic factors and pollution control are evaluated.

Because chemical engineers make extensive use of computers, virtually every course in the program uses them, and modern software is used in the design courses. Because communication skills are important to chemical engineers, courses in speech and writing are included in the major, as are courses in the humanities and social sciences.

Specializations

Biochemical engineering, biomedical engineering, material science, electronic materials processing, environmental engineering.

Other majors to consider

Biochemistry
Chemistry
Environmental health engineering
Microbiology
Nuclear engineering

Careers related to the major

The chemical engineering major has a wide range of careers to choose from following graduation. Graduates may work in: plant operation (production), plant technical services, plant management (supervision), engineering design, marketing, technical sales, corporation management, research and development, college teaching, and product development. Careers in some of these areas become available as the chemical engineer gains experience and cannot be entered directly upon graduation.

For more information

American Institute of Chemical Engineers
345 East 47th Street
New York, NY 10017
(212)705-7338

Civil engineering

Civil engineering majors learn to solve technical problems involved in providing buildings, bridges, airports, transportation systems, foundations, coastal facilities, environmental control systems, and water supply and purification systems. The major prepares students to become involved in the conception, planning, design, construction, operation, and maintenance of these important public facilities.

Interests, skills, and qualities associated with success in the major

Interests. Mathematics, physical sciences, computers, building things, working toward a better quality of life, public service, applying mathematics and science to practical uses.

Skills and qualities. Quantitative ability, mathematics, physical sciences, logical thinking, interpersonal skills, communication skills, teamwork.

Recommended high school preparation

English 4, precollege mathematics 4, laboratory science 2–4, history 2–4, foreign language 1–2, and computer science .5–1. Laboratory science should include chemistry and physics.

Typical courses in the major

Structural Analysis
Soil Mechanics
Hydraulic Engineering
Waste Water Management
Planning and Design
Engineering Materials
Mechanics of Materials
Fluid Mechanics

Structural Design
Geotechnical Engineering
Water Resources
Transportation Engineering
Surveying
Statics
Dynamics
Engineering Measurements

What the major is like

Majors in civil engineering learn to plan, analyze, design, and build structures (buildings, bridges) and systems (transportation, water supply). Bachelor's degree programs in civil engineering typically require between 128 and 136 semester credits. Included are at least 16 credits of mathematics, including calculus and differential equations; 16 credits of basic sciences, including chemistry, physics, and possibly geology and/or biology; 32 credits of engineering sciences; 16 credits of engineering design; and 16 credits in the humanities and social sciences. In addition, the program typically includes some of the following: use of computers, English composition, speech, report writing, engineering economics, and statistics.

A civil engineering program typically includes a broad range of courses in fundamental engineering science and in civil engineering analysis and design. Within civil engineering, probably more than in any other engineering discipline, there are a number of technical areas in which one may specialize. Some of the most typical include the following:

Structural engineering. The planning, analysis, and design of large structures, including bridges, buildings, towers, dams, offshore drilling and exploration facilities.

Environmental engineering. The planning and design of facilities for providing and purifying water and for control of water pollution, air pollution, solid waste management, and disposal of hazardous materials.

Geotechnical engineering. The analysis and design of foundations and retaining walls; the development of excavation techniques and construction methods for tunnels, dams, storage systems for hazardous materials, and other facilities.

Hydraulics/coastal/ocean engineering. The analysis and design of dams, floodwalls, pumping stations, aqueducts, canals, harbor and coastal facilities, irrigation and drainage systems, and navigable waterways.

Transportation engineering. The analysis and design of facilities for all modes of transportation, including highways, airports, railways, aerospace systems, and pipelines.

In addition to preparing students for analysis, planning, and design in technical specialty areas, civil engineering programs provide an excellent base for careers in research and development, construction management, and research and teaching.

Although a four-year bachelor's degree is currently considered preparation for entry into the practice of civil engineering, there are efforts within the profession to make the master's degree the minimum educational prerequisite. At the present time, approximately 40 to 45 percent of B.S. degree graduates eventually complete master's degree programs. About 7 percent complete a Ph.D. in order to pursue careers in research and development, in teaching, and in professional engineering involving highly sophisticated analysis and design.

Specializations

Structural engineering, geotechnical engineering, environmental engineering, transportation engineering, hydraulic engineering, ocean and coastal engineering, community and urban planning.

Other majors to consider

Architectural engineering
Environmental health engineering
Ocean engineering

Careers related to the major

Entry-level positions in civil engineering are found in a wide range of organizations such as engineering firms; government agencies at the city, county, state, and federal levels; construction companies; major corporations; and aircraft companies. As engineers gain experience, career paths may lead to a position as an expert in a technical specialty area or into engineering management. In the future, the master's degree will probably be required for entry into the profession.

For more information   The American Society of Civil Engineers
345 East 47th Street
New York, NY 10017
(212)705-7667

Computer engineering

In the computer engineering major, students learn to design and develop computer and computer-related systems. These systems include software systems, hardware systems, and combined hardware/software systems. Students take courses in basic sciences, mathematics, and engineering science and design.

Interests, skills, and qualities associated with success in the major

Interests. Mathematics, science, computing, quantitative and qualitative games.

Skills and qualities. Computing, basic sciences, mathematics.

Recommended high school preparation

English 4, precollege mathematics 4, biology 1, chemistry 1, physics 1, social studies 3–4, history 2–3, foreign language 2–4, music .5, visual arts .5, and computer science .5–1.

Typical courses in the major

Introduction to Computing	Digital System Design
Computer Organization	Algorithms and Data Structures
Computer Architecture	Programming Languages
Software Engineering	Operating Systems
Computer Systems Design	Artificial Intelligence

What the major is like

In the computer engineering major, students learn how to design and develop computer and computer-related systems. They study computers ranging from supercomputers to microcomputers, and large data base systems and complex real-time control systems. Examples of some of the systems they may work with include integrated manufacturing control systems, aircraft control systems, and small dedicated imbedded systems such as those that run "smart" thermostats.

Computer engineering majors learn computer languages and study computer structure and assembly programming language. They study modeling, data structure, and ways of representing data meaningfully. They examine software/hardware tradeoffs: whether a given function should be accomplished through hardware or by the development of software.

Computer engineering evolved out of electrical engineering in the late 1960s. Computer engineering programs are accredited by the Engineering Accreditation Commission of the Accreditation Board for Engineering and Technology under the Computer Engineering Program Criteria. Accredited programs include study in basic sciences, mathematics, humanities, social sciences, and engineering science and design. The engineering science and design component provides a balanced treatment of hardware, software, and the basic modeling techniques used to represent the computing process. Curricula vary considerably from one program to another, but each provides an integrated sequence that covers algorithms, data structures, digital systems, computer organization and architecture, interfacing, software engineering, programming languages, and operating systems.

As in any major, students have opportunities for in-depth study. The available specializations vary somewhat from one institution to another. All programs in computer engineering have substantial laboratory components in which students gain direct experience with a variety of hardware and software.

All these programs provide the proper foundation for entry into the computer engineering profession. Graduates take positions spanning the spectrum of the field (hardware design, software design, applications, development, etc.) in a wide variety of industrial firms and government agencies.

Specializations

Computer architecture, software engineering, real-time systems, programming languages, artificial intelligence.

Other majors to consider

Aerospace/aeronautical engineering
Computer science
Electrical, electronics and communication engineering
Information sciences and systems
Mathematics

Careers related to the major

Accredited programs prepare their graduates for entry into any area of specialization within the computer engineering profession (design and development, manufacturing, protection, and marketing). Work in these areas can lead later to positions in management. Some graduates use the degree as the basis for further study in such fields as medicine, business, or law. With graduate study in computer engineering, positions in research and university teaching become available.

For more information

IEEE Computer Society
1730 Massachusetts Avenue NW
Washington, DC 20036-1903
(202)371-0101

Electrical engineering

Majors in electrical engineering learn to design and manufacture a broad array of electrical and electronic devices and systems to meet society's needs.

Interests, skills, and qualities associated with success in the major

Interests. Computer languages, computer programming, electronic equipment, quantitative games.

Skills and qualities. Quantitative thinking, working with computers, curiosity, mathematics, physical sciences.

Recommended high school preparation

English 4, algebra 1.5–2, calculus .5–1, geometry 1–1.5, trigonometry .5, laboratory science 3–4, history 2, foreign language 2, and computer science 1.

Typical courses in the major

Linear Circuit Analysis
Electrical Fields
Semiconducting Devices
Integrated Circuit Engineering
Microprocessor Interfacing

Signals and Systems
Microprocessor Systems
Information Transmission
Magnetic Fields

What the major is like

Programs in the electrical engineering major normally contain mathematics, basic sciences, humanities, social sciences, engineering science and design, and electives. Curricula often cover areas such as the following:

Communication systems. Handling of information; radio, television, telephone systems; antennas; laser transmission systems.

Computers. Digital systems; microprocessors; image recognition; speech synthesis; product design and manufacturing; industrial robots.

Power systems. Electrical power industry; transmission, distribution, conservation of electrical energy.

Robotics. Automatic control systems; artificial intelligence; use of computers to design and control robots.

Solid state devices and integrated circuits. New products such as small calculators, minicomputers, electronic controls for automotive and navigation systems, cameras, digital clocks, home appliances, electronic games.

Electrical engineering degree programs typically stress analysis and design. Related programs in electrical engineering technology normally apply engineering methods and technical skills, emphasizing the development of hands-on skills.

A four-year degree is normally required to practice electrical engineering. Qualified students should consider graduate study either directly following the bachelor's degree or after they have had some industrial experience. Part-time or evening study programs are often available in large industrial communities. One-quarter to one-third of all graduates go on to complete the doctoral degree in order to pursue careers in research and teaching.

Specializations

Communication systems, computer engineering, power systems, robotics, solid state devices, integrated circuits.

Other majors to consider

Computer engineering
Engineering physics
Mechanical engineering
Physics

Careers related to the major

Electrical engineering graduates work in many fields, for example: energy conversion systems, process control, instrumentation, information processing, and avionics. They work in the following functions: research, testing, operations and maintenance, teaching, design and development, manufacturing, marketing and sales, and administration. Related activities include systems analysis, product development, production field service and user training. With postgraduate degrees: research, design and development, college teaching, business administration, management, law, and medicine.

For more information
Institute of Electrical and Electronics Engineers (IEEE)
345 East 47th Street
New York, NY 10017
(212)705-7900

Industrial engineering

The industrial engineering major is diverse and people oriented. Students learn to plan, design, and implement complex systems for industry that take into account the availability, capabilities, and needs of people, machines, and materials. Industrial engineering methods are used in various human activities such as health care, manufacturing, transportation, and communications.

Interests, skills, and qualities associated with success in the major

Interests. Leadership, problem solving, improving the quality of life.

Skills and qualities. Oral and written communication, organizational ability, working with people, computer literacy, creativity, designing and improving systems, mathematics.

Recommended high school preparation

English 4, algebra 1, calculus 1, geometry 1, precalculus 1, trigonometry 1, chemistry 1, physics 1, social studies 2, foreign language 2, and computer science 1.

Typical courses in the major

Engineering Economy
Operations Research
Industrial Cost Control
Inventory Control
Organization Management
Human Factors
Production Control

Manufacturing Processes
Simulation
Robotics and Automation
Facility Design
Quality Control
Methods and Work Measurement

What the major is like

Industrial engineering majors learn to use engineering principles to design or improve systems that involve goods and services. Industrial engineering deals with how products are made—of the quality and at the cost wanted. Industrial engineers design the factory where the product is made and determine the system of its manufacture. They design the workstations, automation, and robotics; the material handling system; and the factory control system. They are also highly involved with the management of the factory, from overseeing the plant floor to supervising the company.

Industrial engineers are concerned with the worker's environment and safety. They are also concerned with making a product of high quality, at the lowest possible price, and delivering it when the customer wants it.

Industrial engineers also work in distribution systems—in trucking, airline, postal, maritime, rail, communication, and overnight delivery industries. They work with the procurement, routing, scheduling, and maintenance of vehicles. For example, the problems of getting a package overnight from San Francisco to London are industrial engineering problems. Industrial engineering is becoming international engineering, for companies today know no national borders. Industrial engineers hold positions that require them to travel internationally and therefore to know foreign languages. More and more companies are opening in foreign countries or entering into agreements with foreign companies.

It was in the early 1900s in a hospital room that industrial engineering found one of its earliest applications. Two of industrial engineering's founders, Frank and Lillian Gilbreth, determined with co-workers the "one best way" to perform operations and to train doctors, nurses, and technicians. As a result, operating times dropped drastically and survival rates increased. Today industrial engineers work in such service industries as health care, transportation, lodging, food service, defense, and government.

Because of the many careers possible, industrial engineering majors receive a diverse education in computer systems, mathematics and statistics, design, and management, as well as in the physical and social sciences, including economics.

Specializations

Human factors engineering, manufacturing systems engineering, management systems engineering, operations research.

Other majors to consider

Computer science
Industrial and organizational psychology
Industrial technology
Management science
Manufacturing technology
Mathematics
Mechanical engineering

Careers related to the major

The industrial engineering major can prepare one for careers as an industrial engineer, systems analyst, production control manager, quality control manager, operations research analyst, industrial cost control manager, manufacturing engineering manager, systems designer, plant manager. After graduate work in industrial engineering (the M.S. or Ph.D.) one may work as an engineering scientist.

For more information

Institute Headquarters/Institute of Industrial Engineers
25 Technology Park
Norcross, GA 30092
(404)449-0460

Materials/metallurgical engineering

Programs in the materials/metallurgical engineering major educate students in the science and technology of producing such materials as metals, ceramics, polymers, and their composites in forms and with properties suitable for practical use. The major leads to work that can range from materials production, extraction, and recycling to the design, development, and processing of materials for aerospace, transportation, electronic, energy conversion, and biomedical systems.

Interests, skills, and qualities associated with success in the major

Interests. Nature and the physical sciences, developing processes and systems, problem solving, quantitative and computational games.

Skills and qualities. Creative and critical thinking, quantitative thinking, analytic reasoning, oral and written communication, working with others, mathematics, physical sciences.

Recommended high school preparation

English 3–4, algebra 1.5, geometry 1, trigonometry .5, biology 1–2, chemistry 1–2, physics 1–2, history or social studies 2, foreign language, and computer science.

Typical courses in the major

Materials Science
Electronic Materials
Physical Metallurgy
Failure Analysis
Ceramics
Extractive Metallurgy
Electron Microscopy
High-Temperature Materials

Polymers
Phase Equilibriums
Forming and Fabrication
Corrosion
Composites
Crystallography
Materials Design and Selection

What the major is like

Majors in materials/metallurgical engineering learn to develop materials to meet specific needs. Everything seen and used is made of materials derived from the earth—large buildings and other structures, supersonic aircraft, advanced computers, electronic instruments, robotic systems, and biomedical devices like artificial limbs, joints, and implants. The future will bring expanding needs for new materials with high-performance applications as well as cheap high-volume materials for mass production. New and better processing methods will be needed to provide a continuing supply of minerals and raw materials from leaner and more complex ores. In addition, means of reclamation and recycling of solid waste must be developed to conserve natural resources and protect the environment.

Undergraduate programs normally include mathematics, communication, computer science, basic sciences (chemistry and physics), humanities, social sciences, engineering sciences, and engineering design, along with elective courses. Some programs emphasize a particular material, such as ceramics or polymers. Programs simply designated "materials engineering" probably include instruction in most types of materials.

Engineering science course work includes studies in the structure and properties of materials, material energy balances, transport phenomena, strength of materials, and tools for structural and chemical characterization. The engineering design courses emphasize devising materials, components, systems, or processes to meet particular objectives.

The possibilities for innovation, adaptation, and substitution are unlimited in the materials field. Although much attention is being focused on developing metals, ceramics, polymers, and composites, the ability to engineer new materials to meet specific needs is just being realized. This engineering can be done at the atomic level (as in fiber reinforcement to make a "graphite" fishing rod) or at the macroscopic level such as with bridges, buildings, and appliances.

The ability to engineer materials to exacting specifications has its basis in the development of a variety of tools and capabilities: electron microscopes that permit resolution of the structure and composition of materials at the atomic level, high-speed computers that make it possible to model the behavior of materials and components, and new means of processing material, such as rapid solidification, mechanical alloying, microgravity processing, thin film deposition, and plasma spraying. Students will learn to use these tools in their studies.

The impact and influence of the science and engineering of materials on critical manufacturing and processing industries have given the field a major role in the competitive global economy. In many areas, critical improvements in product performance are limited by available materials. The ability to engineer materials to specifications will make many such improvements possible.

Materials/metallurgical engineering graduates work in production, processing, reclamation, recycling, and selection and design of materials for the following: ground transportation systems, aerospace systems, household appliances, biomedical applications, energy conversion and utilization devices, information and communication systems, optical and optoelectronic components, and electronic and magnetic devices.

More than half of materials/metallurgical engineers begin their first job with a bachelor's degree. The remainder begin their career with a master's degree or a doctorate. The doctoral degree is usually required for careers in research and in teaching at the college level. The B.S. degree may be followed by study in such fields as business administration, management, and law (for example, patent law).

Specializations

Materials engineering, ceramic engineering, metallurgical engineering, polymers.

Other majors to consider

Chemical engineering
Chemistry
Electrical engineering
Mechanical engineering
Physics

Careers related to the major

Materials/metallurgical engineering graduates work in diversified functions including the following: manufacturing, research, technical services, administration, teaching, design and development, sales and marketing, quality control and testing, performance and failure analysis. Advanced degrees can lead to careers in research, design and development, college teaching, administration, management, law, medicine, or business.

For more information

ASM International
Materials Park, OH 44073
(216)338-5151
(800)336-5152

The Minerals, Metals, Materials Society
420 Commonwealth Drive
Warrendale, PA 15086-7514
(412)776-9011
(800)966-4867

American Ceramic Society
735 Ceramic Place
Westerville, OH 43081-2821
(614)890-4700

The Materials Revolution. Tom Forester. Cambridge, Mass.: MIT Press, 1988.

"Advanced Materials: Reshaping Our Lives," *National Geographic*, vol. 176, December 1989, page 746, has useful information on the field.

Mechanical engineering

Mechanical engineering deals with forces and energy in mechanical (solid and fluid) and thermal systems. Students learn to create and build machines, devices, and systems that perform useful services.

Interests, skills, and qualities associated with success in the major

Interests. Mechanical devices, how things work, computers, cars, solving problems, mathematics, physical sciences.

Skills and qualities. Creativity, innovation, oral and written communication, computer programming, organizing projects and people.

Recommended high school preparation

English 4, algebra 2, calculus 1, geometry .5, trigonometry .5, laboratory science 3–4, history or social studies 2, foreign language 2, and computer science 1.

Typical courses in the major

Solid Mechanics
Energy Systems
Mechanical Systems
Fluid Mechanics
Mechanisms
Automatic Controls

Thermodynamics
Materials Science
Manufacturing Systems
Heat Transfer
Design
Engineering Projects

What the major is like

In mechanical engineering, students focus on mechanics (fluids and solids) and heat as forms of energy. They use mathematical calculations to determine what a device will do before building it. They learn to model—to visualize a new device and to convey to others what it would do. And they learn what's involved in manufacturing the things they design, for example, a vehicle, an acoustic system, an engine.

The mechanical engineering major normally includes mathematics (calculus through differential equations) and numerical analysis; basic science (chemistry, physics, and perhaps biology or materials science); humanities and social science; and basic engineering science courses as well as mechanical engineering courses, which include the design of thermal and mechanical systems. Mechanical engineering programs generally emphasize engineering theory and analysis as well as design, with appropriate supporting laboratory and project work in such areas as:

Engineering mechanics. Static and dynamic forces within and on structures, equivalent force systems, dynamics, stresses and strains, and strength of materials.

Materials. Properties of materials, physical metallurgy, metallic and other materials including polymers, ceramics, and composites.

Electrical circuits and systems. Electrical circuits, direct and alternating current, electrical machinery, digital and analog electronic devices, circuits, and control systems.

Thermal systems. Fluid mechanics, thermodynamics, combustion, refrigeration, heat transfer, energy systems, and internal combustion engines.

Mechanical systems. Kinematics and mechanisms, modeling of multicomponent systems, control of mechanical systems, vibrations, component design and analysis, machine design, and dynamics of machinery.

Manufacturing systems. Modern manufacturing systems, robotics, computer-aided manufacturing systems, artificial intelligence, and computers integrated in manufacturing.

Specialty course work or technical electives typically include more in-depth study of acoustics and noise control, automotive engineering, applied solar energy, advanced control system design, biomechanics and biomedical engineering, biotechnology, computer-aided design, composite materials, direct energy conversion, energy system analysis, energy conservation, environmental control systems, gas dynamics, heating, ventilating and air conditioning, nondestructive testing, numerical modeling and simulation, packaging engineering, propulsion systems, polymer processing, robotics, and turbomachinery.

Because computers are used in the solution of many mechanical engineering problems, curricula include considerable computer programming and numerical analysis.

Related programs in mechanical engineering technology focus on the application of engineering methods in support of engineering projects. A technology program emphasizes technical skills and the development of hands-on capabilities.

Cooperative education programs, providing opportunities for full-time employment during alternating academic terms, are offered by many institutions. Such programs are available after a student has completed the basic engineering course work.

Specializations

Automatic controls, bioengineering, energy systems, materials engineering, design, manufacturing systems, thermal systems, automotive engineering.

Other majors to consider	**Aerospace/aeronautical engineering** **Chemical engineering** **Civil engineering** **Electrical engineering** Engineering mechanics Engineering science **Industrial engineering** Nuclear engineering **Petroleum engineering**
Careers related to the major	Mechanical engineers are actively engaged in a wide range of careers in industry, business, government, and universities. Engineers interact with people or machines in research, design, development, testing, manufacturing, operations, marketing, sales, or management. Many mechanical engineers complete advanced degrees in engineering; others continue their education in related fields like medicine, business, or law.
For more information	American Society of Mechanical Engineers 345 East 47th Street New York, NY 10017 (212)705-7722

Petroleum engineering

Petroleum engineering majors receive a broad background in engineering and business as preparation for designing ways to find and extract minerals below the earth's surface, especially petroleum. Students also learn to design the systems used in oil and gas production.

Interests, skills, and qualities associated with success in the major	**Interests.** Solving problems, working with others, international travel, using computers, outdoor activities. **Skills and qualities.** Mathematics, physics, oral and written communication, working with others.
Recommended high school preparation	English 4, precollege mathematics 4, biology 1, chemistry 1, physics 1, social studies 2, history 1, foreign language 2, and computer science 1.
Typical courses in the major	Drilling Production Engineering Reservoir Engineering Mineral Law Formation Evaluation Rock Properties Engineering Economics
What the major is like	Majors in petroleum engineering take approximately one year of course work in mathematics, physics, chemistry, and geology and one year of engineering sciences such as computer analysis methods, electronics, strength of materials, behavior of hydrocarbon fluids, flow of fluids, and

flow of heat. This work gives students the basic problem-solving skills needed to tackle the technical challenges of modern engineering design. Included in the program is course work in the humanities and social sciences.

In the junior and senior years, students take more specialized course work and laboratory work in such areas as well drilling, economic evaluation of mineral properties, mineral law, etc. At least one-half year of engineering design is included in advanced topics. The use of computers is integrated throughout the specialized course work.

Most petroleum engineering majors receive on-the-job training through summer jobs in industry. Major oil companies recruit for both summer and permanent positions on almost all campuses that offer petroleum engineering degrees. The petroleum industry provides a large number of scholarships for students interested in this field.

Specializations

Well drilling, reservoir analysis, geology, environmental protection, petroleum production, formation evaluation, computer applications, economics.

Other majors to consider

Chemical engineering
Geological engineering
Geology
Mechanical engineering
Mining and mineral engineering

Careers related to the major

Graduates of petroleum engineering programs will find positions available with oil and gas companies, service companies and drilling contractors, pipeline companies, consulting firms, and financial institutions. Some jobs primarily involve fieldwork supervising drilling or production operations, and others primarily involve office work. Some positions are highly technical, and others deal mainly with business management. Some of the jobs available are: energy company management, drilling engineer, production engineer, reservoir engineer, research engineer, environmental protection manager, safety manager, computer applications specialist.

For more information

Society of Petroleum Engineers
Career Guidance Committee
222 Palisades Creek Drive
Richardson, TX 75080
(800)456-6863

Health Sciences and Services

BONNIE BULLOUGH

State University of New York University at Buffalo

The health care industry, one of the fastest-growing sectors of the American economy, employs more than seven million workers in a vast array of jobs. The job titles vary, and the training necessary to fill these jobs ranges from brief on-the-job orientation to lengthy postgraduate education. The schools and departments within universities that prepare students for positions in health care are almost universally called schools or departments of health sciences or services. They share a common base in the biological sciences but vary in their other requirements and in the clinical training they offer.

Students are prepared for professional, scientific, and managerial positions in the health care industry. Although some jobs require a master's degree or a doctorate, other interesting and important positions require a bachelor's degree. Moreover, because of their common basis in the biological sciences, graduates of the four-year programs can use their preparation as a stepping stone if they decide to seek advanced training in specialties at the master's and doctoral levels.

Health workers and health care settings

Health care institutions are the usual workplace for most health care professionals. Included are acute care hospitals, long-term hospital facilities, mental hospitals, and nursing homes for short- and long-term care. Each group of health care professionals contributes its own special expertise to the work of these institutions.

When the patient enters the hospital, a diagnostic process usually begins. Medical technologists who are experts in clinical laboratory science carry out a variety of laboratory procedures that facilitate the diagnosis.

For certain diagnoses nuclear technologists are necessary. Applying the principles of nuclear physics to identify cells, they use sophisticated scanning devices to produce pictures that provide detailed knowledge of the inner workings of the body.

Registered nurses not only participate in making diagnoses; they also administer medications and treatments, provide comfort measures, teach patients about their illnesses, and supervise the work of ancillary hospital workers. Pharmacists provide the drugs used in treatment and monitor the drug therapy to make sure it is safe and appropriate. As treatment regimens have become more complex, pharmacists have increasingly been called on to ensure that the various drugs do not interact with each other to harm the patient.

As patients recover, they may need the help of a physical therapist, who teaches them to exercise to regain the function of an injured limb or to position themselves to reduce pain. Occupational therapists may help them alter their lifestyle to adjust to an illness, and speech therapists may teach stroke victims to talk again.

Graduates of programs in medical records administration are hired to organize hospital charts and other data for quick and accurate retrieval. Although computers have made record keeping easier in many ways, they have also made it more complex if only because the quantity of paper has increased. Medical records administrators keep the system from becoming chaotic; thus clinicians receive accurate and timely data about patients. They also preserve records over time to prepare for new admissions or to share important data with providers of ambulatory health care.

Because hospitals are complex organizations, in recent years they have sought out managers who are prepared in schools of health services administration. These managers must be able to work with a variety of people, to implement and monitor complex systems, and to deal effectively with government agencies and insurance companies. The position is fascinating and challenging.

Although other health care institutions use many of the same workers as hospitals do, the emphasis is different. In long-term care institutions—skilled nursing facilities, mental hospitals, and nursing homes—the specialists in rehabilitation are particularly important. They include physical therapists, occupational therapists, speech and audiology specialists, and even specialists in music and art therapy. Without their services patients may remain unnecessarily disabled. The therapists help patients function as well as possible. Nurses in these settings often coordinate the work of the various team members.

Health care is also provided in community settings such as ambulatory clinics, offices, and clients' homes. Other members of the health care team include dental hygienists, who provide preventive dental care by cleaning teeth and teaching oral hygiene. Athletic trainers, a recent addition to the health care team, work on high school, college, and professional playing fields where they give emergency care for trauma, participate in rehabilitation after injuries occur, and teach athletes how to prevent future injuries. Some also work in health clubs and similar sites where they teach adults how to exercise to improve their health.

Much of the work of speech pathologists and audiology specialists is community-based. In schools and clinics they test hearing, evaluate speech problems, and teach clients how to overcome speech problems. Physical therapists also are often community-based.

Education for careers in the health sciences

With the exception of health services administrators, health science majors are linked by core content in the biological sciences. Even majors in medical records administration, speech pathology, and occupational health take one or two biological science courses. A longer sequence is required for majors in pharmacology, nursing, clinical laboratory science, nuclear technology, dental hygiene, physical therapy, and athletic training. This sequence usually includes chemistry, anatomy, physiology, microbiology, and pathophysiology. Physics or pharmacology may be added as appropriate. Because mathematics is a prerequisite for science courses, mathematics is a basic requirement in health sciences.

The fact that so many of the health sciences start with a sequence of courses in the biological sciences facilitates transfer from one major to another if candidates decide early that they have chosen the wrong health science for their talents and interests. It also facilitates postgraduate education in the advanced health science majors (medicine, dentistry, veterinary medicine, and research science). The biological science required for a particular bachelor's degree may not be sufficient for acceptance into graduate-level health science majors, but it certainly provides a good beginning.

Because working with clients is a crucial component of health science jobs, behavioral sciences—psychology, sociology, anthropology—are required. English is a requirement for all health science majors, and a foreign language can be very useful to the health worker.

High school background

The broadest possible academic preparation in secondary school is best for the prospective major in the health sciences. Mastery of basic English and mathematics is essential. Biology, chemistry, and physics are often prerequisites for college programs. Social science increases the understanding of human behavior and is needed for most health care occupations. A foreign language can offer additional opportunities to those health professionals who work directly with the public, because many clients are not fluent in English. Sometimes a premium is paid to a worker who is fluent in Spanish, the language most in demand. Knowledge of another culture may also facilitate communication. Members of ethnic minority groups who have firsthand knowledge of another culture are particularly welcome in the health professions.

Choosing a college

Most of the health sciences and services schools are accredited by the state. Also, the professional organization that speaks for a specific health profession will ordinarily send interested candidates a list of nationally accredited programs. The institution's catalog should indicate the program's accreditation as well as the number of faculty members and their education level. A visit to the campus can help students evaluate the quality of the classroom and laboratory space, the adequacy of the library, and aspects of student life.

Athletic training

Majors in athletic training learn to prevent, recognize, refer, and treat injuries and illnesses sustained by athletes. The study of exercise sciences and the medical aspects of sport, together with clinical experience, prepares students for national certification in the field.

Interests, skills, and qualities associated with success in the major

Interests. Sports, helping others, health and medicine, physical fitness and exercise, daily challenges.

Skills and qualities. Manual skills, science (especially anatomy and biology), problem solving, interpersonal communication, perseverance, loyalty, integrity.

Recommended high school preparation

English 4, precollege mathematics 2.5, biology 1, chemistry 1, physics 1, social studies 1, history 1, foreign language 2–4, and computer science 1.

Typical courses in the major

Anatomy	Physiology
Health	Nutrition
Exercise Physiology	Kinesiology
First Aid	Cardiopulmonary Resuscitation
Psychology	Basic Athletic Training
Advanced Athletic Training	Management Techniques
Rehabilitation Techniques	

What the major is like

The major in athletic training is concerned with the prevention, recognition, and management of athletic, sport, and exercise-related injuries and illnesses. Knowledge of human anatomy, physiology, pathology, and body mechanics is combined with practical skills in two areas: prevention and rehabilitation. Students learn to evaluate and manage injuries in clinical settings. Successful completion of the program qualifies students for national certification, the entry-level standard in this health-care profession.

Students study academic and clinical sciences in order to supervise the conditioning and safety practices of athletic teams and of those who play sports. They learn to develop systems of on-site injury surveillance and to determine through examination whether an injury requires acute care and medical referral. Students also develop background in the management of injuries as members of health care teams so that under the direction of a physician they can administer treatment: whirlpool baths, ultrasound, electrical stimulation, taping, splints, and exercise. They develop critical skills in leadership and communication through extensive clinical interaction with coaches, physicians, administrators, athletes, and parents of athletes.

Students typically begin their programs with elementary science courses and an introduction to athletic training. It is important that students be aware of choices within these programs, because progress in the clinical applications of their skills generally requires the successful completion of prerequisites and exposure to athletic training or sports medicine. While in high school, students should, if possible, work as a student manager or trainer, attend summer athletic training camps, volunteer in sports medicine clinics, and spend time with athletic trainers.

Majors in athletic training receive directed clinical experience of at least 800 hours. Typically, this involves a broad range of sports: contact and noncontact, male and female, team and individual. Clinical settings are both on- and off-campus in athletic training rooms and practice and game facilities. Students may also get clinical experience in sports medicine clinics in hospitals or private settings. At least two academic years are needed to complete this clinical experience.

Specializations

Specialization is not generally available.

Other majors to consider

Counseling psychology
Health science
Nursing
Physical therapy
Physician's assistant
Psychology

Careers related to the major

With a bachelor's degree in athletic training one can find entry-level positions as an athletic trainer in schools, sports medicine clinics, and industrial/government settings. With a master's degree and experience in the field, one can work as an athletic trainer in collegiate and professional sports and be an administrator in sports medicine clinics and agencies. With a doctorate, one can teach and do research on athletic training programs.

For more information

National Athletic Trainers Association, Inc.
2952 Stemmons
Dallas, TX 75247
(214)637-6282

American Medical Association
515 North State Street
Chicago, IL 60610
(312)464-4660

Clinical laboratory science

Students majoring in clinical laboratory science learn to perform medical tests to determine the presence and cause of disease. The program consists of a solid concentration of basic sciences and professional courses in clinical laboratory studies.

Interests, skills, and qualities associated with success in the major

Interests. Solving problems and puzzles, games that involve analytic reasoning, working with complex machinery, computer science, laboratory work, helping others, medicine, biological science, observing and understanding what makes things work.

Skills and qualities. Computation, logic, analytic skills, computer skills, pattern recognition, communication skills, grasp of basic scientific principles, hand-eye coordination.

Recommended high school preparation

English 3, precollege mathematics 3, biology 2–3, chemistry 1–2, physics 1, social studies 2, history 2, foreign language 2, music 1, visual arts 1, and computer science 2.

Typical courses in the major

Botany	Zoology
Human Anatomy/Physiology	Cell Physiology
Genetics	Microbiology
Inorganic Chemistry	Organic Chemistry
Computer Science	Algebra
Statistics	Biochemistry
Hematology	Hemostasis
Microbiology	Immunology
Immunohematology	Education Techniques
Management Techniques	Quality Assurance

What the major is like

The major in clinical laboratory science (formerly called medical laboratory technology) prepares students to apply their knowledge of and skills in the basic sciences to laboratory testing in health care, research, industry, or government agencies. This major may be found in departments of biology, chemistry, natural sciences, or life sciences, or in schools of health professions, allied health and/or nursing, or medicine. Whatever its location, an accredited clinical laboratory science program can be described as follows.

To gain a sound foundation for later clinical studies, students take a number of science courses in the first two or three years of the program. Basic principles of the cell are studied in plants (botany) and in animals (zoology). Courses in human anatomy and/or physiology, genetics, and microbiology follow. Advanced cell physiology may also be studied. Chemistry courses include the study of inorganic and organic compounds and biochemistry. Algebra, statistics, or both are required, and courses in chemical analysis and computer science are useful.

The clinical portion of the program is a cooperative arrangement between a university or college and one or more medical laboratory education programs accredited by the American Medical Association. In this clinical program students spend 12 to 24 months (that is, their third and/or fourth years) learning the theory, procedures, equipment, and practices of clinical laboratory science. During this period in a medical laboratory they learn to test body fluids and tissues to determine the presence, absence, extent, or cause of disease.

Clinical laboratory scientists are also expected to recognize and solve problems in testing, to teach and supervise others, and to participate with physicians, nurses, and other professionals in the health care team by assisting in the interpretation of test results. Courses in education techniques, management and supervision, and quality assurance are therefore also included in the clinical curriculum. Successful completion of the program entitles students to medical certificates in addition to their degrees. They then take national examinations for certification.

Acceptance into a clinical program, after completion of preclinical course work, is competitive and by no means guaranteed. The clinical programs are not obliged by their agreements with local colleges and universities to accept all candidates. Students compete with other applicants for available spaces. In this competition, grades in preclinical courses are critically important. Students should consult with their college advisers about the process of entering the clinical program.

Specializations

Clinical chemistry, clinical hematology, clinical immunohematology, clinical microbiology.

Other majors to consider

Biochemistry
Biology
Biomedical equipment technology
Chemistry
Predentistry
Premedicine
Preveterinary

Careers related to the major

Certified clinical laboratory scientists are in demand in the fields of medicine, industry, research, management, and teaching. Positions that this major leads to include: clinical laboratory scientist (laboratory technologist), research analyst, forensic analyst, industrial technical/marketing representative, risk manager (in health care), infection control officer, environmental health officer, public health/epidemiological control officer, laboratory information manager. Advanced degrees are usually needed to work as a laboratory manager, college teacher, or clinical laboratory program director. With appropriate graduate work, students may become a physician or surgeon, dentist, veterinarian, health administrator, or business manager.

For more information

American Society for Medical Technology (ASMT)
2021 L Street NW, Suite 400
Washington, DC 20036
(202)785-3311

American Medical Association
515 North State Street
Chicago, IL 60610
(312)464-4660

Dental hygiene

Majors in dental hygiene obtain the knowledge and clinical skills needed to provide preventive oral health care. Courses in basic and dental sciences, as well as extensive direct patient care, prepare students to become licensed dental hygienists.

Interests, skills, and qualities associated with success in the major	**Interests.** Working with people, helping individuals maintain their health, detail-oriented activities.

Skills and qualities. Highly developed motor skills of the hand, communication.

Recommended high school preparation

English 3, precollege mathematics 3, biology 1, chemistry 1, social studies 1, and history 1.

Typical courses in the major

Anatomy
Microbiology
Pharmacology
Chemistry
Pathology
Pain Control
Nutrition
Infection and Hazard Control

Patient Management
Radiology
Dental Hygiene Techniques
Preventive Oral Care
Health Education
Dental Materials
Ethics

What the major is like

Majors in dental hygiene learn to provide preventive oral health services. The primary responsibility of dental hygienists is to assist patients in achieving and maintaining oral health. They are therefore required to master a wide range of skills related to oral and dental health and patient education.

Specific training varies from state to state, but students are usually taught to perform the following: patient assessment, which includes a medical history, blood pressure, examination of head, neck, and mouth, and oral cancer screening; exposing dental x-rays; removal of deposits from the teeth (oral prophylaxis); application of decay-preventing agents such as fluoride and fissure sealants; designing and implementing dental health programs; and counseling patients to develop healthful lifestyles.

Many institutions require one to two years of general studies before students enroll in the dental hygiene program, which requires two years to complete. A dental hygiene program may be located in a community college or in a four-year institution. Some programs are affiliated with a dental school.

Students first study basic sciences such as human anatomy, physiology, and pathology in order to gain an understanding of the function of the human body, the process of disease, and the biological and physiological basis of health. Courses in dental hygiene sciences provide the foundation for dental hygiene care and clinical practice. Learning takes place in the classroom, in laboratories, and in clinical experiences. Students develop skills by practicing on models and through direct patient care, which begins in the first year. The provision of dental hygiene services to a large and diverse group of patients in a clinical setting is emphasized.

Much of a dental hygienist's time is spent interacting one-on-one with patients. Students therefore must acquire strong communication and interpersonal skills through courses in psychology, speech, sociology, and patient management.

Outside experiences may include visits to patients in public health clinics, hospitals, child care centers, nursing homes, and correctional facilities. Students may also participate in health fairs, health education presentations, and elementary school activities. Some dental hygiene programs send students to dental offices in the community for real-life experience.

Dental hygiene is a licensed health care profession. Licensure requires graduation from an accredited dental hygiene program plus successful completion of a national written examination and a state's own written and clinical exam.

Specializations   Not generally available.

Other majors to consider   **Medical record administration**
Nursing
Occupational therapy
Physical therapy
Predentistry

Careers related to the major   The majority of dental hygiene graduates work as dental hygienists in private dental offices, although an increasing number work in public health agencies, school systems, hospitals, long-term care facilities, universities, and health care organizations. The major can lead to careers in: clinical dental hygiene, teaching, office management, public health, or sales of dental products. With an appropriate graduate degree, it can enable one to work as a program administrator, researcher, or dentist.

For more information   American Dental Hygienists' Association
444 North Michigan Avenue, Suite 3400
Chicago, IL 60611
(312)440-8900

American Dental Association
211 East Chicago Avenue
Chicago, IL 60611
(312)440-2719
(800)621-8099

Health services management

The major in health services management prepares students for entry-level positions managing a wide variety of health care organizations such as hospitals, nursing homes, insurance companies, and public agencies. The curriculum combines a broad liberal arts background, administrative theory, general management skills, and the more specific knowledge and skills involved in planning and delivering health services.

Interests, skills, and qualities associated with success in the major   **Interests.** Working with people, taking initiative, solving problems, working with data.

Skills and qualities. Oral and written communication, organizational skills, interpersonal skills, understanding and analyzing data, critical thinking.

Recommended high school preparation   English 4, precollege mathematics 4, biology 1, chemistry 1, physics 1, social studies 2, history 1, foreign language 3, and computer science .5.

Typical courses in the major	Introduction to Health Care Economics/Health Economics Organizational Behavior Accounting Statistics Computer/Information Systems Epidemiology Public Health Political Science Health Care Management Health Policy Health Law Ethics Financial Management Strategic Planning Supervised Internship Marketing Health Care

What the major is like

The health services management major is designed for students interested in entry-level positions in the management of health care organizations. The major is typically found in a university's school of business, allied health, or public health.

Health administration students learn how to deliver personal health care to individuals and also to manage effectively health care organizations such as nursing homes, clinics, welfare departments, rehabilitation programs, and general hospitals. Health care delivery is changing dynamically in order to meet the needs of the country's growing population of elderly people, and to improve or change current health care payment systems. Health administrators must be able to understand and solve the complex problems and issues involved in delivering services to people in need.

Students learn to manage the finances of organizations, deal with personnel, understand and comply with the laws that affect health organizations, and to oversee other aspects of administration. They also study how health services and medical care are delivered and examine legal issues related to health care.

The curriculum usually begins with a broad foundation in the liberal arts and focuses on the social sciences, biological sciences, and quantitative skills. In addition, majors typically take basic business courses (organizational behavior, economics, accounting, business statistics) during their first two years.

The health services management program begins in the third year with a series of interrelated courses on the strategies and tactics of health-care management. Programs also require supervised internships (ranging in length from several weeks in the summer to a full semester) within a health care organization, giving students the opportunity to gain practical experience and to apply their classroom learning.

Specializations

Long-term care administration.

Other majors to consider

Business administration
Computer science
Public administration

Careers related to the major

Graduates of health services management programs obtain entry-level positions in management of health care organizations such as hospitals, nursing homes, home health agencies, health maintenance organizations, insurance companies, and public health agencies. The major also prepares one for graduate study in health management, public policy, law, and clinical degree programs.

For more information

Association of University Programs in Health Administration
1911 North Fort Myer Drive, Suite 503
Arlington, VA 22209
(703)524-5500

Medical record administration

A major in medical record administration merges the study of business and medicine. Students prepare to direct medical record departments in varied health care settings by exploring the health care environment, health care organizations, clinical information systems, medical record department operations, and health care reimbursement systems.

Interests, skills, and qualities associated with success in the major

Interests. Leadership, working with people, designing and implementing systems, problem solving, working with detail.

Skills and qualities. Writing and speaking effectively, organization and management, analytic and problem-solving skills, working in groups, working in a changing environment.

Recommended high school preparation

English 4, precollege mathematics 3, biology 1, social studies 3, foreign language 4, and computer science 1.

Typical courses in the major

Clinical Information Systems
Biomedical Computing
Health Care Statistics
Quality Assurance
Medical Record Operations

Hospital Management
Health Care Law
Health Care Delivery Systems
Health Care Financial Management

What the major is like

The major in medical record administration prepares students to supervise and manage medical record departments in a variety of health care settings. In many colleges the major is called health information management. At some, it is referred to as health record administration.

Courses in the first two years of college serve as a foundation both for specialized course work in the major and for the overall development of the student. Typical prerequisites include the biological sciences, computer sciences, statistics, mathematics, accounting, and English.

Students generally begin their specialized course work in the junior year. They study the organization of the health care delivery system in the United States; the organization of hospitals and medical staff; and medical science, including the study of medical terminology and disease processes. They learn about the origin and use of medical records; coding of information contained in medical records; legal aspects of health care, including the U.S. legal system, malpractice, confidentiality and security of information contained in medical records and other medical documents, and hospital risk management. In addition they explore health care financial reimbursement systems, data base management, health information systems management, and learn to analyze health care data to support decision making.

Most classes in the major follow the lecture-discussion format. Students apply the knowledge and skills they learned in the classroom or laboratory in clinical settings, or through individual or group projects. Students may also be asked to prepare oral and written reports.

During the final year of study, each student interns at a health care delivery site for a concentrated period, usually a minimum of four weeks.

Under supervision, the student participates in all aspects of medical record administration, including working on specific projects, supervising employees, and attending medical staff and administrative committee meetings. Students report their clinical experiences to their classmates and program faculty.

On graduation from an accredited program in medical record administration, students are eligible to take the national certifying examination for the Registered Record Administrator (RRA) credential, administered by the American Medical Record Association.

Specializations

Not generally available.

Other majors to consider

Health services management

Careers related to the major

The medical record administration major prepares graduates for entry-level supervisory jobs in the medical record department of a variety of health care settings (hospitals, clinics, long-term care facilities). One may also work as a quality assurance coordinator, utilization review coordinator, or sales representative. With appropriate graduate degrees, one may work as a health care researcher, health care administrator, or medical record educator.

For more information

American Medical Record Association
919 North Michigan Avenue, Suite 1400
Chicago, IL 60611

Accrediting Commission on Education for Health Services Adm.
1911 North Fort Myer Drive, Suite 503
Arlington, VA 22209

American Medical Association
515 North State Street
Chicago, IL 60610
(312)464-4660

Nuclear medical technology

Nuclear medical technology majors learn to use radioactive drugs to diagnose and treat a variety of abnormal health conditions. Students learn to prepare and administer radioactive drugs to patients, operate radiation detection equipment, and perform the calculations or computer analysis needed to complete the patient's examination.

Interests, skills, and qualities associated with success in the major

Interests. Biological sciences, new technologies, helping others, working in a medical setting, working with people.

Skills and qualities. The sciences (particularly biological and physical sciences), working with others, empathy for others, motivation, analytic skills, communication skills, personal organization, working independently.

Recommended high school preparation

English 4, precollege mathematics 3, biology 2, chemistry 1, physics 1, social studies 1, history 1, and computer science 1.

Typical courses in the major

Patient Care
Nuclear Medicine Physics
Radiopharmacology
Radiochemistry
Radionuclide Therapy
Medical Ethics
Diagnostic Procedures

Radiation Safety
Nuclear Instrumentation
Radiation Biology
Radioimmunoassay Procedures
Computer Applications
Clinical Education

What the major is like

Majors in nuclear medical technology learn to use radioactive tracers to study normal and abnormal bodily functions and to treat certain diseases. A radiotracer, or radiopharmaceutical, is a radioactive drug; when administered to a patient, it can be detected outside the body by use of equipment. Under the direction of a radiologist (a physician who specializes in the field), a nuclear medical technologist prepares and administers radiopharmaceuticals; operates equipment that measures the quantity and distribution of the drug in the patient; and performs calculations or computer analysis needed to complete the patient's examination.

In general, nuclear medical procedures can be divided into three areas: organ imaging, radioactive analysis of biological specimens, and radiotherapy. The most commonly performed procedure is organ imaging. When a radiopharmaceutical is administered to the patient, it circulates throughout the body and eventually concentrates in the organ under exploration. For example, the thyroid gland absorbs radioactive iodine, allowing the technologist to photograph the organ with radiation detection equipment.

Students begin their studies by completing foundation courses in human anatomy, physiology, chemistry, physics, mathematics, statistics, and computer analysis. In addition, students take courses in the liberal arts. (Some nuclear medical programs require two years of foundation courses and two years of specialized courses. Students should be clear about the requirements of the program they wish to attend.) On completion of the foundation courses, students apply to an accredited nuclear medical technology program—usually at a medical sciences campus. Students receive a bachelor's degree following four years of study, although some associate degree programs are available. On completion of degree requirements, students must pass a national certified examination before entering the profession.

In the specialized component of the nuclear medical technology program, students attend classes and also receive hands-on hospital experience with patients. The program is demanding and rigorous, and prospective students are encouraged to visit a nuclear medicine department to learn from technologists and program chairmen what is expected of students.

Nuclear medicine is an excellent choice for students who are interested in the biological sciences and would like to work in a medical profession but who do not wish to become a physician or a nurse. On the other hand, many students choose nuclear medicine as their undergraduate major in preparation for medical school.

Specializations

Magnetic resonance imaging, diagnostic medical sonography, radiopharmaceuticals, radiological/health physics.

Other majors to consider

Biology
Clinical laboratory science
Computer science
Nursing
Pharmacy
Physics
Radiograph medical technology

Careers related to the major

On completing the program, students are prepared to work as nuclear medicine technologists. Most jobs are in hospitals. Technologists often move to management positions or choose to specialize in computer applications, radiopharmaceutical preparation, or sales. Choices open to technologists with graduate degrees include jobs as health physicists or radiation safety officers, educators, and administrators.

For more information

American Medical Association
515 North State Street
Chicago, IL 60610
(312)464-4660

Nursing

Majors in nursing learn how to care for those who are ill; how to rehabilitate, counsel, and educate patients; and how to work as part of a health care team in many settings. They study humanities, natural sciences, and nursing theory in order to serve individuals, families, groups, and communities.

Interests, skills, and qualities associated with success in the major

Interests. Students of nursing need to be capable of developing new interests, attitudes, and career aspirations that will enable them to provide intimate helping services to people who need competent, sensitive, humane, and ethical care.

Skills and qualities. Systematic, comprehensive, and clear thinking; clear writing and speaking; independent decision making.

Recommended high school preparation

English 4, precollege mathematics 3, biology 1, chemistry 1, physics .5, social studies .5, anthropology, psychology, sociology, history .5, foreign language 2, and computer science .5.

Typical courses in the major

Human Anatomy
Human Physiology
Nutrition
Organic Chemistry
Sociology
Anthropology
Human Development
Pathology

Mathematics
Physics
Inorganic Chemistry
Psychology
Animal Biology
Microbiology
Pharmacology

What the major is like

The nursing major trains students to provide the care that is needed by all kinds of people. That includes instructing healthy people about good health practices—giving pregnant women information about prenatal care, for example. Nurses give direct care to patients who are infirm, ill, disabled, and dying and also to those who are troubled, lonely, abused, incarcerated, or homeless. Nursing students learn to respond to changing situations and conditions.

Students learn to work as a member of a medical team. Toward this end, they are trained in classrooms, in laboratories, and in a variety of settings where people need nursing care. The curriculum reflects the current need for nurses to serve people in a variety of settings—hospitals, nursing homes, clinics, the home.

In their first two years nursing majors complete liberal arts courses in English, social sciences, the humanities, and natural sciences. They then concentrate on nursing courses, in which they learn to combine knowledge gained in studying the humanities and sciences with nursing theory. They learn how to meet the health care needs of individuals and groups and to respond to changing health needs and services. They learn to evaluate current research to determine its benefit to nursing practice. They examine nurse-client relationships and the organization of health care delivery. They study ethical and practical issues related to death and acute illness. They also examine ways of providing care to culturally diverse communities. They gain clinical practice by working, under supervision, in hospitals, long-term care facilities, schools, community health organizations, mental health/psychiatric institutions, and other settings.

Some programs require a senior internship in which the student works with a practicing nurse and receives academic credit while getting first-hand experience. There may be opportunities for paid summer work experience.

After completing a bachelor's degree, the graduate must pass the National Council of State Boards of Nursing Licensure Examinations for Registered Nurses.

Specializations

The undergraduate program in nursing is usually general. In the future, more undergraduate programs may offer specialization in areas such as critical care or nursing home care.

Other majors to consider

Dental hygiene
Gerontology
Nutritional sciences
Occupational therapy
Pharmacy
Physical therapy
Social work
Speech pathology/audiology

Careers related to the major

The nursing profession is the most rapidly growing occupation for college graduates. The shortage of nursing students is expected to continue into the next century. Men and women educated as professional nurses are and will be in demand in a variety of jobs and settings, among them public and community health agencies, physicians' offices, clinics, hospitals, schools, factories, prisons, wellness centers, the Red Cross, home and foreign missions, youth camps, professional organizations, mental health agencies, the armed forces, rehabilitation centers, in-home care, insurance companies, and private practice.

For more information

The American Association of Colleges of Nursing
One Dupont Circle, Suite 530
Washington, DC 20036
(202)463-6930

National League for Nursing
350 Hudson Street
New York, NY 10014
(212)989-9393
(800)669-1656

Occupational therapy

Majors in occupational therapy learn to treat performance problems due to physical, psychological, social, and developmental problems. Students learn to help patients function independently so that they may work, play, take care of themselves, and relate to others in a productive and satisfying manner.

Interests, skills, and qualities associated with success in the major

Interests. Solving puzzles in creative ways, intellectual challenges, working with people, technology, medicine, health, rehabilitation.

Skills and qualities. Life sciences, logical thinking, listening, articulate verbal and written communication, working with others, flexibility, problem solving.

Recommended high school preparation

English 4, precollege mathematics 3–4, biology 1, chemistry 1, physics 1, social studies 2, history 2, foreign language 2–3, music 1, visual arts 1, and computer science 1–2.

Typical courses in the major

Biology	Research Methods
Statistics	Biomechanics
Human Development	Physiology
Activities Theory	Human Occupation
Pediatrics	Therapeutic Media
Management	Psychology
Sociology	Anatomy
Ergonomics	Kinesiology

Neurological Conditions   Adaptive Equipment
Gerontology   Occupational Therapy Theory

What the major is like   The occupational therapy program is currently offered by approximately 75 colleges and universities, all accredited by the American Occupational Therapy Association, which supplies a list of accredited programs on request. The programs include study of normal maturation, development, and function; the effect and consequence of diseases, trauma, or aging; and the varied ways in which therapists can assist persons whose performance of routine activities has become threatened or impaired by conditions causing physical or psychosocial disabilities.

Occupational therapy majors learn to evaluate people's performance of simple and complex everyday tasks using a variety of assessment tools. Therapists also assess the individual's personal goals within the context of the demands of his or her environment. Using various purposeful activities, in individual or group settings, therapists guide clients to function more independently and to maximize their abilities. In schools, hospitals, health agencies, industry, and residential facilities, occupational therapists work with individuals of all ages who have conditions that cause performance problems. They offer specialized assistance that enables disabled individuals to perform the daily life activities of work, play, self-care, and relating to others in a productive and satisfying manner.

Students receive a foundation in liberal arts and then take courses to master the specific skills of an occupational therapist. Approximately 50 percent of the total course work is taken in the humanities, fine arts, and natural and social sciences, most of it during the freshman and sophomore years. The last two years are generally devoted to the combined theory and practice courses that constitute the actual occupational therapy major.

At some institutions the therapy courses and liberal arts courses are integrated over the full four-year program. At others, the liberal arts component is taken during the first two years and the therapy component follows. At some of these latter institutions, students must apply to enter the therapy program just before beginning the junior year. At others acceptance into the major as a freshman guarantees admission to the program. It is also possible to complete the liberal arts courses at any two- or four-year college and then transfer, as a junior, into the accredited occupational therapy program.

Class size, laboratory facilities, and class formats vary, but all programs integrate field experiences into the program (fieldwork 1). Students observe and then treat patients or clients under the close supervision of occupational therapists at hospitals, schools, or other facilities where occupational therapy is practiced. This fieldwork may be weekly or in a concentrated time block and generally offers students experience in a wide variety of clinical settings.

All programs also include six to nine months of subsequent, full-time fieldwork (fieldwork 2). This work is scheduled in two- or three-month blocks at hospitals, schools, or other agencies. Like fieldwork 1, it is under the supervision of a fully qualified occupational therapist. During this portion of their training, students receive hands-on experience that integrates their academic studies and clinical training in preparation for occupational therapy practice.

After completing an accredited program, students may take the National Certificate Examination, administered in January and July by the American Occupational Therapy Certification Board. If successful, the graduate becomes an occupational therapist, registered (OTR). Many states require their own licenses, usually based on the results of the national examination.

Specializations

Pediatrics, psychosocial dysfunction, rehabilitation, developmental disabilities, infants at risk, academic occupational therapy, school-based therapy, physical disabilities, work and industrial ergonomics, geriatrics, research education.

Other majors to consider

Anatomy
Art therapy
Behavioral sciences
Biology
Music therapy
Physical therapy
Psychology
Recreation therapy
Rehabilitation counseling/services
Social work

Careers related to the major

Health care trends in recent years have resulted in a significant demand for occupational therapists. Job openings for occupational therapists exist in hospitals, health agencies, schools, industries, and private practices. Related careers include case manager, agency administrator, health planner, researcher, industrial ergonomist, and educator. Graduate study in occupational therapy or a closely related area can enhance therapists' job options.

For more information

American Occupational Therapy Association, Inc.
1383 Piccard Drive
P.O. Box 1725
Rockville, MD 20849-1725
(301)948-9626

American Medical Association
515 North State Street
Chicago, IL 60610
(312)464-4660

Pharmacy

Pharmacy majors learn to provide drug products and drug information in all areas of patient care. They also learn to monitor drug therapy in order to ensure that the treatment is appropriate, safe, therapeutically effective, and cost-effective.

Interests, skills, and qualities associated with success in the major

Interests. Chemistry, biology, math, solving problems, helping others, lifelong learning.

Skills and qualities. Written and oral communication, patience, tact, adapting to change, working carefully, thoroughly, and cooperatively under pressure.

Recommended high school preparation

English 4, precollege mathematics 3–4, biology 1, chemistry 1–2, physics 1, social studies 1, speech .5–1, and computer science .5–1.

Typical courses in the major

Chemistry	Microbiology
Biochemistry	Medicinal Chemistry
Calculus	Biology
Organic Chemistry	Computer Science
Anatomy	Physiology
Pathophysiology	Pharmaceutics
Pharmacokinetics	Pharmacology
Pharmacy Law	Pharmacy Practice
Management and Marketing	Therapeutics
Pharmacy Externship	

What the major is like

The major in pharmacy prepares students to provide the drugs used in treatment of disease and to monitor drug therapy. Traditionally, the pharmacist has been concerned with dispensing medicines to fill physicians' prescriptions for patients. Since the early 1960s, however, there has been a growing trend for the pharmacist to work more closely with the physician, other health professionals, and the patient to help assure appropriate use of an ever-increasing spectrum of effective medications. Overall, the pharmacist is expected to provide services that help ensure appropriate, safe, cost-effective, and therapeutically effective drug therapy for the condition being treated. A particular emphasis is educating and motivating patients to manage their drug therapy as it relates to their particular medical condition.

Programs at the 75 accredited colleges of pharmacy in the United States prepare students to provide these services. Some admit students directly into the program from high school; others require one or two years of prepharmacy study. In the first two years of college, almost all programs require general chemistry, organic chemistry, biology, mathematics, microbiology, and general education (including the social and behavioral sciences and English). Some also require physics and computer science.

In the remaining years the curriculum focuses on the physiology and biochemistry of the human body, both in health and on appropriate drugs and drug therapy to diagnose, treat, or prevent disease. Emphasis is placed on monitoring drug therapy for its outcomes and on providing information to patients and other health professionals about drugs. Students also study the management and legal aspects of the profession of pharmacy. Also, all schools of pharmacy require a structured externship/clerkship program in which students work in clinical settings for academic credit.

Majors may work toward a bachelor's degree in pharmacy (five years) or a doctorate in pharmacy (Pharm.D., six years) as the first professional degree. The Pharm.D. is considered an advanced professional degree in that additional courses are required in therapeutics, drug information, pharmacokinetics (the monitoring of blood levels of drugs to determine precise dosage), patient drug therapy monitoring, statistics, pathophysiology (disease processes), and advanced clinical clerkships. Because of the continuing complexity of pharmacy services, it has been predicted that by the twenty-first century the doctor of Pharmacy (Pharm.D.) will be the only professional degree in the field.

Thus, during the next decade, pharmacists will probably provide an even wider range of pharmaceutical services than now—especially in view of the rapid advances in biotechnology and the use of computers. It is likely that pharmacists will use technical personnel to perform tasks that do not require professional judgment. They will use available patient data, information sources, and interpretive skills to provide knowledge about the use and monitoring of drugs. The curricula in schools of pharmacy in the United States are being studied and changed for this increasingly important and complex role of the pharmacist.

Specializations

Hospital pharmacy, community pharmacy, home health care, long-term care pharmacy, nuclear pharmacy, quality control, production, research.

Other majors to consider

Biochemistry
Biology
Chemistry
Health science
Predentistry
Premedicine

Careers related to the major

With a professional degree in pharmacy, one can work as a manager of a pharmacy in a hospital or clinical setting, as a district manager of chain pharmacies, a clinical specialist in pharmaceutical care, or a quality control supervisor in the pharmaceutical industry. With appropriate graduate degrees, one can pursue careers in academia, clinical drug research, medicine, dentistry, or law.

For more information

American Association of Colleges of Pharmacy
1426 Prince Street
Alexandria, VA 22314-8982

National Association of Chain Drug Stores
413 North Lee Street
Alexandria, VA 22314

American Pharmaceutical Association
2215 Constitution Avenue NW
Washington, DC 20037

American Council on Pharmaceutical Education
311 West Superior Street, Suite 512
Chicago, IL 60610
(312)664-3575

Physical therapy

The major in physical therapy prepares students to take state licensure examinations in this field and thus qualify for service in the prevention of disabilities and the rehabilitation of the disabled. Students learn to test, evaluate, and plan a treatment program for patients who are physically incapacitated as the result of accidents or disease and for healthy individuals who wish to prevent injuries in work or recreational settings.

Interests, skills, and qualities associated with success in the major

Interests. Biological and physical sciences, exercise and fitness, people, analytic reasoning.

Skills and qualities. Interpersonal communication, problem solving, visual/spatial perception, natural curiosity, emotional sensitivity.

Recommended high school preparation

English 4, precollege mathematics 3, biology 1, chemistry 1, physics 1, social studies 1, history 1, foreign language 2, and computer science 1.

Typical courses in the major

Anatomy
Human Development
Electrotherapy
Clinical Practicum
Kinesiology
Psychology
Physical Therapy Exercise

Physiology
Neurology
Research
Neuroanatomy
Orthopedics
Health Policy

What the major is like

At most institutions students who want to major in physical therapy enroll in the general college for their first two years. They complete prerequisite courses in biology, chemistry, physics, English, and social sciences before applying to the physical therapy program as juniors. Enrollment in the major is usually limited, and admission is highly competitive. A few institutions admit students to physical therapy as freshmen, and many accept advanced and older, returning students.

The curriculum emphasizes biological sciences during the first year of the program and usually includes human anatomic dissection, pathology, and biomechanics. Subsequently students develop skills in evaluation and treatment. Students learn to test the patient's functional capacity and any sensory, musculoskeletal, neurological, or physiological impairments that result in disability. Treatments often include exercise for increasing strength, endurance, coordination, and range of movement; the application of heat, cold, electrical stimulation, or ultrasound to relieve pain and stimulate muscular activity; and patient education in functional activities, use of assistive devices, and injury prevention.

Students spend many hours in physical therapy laboratories practicing evaluation and treatment techniques on one another, and throughout the curriculum they also work with patients in clinical experiences. Most programs conclude with 12 to 16 weeks of full-time clinical experience. The entire program requires 21 to 24 months.

All physical therapy education programs are accredited by the Commission on Accreditation in Education of the American Physical Therapy Association and meet specified national standards. Entry-level programs are also offered at the master's level at some institutions; the trend within the profession is toward such advanced education.

Specializations

Cardiopulmonary disorders, geriatrics, orthopedics, sports, electrophysiology, neurology, pediatrics.

Other majors to consider

Athletic training
Occupational therapy
Predentistry
Premedicine
Recreation therapy

Careers related to the major

Physical therapists work in hospitals, extended-care facilities, home health agencies, public and private schools, industry, programs for the developmentally disabled, and private clinics. Physical therapists may advance their careers by working toward certification as clinical specialists, obtaining advanced academic degrees, or accepting administrative, teaching, or research positions.

For more information

American Physical Therapy Association
1111 North Fairfax Street
Alexandria, VA 22314
(703)706-3245
(800)999-2782

Speech pathology/audiology

Students who major in speech pathology and audiology (speech therapy and hearing therapy) receive training in the identification and treatment of human communication disorders. They learn about the normal processes of speech and language development, why problems may occur, and what can be done to minimize their impact.

Interests, skills, and qualities associated with success in the major

Interests. Working with children, working with adults, identifying and solving behavioral problems, applying technology to human needs.

Skills and qualities. Oral and written communication skills, creativity, working cooperatively in groups.

Recommended high school preparation

English 3, precollege mathematics 2, biology 2, chemistry 1, physics 1, history or social studies 2, and computer science 1.

Typical courses in the major	Language Development	Articulation
	Speech and Hearing Science	Fluency Disorders
	Clinical Experience	Voice Disorders
	Hearing Testing	Language Disorders
	Diagnostics	Anatomy

What the major is like

The undergraduate major in speech pathology/audiology, which prepares students for subsequent professional study at the master's level, provides an understanding of normal and defective hearing and speech. Students learn to identify and evaluate human communication disorders and study available treatment. In introductory courses, they study normal voice, speech, and language processes and the symptoms of disorders. Through the study of anatomy and physiology, they learn the physical bases of how people produce and perceive speech. They examine what might cause speech and hearing problems and how treatment programs are formed and carried out. They read research reports on speech disorders in order to apply findings to treatment programs and to determine what further research needs to be done. They may study stuttering, voice disorders, aphasia, and other common disorders.

While students are pursuing their major, they also complete requirements in academic areas that support the core courses of the major. These typically include biology and physical sciences, behavioral and social sciences, and course work in liberal arts and sciences as required by the specific institution.

The typical curriculum in speech pathology and audiology is additive: each succeeding course is based on knowledge and skills developed in previous courses. Students often start the major as freshmen with an introductory course and proceed with courses in normal and abnormal processes in speech, language, and hearing behavior.

Although most courses follow the lecture format, technological advances provide varied learning experiences—for example, interactive computer instruction and the use of video and laser disk programs.

Undergraduate students usually get clinical experience by working in the college speech and hearing clinic, under close supervision, with children and adults who need to have problems diagnosed or treated.

After receiving their undergraduate degree, students typically complete the master's degree, which is required in most states for certification in this field.

Specializations

There are no specializations at the undergraduate level.

Other majors to consider

Biology
Health services management
Psychology
Sociology
Special education

Careers related to the major

The undergraduate degree in speech pathology/audiology is a preprofessional degree. That is, in nearly all states the practitioner must hold at least a master's degree in order to practice as a speech pathologist or an audiologist. Graduate programs in this field are offered by colleges and universities in every state. There have never been greater opportunities to enter this challenging, fulfilling profession in settings like these: hospitals, schools, rehabilitation centers, community speech and hearing clinics, centers for the developmentally disabled, nursing care facilities, research laboratories, colleges and universities, day care centers, health departments, and private practice.

For more information
American Speech-Language-Hearing Association
10801 Rockville Pike
Rockville, MD 20852
(301)897-5700

Home Economics

SHARON REDICK

Ohio State University

All home economics majors focus, directly or indirectly, on issues pertaining to the family. In all cultures, individuals and families have had to decide how best to feed, clothe, and nurture families, care for children, manage resources, and provide shelter. In the past, families were self-sufficient and produced most of the goods and services needed to solve these everyday practical problems. As technology and science have advanced and society has changed many of the goods and services are purchased rather than produced by families.

Today's technology-based societies need home economics majors to help provide information, gained through research, about families and individuals as consumers and decision makers. This information relates to clothing, child care, elder care, food, money, housing, and other issues of resource management. Beyond its importance to consumers, information is needed to help individuals and families make decisions on how to interact, develop satisfying relationships, and acquire reasoning skills.

Home economics programs are called different names at different colleges. After "home economics," the second most common name is "human ecology." Other frequently used titles are family sciences, family studies, family and consumer sciences, and family resources. Regardless of the name, the programs hold true to their mission—that is, preparing professionals who are committed to the well-being of families.

Home economics/human ecology professionals approach the family and its daily living pattern as an integrated system with many parts. Thus the entire environment (political, social, economic, and ecological)—its impact on the family and the family's impact on society—is important. Students in home economics/human ecology programs learn that family structure, lifestyles, consumption patterns, and health may be viewed as an ecosystem interrelated with other aspects of society.

Home economists become involved in societal issues that directly affect families, such as homelessness, hunger, poverty, child abuse, family violence, teenage pregnancy, and child care. They are a voice for families at local, state, national, and international levels and are recognized by the United States Congress as one of the most effective lobbyist groups. Home economists become involved individually as well as collectively through their professional associations. Each specialty has a professional association as well as an original agency, the American Home Economics Association (AHEA), which was established nearly one hundred years ago and continues to serve today.

A career in home economics/human ecology or any one of its specialties is unique in that the professional's ultimate focus is on the well-being of the family and its relation to the environment. Relying on strong research, home economics/human ecology professionals seek and offer solutions to the problems of today's families. They know that their contribution will be measured by the ability of families to function effectively now and in the future.

To prepare for a career in home economics, students should have a strong college preparatory program in high school. While not required, high school home economics courses are recommended. In college, students enroll in a specific major such as home economics education, nutrition, family studies, textile science, housing, fashion merchandising, hospitality management, child studies, consumer economics, or family finances. Each major includes a strong background in liberal arts or general education. Students are expected to have or to develop computer skills. At the heart of the education of the home economics graduate, regardless of major, is the development of professional skills and a focus on family well-being. Skills common to each major in the field include planning, organizing, managing, relating to people, leadership, critical thinking, and decision making. Most majors include field experiences or internships.

Undergraduate study of home economics/human ecology prepares a student for graduate and professional degrees. Bachelor's, master's, and doctoral degrees can be earned in each of the majors discussed; however, the undergraduate programs are also good preparation for other professional degrees. For example, the food science and nutrition major is excellent preparation for medicine, and family and consumer resource management is a good background for law. Textile science becomes a good foundation for advanced work in chemistry. The major in individual and family development serves as preparation for advanced work in psychology or sociology. Home economics education is a good foundation for advanced degrees in curriculum development, supervision, or educational administration.

To select an appropriate college program, students should evaluate the number of faculty, the number of students, the number of course offerings in each major, the variety of majors offered, available field experiences and internships, program accreditation by professional agencies, the success of graduates, availability of graduate programs, research being conducted, student organizations, and opportunities for student involvement. A visit to the campus provides students with an opportunity to ask questions about these matters, to see classrooms and laboratories, and to interact with faculty and students. If possible, students should tour colleges with a current student.

Home economics graduates bring to their employers an integrated knowledge and understanding of today's families and their environment. They are committed to helping families function in ways that promote the development of mature, healthy, and productive citizens. And, they have the skills and knowledge needed in today's labor market plus a commitment to the basic unit in our complex society—the family.

Day care administration

In the day care administration major students learn to manage programs that provide educational or social services to young children and their families. Students gain knowledge of child development and develop skills in teaching young children, in supervising staff, and in business management.

Interests, skills, and qualities associated with success in the major

Interests. Leadership, management, supervising people, starting and administering programs, working with children.

Skills and qualities. Organizational and managerial skills, program development and evaluation, oral and written communication, ability to identify, analyze, and solve problems, interpersonal communication.

Recommended high school preparation

English 4, precollege mathematics 3–4, biology 2, social studies 2, history 2, computer science 1, and home economics 2.

Typical courses in the major

Child Development
Environmental Organization
Community Relations
Financial Management
Administration and Supervision

Early Childhood Curriculum
Child Guidance
Child Psychology
Organizational Behavior

What the major is like

The major in day care administration prepares students to direct and administer educational, social service, and therapeutic programs for young children and their families. The undergraduate program combines classroom instruction and practical experience to prepare students for entry-level positions—as well as for advanced education—in this field. The classroom instruction includes survey courses that focus on child development, behavior, and learning, followed by advanced work in, for example, the observation and assessment of children's development.

Students may choose to concentrate on a specific period of development, such as development in infancy (if the interest is infant day care), development in early childhood (for students planning to direct preschool or Head Start programs), or development in middle childhood (school-age child care). Methods classes follow; these are combined with fieldwork with children, parents, and teachers, and focus on planning and implementing curriculum, organizing the educational environment, guiding children's behavior, and observing and assessing children's development. Additional course work in business management, finance, marketing, and organizational psychology completes the program.

Majors in day care administration gain practical experiences developing programs, supervising staff, and administering a day care center. They complete their supervised fieldwork by applying what they have learned to for-profit child care programs, nonprofit child care programs in social service agencies, government programs in child care such as Head Start, and corporate-sponsored child care and other employer-assisted programs for working parents.

Specializations

Early childhood education, early childhood special education.

Other majors to consider

Child development, care and guidance
Early childhood education
Elementary education
Special education

Careers related to the major

With more women in the work force, a focus on quality early childhood education, and growing corporate support for employer-assisted child care, there is increasing need for child care administrators. Careers the major may lead to include day care, preschool, or early childhood education program director; Head Start director; administrator of social, educational, and therapeutic services for young children. With graduate degrees one can teach in colleges or do research.

For more information

National Association for the Education of Young Children
1834 Connecticut Avenue NW
Washington, DC 20009-5786
(800)424-2460

Child Care Information Exchange
P.O. Box 2890
Redmond, WA 98073
(206)883-9394

Family/consumer resource management

In the family/consumer resource management major students learn to analyze individual's and families' needs and behavior as consumers. Students learn to serve consumer interests in government, business, and education.

Interests, skills, and qualities associated with success in the major

Interests. Working with people, solving problems.

Skills and qualities. Oral and written communication skills, creative and critical thinking, solving problems, organization, understanding and analyzing numerical data, negotiation and mediation.

Recommended high school preparation

English 4, precollege mathematics 3, laboratory science 2–3, history or social studies 3, foreign language 2, and computer science 1.

Typical courses in the major	Family Resource Management	Consumer Information
	Consumer Behavior	Family Economics
	Personal/Family Finance	Housing
	Publicity Media and Methods	Marketing
	Negotiation and Mediation	Newswriting
	Principles of Advertising	Public Relations
	Economics	Accounting
	Business Law	Public Policy Administration

What the major is like

In the family/consumer resource management major students learn to identify, analyze, and evaluate family and consumer needs, problems, and behavior. Students prepare for professional leadership in serving family and consumer interests in such areas as government, education, business, and the media. The major also helps students deal with consumer decision making, economics, and problems. Students learn to analyze how individuals and families use resources (capital, time, money) to achieve their desired quality of life. The major provides an understanding of the consumer's needs and behavior in the marketplace, as opposed to the seller's perspective. The major is sometimes called consumer science, family/consumer studies, family/consumer economics, or family ecology.

The program typically includes courses in English, social sciences, humanities, physical and biological sciences, statistics, and analytic methods. Introductory courses in business, economics, journalism, political science, and social work complement the courses in the major.

Courses specific to the major deal with consumer information, behavior, legislation, and decision making as well as budgeting, personal/family finance, public policy affecting families and consumers, the consumer in the marketplace, and consumer issues and problems. Courses taken outside the major allow students to develop depth in related areas, such as political science, marketing, other business disciplines, communication, psychology, or social work. The senior year offers opportunities for small seminar classes, independent study, and internships.

Specializations

Consumer affairs in business, consumer affairs in government, consumer relations, consumer education, family economics, housing, personal financial counseling, personal financial planning, consumer research.

Other majors to consider

Business administration
Economics
Finance
Health services management
Housing and human development
Marketing
Psychology
Public administration
Social work
Sociology

Careers related to the major

The graduate of a family/consumer resource management program can find entry-level positions in consumer affairs, consumer relations, sales management, customer service, consumer advocacy, personnel management, marketing, financial planning and counseling, housing administration, community services, and home economics. The major can also serve as preparation for graduate work outside the consumer science field, in areas such as law, business, public administration, and banking.

For more information

Society of Consumer Affairs Professionals in Business
4900 Leesburg Pike, Suite 400
Alexandria, VA 22302
(703)519-3700

American Home Economics Association
1555 King Street
Alexandria, VA 22314
(800)424-8080

American Council on Consumer Interests
University of Missouri
240 Stanley Hall
Columbia, MO 65211
(314)882-3817
(800)424-8080

Fashion merchandising

In the fashion merchandising major, students learn how to manufacture fashions consumers want and effectively sell those fashions.

Interests, skills, and qualities associated with success in the major

Interests. Current trends in apparel, arts, furnishings, travel and leisure, and food; business trends; fabrics and other fashion materials; fashion and fashion designers.

Skills and qualities. Flexibility, quantitative analysis, negotiation, motivating people, leadership, organizational ability, written and oral communication, self-motivation, tolerance of stress.

Recommended high school preparation

English 4, precollege mathematics 4, biology 1, chemistry 1, social studies 1, history 2, foreign language, visual arts 1, speech .5–1, and computer science .5–1.

Typical courses in the major

Textiles	Fashion Analysis
Merchandising Management	Merchandise Planning
Marketing	Accounting
Economics	Consumer Behavior
Mathematics	Historical Costumes

What the major is like

Students learn to sell fashions in fashion merchandising programs that are most often found in departments of home economics/human ecology or of textiles and clothing, and occasionally in schools of business. Wherever the program is housed, students usually begin the major with classes in writing, speech, mathematics, history, social science, and natural science. During the freshman or sophomore year, they take courses such as fashion analysis and textiles, which introduce them to the terms they need to communicate with others in the fashion industry and build their knowledge of fashion products. In advanced courses students learn to organize and operate a clothing retail business; to plan, promote, and manage merchandise inventories; and to calculate retail figures for a profitable business. Merchandising students may also study historical and multicultural costumes, a field they later draw on to develop special promotions or store events that feature a particular line of merchandise.

Many programs offer internships or field experiences for college credit. Some also offer study tours of major U.S. fashion markets such as New York, Dallas, and Los Angeles, or of European fashion centers. Fashion merchandising students also gain experience using spreadsheets and data base programs on personal computers, which are important tools on the job. Group projects are assigned in advanced courses to help students become effective team players.

The major prepares students for managerial positions in fashion retailing and manufacturing. Through course work, they can prepare to manage a retail firm, to buy goods for a firm, or to work with designers in planning the overall fashion message for an apparel manufacturer. Fashion retailing is a highly competitive industry, and the pace is fast.

Specializations

Retailing, personnel management, textiles, historical costumes/textiles, apparel manufacturing, operations management, international business, speech, art, advertising.

Other majors to consider

Business administration
Hotel/motel and restaurant management
Journalism
Marketing

Careers related to the major

Graduates of fashion merchandising programs have numerous opportunities for careers with department stores, specialty stores, and catalogs. Top students can land positions in executive training programs with major retailers; after the one- or two-year training program, trainees are promoted to buyer. Some typical entry-level jobs are: merchandiser for store or catalog; store manager; personnel manager; operations manager; fashion coordinator; journalist; information director for a fashion-related company or trade association; public relations director.

For more information

International Textile and Apparel Association
P.O. Box 1360
Monument, CO 80132
(719)488-3716

Food sciences and nutrition

Students who major in food science and nutrition study the properties and processing of food before consumption (food science) and the chemical processes of digestion and the use of nutrients (nutrition).

| Interests, skills, and qualities associated with success in the major | **Interests.** Social, health, economic, and political issues involved in food production and availability; chemical reactions and what happens to food when it enters the human body; solving problems. |

Skills and qualities. Oral and written communication, analytic and organizational abilities, critical thinking.

Recommended high school preparation

English 4, precollege mathematics 3–4, biology 1, chemistry 1, physics 1, social studies 2, history 2, foreign language 2, computer science 1–2, and nutrition 1.

Typical courses in the major

Biology
Bacteriology
Food Systems Management
Biochemistry
Food Chemistry
Physical Chemistry

Physiology
Nutrition
Marketing
Organic Chemistry
Diet Therapy

What the major is like

The food science and nutrition major is usually found at large universities in schools or colleges of home economics, agriculture, human ecology, family and consumer sciences, health and human services, or applied sciences. At some institutions food science and nutrition are separate majors; at others, they are one major and students may specialize in either food science or nutrition.

In their first two years of study, students expand their foundation in high school mathematics and science with more chemistry, biochemistry, physiology, and microbiology. They also take courses in sociology and psychology. If students plan to focus on dietetics or nutrition education (working directly with individuals and families to promote health and well-being) they take courses in education and communication. To prepare to work in the business world, students should take courses in business administration, marketing, and public relations. Because computers are used for word processing and data management, courses in that area prove invaluable.

Students later pursue a sequence of studies in either food science or nutrition or both. In food science they learn about food production, processing, packaging, storage, distribution, and preparation. They also learn what makes food pleasing or displeasing to one's sight, smell, and taste.

In nutrition courses students study food selection, preparation, consumption, and digestion. They take courses in food preparation, food chemistry, and basic and advanced nutrition. Although heavy emphasis is placed on the chemistry involved in these processes, students also study the psychological and behavioral aspects of food choices and consumption.

New technologies have drastically changed the way producers grow and harvest food; how processors and distributors treat, package, store, and transport food; the marketing and advertising of food; where food is sold; the degree of preparation of food before it enters the home; the available knowledge about the relation of nutrition to health, especially in the causes and treatment of chronic diseases; food storage and preparation in the home; and the variety of available products from all over the world. At the same time, fad diets, eating disorders, substance abuse, and nutrient-drug interactions threaten health and well-being. Therefore, careers in nutrition and food science provide many opportunities for making important contributions to our world.

Specializations Education, business administration, food systems management (hotel, restaurant, institution), journalism, chemistry.

Other majors to consider
Biochemistry
Business administration
Chemistry
Hotel/motel and restaurant management
Journalism
Marketing
Nutritional education
Nutritional sciences
Physical education

Careers related to the major A bachelor's degree in food science and nutrition provides the knowledge, skills, and abilities for the following careers: nutrition educator working in continuing adult education, children's education (schools, day care centers, campus), or corporate fitness centers; product representative for a food or pharmaceutical company; dietitian helping patients meet special food selection needs; laboratory technician; food editor for a newspaper or magazine; writer of educational materials; food purchasing manager for a large service operation such as a corporate cafeteria, university dormitory, or resort; community nutrition counselor working for a public health agency.

For more information American Home Economics Association
1555 King Street
Alexandria, VA 22314

Society for Nutrition Education
2001 Killebrew Drive, Suite 340
Minneapolis, MN 55425-1882
(612)854-0035
(800)235-6690
(612)854-7869 (fax)

American Dietetic Association
216 West Jackson Boulevard
Chicago, IL 60606-6995

Home economics

Students who major in home economics study the relationships between people and aspects of their environments such as food, clothing, housing, and finances. Graduates are able to help people solve problems related to their everyday lives.

Interests, skills, and qualities associated with success in the major **Interests.** Working with people individually or in groups, helping people make decisions and solve problems.

Skills and qualities. Analyzing and synthesizing diverse subject matter and applying it to various situations, working with people.

Recommended high school preparation	English 4, precollege mathematics 3, biology 1, chemistry 1, social studies 1, history 1, and computer science 1.

Typical courses in the major

Basic Nutrition
Marriage and the Family
Consumer Economics
Child Development
Meal Management
Food Science

Nutrition in the Life Cycle
Family Financial Management
Apparel Production
Apparel Merchandising
Human Development

What the major is like

The home economics major is interdisciplinary and provides a broad background in many areas concerned with the well-being of people of all ages. At large institutions the program may be located in divisions of human ecology, human environmental sciences, or family and consumer sciences. The major begins with course work in the liberal arts. Students then choose courses in areas such as family studies, housing, interior design, textiles and clothing, food sciences and nutrition, and family/consumer economics and resource management. Students learn to analyze and integrate this information and to apply it to individual and family concerns, such as how people manage money, raise their children, plan meals, etc.

At most universities students can specialize in a certain subject and in a related professional area—for example, economics or journalism. Students who are interested in helping families may specialize in human development and family studies; those interested in consumer affairs may specialize in family/consumer economics and resource management. Other possible specialities are clothing and textiles, housing and interior design, and dietetics. Opportunities for international and crosscultural experiences are often available in home economics programs.

Through course work and internships or other supervised practical experiences, students prepare for a variety of professional roles in business, government, education, publishing, and human services.

Specializations

Family and community services, fashion design/merchandising, consumer economics, resource management, food sciences and nutrition, home economics journalism and communication, home economics education, international studies in home economics.

Other majors to consider

Business administration
Chemistry
Communications
Fine arts
Journalism
Psychology
Secondary education
Social work
Sociology

Careers related to the major

Varied careers are available to home economics graduates, particularly those who choose to specialize. The strength that home economists bring to professional positions is not only depth in subject matter but also an overall understanding of consumers and families in their environments. Some possible careers are: community services director, consumer services representative, consumer affairs director, financial planner, cooperative extension services agent, nutrition educator, home economics teacher, curriculum development specialist, journalist, editor, Peace Corps or Vista volunteer, sales representative, product designer.

For more information   American Home Economics Association
1555 King Street
Alexandria, VA 22314
(800)424-8080

Home economics education

Majors in home economics education can prepare to become consumer and homemaking teachers for preschool through adult education in subjects related to the family. They study various aspects of family life including human development, nutrition, and decision making, in addition to teaching strategies.

Interests, skills, and qualities associated with success in the major

Interests. Family life, using current technology, working with people.

Skills and qualities. Communicating well and easily, organizing work, critical and analytical thinking, being practical, creativity.

Recommended high school preparation

English 4, precollege mathematics 2, biology 1, chemistry 1, history or social studies 2, foreign language 2–3, visual arts 1, computer science 1, and home economics 1.

Typical courses in the major

Human Development	Family Relationships
Family in Society	Financial Management
Food Preparation	Nutrition
Housing	Psychology of Clothing
Consumer Management	Textiles
Clothing Construction	Learning Theories
Educational Philosophy	Educational Psychology
Instructional Media	Computers in Education
Curriculum Development	Student Teaching

What the major is like

The home economics education program builds on a foundation of courses in the natural and social sciences, mathematics, communication, and the arts and humanities. Required courses enable students to gain knowledge of how families interact with communities, schools, businesses, hospitals, and other social agencies and institutions; human growth and development—physical, intellectual, emotional, and social—and the needs of the individual throughout the life span; the roles and interrelationships of family members at all socioeconomic levels; the stages of family life; human nutrition and the role of food in the behavior and health of individuals; the relationship of design and environment to human behavior; management theory and application, including individual and family decision making.

In addition, majors study learning theories, classroom management, computers and instructional media, education philosophies, teaching strategies, testing techniques, and curriculum development. Student teaching is generally required.

Home economics education majors learn to perform in an informational society and a global community. They are committed to the profession's unique focus on the family. They develop the ability to lead a project and coordinate a group to accomplish goals; to examine issues within a democratic society; to analyze problems and new ideas and take action with knowledge of the risks and benefits involved. They learn how to think independently and communicate decisions.

Home economics education programs are generally found in schools or colleges of home economics, agriculture, or education. Some home economics programs have changed the name to human ecology, family studies, or human development. Home economics education majors are offered in state land-grant colleges and universities and also in many private institutions.

Specializations	Occupational home economics, extension education.
Other majors to consider	**Early childhood education** **Family/consumer resource management** Fashion design **Food sciences** **Hotel/motel and restaurant management** **Individual and family development** **Marketing** Nutritional sciences Textile technology
Careers related to the major	The home economics education major can lead to jobs as a home economics teacher in elementary or secondary schools; occupational home economics teacher in secondary, postsecondary, or adult programs; cooperative extension family life specialist; cooperative extension 4-H specialist; adult education teacher; preschool teacher; administrator of vocational education; educational specialist in business or industry. Supervisory positions usually require an advanced degree and professional experience.
For more information	American Home Economics Association 1555 King Street Alexandria, VA 22314 (800)424-8080

Hotel/motel and restaurant management

The hotel/motel and restaurant management major introduces students to the principles of managing these key components of the hospitality industry.

Interests, skills, and qualities associated with success in the major

Interests. Working with people, problem solving, attention to detail, leadership.

Skills and qualities. Oral and written communication, organizing ability, creativity, ability to work under pressure and meet deadlines.

Recommended high school preparation

English 4, precollege mathematics 2, laboratory science 2, social studies 2, foreign language 2, speech 1, computer science 1, and food science 1. Spanish is recommended if offered at your high school.

Typical courses in the major

Hospitality Law
Institutional Purchasing
Convention Marketing
Principles of Marketing
Hotel/Restaurant Accounting

Tourism Development
Facility Maintenance
Food Preparation Laboratory
Food and Beverage Management

What the major is like

Hotel/motel and restaurant management programs may be separate divisions of a university or part of its school of business or home economics. When part of a business school, the program tends to include many business courses adapted to the unique conditions of operating a hotel or restaurant; when the major is associated with a school of home economics, dietetics and hands-on food preparation may be stressed.

Nearly every program will begin by providing a two-year foundation of courses in the liberal arts and business management. The final two years are usually devoted to laboratory work and analysis of case studies.

Most programs are structured to provide broad exposure to the many facets of the tourism industry. Courses cover such topics as food and beverage cost control, maintenance of facilities (including sound control, swimming pool maintenance, blueprint reading), quantity food production, principles of accounting, human resources management, convention management, purchasing (everything from beef to bedding supplies), menu design, laws related to the industry, managing a kitchen, and marketing. Students may study the dynamics and psychology of the tourism industry. Some programs have a food preparation emphasis, and students take courses in baking, cooking, wine selection, and kitchen management.

Some universities rely heavily on a lecture and case-study format while others use operating hotels and restaurants as laboratories. Industry leaders frequently appear as guest lecturers. Most programs require paid, hands-on experience in the field.

Programs usually permit some specialization during the final semesters to reflect student career preferences. Elective courses in food production, accounting, computer application, languages (especially Spanish), marketing, or facility design meet these individual needs. Students will also learn to use computers, data analysis, market research, and other facets of management decision making.

Specializations

Hotel/motel management, fast food management, sales and marketing, facility design, restaurant management, human resource management, group and convention sales.

Other majors to consider

Business administration
Food sciences and nutrition
Hospitality and recreation marketing
Real estate
Tourism
Transportation and travel marketing

Careers related to the major

Graduates of hotel/motel and restaurant management programs usually begin their careers as entry-level managers in a national hotel or restaurant chain. Career progress often involves frequent relocation within a corporation and to other companies. Promotions may lead to positions as general manager of a segment of the corporation or to assignments in corporate headquarters. Graduates may also take jobs with companies that supply food, beverages, and equipment to hotels and restaurants. Some work with trade associations; others own and manage their own businesses. An advanced degree is required to be a college teacher.

For more information

American Hotel and Motel Association
1201 New York Avenue NW
Washington, DC 20005
(202)289-3100

Housing and human development

In the housing and human development major students learn to analyze the use of and investment in housing and its impact on families, the community, and the larger economy and society.

Interests, skills, and qualities associated with success in the major

Interests. Working with people, serving others, real estate, home automation, the family, marketing, management, interior design, environmental design, finance.

Skills and qualities. Computer skills, analytical skills.

Recommended high school preparation

English 4, precollege mathematics 3, biology 1, chemistry 1, physics 1, history or social studies 3, foreign language 2, and computer science 1. One year of music or visual arts is also recommended.

Typical courses in the major	Introduction to Housing	Federal Housing Developments
	Housing Alternatives	Demographics
	Home Technology	Family Resource Management
	Interiors and Furnishings	Home Management
	State and Local Developments	Principles of Family Finance

What the major is like

In the housing and human development major students learn to analyze the use of and investment in housing and its impact on families, the community, and the larger economy and society.

All students in this major receive a general background in liberal arts, mathematics, natural sciences, and social sciences before beginning their work in the major and, eventually, choosing a specific concentration.

Within the major, students study housing needs (safety, types of dwellings, home ownership) and learn how housing policies, particularly financial programs, affect families. Many programs cover the history of government regulation and taxation and their effect on housing. Factors affecting family well-being are studied, such as affluence, poverty, and access to public services such as health care and education. Students may study consumer legislation and lobbying efforts related to housing.

Students then go on to use this background to examine local, state, and federal housing policies and practices. Some use analytic skills to study supply and demand mechanisms. Others use mechanical skills to aid in the understanding of home technology. And still others use more personal social skills to aid housing programs for the elderly, the handicapped, or single-parent households.

Students may choose to specialize within the major. Those who wish to focus on housing policy can take additional course work in political science or economics. Those with an interest in design might take courses in environmental or interior design. Other related course options include business, education, real estate, sociology, and insurance.

People seeking degrees in housing can be very creative in designing programs and career paths to match their interests and abilities. But all housing students share a desire to understand the various aspects of housing and to participate, in innovative ways, in the future accommodations of our culture.

Specializations

Real estate, engineering, environmental design, merchandising, business, journalism, landscape architecture, textiles, interiors.

Other majors to consider

Civil engineering
Management science
Marketing
Political science and government
Psychology
Sociology

Careers related to the major

Graduates of housing and human development programs can find jobs with real estate companies, state and federal agencies, public utilities, historic preservation firms, financial/mortgage institutions, and trade organizations. They may also work as extension agents, property managers, or consumer affairs specialists.

For more information

American Association of Housing Educators
Texas A & M University College of Architecture
College Station, TX 77843-3137

Individual and family development

The individual and family development major focuses on interpersonal relationships and human development from infancy to old age. Students are introduced to theories of development with an emphasis on techniques to improve quality of life for individuals and families.

Interests, skills, and qualities associated with success in the major

Interests. Helping others, family and individual well-being, prevention and elimination of problems facing people in their daily lives.

Skills and qualities. Working with people, critical thinking, effective communication, openness and curiosity about interpersonal and family dynamics, self-motivation, taking initiative.

Recommended high school preparation

English 4, precollege mathematics 3, biology 1, chemistry 1, social studies 1–2, history 1, and foreign language 1–2.

Typical courses in the major

Infancy and Development
Adolescence
Interpersonal Relationships
Parent Education
Marriage and Family Therapy

Early and Middle Childhood
Aging
Patterns of Family Interaction
Minority Families

What the major is like

Majors in individual and family development learn to identify the characteristics of healthy individuals, marriages, and families. With this knowledge, students prepare to use information from their course work to help individuals and families solve problems and strengthen their relationships.

The name of the major varies; it may be called family and child development, individual and family studies, family resources and human development, child development and family relations, or human development and family studies. The location of the major also varies. For example, at large state universities it may be housed in the college or school of human ecology, human sciences, human development, home economics, family and consumer resources, or applied sciences.

Whatever the particular name and structure of the program, students learn about normal development in infancy, early and middle childhood, adolescence, adulthood, and aging. Childhood topics likely to be covered include the effects of the family on the social, cognitive, and language development of children. Special topics may be child abuse, parent-child relationships, the effects of day care on children, and the effects of divorce on children. Issues relevant to adolescence are parent-child relationships, peer relationships, sexuality, teen pregnancy, and substance abuse. Students interested in the elderly study the biology of aging, health care issues, retirement, family roles in later years, public policy, and the state of being a widow or widower.

Course work also focuses on the interpersonal dynamics, communication, and problem-solving skills found in successful premarital, marital, family, and friendship relationships. In addition, students learn the characteristics and internal dynamics of various types of families—intact, divorced, single-parent, dual-career, and step-families. Course work may also focus on the relationship between families and the larger society, including the world of work, the education system, and religious institutions.

Students should take advantage of internships or fieldwork. These supervised professional experiences may be in human services agencies or organizations, in day care programs, in hospitals, with children, with crisis hot lines, or at shelters for runaways, battered women, or abused children. The internships may be in juvenile delinquency prevention programs, in directing or organizing activities for the elderly in health care or retirement settings, or in assisting the activities director in a resort or hotel.

Specializations

Early childhood development, school-age children and adolescence, adult development and aging, family life education, interpersonal relations, family relations.

Other majors to consider

Education
Psychology
Rehabilitation counseling/services
Social work
Sociology
Special education

Careers related to the major

The major in individual and family development prepares students for a variety of careers with children, parents, single adults, couples, and families. Examples include: child life specialist in hospitals; day care teacher or administrator; parks and recreations activities director; Scout or YMCA/YWCA director or staff worker; cooperative extension or 4-H agent; drug/alcohol/rehabilitation counselor; mental health center director or staff worker; parent educator; family life specialist in industry; crisis center director or staff worker. With appropriate graduate degrees one can work as a marriage and family therapist, college teacher, researcher, church-based program director, or director or teacher in a university laboratory school.

For more information

National Council on Family Relations
3989 Central Avenue NE, Suite 550
Minneapolis, MN 55421-3921
(612)781-9331

Textiles and clothing

The textiles and clothing major leads to careers that focus on the interplay of design, business practices in the industry, and consumer needs. Students gain a general knowledge of the production, distribution, consumption, and performance of textiles and apparel.

Interests, skills, and qualities associated with success in the major	**Interests.** Working with textiles, making decisions, taking initiative, working with people.
	Skills and qualities. Creativity, assertiveness, leadership, organization, thinking analytically, making clothes, communicating.
Recommended high school preparation	English 4, precollege mathematics 4, chemistry 1–2, social studies 1, history 2, foreign language 4, visual arts 1.5–2, speech 1, and computer science 3–4. Two years of clothing construction are also recommended.

Typical courses in the major

Textile Fundamentals	Historic Textiles and Costumes
Apparel Design	Tailoring
Apparel Industry	Figure and Fashion Illustration
Sociology of Clothing	Textiles in Nonapparel Uses
Clothing Construction	Flat Pattern
Mass Production of Apparel	Textile and Clothing Economics

What the major is like

The major in textiles and clothing provides a general knowledge of the production, distribution, consumption, and performance of textiles and apparel. Students gain skills in such areas as clothing selection, coordination, and construction; design; compatibility of fabrics and sewn products; care and renovation of clothing; and quality control.

The major may be offered in a university's college of arts and sciences or in home economics, and it may lead to a bachelor of science (with an emphasis in physical science) or a bachelor of arts (with an emphasis in arts and humanities). The textiles and clothing major provides a broad background in the liberal arts; approximately half of the course work is in the humanities, fine arts, mathematics, and social sciences. Students are encouraged to select liberal arts courses that enhance and complement their personal interest in fields such as art, journalism, or foreign languages. They also generally take some textiles and clothing courses in the freshman year. The field is introduced by beginning courses in textile fundamentals, clothing construction, and consumer clothing problems.

In many textiles and clothing courses, knowledge gained through lectures is applied in laboratory or studio assignments in design, textiles, and art. In-class application of industry procedures and equipment provides practical experience. The emerging technology used in the textiles and clothing industry has required the introduction of computer-aided design and computer-aided manufacturing into some programs.

Many colleges and universities offer internships in which students earn credit while getting firsthand experience in the industry. Furthermore, many programs provide off-campus fashion study and tours of manufacturing and fashion centers, including professional visits to retail stores, design houses, and textile factories, and cultural visits to museums and historic sites.

Specializations

Textile design, journalism, apparel design, marketing.

Other majors to consider

Fashion design
Fashion merchandising
Fine arts
Home economics education
Marketing
Psychology
Textile engineering
Textile technology

Careers related to the major

The textiles and clothing major prepares the graduate to work as a retail sales manager; educational representative for fabric, pattern, sewing machine, and notions firms; textile and apparel advertiser and promoter; quality control analyst; sales representative; sample maker; clothing coordinator; wardrobe planner; extension specialist; research assistant in textiles; textile or apparel designer; conservator of historical textiles and costumes. With specialized training, one may work as a textile chemist, textile engineer, or college teacher.

For more information

International Textile and Apparel Association
P.O. Box 1360
Monument, CO 80132
(719)488-3716

American Association of Textile Chemists and Colorists
P.O. Box 12215
Research Triangle Park, NC 27709-2215
(919)549-8141

Humanities

HEIDI BYRNES

Georgetown University

When high school students plan for life after graduation, many have conflicting sentiments. Most realize that obtaining a college degree is almost a necessity, if only for future economic well-being. Yet, for many, the additional purposes of college study, let alone a choice of major, are considerably less clear. The decision-making process is more bewildering in part because of the imprecise relationship between a major and a career after college. And, finally, there is the often-unarticulated but powerful sense that one is not quite ready to tackle the big issues. Somehow, the task of becoming a whole and educated person is still ahead.

An education in the humanities speaks to all of these issues. What are the humanities, and why should students preparing for life in the twenty-first century study them? The answers to these interrelated questions offer a look at how the humanities are presented in colleges and universities and suggest connections between humanistic studies and satisfying careers.

The humanities concern us with the realm of thought and intellect, with values and beliefs, and with the need for connectedness and a sense of place. In the realm of thought and intellect, the critical realization is that what we generally consider to be "facts" about our reality are actually interpretations of it that we construct. By far the most powerful tool in that creative construction is language, which reflects our social nature as well as our individuality. As a social phenomenon, language defines and maintains a group, preserves its past and charts its future, and gives its members a sense of belonging and security. As a creative individual act, language reflects choices about what one wants to say, how one wants to say it, to whom, and with what purpose. We act through language, and through that action and interaction we become ourselves.

Not surprisingly, then, the humanities focus on language–both one's native tongue and other languages–and its uses. Such instruction is often narrowly perceived as being focused on superficial features such as grammar or vocabulary. Its real aim, however, is to enhance our ability to comprehend and analyze messages, spoken or written, and to communicate our own messages through speaking or writing. Correct grammar and vocabulary contributes to that success. But more important is an awareness of how language works: how it builds on powerful unspoken presuppositions, how it influences our thinking, and the thinking of others, how it changes over time, how it varies between social groups, and what it reveals about their perception of reality.

Given the interpretive nature of language, values and beliefs are naturally a central concern in the humanities. We face at least two major dichotomies: (1) our society seems driven by "facts" but is moved by values and beliefs; and (2) our values and beliefs are culturally constructed, but there are truths and norms that transcend all cultures. It is in sorting out these oppositions that the humanities see their purpose. What can be understood as relative, and what must be understood as essential? What deserves to be accepted deferentially, even though it is unfamiliar, and what has to be rejected because it denies the essential dignity of men and women? What should be changed, and what is our vision for such change? In a whole range of human activities–in private interaction as well as in public policymaking, in the economic sector as well as in education, health care, industry and the arts–such questions are being posed and their answers require a keen awareness of society's values and beliefs.

An awareness of these values and beliefs is best gained through seeing our own activities in relation to the larger scheme of things. Who were the people and events that came before us that made us what we are? How were they shaped by their environment and role in time? What is our sense of place within this larger continuum of human history?

By providing such intellectual tools, a humanities education empowers young adults to be decision-makers. They will have honed their skills of analysis through astute listening and critical reading, and increased their ability to argue persuasively in oral or written presentations. On the surface, these may seem to be mere language skills. In reality, however, these are the skills of critical thinking that apply in any professional setting, from law to medicine, from business to technology, from engineering to manufacturing. The ability to distinguish between valid evidence and unsupported opinion, to acknowledge one and dismiss the other, is critical everywhere.

Small wonder, then, that liberal arts education has withstood the test of time. Indeed, some of the professions requiring advanced schooling that are closely associated with rigorous training in a highly specialized field–among them, medicine, business, law, and computer science–have recently reiterated the value of a broad undergraduate education in the humanities. And other fields as well–in administration, finance, and the service sector–often prefer someone who first obtained a broad ability to reason and to place events in a larger framework over someone who specialized too early and thus is less adaptable to developments that are, as yet, totally unpredictable.

In the United States, a humanities education that includes proficiency in another language speaks to the country's identity in several ways. As a political and national entity, America has traditionally viewed itself as an immigrant country that subscribes to the cultural and political ideal that social harmony among distinct ethnic groups is not only possible but gives the country its special character and value. In the future, as increasing waves of immigration reach these shores, the American ideal of unity in diversity, not to mention the permissibility of diversity, is likely to come under severe strain.

In addition, the level of awareness and sophistication that all of us have about cross-cultural differences has political, economic, and social implications for everyone. We must become citizens of the world.

If you are open-minded toward yourself and others, willing to grow, and desire to put yourself to the test of rigorous thinking, your attitude is in tune with the growth that college study promises. You may thrive in a major in the humanities.

American literature

Through the study of fiction, prose, poetry, and drama, American literature majors study the historical development of the culture in which they live. Students learn about the forces—intellectual, economic, geographic, and social—that have shaped their own character.

Interests, skills, and qualities associated with success in the major

Interests. Sensitivity to language, the power of ideas, exploring the development of different regional and ethnic traditions that make up American culture.

Skills and qualities. Assessing conflicting points of view.

Recommended high school preparation

English 4, laboratory science 1, social studies 1, history 2, foreign language 2, visual arts 2, and computer science 1.

Typical courses in the major

Survey of American Literature
The American Novel
American Drama
Native American Literature
Melville
Faulkner

The American Renaissance
American Poetry
Black American Literature
Literature by American Women
American Autobiography

What the major is like

Although American literature is comparatively young (only about 400 years old), its variety and richness are a source of joy and understanding. American literature began in the oral songs and tales of native Americans. It continued through the literature of white exploration and settlement during the sixteenth and seventeenth centuries. As soon as English Puritans began arriving in New England, they developed a prolific literary culture that included histories, biographies, and poetry as well as sermons. The Puritan influence expanded through the poetry of Edward Taylor and the prose of Jonathan Edwards and was transformed in the mid-nineteenth-century writings of Nathaniel Hawthorne, Ralph Waldo Emerson, Henry Thoreau, Emily Dickinson, and Harriet Beecher Stowe. Although New England dominated American writing until the Civil War, both the Middle Colonies (in the works of Benjamin Franklin, James Fenimore Cooper, Herman Melville, and Walt Whitman) and the South (in the works of William Byrd, Thomas Jefferson, and Edgar Allan Poe) developed different ways of life, and different literatures, which were and are no less important. Alongside well-known white literature, necessarily dominant in a print culture, other lively and often subversive traditions flourished: fugitive slave narratives, Native American protest speeches, folk songs, and frontier humor.

After the Civil War, American literature developed so many varied voices, literary movements, and major authors that it is impossible to summarize. A few highlights are the development of realism in fiction (William Dean Howells, Henry James, Stephen Crane, Edith Wharton, and

Theodore Dreiser); the growth of Midwestern, Western, and Southern regional literature (Willa Cather, Sherwood Anderson, Frank Norris, John Steinbeck, Flannery O'Connor, Eudora Welty); America's lead in the exciting revolution of international modernism in poetry (Ezra Pound, T.S. Eliot, Marianne Moore, Wallace Stevens, William Carlos Williams); the three ever-popular Modernist novelists of the 1920s (Ernest Hemingway, F. Scott Fitzgerald, and William Faulkner); the emergence of major American drama (Eugene O'Neill, Arthur Miller, Tennessee Williams); the increasing prominence of black American literature (Langston Hughes, Zora Neale Hurston, Richard Wright, Ralph Ellison, and James Baldwin); the uneasy self-conscious affirmations of post-World War II fiction (Saul Bellow, Vladimir Nabokov, Norman Mailer, John Updike); the grimness of post-World War II poetry (Robert Lowell, John Berryman, Elizabeth Bishop, and Sylvia Plath); the revolt of the Beat Generation (Jack Kerouac); the recent achievements in Native American writings in English (N. Scott Momaday, Leslie Silko, James Welch, Louise Erdrich) and in literature by and for women (Adrienne Rich, Ann Beattie, Joan Didion, Toni Morrison).

Insofar as American literature has one story, it is one of growing variety, diversity, and power of separate yet related traditions. To experience such growth is to learn to understand and tolerate differences between men and women as well as those among peoples, races, and regions. From such tolerance and understanding each of us can find the inner power to help make a better world. At the very least, the American literature major learns to read, write, and think about the many worlds within "America" with far greater discrimination and clarity.

Specializations	Creative writing, American civilization, literature of the new world.
Other majors to consider	**Afro-American studies** **American studies** **Comparative literature** **English** Native American languages **Political science and government**
Careers related to the major	The American literature major prepares students for jobs in business, public administration, education, and government. It is good preparation for professional study in law, business, or medicine.
For more information	The Modern Language Association of America 10 Astor Place New York, NY 10003 (212)475-9500 National Council of Teachers of English 1111 Kenyon Road Urbana, IL 61801 (217)328-3870

Chinese

In the Chinese major students develop skills in spoken and written Chinese and study Chinese history, literature, culture, and civilization.

Interests, skills, and qualities associated with success in the major

Interests. Chinese people, culture, history, and civilization; fine arts; dramatic arts; literature and drama; martial arts; travel and exploration.

Skills and qualities. Learning foreign languages, awareness of Chinese culture, values, and history.

Recommended high school preparation

English 4, precollege mathematics 4, laboratory science 1, social studies 1, history 2, foreign language 4, music 1, and visual arts 1. Students should take Chinese if it is offered at their high school.

Typical courses in the major

Elementary Chinese
Intermediate Chinese
Modern Chinese Short Stories
Modern Chinese Theater
Chinese Novels
Chinese Linguistics
Chinese Religions

Advanced Chinese
Advanced Classical Chinese
Modern Chinese Fiction
Chinese Art
Chinese Music
Chinese History

What the major is like

The scope and content of Chinese programs vary. Generally an advanced level of spoken and written Chinese is required for students who major in the field, along with reading courses in Chinese literature, history, politics, and philosophy. Other courses in Chinese culture, literature, and history—conducted in English—are also included.

Except for English, Chinese is spoken by the greatest number of people (more than a billion), and Chinese culture is one of the oldest in the world. Unlike speakers of English, most speakers of Chinese share a common ethnic origin. There are many dialects in China, such as Fukienese, Hakka, and Wu. The most popular dialect is Mandarin, the official language of China, spoken by roughly 800 million Chinese. Cantonese, a widely used dialect, is spoken by more than 50 million, including overseas Chinese in Hong Kong, Southeast Asia, and North America. For English speakers, it is said that "Chinese is easy to learn, but difficult to master." Once the four tones and a basic vocabulary are learned, it is not difficult to speak the language because the grammar is user-friendly.

The study of Chinese language and culture has had a place in American colleges and universities for over a century. In the nineteenth century it was restricted to a small group of institutions. But military needs in World War II and broader international concerns since the 1960s stimulated American interest to the point that now over 300 colleges (and half that many high schools) offer instruction in Chinese for a language requirement, a certificate, or a degree. In institutions that offer a degree in Chinese, the major may be housed in departments that teach only modern languages, teach East Asian languages and culture, teach East Asian languages and literature, teach comparative literature, teach linguistics or offer second language education, including bilingual education. Majors in Chinese often minor in one of the humanities or social sciences.

Whatever the program's location and specific requirements, at most colleges the Chinese major has the following goals, with varying emphasis: (1) mastery of the Chinese language; (2) development of powers of critical analysis by comparing cultures and languages; and (3) appreciation of Chinese literature and culture.

Programs that emphasize the first category (Chinese language) offer a series of language-skill courses. Programs that concentrate on the second category examine different language structures, concept formulation, cultural traits, and the contrast between Chinese and Western traditions in courses such as Chinese linguistics, comparative literature, and cross-cultural studies. Programs that stress the third category emphasize understanding and appreciating the Chinese people and their history and culture through readings in Chinese literature (in Chinese and in English) and courses in Chinese calligraphy.

Students in the Chinese major gain increased insight into their own American attitudes, values, and beliefs as well as into those of the Chinese. They thus gain a cultural perspective from which to view the behavior and customs of others.

Specializations

Chinese language, Chinese culture, Chinese civilization, Chinese literature, Chinese cross-cultural studies, linguistics, Chinese drama, Chinese theater, Chinese calligraphy.

Other majors to consider

Anthropology
Asian studies
Comparative literature
Fine arts
History
International relations
Linguistics
Philosophy
Religion

Careers related to the major

Chinese majors pursue many different careers. Many become language teachers, but an increasing number enter business firms dealing with overseas markets. Various branches of the government and of international organizations need experts with knowledge of China and the Chinese languages. Some graduates complete a doctorate in Chinese and become college teachers.

For more information

Chinese Language Teachers Association
211 Jones Hall
Princeton University
Princeton, NJ 08544-1008
(609)258-4279

Classics

Classics majors immerse themselves in two cultures fundamental to the West—the cultures of ancient Greece and ancient Rome. Students explore the literature, history, art, philosophy, and architecture of those civilizations. Connecting with the past creates a sense of belonging to humanity and participating in human achievement and evokes reflections on the present.

Interests, skills, and qualities associated with success in the major

Interests. Language, literature, exploring the past, acquiring a broad liberal education.

Skills and qualities. The self-confidence to tackle life with imagination; skills of analysis and criticism.

Recommended high school preparation

English 4, precollege mathematics 4, laboratory science 4, European history 1, and foreign language 3–4. Students should take Latin or Greek if offered.

Typical courses in the major

Mythology
Elementary Latin
Beginning Greek
Ancient Drama
Plato
Vergil

Intensive Greek
Intensive Latin
Attic Greek
Homer
Catullus
Greek and Roman Civilization

What the major is like

In the classics major, students learn Latin, Greek, or both, and in so doing learn about language itself, the primary intellectual tool. The term classics refers to the literature of the ancient Greeks and Romans. Its themes, forms, and images have inspired generation upon generation of readers and writers. Students learn different methods of interpreting literature—methods that take account of audience, context, transmission of the text, and modern theory. They learn to distinguish reliable from unreliable evidence and to use evidence honestly and creatively to understand others' arguments and create their own. These skills are useful in any career.

The oldest surviving classical text, and hence one of the oldest surviving texts of Western literature, is the Iliad of Homer. Although Homer probably composed and sang his heroic, epic poetry in the ninth century B.C., he incorporated many songs and themes from far earlier times; the Trojan War, the setting of the Iliad, is dated to the twelfth century B.C. Homer and his successor, Hesiod, reveal wonderful and self-conscious societies just beginning to develop the complex intellectual, cultural, and political life of the Greek city-state, the polis.

Later Greek poets—Sappho and Pindar, for example—composed their songs for their own aristocratic audiences. Aeschylus, Sophocles, and Euripides provided tragedies, and Aristophanes wrote comedies, for democratic Athens. Their plays are still among the most powerful and beautiful (and in the case of Aristophanes, the funniest) in Western literature. Even if their names seem strange, their works are immediately engaging. Other Greek writers—Herodotus, Thucydides, Plato, Aristotle, Demosthenes—

developed history, philosophy, rhetoric, and literary theory. They asked fundamental questions about human existence, knowledge, politics, ethics, and beauty that continue to engage us today.

The Roman republic began as a small city-state in the sixth century B.C., gradually gained control of all Italy, defeated Hannibal and Carthage for control of the western Mediterranean world, and finally seized command of all the countries around the Mediterranean Sea. The existing Latin literature begins with the lively comedies of Plautus in the third century B.C., when Rome was already a great power. The comedies of Terence, the philosophical poetry of Lucretius, the love poetry of Catullus, the accounts of Caesar's conquest of Gaul (roughly, modern France), and the great philosophical and legal orations of Cicero—all are part of the turbulent culture of the late Roman republic.

In 29 B.C., after a century of civil war, Augustus founded the Roman empire and established the Pax Romana, the Roman Peace, in the Mediterranean world, which Rome ruled until the fourth century A.D. In the first century of that period came the greatest flowering of Latin literature: the poets Vergil, Horace, and Ovid, the satirist and poet Juvenal, the historians Livy and Tacitus, the statesman and playwright Seneca, and later the novelist Apuleius. Their literary forms shaped European literature. But as important as the literature—despite Horace's conviction that poetry is the most enduring of all monuments—are the so-called practical Roman creations: mighty architectural and civil engineering works, legal codes, and principles of governing. These, too, have shaped European culture.

Students of the classics learn about the grand intellectual tradition of Western humanism, spawned in Italy in the fourteenth century by Petrarch and carried on by hosts of others inspired to go to the very sources of our civilization. Beyond acting as curators of a great literary tradition, students discover new meaning in the literature of the ancient Greeks and Romans, so that it remains alive today. They also pursue archaeology, a field in which something new turns up with great regularity.

Specializations	Latin, Greek, classical civilizations, archaeology.
Other majors to consider	**Anthropology** **Art history** Folklore and mythology **History** **Linguistics** Other literature and language majors **Philosophy** **Political science and government**
Careers related to the major	The classics major prepares one for a variety of jobs in business, government, education, or social services, in large and small companies or in public organizations. With appropriate graduate study it can lead to careers in medicine, law, and other professions.
For more information	American Philological Association Department of Classics Fordham University Bronx, NY 10458 (212)579-2994

The Odyssey. Robert Fitzgerald, translator. New York: Random House Vintage Classics, 1990.

Antigone. Robert Fagles, translator. In *Three Theban Plays*. New York: Penguin Classics Series. 1984.

Comparative literature

Majors in comparative literature study the literature of different countries, cultures, and languages. They explore their poetry, prose, and drama and consider the relation of literature to other arts and to other fields of study.

Interests, skills, and qualities associated with success in the major

Interests. Literature, foreign languages, differences between cultures as expressed in their languages and works of art.

Skills and qualities. Reading critically, communicating articulately, appreciating different cultures.

Recommended high school preparation

English 4, laboratory science 1, social studies 1, history 3, foreign language 4, music 1, visual arts 1, and computer science 1.

Typical courses in the major

Medieval Epic	History and the Novel
Tragedy	The Novel of the Self
Romanticism	Gender and Literary History
Proust, Mann, and Joyce	Narrative Technique

What the major is like

Comparative literature majors study at least two literatures in the original languages and focus on subjects that go beyond national, historical, and language boundaries. These may include literary movements (for example, Romanticism, surrealism), literary periods (the Renaissance), literary forms (the novel), literary issues (the treatment of science and technology), and literary theory and criticism. Just as art history students study the art of other countries and botany students study the plants of more than one region, so do students of comparative literature study more than one body of literature. Most American students choose English or American literature as one of their two literary fields. They also study at least one foreign language and culture and compare the two cultures and their literature. They may also study the relation of literature to other creative fields such as painting, photography, film, or sculpture, and the relation of literature to other disciplines such as anthropology, psychology, or history. The field is strongly interdisciplinary, and the possibilities for comparative study are virtually limitless.

Most departments or programs of comparative literature require one or more courses in a discipline that introduces students to comparative analysis. These courses suggest new ways of reading; some focus exclusively on the text, others consider the society and culture in which the text is created and read, and still others concentrate on the relation between the text and its author or the text and its readers. Students learn the many traditions authors draw on when they create poems, plays, and novels.

These introductory courses and others may be supplemented with advanced literature courses in the original languages from two or more other countries. Most colleges and universities offer the study of English, French, Spanish, German, Latin, and Greek; others offer Russian, Japanese, Chinese, Arabic, Polish, or other languages. Because literature is studied in these language departments, students encounter a variety of critical approaches.

The major in comparative literature requires a great deal of reading and writing—some of it, of course, in a foreign language. Students thus learn to communicate and to think logically and creatively. Study abroad can be an exciting and important part of the program.

The potential scope of the major, which emphasizes originality and creativity, allows contact with the greatest range of literary works of any program in the humanities.

Specializations

Many students in comparative literature designate one of their literatures as major and the other as minor to indicate a greater degree of concentration in one. Some programs also offer concentrations in literature and the arts.

Other majors to consider

Anthropology
Dramatic arts/theater
English
Film arts
Foreign languages (multiple emphasis)
Linguistics
Other foreign languages
Other literature and language majors
Philosophy
Women's studies

Careers related to the major

The comparative literature major can lead to jobs in journalism, business, education, publishing, government, or radio, television, or film. With appropriate graduate degrees it can lead to careers in law, international business, and college teaching and research.

For more information

American Comparative Literature Association
Comparative Literature Department
3010 JKHB
Brigham Young University
Provo, UT 84602
(801)378-1211

Creative writing

The creative writing major is designed to help students become novelists, poets, playwrights, screenwriters, or essayists.

Interests, skills, and qualities associated with success in the major	**Interests.** Drama, poetry, fiction, film, language. **Skills and qualities.** Writing, openness to revision, patience.
Recommended high school preparation	English 4, precollege mathematics 1–2, biology 1, chemistry 1, physics 1, social studies 2–3, history 2–3, foreign language 4, music 1–2, visual arts 1–2, and computer science 1.

Typical courses in the major

Composition
Poetry Writing
Exposition Writing
Argumentation
Advanced Writing

Fiction Writing
Journalism
Topics in English Composition
Playwriting

What the major is like

The creative writing major closely resembles the English major. Much of the course work is similar in the two programs—in particular, the study of composition and of varied works in drama, prose, and poetry. But for students in the creative writing major, their own writings are used as primary texts in writing workshops. Workshops are often taught by professional, published authors whose goal is to develop the creative talents of their students.

In general, the course work for the creative writing major is divided among literature courses, writing workshops, and liberal arts requirements in the sciences, mathematics, and other humanities. Two degrees are offered: the Bachelor of Fine Arts and the Bachelor of Arts in English with a writing emphasis. The B.F.A. requires more time in writing workshops. The B.A. stresses literature and composition; courses in writing are added to, or may replace, courses in the regular English major. In many colleges, students enter writing courses on the recommendation of the instructor teaching the course; this recommendation is based on writing samples or previous writing courses.

Writing workshops tend to be specific to a particular form of writing—essay, prose, drama, short story, or poetry. Students in essay writing learn how to design an argument, study techniques of analysis and persuasion, and explore the relation between voice and purpose. In poetry writing they experiment with meter, image, tone, and organization; in a fiction course, they may focus on characterization, dialogue, and plot. In most courses, students will analyze the work of their fellow students.

The major encourages the fine art of writing and can be followed by one of many graduate writing programs. A focus on creative writing may lead to work in publishing, or other fields that require writing skills. Some writers, of course, make an independent living from writing, but usually they supplement their income with other work.

Specializations

Poetry, fiction, playwriting, screenwriting, creative nonfiction.

Other majors to consider

Art history
Dramatic arts/theater
Education
* **English**
Journalism

Careers related to the major

The creative writing major can lead to jobs in advertising, teaching, publishing, communications, journalism, and arts administration. It prepares one for graduate and professional work in law and business.

For more information Associated Writing Programs
Old Dominion University
1411 West 49th Street
Norfolk, VA 23529-0079
(804)683-3839

English

English majors study important works of literature—drama, prose, poetry—focusing on the point of view, organization, and language of the works. In addition to developing critical and analytical reading skills, students get practice in language use and composition.

Interests, skills, and qualities associated with success in the major

Interests. Reading, talking, and writing about literature; music, theater, and film.

Skills and qualities. Speaking easily and well, writing and revising.

Recommended high school preparation

English 4, precollege mathematics 3, laboratory science 2, history 3–4, and foreign language 3–4. History courses should include world and American history.

Typical courses in the major

History of the Novel	Continental Masterpieces
Chaucer	Shakespeare
Milton	The Epic
Contemporary Literary Theory	New Voices in Literature
Medieval Literature	Poetry
Victorian Literature	English Drama
The Romantics	The Modern Short Story
Modern English Grammar	

What the major is like

The goal of the English major is the understanding of English and American literature in prose and verse. In some universities "literature" may include any works that have been recorded—newspapers, technical and nontechnical reports, documentaries, magazines, films; in others, the term is restricted to works in poetry, prose, and drama in English, American, and comparative literature. The major usually requires 8 to 10 courses that acquaint the student with technical issues in reading and writing.

Whether literary works are approached historically, psychologically, generically, or sociologically, students are introduced to the terms used by scholars and critics. Students learn about point of view, explication, tone, irony, metaphoric language, image, structure, allusion, affective reading, and the various aspects of a literary text—for example, its sources and its historical context. Students are also introduced to the definition of audience, the ways in which pieces of literature can be instructive, and how texts affect their audiences' beliefs and emotions.

Courses in literature enable students to realize better how readers are guided by the text; courses in writing enable them to practice many of the techniques they learned from reading the work of others. Students become increasingly sensitive to the subtleties of language and to the influences of what they read and hear. They learn the logic or the illogic of an argument, the moral positions found in literature, the ways experiences are organized, and thoughtful reactions to psychological and emotional persuasions.

The English major requires much writing and reading as well as library research. Students are given a historical perspective from which to judge their language in prose and verse and learn to write and speak effectively in various forms. They also learn to think creatively and logically.

The English program may be housed in a department that teaches only American and English literature or in a department that teaches classical literature and language as well as those of other nations (Spanish, French, German, Russian, Chinese, or other).

Specializations	American studies, comparative literature, creative writing, critical theory, drama, film, journalism, linguistics.
Other majors to consider	**Advertising** **American studies** **Comparative literature** **Creative writing** **Dramatic arts/theater** Foreign languages **History** **Linguistics** **Philosophy** **Women's studies**
Careers related to the major	The English major prepares one for careers in journalism, publishing, radio and television broadcasting, elementary or secondary school teaching, management, social work, and technical writing. With graduate or professional study, it can lead to careers in college teaching, law, or other professions.
For more information	The Modern Language Association of America 10 Astor Place New York, NY 10003 (212)475-9500

English education

The major in English education prepares students to teach literature, language skills, and composition in middle and secondary schools.

Interests, skills, and qualities associated with success in the major

Interests. Nature and history of languages; reading and discussing classic and contemporary literature; expository, journalistic, and creative writing; the personal and linguistic development of children and teenagers.

Skills and qualities. Working with teenagers, communicating effectively, guiding discussions.

Recommended high school preparation

English 4, precollege mathematics 2, laboratory science 2, social studies 1, history 3, foreign language 3, music 1, visual arts 1, and computer science 1. One year of drama, journalism, or speech is also recommended.

Typical courses in the major

Modern English Linguistics
World Literature
Major English Writers
Major Literary Types
Learning Theories
Multicultural Education
Methods of Teaching English
Literature for Adolescents
Expository Writing
Theories of Literary Criticism
Major American Writers
Adolescent Development
Social Foundations
Exceptional Learners
Student Teaching

What the major is like

Majors in English education, preparing to teach in middle, junior high, or senior high schools, take about a third of their courses in general education—that is, in the sciences and mathematics, history and social sciences, humanities and arts. An additional 40 percent of their course work is in English and such related subjects as theater. They take a limited number of electives, several professional education courses, and one or more courses in the teaching of English, including student teaching.

Professional education includes courses in child and adolescent development to help prospective English teachers understand the intellectual, physical, psychological, and social development of their students. The program usually includes background in the historical development of the American school system and insights into how schools function.

Prospective English teachers then go on to courses that deal specifically with the teaching of literature, composition, and language. They learn how to select and present works of literature and to design writing programs that develop composition skills, vocabulary, spelling, and standard English grammar. Student teaching, in the senior year, usually consists of a full day in a middle, junior, or senior high school for 10 to 15 weeks. The student teacher, working with a teacher from the school, plans and carries out instruction.

Typically, colleges and universities offer one or more of the following programs to prepare English teachers: (1) A major in English with a minor in education leads to a bachelor's degree in English and a recommendation for certification as an English teacher. (2) A major in English education with English courses similar to the English major leads to a bachelor's degree in education. (3) A major in English or a related subject such as journalism, without an undergraduate program in professional education, is followed by postgraduate education studies and student teaching. In this program the student may also complete the work required for a master's degree in English.

Specializations

Literary history and criticism, rhetoric and composition, creative writing, journalism, linguistics, drama, speech, middle school education, high school education.

Other majors to consider	**Communications**
	Dramatic arts/theater
	Elementary education
	History
	Journalism
	Literature and language majors
	Philosophy
	Psychology
	Special education
	Women's studies

Careers related to the major	The English education degree can lead to a job as a teacher of English language arts in grades 6 through 12. With additional, specialized training it can lead to careers as a school librarian, special education teacher, journalist, social worker, technical writer, or radio, television, or film writer. With appropriate graduate study, one can become a curriculum specialist, school principal, or college teacher.

For more information	National Council of Teachers of English
	1111 Kenyon Road
	Urbana, IL 61801
	(217)328-3870
	The Modern Language Association of America
	10 Astor Place
	New York, NY 10003
	(212)475-9500
	National Education Association
	1201 Sixteenth Street NW
	Washington, DC 20036
	(202)833-4000
	American Federation of Teachers
	555 New Jersey Avenue NW
	Washington, DC 20001
	(202)879-4400

French

Majors in French study the French language, literature, and culture as found both in France and in other French-speaking areas of the world.

Interests, skills, and qualities associated with success in the major	**Interests.** Reading, talking, and writing about literature; the links between language, history, and culture.
	Skills and qualities. Fluency in speaking and writing, composing and revising written works, a good ear for music.

| **Recommended high school preparation** | English 4, precollege mathematics 2, biology 1, chemistry 1, physics 1, history 2, and foreign language 4. |

Typical courses in the major

French Composition	Intermediate Grammar
French Theater	French Literature
French Conversation	Stylistics
Commercial French	French Phonetics
Realism and Naturalism	Twentieth-century Poetry

What the major is like

Students who major in French study the language, literature, and cultural background of the people of France and other French-speaking regions. Traditionally, the culture of France and the French language spoken in Paris, its capital, have dominated the major. Since World War II, however, French studies have generally been broadened to include the languages and cultures of territories formerly under French control, such as Algeria, the Ivory Coast, Lebanon, and Indochina. These changes underscore the importance of the French language, one of the world's foremost international languages since the eighteenth century.

Most programs combine two basic tracks. First, there is the study of the language—grammar, structure, and pronunciation. In a series of grammar, composition, and conversation courses, students learn all four language skills: reading, listening, speaking, and writing. Second, students explore French literature. For richness, diversity, and prestige, French literature is striking. Some classes examine classics, such as the theater of Molière, Corneille, and Racine; others study the poetry of the Renaissance or the novels of Flaubert. In yet others, students may read newspapers, magazines, and technical reports, or they may view films.

These two areas of course work are obviously related. While students pursue fluency and accuracy in language courses, they broaden their basic language skills by discovering how various texts use the language and the culture. Literature and language courses are thus closely interwoven in the major; indeed, they are inseparable.

Although many students who major in French have been exposed to the language before entering college, it is possible to begin studying the French language in the freshman year and start the major course work in the junior year. Generally, a minimum of 12 semester courses in upper-level French is required. In many institutions study abroad is strongly encouraged; either in a summer program or in the junior year. Many colleges and universities sponsor study-abroad programs, for exposure to a French-speaking culture is a significant, although not indispensable, aspect of the major. In efforts to provide similar experiences in the United States, many French departments sponsor film series, lectures, theatrical performances, and informal social gatherings where students speak and hear French. Students are encouraged to view their peers and their instructors as members of one community bonded by similar interests and engaged in similar pursuits.

The French major is generally offered in a department of Romance languages and literatures (that is, languages derived from Latin, including Spanish, Portuguese, Italian, Rumanian), although in smaller institutions it may be in a department of foreign languages, where such languages as German, Russian, and Chinese are also taught. Students often minor in one of these other languages, or they may combine their major with political science, history, philosophy, English, business, or journalism.

Specializations

Not generally available.

Other majors to consider	**English** **European studies** **History** **Linguistics** Other literature and language majors **Philosophy** **Political science and government**
Careers related to the major	The French major can lead to jobs in secondary school teaching, translation, tourism, international business, journalism, and publishing. With appropriate graduate degrees, one can work in research, law, diplomacy, banking, and marketing.
For more information	The Modern Language Association of America 10 Astor Place New York, NY 10003 (212)475-9500

German

Students who major in German explore a rich literary, philosophical, and scientific tradition. They study the language, literature, and culture of Germany, Austria, and much of Switzerland.

Interests, skills, and qualities associated with success in the major	**Interests.** Literature, history, German culture, a liberal education. **Skills and qualities.** Learning languages.
Recommended high school preparation	English 4, precollege mathematics 2, laboratory science 2, history 3, and foreign language 4. History should include world or European history, and foreign language should be German if possible.
Typical courses in the major	Elementary German German Conversation Intermediate German German History and Culture German Literature Age of Goethe Romanticism Postwar Literature German Drama German Poetry German Film Modern German Literature
What the major is like	The major in German includes many aspects of the language, literature, and culture of Germany, Austria, and much of Switzerland. Although some students learn the language before entering college, many do not begin to study German until their first year. Students then use the language to explore increasingly complex texts in courses that are taught in German and tend to have small enrollments. The curriculum may offer a major in either German literature or German studies. The German literary tradition is remarkably rich and con-

tinues to be today. Students read not only eighteenth- and nineteenth-century authors like Goethe, Schiller, and Heine, and major figures from the first part of this century (for example, Kafka, Rilke, Brecht), but also great contemporary writers like Dürrenmatt, Frisch, and Grass. Courses in German film are becoming increasingly common. And, like any other literature major, the German major considers literary theory.

German studies may cover anything from the works of great philosophers like Kant, Hegel, and Marx to contemporary political science. Many departments offer surveys of German intellectual history that explore art, literature, music, philosophy, and science. Others join with other disciplines, such as history, to present topics like the rise of Hitler. A few programs have ties to departments of business administration and teach language courses in business German.

The major typically includes time abroad, in either academic or work programs. Colleges that have their own programs abroad generally offer courses taught by special staff; students live in dormitories, apartments, or local homes. Most of the stronger junior-year-abroad programs accept students from various institutions. Colleges without their own programs generally permit, or even encourage, qualified students to attend them.

Many American colleges and other organizations help students find vacation employment in German-speaking countries, thus strengthening their command of the language.

Specializations

German literature of a particular period, German area studies, Germanic linguistics, German intellectual history.

Other majors to consider

Comparative literature
English
History
Linguistics
Music
Other foreign languages
Philosophy
Political science and government

Careers related to the major

A mastery of German is valuable in almost any academic field, as well as in international business and diplomacy. German majors tend to pursue a rich variety of careers. Many become secondary school teachers or college teachers, or enter jobs in government, business, or journalism. With appropriate professional study, one can enter the fields of medicine and law.

For more information

American Association of Teachers of German
112 Haddontowne Court, No. 104
Cherry Hill, NJ 08034
(609)795-5553

History

History majors expand their knowledge and understanding of the past. Working with written, oral, visual, and artifactual evidence, they examine the causes, contexts, and chronologies of historical events, thus cultivating a sense of continuity and change in human experiences.

Interests, skills, and qualities associated with success in the major

Interests. Curiosity about when, where, and why historical happenings occurred; what it was like to have lived in different times and places and to have known historical figures.

Skills and qualities. Reading carefully, writing clearly, speaking articulately, thinking analytically, synthesizing information, interpreting facts, expressing ideas with clarity and precision.

Recommended high school preparation

English 4, precollege mathematics 3–4, biology 1, chemistry 1, physics 1, social studies 2, history 2–3, foreign language 2–4, and computer science 1.

Typical courses in the major

Western Civilization	East Asian Civilization
Ancient Greece	Ancient Rome
Tudor and Stuart England	Modern England
Precolonial Africa	American History
U.S. Constitutional History	U.S. Economic History
Modern Latin America	Medieval History
Renaissance and Reformation	Historical Research
The French Revolution	

What the major is like

Working with written, oral, visual, and artifactual evidence, history majors examine the causes, contexts, and chronologies of historical events. They thereby expand their knowledge of the past, and gain an understanding of continuity and change in human experience.

The study of history does not need to be sequential. There are prerequisites for advanced work, but students typically do not take courses in a fixed order. Rather, they devise a program that meets their own interests and also fulfills requirements found in most institutions: one or two introductory courses, one or more courses that acquaint students with cultures and histories other than their own, a course in historical methods, and a research seminar.

The courses in the history major usually focus on time periods, nations, geographic areas, distinctive historical perspectives, and themes, often in combination (for example, Civil Rights in the United States, 1945 to 1970; Women in Nineteenth Century Europe). The major helps students to understand the purposes, principles, and methodologies involved in the study of history and to grasp both particulars and universals of societies past and present. It also explores questions of judgment and interpretation, of good and bad, of right and wrong.

History majors read extensively and develop and demonstrate writing skills through essay exams, book reviews, and research papers. They use libraries extensively, and must be able to do computer-aided research. If their studies in history have a social science orientation, even more computer competence is required. Because history students must do archival research and interviewing, and their courses rely on lectures and discussion, they must have precise listening and speaking skills.

Specializations

Many history programs enable students to concentrate on a geographic region or time period, or perhaps on a nation or topic.

Other majors to consider

American studies
Classics
Economics
English
Geography
International relations
Political science and government
Sociology
Speech

Careers related to the major

The history major prepares students for careers demanding the knowledge, understanding, perspective, skills, and sensitivities gained through studying history. Such careers are found in business, government, nonprofit agencies, and elementary and secondary schools. Graduate work in history leads to careers in teaching at the secondary and college levels, as well as in museums, archives, and historical and government agencies. The history major also prepares students for advanced studies in law, business, medicine, and other professions.

For more information

American Historical Association
400 A Street SE
Washington, DC 20003
(202)544-2422

Italian

Majors in Italian study the language, literature, culture, and history of Italy, birthplace of the Renaissance and an artistically rich country. Students also learn about contemporary Italian society.

Interests, skills, and qualities associated with success in the major

Interests. Foreign languages, architecture, music, history, literature, film, contemporary European politics and economics.

Skills and qualities. Learning foreign languages, understanding foreign cultures, sensitivity to art, especially to literature and the visual arts.

Recommended high school preparation

English 4, precollege mathematics 3, laboratory science 2, social studies 1–2, history 2–3, and foreign language 4. The study of Latin and 1 to 2 years of music or visual arts is highly recommended.

Typical courses in the major	Elementary Italian	The Renaissance
	Intermediate Italian	Dante
	Advanced Italian	Nineteenth-century Literature
	Twentieth-century Literature	Italian Masterworks
	Italian Theater	Italian Cinema
	Italian Civilization	

What the major is like

The major in Italian usually includes study of both language and literature, with the underlying theme of Italian culture and civilization. Students who don't already know the language begin with elementary Italian, a two-semester course in which they study the basic grammar and learn to speak, read, and write simple Italian. Students who have completed this course (or its equivalent before entering college) go on to intermediate Italian, a two-semester course usually taught entirely in Italian, in which they review their grammar and practice listening, speaking, reading, and writing.

Many students who take the intermediate course plan a junior year in Italy. Many American programs in Italy require two years of college Italian because their own courses, or courses students take at Italian universities, are taught entirely in Italian. Intermediate Italian has another goal: to prepare students for the study of Italian culture, especially literature and history, during their junior year abroad or in advanced courses at home. Most intermediate courses include poetry and prose, often teach the analysis of literature, and introduce students to Italian history and culture and contemporary Italian society.

In advanced Italian, which emphasizes conversation and composition, students discuss and write about historical and contemporary aspects of Italian culture and civilization.

Italy's greatest poet is Dante Alighieri, author of the *Divine Comedy*. Thus the Italian major usually requires a course in Dante, in which students read part or all of the poem in the original. Most programs in Italian also include study of Italian Renaissance literature, especially the writings of Boccaccio and Petrarch, sometimes the epic poems of Ariosto and Tasso, and often the writings of Machiavelli and Galileo. Also important to Italian literature is the early nineteenth century, the period of Romanticism in Italy. Most colleges therefore expect their Italian majors to learn about the writer Ugo Foscolo and the poet Giacomo Leopardi, as well as the Italian novelist Alessandro Manzoni, author of *I promessi sposi (The Betrothed)*.

Twentieth century Italian literature is very popular with majors. The course includes the best Italian writers of our time—Pirandello, Svevo, D'Annunzio, Pavese, Moravia, Pasolini, Buzzati, Morante, Ginsburg, and Calvino—and the poets Montale, Ungaretti, Saba, and Quasimodo. Some institutions offer a course in masterworks of Italian literature, which treats in depth the writings of one or more great Italian writers or offers a survey of Italian writers from Dante to the present. Many Italian programs show contemporary Italian films in the contemporary Italian literature course, or they may offer a specific course in Italian cinema in which students study the films of such famous Italian directors as De Sica, Visconti, Fellini, Antonioni, Pasolini, Bertolucci, and Wertmuller. Italian opera may be studied in one or more required courses.

Specializations

Italian studies.

Other majors to consider	**Art history** **Comparative literature** **European studies** **Fine arts** **French** **History** Latin **Music** **Political science and government** **Spanish**
Careers related to the major	The Italian major can lead to careers as an Italian teacher, translator, studio artist, art historian, architect, or industrial designer, and careers in music, film, government, international politics, or international business. Appropriate graduate study is required for some of these careers. College teaching and research are options with a doctorate.
For more information	The Modern Language Association of America 10 Astor Place New York, NY 10003 (212)475-9500

Japanese

Majors in Japanese engage in intensive language study and read Japanese literature in translation as well as texts on Japanese history, religion, arts, and society. In learning about Japan's past and present, students discover the crucial role traditional values continue to play in a very modern Japan.

Interests, skills, and qualities associated with success in the major	**Interests.** Travel, other cultures, foreign languages, the Japanese language and culture, business, and government. **Skills and qualities.** Foreign languages and humanities such as English and history.
Recommended high school preparation	English 4, precollege mathematics 3, laboratory science 3, social studies 1–2, history 2, and foreign language 3–4. History should include world history. A year spent in Japan on an exchange program is ideal, although not essential, preparation for this major.
Typical courses in the major	Beginning Japanese Japanese Culture Intermediate Japanese Advanced Spoken Japanese Advanced Japanese Japanese Linguistics Classical Japanese Literature in Translation Japanese Drama History of Japan Arts of Japan Japanese Religion

What the major is like

The major in Japanese generally requires three to four years of study in modern Japanese. The first two years are likely to be especially intensive—often 6 to 8 hours of class and language lab per week. In institutions that have extensive programs, students may have a variety of choices at advanced language levels—courses that emphasize a particular skill (speaking, reading, composition, translation) or kind of text (literary, social science). Classical Japanese may be optional or required. Some universities are now introducing separate programs in business and technical Japanese, limiting the selection of materials and aiming at a reading knowledge only; such courses may be open to majors although they are not intended primarily for them.

If Japanese is a specialization within a broader major in Asian or East Asian studies, as it is at many smaller colleges, the language requirement is often only two years. This usually gives the student proficiency in conversational Japanese but limited reading ability.

A great many students of Japanese choose double majors, combining Japanese with such areas as international relations, business, economics, engineering, computer science, linguistics, and education.

A cultural component always accompanies language study. Because one of the most enjoyable ways to learn about a culture is to read its literature, a survey of Japanese literature in translation is always required, usually in a yearlong sequence of courses spanning the period from the eighth century to the present. Highlights include Murasaki Shikibu's monumental eleventh-century romance, *The Tale of Genji*; the poetry of haiku master Matsuo Bashō; and the novels of Nobel Prize winner Kawabata Yasunari. Where the emphasis on literary studies is strong, specialized courses on individual authors, genres, periods, topics, and literary analysis are offered—generally in translation but sometimes including limited readings in Japanese.

Students further their understanding of Japanese culture by selecting courses in fields like religion, history, art history, anthropology, and political science, or they may choose a single, broad-ranging course covering each topic briefly. Where Japanese is part of a broader Asian studies major, requirements may include courses on other Asian countries as well. These courses not only provide information about Japan and the Japanese (or other Asian peoples)—how they lived and thought in the past, what makes them tick today—but also show students different ways of experiencing life and the world around them. Students thus gain new perspectives from which they can reflect on their own culture.

To give majors firsthand experience with the language as well as with Japanese society and culture, many institutions offer students opportunities to live and study in Japan.

Specializations

The most common specialization is Japanese literature. At smaller colleges, Japanese may itself be a specialization within an Asian or East Asian studies major.

Other majors to consider

Anthropology
Area studies
Asian studies
Comparative literature
East Asian studies
History
International business management
International relations
Linguistics

Careers related to the major

The Japanese major provides linguistic skills and cultural knowledge that are increasingly sought by a wide variety of employers in business, law, journalism and publishing, government (both federal and state), and cultural exchange organizations. College teachers of Japanese are in great demand (an advanced degree is required); high school teachers are increasingly needed. The major is often a doorway to jobs with Japanese firms in the United States or Japan. With advanced training or experience, some Japanese majors establish themselves as independent translators, interpreters, or consultants.

For more information

The Association of Teachers of Japanese
40 Middlebury College
Middlebury, VT 05753

Linguistics

Linguistics majors study the common properties of the world's languages. Students examine the extraordinary skills involved in the apparently ordinary tasks of speaking, writing, listening, and reading and explore the history and structure of specific languages.

Interests, skills, and qualities associated with success in the major

Interests. Language, foreign languages, word games, puzzles, how people talk and express themselves.

Skills and qualities. Learning foreign languages, problem solving, verbal ability.

Recommended high school preparation

English 4, precollege mathematics 3–4, biology 1, physics 1, social studies 2, history 2, foreign language 4, and computer science .5–1. More than one foreign language should be studied if possible.

Typical courses in the major

Introduction to Linguistics	Languages of the World
Phonetics	Phonology
Morphology	Syntax
Semantics	Historical Linguistics
Dialectology	Writing Systems

What the major is like

Linguistics is a modern and rapidly growing discipline, with roots in the traditional fields of grammar, rhetoric, and logic, as well as in anthropology and the study of specific ancient and modern languages. First offered as a college or university major in the late 1930s, it is now available at well over 100 institutions. At half these institutions the major is offered in a department of linguistics, and at others it is in a department that combines linguistics with another discipline. Or it may be administered by an interdisciplinary committee drawing faculty and resources from such fields as English, the classics, modern foreign languages, anthropology, philosophy, psychology, and speech.

A major focus of linguistics today is the study of the common properties of the world's languages, which number about five thousand. Students also focus on the unique properties of individual languages in order to reach a deeper understanding of those properties and of the people who speak those languages.

Because most students do not discover linguistics until they enter college, the major usually begins with a general introductory course in the field. This is followed by specific courses in the study of language, including phonetics and phonology (study of the sounds of speech and how they function in language), morphology (study of the structure and function of words), syntax (study of how words combine to form phrases or sentences), and semantics (study of meaning and use). These subjects make up the core of contemporary linguistic study.

A major in linguistics may consist solely of courses in the core, but more often the major combines these subjects with study of specific languages or families of languages and their relation to the cultures in which they are used, with comparative and historical studies of different languages and dialects, and with methods for investigating little-known languages and dialects.

In addition, the linguistics major may explore such topics as how children acquire language; how people actually produce and understand written, spoken, and signed language; how language disorders can be diagnosed and treated; how languages can be taught most effectively; how the use of specific languages and dialects has been fostered (or discouraged) by government policy; and how computers can be designed and programmed to understand and produce language.

Specializations

Linguistics theory, psycholinguistics, language and education, computational linguistics, history and structure of a specific language.

Other majors to consider

Anthropology
Classics
Comparative literature
Computer science
English
Philosophy
Psychology

Careers related to the major

The linguistics major can lead to jobs in business, particularly international business, public relations, software design and marketing, English as a Second Language teaching and research, foreign language teaching and research, health-related professions such as speech pathology and language disorders, industrial research and development (in speech recognition, natural language processing, text analysis and interpretation, electronic dictionary design and preparation, artificial intelligence), college teaching and research, and law. Some of these fields require appropriate graduate study.

For more information

Linguistic Society of America
1325 18th Street NW, Suite 211
Washington, DC 20036
(202)835-1714

Center for Applied Linguistics
1118 22nd Street NW
Washington, DC 20037
(202)429-9292

Philosophy

Philosophy majors participate in a tradition of thought as old as civilized life and as new as artificial intelligence and medical ethics. They examine issues of morality, reality, and knowledge. Students learn to think clearly and to support their beliefs with good reasons.

Interests, skills, and qualities associated with success in the major

Interests. Word games, solitary meditation, argument with family and friends, puzzles, reading, asking "why" questions, seeing connections between different things.

Skills and qualities. Writing, debating, seeing other people's points of view, concentrating on one thing, thinking logically, mathematics.

Recommended high school preparation

English 3, precollege mathematics 1, laboratory science 2, and history 2.

Typical courses in the major

Ethics	Logic
History of Philosophy	Metaphysics
Political Philosophy	Theory of Knowledge
Philosophy of History	Philosophy of Science
Philosophy of Religion	Plato
Aristotle	Locke
Kant	Hegel
Aesthetics	

What the major is like

Philosophy differs from other fields of study in that it is the most general of all: no bit of information, no religious or moral tradition, no part of science is off limits to the student of philosophy. Philosophy majors consider the entire universe, human and nonhuman, to be their subject matter. At the same time philosophy tends to favor certain ways of thinking over others. Philosophy students must learn to give reasons for their beliefs while being unafraid to speculate boldly. Hence most teachers of philosophy consider themselves successful if their students become disciplined, imaginative thinkers.

Beginning courses in philosophy are designed for students with little preparation in this field because few secondary schools offer philosophy courses. Virtually every program has introductory courses in problems in philosophy, as well as courses in the history of philosophy. Courses in philosophical problems may be taught by reading in major areas, such as ethics (moral conduct), metaphysics (the nature of reality), logic, epistemology (the study of knowledge), and aesthetics (the nature of art), or by studying a range of particular topics, such as free will, the existence of God, what makes a good society, the nature of persons. Surveys of the entire history of philosophy, beginning with the Greeks, usually take at least one school year to complete and may take two or more.

Many of the questions asked by adult philosophers are ones they asked as children: How did the world begin? Do animals have their own language? Could I be someone else? Philosophy is much concerned with such seemingly simple questions; in fact, part of the fascination of philosophy is its capacity to reveal the complexity and subtlety of such apparently simple matters. On the other hand, philosophy also tries to expose the muddled thinking so commonly read and heard every day. Thus, philosophy tries to bring students' attention back to questions that are basic and profound as well as to clear their heads of fuzzy thinking and weak arguments.

As students progress through the major, taking courses in the history of philosophy, in major figures (such as Plato, Aristotle, Aquinas, Descartes, Hume, Kant, Hegel, Wittgenstein, Dewey), and in particular problems (language, consciousness, scientific "truth," social and political justice), they are expected to master the arguments of other philosophers. But they are increasingly expected to "do" philosophy on their own. At many colleges and universities they therefore work closely with their professors, sometimes writing long theses in their senior year.

Philosophy departments at large universities with graduate programs ordinarily have special strength in some particular area or areas of philosophy (e.g., ethics and moral philosophy, phenomenology, philosophy of language, history of philosophy, political philosophy). Departments at colleges that do not have graduate programs tend not to be specialized. Both sorts of departments, however, offer undergraduates a full range of courses and topics. Limitations on the scope of offerings are usually determined by the size of the department—the more professors in the department, the wider the variety of subjects taught.

Specializations

Applied philosophy, business ethics, medical ethics, philosophy for children, mathematical logic, cognitive science, feminist philosophy.

Other majors to consider

Biology
Chemistry
Classics
English
History
Mathematics
Music
Physics
Religion

Careers related to the major

Philosophy majors find their training useful in a variety of fields. They have developed general analytic and organizational skills, which they can transfer from one career area or job to another. They have the flexibility and capacity for growth that employers find valuable. Many enter jobs in business, journalism, computer science, public administration, teaching (all levels), publishing, and public relations. With appropriate graduate work they find careers in law, the health professions, and college teaching.

For more information

American Philosophical Association
University of Delaware
Newark, DE 19716
(302)831-1112

Religion

Students who major in religion become familiar with various religious traditions. They also learn to use a range of approaches when examining religion—historical, textual, psychological, philosophical, sociological, and anthropological.

Interests, skills, and qualities associated with success in the major

Interests. Different cultures and societies, past and present; world religions; understanding perennial human problems and mysteries, such as birth, growth, love, death, grief.

Skills and qualities. Oral and written communication, teamwork, learning foreign languages, reading carefully and critically.

Recommended high school preparation

English 4, precollege mathematics 2, biology 1, chemistry 1, physics 1, social studies 2, history 2, foreign language 3, music 1, visual arts 1, and computer science 1.

Typical courses in the major

Introduction to Religion
Judaism
Hinduism
Christianity
Buddhism
Islam

Religions of China
American Religions
Existentialist Theology
Religions of Japan
Religion and Moral Issues
Critiques of Religion

What the major is like

Students of religion learn to differentiate between *participating* in a religious tradition—its stories, rituals, symbols, beliefs, social and institutional structures, and behaviors—and *understanding* that tradition regardless of participation. The study of religion enables students, like other liberal arts majors, to understand their subject through a combination of approaches or methods of study.

First, the study of religion involves many cultures and traditions. By learning to discern similarities and differences *between* religious traditions, students recognize and appreciate differences *within* a religious tradition. Students come to realize that understanding may arise not only from active participation in a religion but also from empathetic study of it.

Second, every religious tradition can yield insights and understanding through critical inquiry. Recognizing other religious points of view expands students' awareness. Learning what meanings another religion attaches to such human concerns as birth and death, joy and sorrow, peace and war, makes what was previously unfamiliar less so. Students learn nuances, multiple levels of meaning, and skills of interpretation that challenge, contradict, test, and deepen their preconceptions and understanding. The previously familiar becomes somewhat less taken for granted.

Third, students learn to think critically and imaginatively. They study religion independently of the affirmations of participants in a religion and of criticisms from its opponents. Historical investigation, psychological inquiry, social analyses, anthropological and ethnological investigations, feminist criticism, and linguistic analysis are but some of the methods widely used in the study of religion.

Most programs require an entry-level course in at least two religious traditions: Christianity, Judaism, Buddhism, Hinduism, Islam, religions of China, religions of Japan, or American religions. Students then generally take an intermediate-level course in each of these two traditions. At least one course will examine various approaches to the study of religion. A seminar may take an in-depth look at an issue or type of religion.

Which traditions are studied and which approaches are used vary according to the department or program. But in all institutions, understanding, comparative study, and critical and imaginative inquiry are the tools of the religion major.

Specializations

Textual studies, religious thought, history of religion, historical traditions, religion and social sciences, religion and culture.

Other majors to consider

Afro-American studies
Anthropology
Art history
History
Jewish studies
Philosophy
Psychology
Sociology
Women's studies

Careers related to the major

Like majors in most of the liberal arts, a major in religion provides sound preparation for careers in many fields of work. It also prepares a student for professional and graduate study in business, law, medicine, counseling, psychology, higher education, secondary education, and other fields. The major may lead to careers managing religious institutions, though graduate work is usually required.

For more information

American Academy of Religion
1703 Clifton Road NE
Suite GS
Atlanta, GA 30329-4019

Council of Societies for the Study of Religion
Mercer University
Macon, GA 31207
(912)741-2376

Russian

The Russian major offers a wide range of courses in Russian language, literature, culture, and civilization. With language as the basic tool, students investigate the Russian world and its people, thereby gaining a broader understanding of the unique historical, geographic, and cultural factors that have contributed to the development of the Russian language.

Interests, skills, and qualities associated with success in the major	**Interests.** Russian culture, humanities, language, literature.

Skills and qualities. Learning foreign languages, being open-minded, perseverance. |
| **Recommended high school preparation** | English 4, precollege mathematics 2, laboratory science 2, history or social studies 3, and foreign language 2. If possible, Russian should be the foreign language taken and history should include world, European, or Russian history. |
| **Typical courses in the major** | Beginning Russian · Phonetics and Intonation · Intermediate Russian · Conversation and Composition · Advanced Russian · Survey of Russian Literature · Russian Theater and Drama · Chekhov · The Russian Short Story · Gogol · The Russian Novel · Pushkin |

Typical courses in the major

Beginning Russian
Intermediate Russian
Advanced Russian
Russian Theater and Drama
The Russian Short Story
The Russian Novel

Phonetics and Intonation
Conversation and Composition
Survey of Russian Literature
Chekhov
Gogol
Pushkin

What the major is like

Russian, the language of one of the world's great literatures, is central to modern international relations, business, and science. Russian majors study the language and read Russian literature; they also study Russian culture and civilization, Russian and European history, and other related disciplines.

The Russian major generally requires three to four years of language study. The first two years usually require a minimum of five to six hours per week of class and language lab time. Some colleges offer intensive Russian language courses, which require eight to twelve hours per week. The goal is to enable students to communicate orally and in writing.

Upper-level Russian language courses are designed to help the students communicate effectively (beyond the basics) with Russian speakers on a variety of topics. The choice of courses at the advanced level depends on the department and the strength of its program. Ideally, choices include courses in conversation and composition and Russian literature in the original, and also a course that emphasizes a specialized area such as language of the Soviet press, business language, scientific Russian, or social sciences. The variety of offerings allows students to pursue individual interests. During the senior year students majoring in literature often participate in a senior seminar on a literary topic.

Courses in Russian literature and Russian culture and civilization in translation allow students to explore Russian literature and culture in English.

At colleges where Russian is a part of a broader Russian studies major, students usually must take at least two to three years of Russian language as well as courses in Russian literature. Russian studies programs emphasize the social sciences (history, political science, economics). A strong program allows students to select courses in such subjects as Russian intellectual history, religion (Russian orthodoxy), and Russian art and music.

The study process is made more enjoyable by activities such as a Russian club, Russian house, Russian language table, Russian choral group, and Russian lectures, films, excursions, and radio broadcasts. Since glasnost, the number of study programs and exchanges in Russia has grown significantly, and opportunities to study in Russia have increased markedly. These programs are usually administered by individual institutions or groups. Majors in Russian now have the opportunity to spend a summer, a semester, or even a full year studying and living in the former Soviet republics, thereby immersing themselves completely in the language and culture of the Russian people.

Many students double-major in Russian and international relations, business, economics, education, computer science, linguistics, or another language and literature.

Specializations Russian literature, Russian language.

Other majors to consider

Anthropology
Comparative literature
Fine arts
History
International business management
International relations
Linguistics
Political science and government
Slavic languages (other than Russian)

Careers related to the major

The Russian major prepares one to teach Russian in a high school or primary school (with the appropriate teaching credential). Many graduates find employment in government or business. With a doctorate, one may teach in a college or university. Many Russian majors pursue careers or advanced degrees in other fields such as law, business, computer science, anthropology, geology, sociology, or medicine.

For more information

American Association for the Advancement of Slavic Studies
Jordan Quad, Acacia Building, Stanford University
125 Panama Street
Stanford, CA 94305-4130
(415)723-9668

American Council of Teachers of Russian
Study Programs in the USSR
1776 Massachusetts Avenue NW, Suite 300
Washington, DC 20036
(202)833-7522

Spanish

Majors in Spanish develop competence in the language and explore the history of the Spanish language, literature, and culture in Spain and Spanish America.

Interests, skills, and qualities associated with success in the major

Interests. Language, communication, literature, diverse cultures, liberal education, travel.

Skills and qualities. Oral and written communication, good interpersonal skills, a good ear for language and patterns in communication, a balance between analytical and creative skills.

Recommended high school preparation	English 4, precollege mathematics 1–2, biology 1, chemistry 1, physics 1, social studies 1, history 2–3, foreign language 2–4, music 1, and visual arts 1.

Typical courses in the major

Intermediate Spanish	Advanced Composition
Spanish Peninsular Literature	Spanish American Literature
Culture and Civilization	Spanish Renaissance
Latin American Novels	Cervantes
Business Spanish	Phonetics
Applied Linguistics	

What the major is like

In general, Spanish majors focus on using the Spanish language during their first two years of study. If possible, students interested in a Spanish major should take at least two years of Spanish (preferably more) in high school and then hone the basic skills (speaking, listening, reading, writing) at college.

In their freshman and sophomore years, students will take courses conducted in Spanish that allow them to converse and practice writing; read literature from both Spain and Spanish America; and explore various paths leading to careers in teaching, business, social work, government, etc.

During their junior and senior years, students take advanced work in speaking and writing skills. They may study phonetics and do creative writing in Spanish. They also study Hispanic literature, usually that of both Spain and of Spanish America.

Spanish majors become familiar with the sweep of Spanish-language literature, including the medieval epic *The Poem of the Cid* and the literature written when Christians, Jews, and Moors shared the Iberian Peninsula; the early Renaissance Spanish classic *La Celestina*; the picaresque novel (*Lazarillo de Tormes*); the writings by the mystics; the great Spanish dramatists of the Golden Age (Lope de Vega, Tirso de Molina, Calderón de la Barca); the baroque masterpiece *Don Quijote*; and the neoclassical, romantic, realist, and modernist works.

Spanish majors also study the literature of Spanish America, which began its development in 1492 and has gained prominence in the present world, which is beginning to be familiar with the names Borges, García Márquez, Fuentes, and Vargas Llosa.

The major may offer courses in teaching methodology and applied linguistics, often in collaboration with the institution's school of education. Many programs—responding to students' increasing interest in using Spanish in their careers—offer business Spanish and medical Spanish as well as the history and culture of Spain and Spanish America (apart from courses in the history department). Bilingual translation may be an elective. Almost all programs encourage a semester, a year, or a summer of study in a Spanish-speaking country.

Specializations

Spanish literature, Spanish American literature, language teaching, business Spanish, translation.

Other majors to consider

Anthropology
Communications
European studies
History
International business management
International relations
Latin American studies

Linguistics
Other literature and language majors
Political science and government

Careers related to the major

The Spanish major prepares one for a range of positions in government or business, especially those demanding mastery of a foreign language. Graduates can find jobs in business, banking, social services, teaching, government, translating/interpreting, and international student exchange organizations. With appropriate advanced degrees they may work in law or in medical professions as a physician, nurse, or hospital administrator, and they will be especially valued in bilingual communities.

For more information

The Modern Language Association of America
10 Astor Place
New York, NY 10003
(212)475-9500

Interdisciplinary, Area, and Ethnic Studies

HANS PALMER
Pomona College

Over the last 20 years new majors have focused on area studies, ethnic studies, and other complex issues. Many of these majors are interdisciplinary both in approach to their subjects and in new methods of analysis. Actually, the movement toward such majors is not all that new; rather, there has been a recent increasing interest in these fields as educators come to realize, again, the complexity of many issues.

The stimuli have come from a number of sources: the awareness that long-standing problems have been inadequately addressed by traditional methods (for example, problems of the city); the emergence of new ways of looking at old problems (feminist approaches to questions of peace and war); the appearance of new problems and concerns (the global environment); and the development of new methods and even new disciplines (sociobiology). The new kinds of study have allowed colleges and universities to address many questions that seemed immune to older approaches and have enabled students and faculty alike to break new ground. Some majors are truly *inter*disciplinary because they arise from the combination of existing methods and disciplines. Others are *multi*disciplinary because a problem, an event, or a situation is analyzed from a number of perspectives at the same time. Often, questions of values and ethics are central to the major and its materials and methods.

Some new majors group themselves around contemporary issues. Among them are international relations, public policy analysis, environmental studies, and women's studies. Although these majors may focus on parts of larger problems, most focus on the development of new methods and application to specific events and issues. For example, an international relations major may want to analyze the political, economic, historical, and cultural aspects of international problems while at the same time emphasizing a part of the world that is of special interest, say the Middle East. A women's studies major may emphasize feminist approaches to social and individual problems while simultaneously delving into the role of women in the arts, in the labor force, or in science. Some majors in this category may be interdisciplinary, others multidisciplinary. Often the approach varies, depending on the interests of the faculty and the students.

Other majors in these groups cluster around an area. These include African studies, Latin American studies, and Middle Eastern studies. Many of these programs are multidisciplinary because they bring together many approaches at the same time. Such programs focus on the politics and history of a region; yet the emphasis may be on the culture and sociology of the people. In other instances a program may emphasize the uniqueness of a people and their civilization.

Several programs concentrate on ethnic, linguistic, or religious groups. In this category are Afro-American studies, Jewish studies, and Latin American studies. These programs focus on the experiences of a given group: their history, their economic position and participation, their political situation, and often their unique psychological perspectives. Some programs analyze the contributions of members of these ethnic groups across a wide variety of activities: the arts, professions, sciences, and commerce. These programs often focus on how members of ethnic groups see themselves and how they are seen by others in their societies. Other courses in these majors track specific experiences and contributions. Considerable emphasis may be placed on a particular historical event or experience—for example, the Holocaust, or slavery in the pre-Civil War United States.

Often these programs focus on one problem or issue from differing viewpoints. Widely divergent perspectives may be introduced. For example, a program in urban studies can incorporate skills and insights from biology, geography, demography, economics, political science, cultural anthropology, and sociology. It can even include materials from civil engineering and philosophy and ethics.

Interdisciplinary, area, and ethnic studies programs are organized in different ways. Some are housed in special departments or in specific divisions of the college or university such as the humanities or the social sciences. Or the major may be freestanding, unconnected to a specific division. Other programs are within departments, and some serve as special resources for an individual department or a cluster of departments. In such cases the major can be joined with a disciplinary major and also be a freestanding major. For example, women's studies or public policy majors can be linked to specific department majors to provide a special emphasis or direction. Some interdisciplinary, ethnic, and area programs are supervised by special committees composed of members from individual departments. Students may pursue interdisciplinary majors on an individual basis, designing their program from a menu of relevant courses, subject to guidelines and with the help of an adviser or supervisor linked to the major.

Many interdisciplinary majors feature hands-on experiences. Students in urban studies may take internships with city agencies or with volunteer groups. Other students may study abroad or in the national or state capital to gain firsthand experience and evidence to illuminate and enrich their classroom work. In most interdisciplinary, area, and ethnic majors there is a senior exercise that brings together the various parts of the major. The exercise may be in the form of a thesis, a long paper, or an oral presentation. It may be a portfolio of papers or projects. It may feature several components. The senior exercises give students the opportunity to review and integrate what they've learned so that the work becomes truly the students' own.

Interdisciplinary, area study, and ethnic programs appeal to many different students. Some major in these fields because they have a taste for

complexity; they often find that the issues and methods emphasized in such programs are attractive because they are not easily identifiable in airtight categories. Other students are drawn because the programs seem to emphasize newness and openness. Similarly, some students are intrigued because these programs may encourage them to strike out on their own, using new insights and new methods to solve problems and issues that remain undefined and unsettled. (In other settings these students might have designed special majors for themselves.) For other students these programs touch on values and moral imperatives important in their own lives. For still others there is great interest in studying their own roots. Often area studies, as well as ethnic or religious studies, are selected on those grounds.

Graduates of interdisciplinary, area, or ethnic programs have numerous career opportunities. The special skills and abilities to deal with complexity and ambiguity are valued in an increasingly complex world in which problems often appear intractable. Furthermore, the ability to integrate both materials and methods from several fields enables graduates to offer employers enviable sets of analytic and expository skills which are of growing importance in today's world.

African studies

In the African studies major students investigate the ways in which, over time, African peoples have structured their lives, their livelihoods, their arts, and their social relations. Students also consider the impact of Africa and Africans on today's world.

Interests, skills, and qualities associated with success in the major

Interests. Learning about various peoples, cultures, and social systems; international relations and foreign affairs; reading, languages, travel.

Skills and qualities. Broadmindedness and natural curiosity; enjoyment of diversity; willingness to reexamine customary beliefs; openness to non-Western ideas.

Recommended high school preparation

English 4, precollege mathematics 2, biology 2, history or social studies 4, foreign language 4, music 2, visual arts 2, and computer science 2.

Typical courses in the major

Peoples of Africa
Independence
African Literatures
Environment and Social Change
African Religion
Nineteenth-century Africa
Black Nationalism

Art of West Africa
African Film
Pan-Africanism
Government and Politics
Economics of Developing Countries
African Languages

What the major is like

African studies is a liberal arts major that creates an understanding of continuity and change in African civilizations. Through courses in various disciplines, students consider the human experiences that from earliest times have taken place on the African continent. The program acquaints students with African literature, history, political science, economics, and anthropology. It instills an appreciation of African arts. Students develop their powers of critical analysis.

The intention of the major varies from campus to campus. At some institutions, African studies examines the development and expressions of diverse national cultures. Such programs equip students with the skills needed to observe and interpret cultures very different from their own. Students learn to relate their study of the African continent to the broader study of the culture and history of all human beings. Other programs focus on African views on such issues as European colonialism, apartheid, the Atlantic slave trade, postcolonial structures of control and domination, wars of independence, and Pan-Africanism, thereby enabling students to interpret the role Africa plays in today's world.

The major is structured in various ways, depending on an institution's resources. Ideally, at large universities there is an African specialist in each department of the humanities and social science divisions whose efforts are coordinated by the African studies program. A small college may offer seminars and tutorials in which students explore selected themes in depth.

Some institutions emphasize proficiency in an African language, which students gain from intensive exposure to African source materials. Still others encourage an extended period of study in Africa—a summer, a semester, a year—in a program designed to fulfill specific academic objectives. All programs use visiting faculty, film, and lecture series, conferences, and field trips to enrich their curricula.

Specializations

African Francophone or Anglophone literature, African history, African art history, African politics, ecology in Africa, archaeology in Africa, African languages.

Other majors to consider

Afro-American studies
Anthropology
Archaeology
Art history
Geography
History
International relations

Careers related to the major

The African studies major can lead to careers in international service agencies, banking and finance, journalism, government, education, and publishing. With appropriate graduate or professional degrees, one can pursue law, university research and teaching, business, and other professions.

For more information

Dr. Edna Bay
African Studies Association
Emory University
Credit Union Building
Atlanta, GA 30322
(404)329-6410

Afro-American studies

In Afro-American studies, students become familiar with the history, literature, art, and lives of black people in America. They study the contributions of persons of African descent to world civilizations and learn how these contributions have frequently been distorted, ignored, or denied.

Interests, skills, and qualities associated with success in the major

Interests. Ability to shift perspective and to synthesize different points of view.

Skills and qualities. Reading critically, writing well, understanding different types of people, objectivity, openmindedness.

Recommended high school preparation

English 4, precollege mathematics 2, laboratory science 1, history or social studies 4, foreign language 4, music 1, visual arts 1, and computer science 1.

Typical courses in the major	Afro-American Literature	Afro-American History since 1865
	Afro-American Psychology	Slavery in the Americas
	History of Africa	The Sociology of Black Women
	The Black Family	African Literature
	Blacks in Latin America	Caribbean History and Society

What the major is like

The major in Afro-American studies is an interdisciplinary program for students who want a comprehensive understanding of Africa and the descendants of African peoples. Studies include the history, literature, art, and societies of blacks. Whether the department is titled African and Afro-American studies, Afro-American studies, or black studies, students master the perspective of more than one field and gain knowledge of Africa as well as of black people in the Americas. In some colleges African studies is separate from Afro-American studies, but students majoring in Afro-American studies are usually expected to take one or more African studies courses.

Ordinarily students begin with an introductory course that examines the history of Afro-American studies, prepares them for interdisciplinary work, and places black history in the context of world history. Such a course usually has the dual purpose of combating negative stereotypes of black people and demonstrating the contributions persons of African descent have made to world civilizations. Students read history, literature, and studies about black people by anthropologists, economists, political scientists, psychologists, theologians, and sociologists. In most introductory courses students also study music, dance, and the arts of black people. Throughout, the emphasis is usually on how black people see themselves and how they are seen by others. Slavery is viewed from the perspectives of both the slaveholder and the slave: Students are asked to reconcile different viewpoints, sort out the emotions of whites and blacks alike, master their own feelings about race, and reach a balanced conclusion about the enslavement of Africans and its effect on whites and blacks today.

Advanced courses build on this interdisciplinary introduction. At some institutions students are free to pursue specialized paths. At large universities, students interested in the arts take courses in art, literature, and music; those interested in the social sciences take courses in anthropology, economics, political science, psychology, and sociology; and those interested in the black past take history courses. At small colleges, these paths may be combined so that some students may center their studies on art and literature and others focus on history and social sciences. Most black studies courses have an interdisciplinary component; for example, students who study Afro-American literature are reminded of the social contexts within which black writers work. At many colleges a double major is possible, and students major in premedicine and Afro-American studies, social work and Afro-American studies, or economics and Afro-American studies.

Many Afro-American studies departments require a senior project or a seminar to enable students to reflect on what they have learned. At colleges in large cities, the project may involve the student with the local black community, giving them the opportunity to work together on matters of mutual concern.

Specializations

Afro-American history, African literature, African history, Afro-American literature, black music, social scientific perspectives of black Americans.

Other majors to consider	**African studies**
	Anthropology
	Caribbean studies
	Hispanic American studies
	History
	Latin American studies
	Political science and government
	Psychology
	Social work
	Sociology
	Women's studies

Careers related to the major

Afro-American studies prepares students for careers in education, social service, public administration, business, and a range of other areas. It is also excellent preparation for graduate or professional study in law, business, religion, medicine, or social work. A degree in Afro-American studies is useful for those who plan to study or work abroad because it prepares students to work with diverse peoples.

For more information

National Council for Black Studies
Memorial Hall East
Indiana University
Bloomington, IN 47405
(812)855-3875

American studies

The major in American studies integrates courses in American history, literature, and the arts to give students a comprehensive understanding of American society and values.

Interests, skills, and qualities associated with success in the major

Interests. American life, music and art, literature, ethnicity, politics, American values and morals.

Skills and qualities. Written and oral expression, creative analysis, integrating different subjects and fields.

Recommended high school preparation

English 4, precollege mathematics 1, biology 1, chemistry 1, physics 1, social studies 2, history 2, foreign language 3, music 2, and visual arts 2.

Typical courses in the major

American Civilization
Women in American Society
American Literature
Blacks in American Society

American Film
The American Wilderness
American Art

What the major is like

American studies is an interdisciplinary major in which students pursue diverse approaches to American history, literature, and the arts. Although programs vary according to faculty strengths and college requirements, all have a common aim: understanding the core of American society and values, past and present.

Three kinds of courses typify American studies programs. For freshmen and sophomores, survey courses trace American culture and society from colonization to the 1980s. These courses introduce the various disciplines relevant to American studies. For example, topics in the first semester may include American immigration (history), the rise of distinctive American architecture (art), and the evolution of colonial politics (political science), all as part of the study of pre-Revolutionary society. Subjects in the next semester may be family life and urbanization (sociology), the rise of modern American advertising (history), and the origins of American realism in the 1880s and 1890s (art and literature).

During the junior and senior years, students typically focus on two or three aspects of American culture and society. Each student consults with a faculty adviser and develops an area of interest. In the most common concentration, history and literature, course work might be in American political history, modern American literature, and film. But other combinations are also available. Students whose interest is the social sciences, especially politics, take courses in history, political science, and sociology. Students who want to explore American pluralism (diverse peoples in a common culture) take courses in ethnic studies, sociology, religion, and history. American studies majors are typically stimulated by this interdisciplinary approach. For instance, students often comment that they more fully understand American literature, art, and film by studying American political and economic development.

American studies programs usually provide senior seminars, which build on students' previous course work. Although these seminars vary considerably from one institution to the next, most examine the development of American society and culture through advanced readings. Other seminars concentrate on a particular period, perhaps the 1950s or the 1960s. Some programs also allow students to develop major research projects, historical or contemporary. These projects are exceptionally rewarding because they engage the students' emerging interests and reflect their developing skills and knowledge.

The interdisciplinary focus of American studies encourages frequent faculty contact and substantial undergraduate interaction. Faculty members are usually highly committed and responsive, and most classes are relatively small. The students develop a strong bond that makes American studies as enjoyable as it is useful.

Specializations American art and literature, ethnic studies, American film, women's studies, nineteenth-century American culture, twentieth-century American culture.

Other majors to consider

Anthropology
Art history
Comparative literature
Ethnic studies
Fine arts
History
Literature and language majors
Political science and government
Sociology

Careers related to the major The American studies major prepares one for careers in a wide range of areas, including education, journalism, politics, publishing, social services, editing, and writing. With appropriate graduate training, American studies majors may pursue careers in college teaching, curating, museum administration, law, business, or other professions.

For more information

American Studies Association
University of Maryland
2140 Taliaferro Hall
College Park, MD 20742
(301)405-1364

Asian studies

The major in Asian studies is designed to provide a background in Asian languages and cultures. Programs may focus on one part of Asia (Japan, China, Korea, Southeast Asia, or South Asia) or involve comparative study of the entire region. Students usually study an Asian language and take a range of social science and humanities courses to gain insight into Asian cultures, societies, history, politics, and economics.

Interests, skills, and qualities associated with success in the major

Interests. Other cultures and languages, travel, new experiences, learning a foreign language and culture, achieving new perspectives for understanding our own culture.

Skills and qualities. Oral and written communication, adapting to other cultures, curiosity.

Recommended high school preparation

English 4, precollege mathematics 2, laboratory science 2, social studies 2, history 2, and foreign language 2–4. Travel or residence abroad is useful, either as part of a formal exchange student program or as an individual or family experience.

Typical courses in the major

Chinese Civilization
South Asian Civilization
Buddhist Thought and Values
Religions of India

Modern Japan
Oriental Philosophy
Masterpieces of Asian Literature

What the major is like

The Asian studies major involves the study of the languages, cultures, religions, societies, and political and economic characteristics of all of Asia or of one of its major subdivisions: Japan, China, Southeast Asia, or South Asia. The program usually includes interdisciplinary courses that survey a wide range of topics in the social sciences and humanities. A broad historical and contemporary overview of the region is provided. With this background, students then choose additional courses in specific fields such as history, anthropology, political science, and religion.

Programs may cover traditional aspects of Asian culture, the impact of the prominent religions (Hinduism, Buddhism, Islam, Taoism, and Shinto), the history of the major art forms (architecture, music, literature, and film), the role of women, and interaction with the West.

Central to any program in Asian studies is the study of an Asian language (for example, Chinese, Japanese, Korean, Thai, Hindi); this is critical to understanding the cultures of the region. Asian languages are not difficult but they are different from ours, and it is exciting to discover, through their languages, the characteristics of the various cultures of Asia. Intensive summer programs in the United States and Asia, together with one-year programs in Asia, enable students to acquire additional language training and practice. Many Asian studies programs encourage students to spend a summer or year in some part of Asia. The experience of living in Asia is very rewarding.

In general, work in Asian studies builds considerable solidarity and interaction among Asian studies majors and close relations with faculty, all of whom share the commitment to increasing our knowledge about and contacts with Asia. With half the world's population and the most rapidly growing economies, Asia will be a dominant force in the next century. It is exciting to become a part of the group which will foster understanding and enhance interaction with the Asian people.

Specializations

An Asian language, East Asian literature, South Asian literature, anthropology, history, geography, political science, religion, art, history.

Other majors to consider

Anthropology
Art history
Comparative literature
History
International business management
Philosophy
Political science and government
Sociology

Careers related to the major

Asian studies graduates often pursue teaching or careers in the government, with foundations, in journalism, communications, international business, and international law. Teachers with special knowledge of Asia are needed at graduate, undergraduate, and secondary levels. There are positions in government agencies (State Department, development agencies, CIA) and in private foundations and international agencies. Businesses, particularly banks, seek Asia specialists to work overseas; international law firms also provide opportunities for Asia generalists and specialists. In general, the more language training a student has, the more jobs will be available to him or her.

For more information

Association for Asian Studies
University of Michigan
One Lane Hall
Ann Arbor, MI 48109

Environmental studies

Environmental studies is concerned with the effects of human activities on the environment from the perspectives of the natural and engineering sciences, social sciences, and humanities. Students majoring in the field study regional, national, and global environmental problems.

Interests, skills, and qualities associated with success in the major

Interests. The environment, solving environmental problems.

Skills and qualities. Quantitative analysis, natural sciences, integrating the insights of various disciplines into a unified perspective.

Recommended high school preparation

English 4, precollege mathematics 3–4, biology 1, chemistry 1, physics 1, social studies 2, and history 2.

Typical courses in the major

Ecology
Wildlife Management
Environmental Geology
Environmental Policy
Energy Policy
Environmental Health
Environmental History

Conservation Biology
Environmental Chemistry
Environmental Economics
Environmental Ethics
Land Use Planning
Environmental Education

What the major is like

The rapidly growing interest in environmental studies as an undergraduate major is a result of the increasing awareness of human impact on the environment. Environmental studies differs from related majors such as environmental science and environmental engineering in its greater emphasis on social sciences and humanities. Colleges and universities offer environmental studies as a liberal arts program, focusing less on technical training than on general comprehension of environmental problems.

Typically students begin the major with introductory courses in the natural sciences (usually biology and/or chemistry) and the social sciences. Environmental studies students take at least half their courses in biology, chemistry, and geology. Students with especially strong natural science interests may combine a concentration in a science with courses in environmental studies.

Some programs include some advanced courses in the social sciences, environmental economics, and environmental history. Economics is particularly important, because policymakers often use economic analysis to determine possible solutions to such problems as pollution, resource depletion, and land use. Environmental politics is important in order to understand the context in which policies and programs are created and carried out. Some programs also offer study of environmental problems in foreign countries, for example, the depletion of forests and the growth of deserts as well as such global problems as the so-called greenhouse effect.

In programs that include humanities, courses are commonly offered in environmental philosophy and ethics as well as in art, religion, and literature. An understanding of attitudes toward nature expressed in these areas helps us comprehend human relations with the environment.

Students can often get hands-on experience in solving environmental problems through fieldwork and internships. However, careers in the field increasingly require technical training at advanced levels and usually graduate work. The liberal arts education in environmental studies does not replace advanced specialized training, but it provides excellent preparation for such training.

Specializations Natural sciences, social sciences.

Other majors to consider
Agricultural education
Biology
Business administration
Chemical engineering
City, community, and regional planning
Environmental science
Forestry
Geology
Science education
Wildlife management

Careers related to the major Graduates of environmental studies programs can find jobs in lobbying, management of environmental organizations, journalism, environmental education (as a park naturalist, for example), or toxic waste disposal. After appropriate graduate work, they can find careers in air or water quality planning, solid waste planning, land use planning, fisheries and wildlife management, policy analysis, environmental law, laboratory research, resource economics, or college teaching.

For more information Conservation Directory
National Wildlife Federation
1400 Sixteenth Street NW
Washington, DC 20036-2266
(202)797-6800

European studies

European studies is an interdisciplinary major for students who want to increase their understanding of the history of European civilization and their knowledge of present-day Europe.

Interests, skills, and qualities associated with success in the major **Interests.** History, politics, economics, social change, art, music, theater, comparative literature, languages and linguistics, philosophy and religion.

Skills and qualities. Learning languages, summarizing and analyzing readings, reasoning cogently and clearly, writing lucidly and correctly.

Recommended high school preparation	English 4, precollege mathematics 2, laboratory science 1, social studies 2, geography .5, history 2–4, and foreign language 4. One year of music or visual arts is also recommended.
Typical courses in the major	Politics of Eastern Europe Spanish Civil War Greece and Rome Classicism and Romanticism The Austro-Hungarian Empire Avant-garde Art in Europe The French Revolution
What the major is like	The study of European civilization from antiquity to the present is a vast interdisciplinary enterprise. It comprises the political, social, and economic history of Europe from about 1000 B.C. to the present; the history of European art, music, religions, philosophy, and literatures in over a dozen tongues; the history of Europe's contributions to science, mathematics, and technology; and the study, often comparative, of politics, religion, philosophy, and the arts in present-day Europe.

The introduction to this wealth of material takes one of two forms: (1) a survey course in European civilization, or (2) a course designed to deal with a chosen era of European history (the Renaissance, the Age of Reason, the Romantic period) or with the culture of a single country of modern Europe (France, Germany, Spain). Occasionally both approaches are used.

Whatever form the introduction takes, the student usually works out the rest of the course work with an adviser or an advisory committee. In other words, after introductory courses, the European studies major is self-designed to fit the student's interests, talents, and background, although sometimes there are distribution requirements—typically two courses in history and two or three in languages and literature. For example, the student who has studied Latin and has an interest in the medieval period may wish to take further work in Latin and courses in medieval history, philosophy, theology, and medieval literature. Or if the student speaks some German and has a special interest in modern Austria, after some basic work in economics and comparative politics he or she may design a program focusing on the position of Austria within the political and economic picture of contemporary Europe. For the student who has learned some Polish at home, after preparation in history and comparative politics, he or she may concentrate on Poland's current transition from a socialist country under the shadow of the Soviet Union to a democracy. As another example, the student who is interested in the relation of music to painting in the early twentieth century may want to acquire the necessary background in music and art and fill the rest of the major with special courses in this area. The possibilities are almost limitless.

European studies programs may recommend, or even require, that majors spend a semester or a year (usually the junior year) in Europe. Living and studying in Europe and using a language other than English (except in the United Kingdom and Ireland) is an irreplaceable way to find out what it is like to be a European. Institutions that do not have their own study-abroad program usually honor work taken under the auspices of another institution. Another way to study abroad is to enroll at a European university whose credits will transfer to U.S. institutions.

Students may be required in the senior year to complete a special project related to their area of concentration. This valuable exercise focuses and clarifies their ideas.

Specializations	Comparative literature, comparative government, comparative economic systems, medieval Europe, Renaissance Europe, seventeenth-century

Europe, eighteenth-century Europe, nineteenth-century Europe, contemporary Europe.

Other majors to consider

Art history
Classics
Comparative literature
History
Literature and language majors
Music
Philosophy
Political science and government
Religion

Careers related to the major

The European studies major prepares one for jobs with companies that do business in Europe (banks, travel agencies), or with government, charitable, or research agencies operating in Europe. With graduate training, it can lead to careers in secondary school or college teaching, law (especially legal work for European and U.S. companies that do business together), and with the U.S. foreign service.

For more information

Council for European Studies
Box 44 Schermerhorn Hall
Columbia University
New York, NY 10027

International relations

International relations majors study the historical, political, economic, and sociocultural relations among countries and other participants in the international community. Students develop proficiency in a foreign language as they progress toward global knowledge, literacy, and communication skill.

Interests, skills, and qualities associated with success in the major

Interests. World history, politics, government, social sciences, languages.

Skills and qualities. Learning foreign languages, working with people, sensitivity to diverse peoples and cultures.

Recommended high school preparation

English 3–4, precollege mathematics 2–3, laboratory science 1, social studies 2–4, history 2–4, foreign language 3–4, and computer science 1–2.

Typical courses in the major

International Relations
World History
Microeconomics
Macroeconomics
War and Society

Comparative Government
International Law
U.S. Foreign Policy
The NATO Alliance
Japanese History

International Relations Theory   International Economic Relations
The Middle East   Politics of North Africa
Aftermath of the Cold War

What the major is like

The major in international relations incorporates the importance and excitement of rapid change in international events while responding to the growing need for educated people to perform in an increasingly interdependent world. Global knowledge, cross-cultural literacy, sensitivity in communication and interactions, and comfort in a world of diversity are goals of an international relations program.

The core of the major is an introduction to those disciplines that treat the relations between and among sovereign states and other international participants. These fields typically include political science, economics, history, sociology, and foreign languages. Thus the major is not confined to any one social science but rather is both multi- and interdisciplinary, mirroring the real world of international affairs.

Introductory courses generally begin with a study of the historical background of today's international system, followed by a consideration of the basic elements of the international scene. Attention is given to major current issues. Introductory courses typically end with a consideration of attempts to construct and maintain world peace. Advanced courses build on the political, economic, historical, and other social science dimensions of the introductory courses.

Since the spring of 1992, with the collapse of the USSR and its Eastern European empire, new issues have replaced those that concerned the international community during the Cold War. The industrial democracies face the task of providing some assistance to the former Soviet empire, but also have their own serious economic problems to solve. The new and developing countries are no longer united in demands against the developed countries. Instead, they have their own policies and record of development, yet seek aid from the developed states. It is a new and challenging scene for students to master, and economic issues dominate.

The major is often a multidisciplinary program administered by a committee of professors from various departments. Or, colleges may offer a concentration in international relations within a regular departmental major—usually political science. There are few international relations departments as such because most professors teaching the courses have positions in their home departments of political science, history, or economics.

A typical sequence of studies includes an introduction to international relations (usually offered by the political science department), introductory courses in micro- and macroeconomics, one or two courses in world history, and an introductory course in sociology or anthropology. Advanced courses in each of these departments follow, together with electives in various disciplines as determined by the institution's international relations program. Other requirements may be a seminar in the student's area of concentration as well as proficiency in a relevant foreign language.

Because the program in international relations usually has more demanding courses than ordinary social science programs, plus the foreign language requirement, graduates are viewed as strong competitors in the postgraduate world of study or work.

Specializations

Diplomacy and world order, international economics, comparative politics, cultural foundations of international relations, international environmental studies, international human rights.

Other majors to consider	**Anthropology** **Comparative literature** **Economics** Engineering **Environmental studies** **Geography** **History** Literature and language majors **Political science and government** **Sociology**
Careers related to the major	International relations graduates are eligible for entry-level positions in the federal civil service (especially the departments of State, Defense, Agriculture, and Treasury). Many graduates take positions with members of Congress or Congressional committees. Other options are paralegal positions with law firms and public service legal agencies, jobs in corporations and banks engaged in international business, and positions with a wide variety of nongovernmental organizations such as Amnesty International. Graduate degrees in international relations considerably enhance career options, especially in the Foreign Service and international business.
For more information	American Political Science Association 1527 New Hampshire Avenue NW Washington, DC 20036 (202)483-2512 Foreign Policy Association 729 Seventh Avenue New York, NY 10019 (212)764-4050

Jewish studies

Jewish studies majors explore the experiences of the Jewish people over the past 3,500 years, from Biblical times to the present. Students are exposed to the various civilizations in which the Jews have lived and study their interactions. They study such diverse subjects as the Bible and current events.

Interests, skills, and qualities associated with success in the major	**Interests.** History, the social sciences, the humanities. **Skills and qualities.** Reading intelligently, thinking critically, effective oral and written communication.
Recommended high school preparation	English 4, precollege mathematics 3, laboratory science 2, and history or social studies 2. Although it is not essential to take courses in the Hebrew language, doing so wherever possible may enable students to receive credit for advanced placement in the Hebrew language and also to take

courses that require a reading knowledge of Hebrew earlier than usual in the college career.

Typical courses in the major

Hebrew Language/Literature	Yiddish Language and Literature
Introduction to the Bible	The Ancient Middle East
Rabbinic Literature	Modern Jewish History
Classical Jewish History	Jewish Philosophy and Thought
Modern Near Eastern Studies	Contemporary Jewish Studies
Zionism	The Holocaust

What the major is like

A major in Jewish studies is a unique opportunity for Jewish students to explore their culture in an objective academic setting and for non-Jewish students to broaden their understanding of Judaism, a central foundation of Western civilization, Christianity, and Islam. Because of the widespread geographic distribution of the Jews over the centuries, courses in Judaic studies familiarize the student with many aspects of the human experience, often from a completely new perspective. Areas covered include archaeology, Biblical times, the Hellenistic period, early Christianity, Christian Europe, and the Islamic world. Of special interest is the modern period, with the emergence of Hasidism, the beginnings of secularization, the origins of reform and conservative Judaism, the phenomenon of Jewish socialism, the development of modern anti-Semitism culminating in the Holocaust, the growth of the American Jewish community, and above all the founding of the State of Israel. The study of Israel includes the gathering of exiles from all over the world, the revival of the Hebrew language, new forms of social organization such as the kibbutz, the conquest of the desert, the struggle to maintain a democratic state in a hostile Middle East, and numerous Arab-Israeli wars.

Depending on the institution, the Jewish studies major is either in a special department of its own or is an interdisciplinary program with faculty from various departments. In some cases, Jewish studies is offered by a department of religion or of Near Eastern civilization. Although in theory these different settings could represent different conceptions of Jewish studies, in practice they usually are simply a reflection of practical considerations at any given university. Less extensive majors may consist essentially of courses in religion and the modern period, given by two or three professors, while others may feature a dozen or more specialists in various disciplines and periods. As a rule, except for classes in Hebrew literature, the language of instruction is English. The larger and more comprehensive programs usually offer a sequence of courses in Hebrew texts.

Specializations

The Bible, Jewish history, Jewish thought, Jewish literature.

Other majors to consider

Anthropology
History
International relations
Literature and language majors
Philosophy
Religion

Careers related to the major

The major in Jewish studies can lead to careers in business, education, government service, social work, and other careers that require a liberal arts education. It is also sound preparation for a range of graduate or professional programs, for example, in law or medicine. The major also qualifies students for a career in Jewish scholarship, Jewish education, Jewish communal service, and the rabbinate or cantorate; graduate degrees are necessary for all of these except entry-level Jewish education jobs.

For more information   Association for Jewish Studies
Harvard University
Widener Library M
Cambridge, MA 02138

Latin American studies

In the Latin American studies major, students take a range of courses in the humanities and social sciences in order to become familiar with Latin American culture, literature, languages, society, history, and economics.

Interests, skills, and qualities associated with success in the major

Interests. Foreign culture, language, travel.

Skills and qualities. Oral and written communication, learning new languages, flexibility.

Recommended high school preparation

English 4, precollege mathematics 2, laboratory science 2, social studies 2, history 2, and foreign language 3–4. Participation in a foreign field program or personal travel is recommended.

Typical courses in the major

Colonial Rule in Latin America   Revolutionary Change
Cultures of Latin America   Slavery in Latin America
Current Latin American Politics   Portuguese
Latin American Literature   Spanish
The U.S. and Latin America

What the major is like

The major in Latin American studies is interdisciplinary and provides an understanding of the cultures, languages, literatures, history, economics, and societies of the diverse area known as Latin America, which reaches from Mexico to Argentina and Chile. (Some programs include the Caribbean as well.) Most programs include core seminars or lecture classes designed to develop this understanding. Typically these courses—plus a selection of other, general courses—account for 60 percent of the major. Students then focus on a geographic area or a topic (revolution, or modern Latin American literature, for example).

Though interdisciplinary in nature, some programs require students to take their concentration in one department (for example, Mexican history within the history department). Other programs permit concentrations that cut across departments (revolution and social change, or business and economics). Generally students also take at least two years in one of the major languages of Latin America—Spanish and Portuguese.

Majors are encouraged (but not required) to study for a summer or for up to a year in Latin America in a program sponsored by their own or another institution.

Specializations

Economics, history, political science, Spanish or Portuguese literature, geography, sociology, anthropology, international business. Many of the larger interdisciplinary programs are quite flexible, allowing self-designed concentrations by topic or geographic area.

Other majors to consider

Anthropology
History
International business management
International relations
Portuguese
Spanish

Careers related to the major

Latin American studies graduates are prepared for a variety of professions. Graduates often pursue careers in government (CIA, State department, or development agencies); teaching, international business, or law.

For more information

Consortium of Latin American Studies Programs
Tulane University
Center for Latin American Studies
New Orleans, LA 70118
(504)865-5164

Center for Latin American Studies
University of Pittsburgh
4E04 Forbes Quadrangle
Pittsburgh, PA 15260
(412)648-7392

Middle Eastern studies

Students who major in Middle Eastern studies take a variety of courses in the culture, history, politics, and religions of the Arab world, Turkey, Iran, and Israel, and study at least one of the area's major languages—Arabic, Persian, Turkish, and Hebrew.

Interests, skills, and qualities associated with success in the major

Interests. Current events, different cultures.

Skills and qualities. Learning languages.

Recommended high school preparation

English 4, precollege mathematics 3, laboratory science 2, history or social studies 4, and foreign language 4. History courses should include world history if available. Latin can be particularly helpful since it strengthens a student's grasp of grammar.

Typical courses in the major	Arabic Literature in Translation	Islamic History and Civilization
	Modern Middle Eastern History	Islamic Religion
	Middle East Politics	Peoples of the Middle East
	Arabic Language	Hebrew Language
	Turkish Language	Persian Language

What the major is like

Middle Eastern studies developed in the 1950s as part of an initiative aimed at training specialists to help the United States meet its increased global responsibilities and commitments in the aftermath of World War II. Most programs were originally at the master's level and concentrated on interdisciplinary training—that is, teaching students a little about history, political science, literature, and religion instead of requiring a concentration in a single department or discipline. The undergraduate major arose later and is available at about 50 universities.

Unlike the graduate programs, the undergraduate major is often administered by a single department, usually a Middle Eastern languages and literatures department, though sometimes by a center for Middle Eastern studies. Consequently, the undergraduate major is sometimes less interdisciplinary than are graduate programs and focuses more on culture and language than on the social sciences.

In a typical program, students take an introductory survey course covering the basic geography, history, and religious traditions of the area. In the following year, they take one or two specialized courses in history, political science, anthropology, religion, or literature in translation. If these courses prove interesting, the student should begin language study early enough to complete at least two full years before graduation. It takes at least three years of Arabic and two years of Turkish, Persian, or Hebrew to become minimally competent in these languages. (At some institutions, other languages such as Armenian, Kurdish, or Berber are available.) If Middle East language courses are not offered, every effort should be made to take them at a neighboring college or as independent study, particularly if the student intends to apply to graduate programs in the field.

Students should inquire into the exact definition of Middle Eastern studies at colleges of their interest. In some instances, the major may not be well adapted to students whose interests are contemporary affairs or politics. Such students will sometimes be better served by majoring in history or political science and taking a Middle Eastern language on the side. Most programs discourage students from concentrating on a single country even though the language they choose may be spoken only there (Turkish, Persian, Hebrew). Instead, programs expect students to become broadly familiar with the history of the region and particularly with the Islamic religion.

Specializations

Language often determines a student's concentration. For example, students of Turkish may take more courses in Turkish history and literature than their colleagues studying Arabic. But specialization at the undergraduate level is usually within the broad interdisciplinary framework of the major.

Other majors to consider

Comparative literature
History
International relations
Islamic studies
Political science and government

Careers related to the major	Graduates of Middle Eastern studies programs often take jobs with banks, multinational corporations, nonprofit organizations and foundations, or with the diplomatic service, the intelligence services, or the government. Some become journalists. Many students proceed to graduate school to learn more about the Middle East. Others combine their expertise with a degree in law or business with the objective of finding employment with international law firms or businesses with Middle East interests.
For more information	The United States Department of Education supports 12 Middle East National Resource Centers. Information about Middle East Studies majors can be obtained by writing to the Director or the Outreach Coordinator of the Middle East National Resource Center at any of the following universities: University of California at Berkeley, Harvard University, Columbia University, University of Arizona, University of Chicago, University of Washington, University of Utah, University of Texas at Austin, Princeton University, New York University, University of California at Los Angeles, University of Pennsylvania.

Urban studies

Students who major in urban studies learn to analyze a variety of social, physical, and economic problems in cities. They learn to approach urban issues creatively, with the goal of improving city life.

Interests, skills, and qualities associated with success in the major	**Interests.** History, cities, communities, government, people's well-being, quality of life. **Skills and qualities.** Verbal and analytic skills, perseverance.
Recommended high school preparation	English 4, precollege mathematics 2, biology 1, chemistry 1, physics 1, social studies 2, geography 1, history 2, foreign language 2, visual arts 1, and computer science 1.
Typical courses in the major	Community Development Economic Development Spatial Analysis Cultural Pluralism Minority Issues Social Institutions Local Government Group and Intergroup Relations Intergenerational Issues
What the major is like	Underlying all course work in the urban studies major are an appreciation of cities as centers of civilization and a hope for their continued service in that role. Programs therefore generally have two goals: understanding complex urban phenomena and learning to deal with them. Students analyze urban reality and learn to approach it creatively, with the intention of making life better in the city. Typical courses cover a wide range of topics: health care issues; problems stemming from class, race, sex, or age; physical design; fiscal and economic systems; community organization; and many other aspects of

city life. Students learn to address urban problems with proper regard for existing legal, social, political, and governmental systems. Management, planning, politics, and urban design become tools of change.

Introductory courses cover urban history, urban social structure, urban form, and regional economics. Advanced courses explore an array of important concerns, from social welfare issues to transportation and infrastructure design, from fiscal policy and government administration to housing, education, health, and community organization. Students may specialize in any of these topics. Or, they may combine their urban studies major with work in the traditional social sciences, humanities, arts, and natural sciences. Toward the end of their program, students may do internships or field research.

Specializations

Environmental psychology, social and human services, policy and politics, physical design, criminal justice and deviancy.

Other majors to consider

City, community, and regional planning
Civil engineering
Environmental studies
Health services management
Housing and human development
Labor/industrial relations
Management science
Parks and recreation management
Political science and government
Social work

Careers related to the major

Many graduates of urban studies programs proceed directly to careers as social service workers, policy analysts, or urban planners and as entry-level professionals in virtually every branch of local, state, and national government. Some pursue professional or graduate degrees in law, social work, criminal justice, education, or planning.

For more information

Urban Affairs Association
University of Delaware
Newark, DE 19716
(302)831-2394

Women's studies

Women's studies puts women and gender at the center of inquiry in a major that typically includes courses from the humanities, social sciences, and natural sciences. Women's studies both adds to existing knowledge about women and generates new perspectives on what is already known about human history and culture.

Interests, skills, and qualities associated with success in the major	**Interests.** How societies are organized, especially the roles of women and men; openness to new ideas and a desire to ask questions; seeing the connections between ideas, systems, and people.
	Skills and qualities. Analyzing arguments, thinking critically, listening, working with others, writing and speaking, developing a greater respect for diversity.
Recommended high school preparation	English 4, precollege mathematics 2, biology 1, chemistry 1, physics 1, social studies 1, history or social studies 2–3, foreign language 2, music 1, and visual arts 1.
Typical courses in the major	Gender, Race, and Class Feminist Theory Women and Literature History of Women of Color Psychology of Women Women and Politics

What the major is like

The major in women's studies is interdisciplinary and seeks to understand what it means now, and has meant in the past, to be a woman. It also examines the concept and the uses of gender, that is, the varying and changing meanings societies attach to being women and men. Because gender reflects and determines differences of power and opportunity, students of women's studies become adept at analyzing systems, asking searching questions about equality, and gaining confidence in their own power to transform the world they live in.

Women's studies began in the late 1960s in an effort to compensate for the invisibility in most college courses of information about women. However, what began as an effort to fill in the gaps has now become a comprehensive analysis of all knowledge, all periods, all information. In addition, then, to giving students the results of new research about the half of humanity and human culture that had been overlooked, the women's studies major generates new perspectives on and questions about existing knowledge, accepted beliefs, and unexamined norms.

Women's studies looks at differences between women and men as society has defined them over time, and also at differences among women themselves. Gender is a focus of analysis but is part of a complex matrix of class, race, age, ethnicity, nationality, and sexual identity. As a result, for many students, women's studies becomes a window on the rest of the world.

Over the years women's studies has concerned itself with not only what is taught, but how it is taught. Classes seek to foster dialogue, create a safe arena in which to disagree, and challenge students to engage with difference. There is much more attention to group work, self-defined papers and projects, discussion, methods of presentation, variety in course assignments, and invitations to tie theory to personal experience.

For many students the women's studies major is far more than an intellectual experience. It transforms their lives. It helps them to both understand their current lives and have the courage to see themselves as capable of shaping their worlds.

Almost all departments have been affected by the dynamic and challenging new scholarship about women produced in ever-increasing quantity over the last 20 years. A typical women's studies program therefore includes courses offered within women's studies itself as well as courses offered by traditional departments. A women's studies major normally offers an introductory women's studies course; a series of electives equally distributed among the humanities and the social sciences and, where possible, the natural sciences; and a final capstone experience in the form of a senior seminar, a field study/internship, or an independent study. Increasingly, women's studies programs are also adding to the major a course requirement on feminist theory as well as one on race, ethnicity, or non-Western culture.

The major offers students unusual flexibility and permits them to tailor their program to specific disciplinary or thematic interests. Almost half of women's studies students double-major because the program permits—indeed encourages—them to take courses outside the interdisciplinary courses of the major.

Specializations

Women and social institutions, women, art and literature, gender and American ethnic studies, cross-cultural analyses, feminism, science, and technology.

Other majors to consider

American studies
Anthropology
Business administration
Communications
Ethnic studies
Fine arts
History
Philosophy
Psychology
Sociology

Careers related to the major

The women's studies major prepares a student for a wide range of employment. Graduates will find jobs in education (all levels), social services, business, government, health services, communications and film, and (with appropriate graduate degrees) in college teaching and research, law, and medicine.

For more information

The National Women's Studies Association
University of Maryland
College Park, MD 20742-1325
(301)405-5573

"Liberal Learning and the Women's Studies Major" is available for $2 from the National Women's Studies Association.

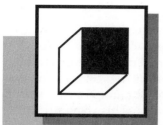

Mathematics

JOHN KENELLY
Clemson University

Majoring in mathematics prepares a student for a lifetime of intellectual growth, change, and rewarding work. Mathematicians use numbers and do arithmetic; but logical thinking and analysis are their game.

There are many interesting questions that students may not think of answering with mathematics. Here are some examples. How do flocks of birds avoid collision in flight? Why do all rivers meander in the same way, and what happens when the pattern is disturbed? What type of electrocardiogram wave patterns predict heart problems? How can meteorologists build a better weather prediction system? Recent developments in mathematics—for example, chaos theory and fractals—are starting to answer these and other equally intriguing questions.

Along with the growth of computer science and computing, the expanding uses of mathematics have moved the subject from a support role for the sciences to the core of most academic disciplines. Mathematicians have thus become important members of almost every research and development team. Math's broad universal usefulness makes it an ideal major for students who wish to delay choosing a field of work while they search out and discover their personal interests and goals.

Mathematics is an academic discipline that overlaps, and applies directly to, most other subjects. Thus, preparing for study in math requires pursuing a broad, diverse curriculum. If mathematicians are going to use their skills in science, business, education, social studies, and the arts, they should be knowledgeable in the basic aspects of these areas. Although no student can include all these areas in a college program, each student can include study in areas of greatest personal interest. Some mathematics majors might concentrate heavily in the physical sciences, whereas others might take courses in economics and accounting. Students who combine mathematics with the arts find this a helpful mix for careers in computer graphic arts and technical animation. These are just examples.

Many mathematicians use computers extensively because they provide the answers within much of mathematical study. However, using computers does not make them computer scientists any more than the extensive use of mathematics turns computer scientists into mathematicians.

Mathematics deals with abstract systems and the study of patterns. In brief, mathematicians create and study mathematical models. During the elementary grades, the student begins the abstract processes of counting and drawing. These continue through high school, where the student learns algebra, with its abstractions (variables, equations, graphs) of problem-solving elements, and geometry, with its abstractions of spatial relations and the reasoning process. Mathematics continues to extend and refine the study of systems and patterns throughout higher education. In college, students will learn about such contemporary areas as graph theory, linear algebra, numerical methods, dynamic systems, operations research, and statistics. In sharp contrast to the material presented in high schools, college-level mathematics courses concentrate on content that has been newly created or has undergone dramatic change as a result of research developments in the last several decades. This dynamic study prepares them for careers that will deal with significant mathematics yet to be discovered.

In high school, prospective mathematics majors should prepare for their college studies by taking a full academic program. In addition to four years of mathematics and English, the program should include college preparatory science, social studies, foreign language, arts, and computer science courses. The science studies should include laboratory courses in which students reach conclusions supported by theory and verified through experimentation. The social studies courses should include world history and social and political history as well as the interpretation of charts and substantial quantitative information. Reading assignments should stress integrating multiple sources of information and synthesizing complex quantitative data. Foreign language study prepares students to participate in the world society and explore the subtle elements of language. Since mathematics often involves the study of subtle properties in a simplified setting, the ability to handle subtle language elements is an important skill.

Because studying the arts sharpens the ability to visualize and to think in abstract terms, it is not surprising that many great mathematicians are also, for example, accomplished musicians. Computers are important in all fields, and mathematics is no exception. In addition to studying programming, mathematics majors should learn to use applications software such as word processing, spreadsheets, data bases, and graphing software. And all students should learn touch typing!

When students who plan to major in math enter college, they are usually expected to begin with calculus, which many will have already studied in high school. Calculus is the mathematical study of change—a universal element in every academic discipline. The calculus course covers a wealth of applications while integrating many of the concepts of algebra and geometry.

In college mathematics courses the essentially simple high school treatment of solving simultaneous linear equations is greatly expanded in linear algebra and linear programming courses.

The theory and understanding of random events, as well as the analysis of data, create a whole new world of challenges and excitement. As computers take most of the drudgery out of statistics, researchers will be able to inject more critical analysis and thinking.

As fast as mathematics is changing, its fundamentals remain the same. Abstract simplified models are universal. Therefore, whatever the nature and details of future varieties, the basics are the same. Those who study one have studied the other.

While the need for mathematicians has been dramatically increasing, the supply of mathematics majors has fallen. From a high of 4 to 5 percent of the entering freshmen in the 1960s, the number of students currently entering the field has declined to one-tenth of that proportion. Mathematics is considered to be a difficult subject, and, on average, from the ninth grade to the Ph.D., about half of the students drop out each year. Yet, the

challenges of a demanding curriculum attract and hold many of the best. Good mathematics students often excel in many areas.

This combination of increased demand and reduced supply has created a rich set of career opportunities for mathematics majors. Because the number of female and minority mathematics students is very small, there are now especially attractive mathematical career opportunities for members of these groups in business, industry, government, and education.

Mathematics majors can anticipate a career that draws on their potential for growth and flexibility. The major is designed to develop reasoning capabilities and not to "coach" students in specialized techniques. Whether you intend to pursue a career in government, industry, or teaching, you owe it to yourself and your future to develop a broad background. As quantitative methods expand and join the wide applications of computer techniques and methods, there will be a growing need for more mathematics majors.

Mathematics

Mathematics majors develop the abilities to explore, conjecture, and reason logically as well as the ability to use various mathematical methods effectively to solve problems. Mathematics is both a discipline and a tool used extensively in the sciences, medicine, business, industry, and government.

Interests, skills, and qualities associated with success in the major

Interests. Problem solving; games requiring analytic reasoning such as bridge, chess, backgammon; solving puzzles; working with numbers; art; music.

Skills and qualities. Computational skills, pattern recognition, analytic skills, logic.

Recommended high school preparation

English 4, algebra 2, geometry 1, precalculus 1, biology 1–2, chemistry 1–2, physics 1–2, social studies 1, foreign language 2, and computer science 1–2. Advanced Placement Calculus is recommended if offered.

Typical courses in the major

Calculus
Analysis
Statistics
Set Theory
Differential Equations

Linear Algebra
Numerical Analysis
Modern Algebra
Applied Mathematics

What the major is like

Mathematics majors learn to explore, conjecture, and reason logically and to use mathematical methods in solving problems. Mathematics is much in demand by the sciences, medicine, business, industry, and government. This demand has intensified dramatically since computer technology has made the analysis of numerical data easy and accessible, and it will continue to grow as technology advances.

Math majors usually take a core sequence of courses in calculus. The calculus was developed independently in the seventeenth century by Gottfried Wilhelm Leibniz and Isaac Newton to analyze changes in physical quantities—for example, the minimum distance between two planets or the maximum profit in some business enterprise. Through calculus one can determine lengths of curves, areas of regions, and volumes of solids, or investigate the velocity and acceleration of moving objects.

Thanks to technological advances since World War II, the undergraduate curriculum now includes courses in combinatorics and discrete methods, which consider the finite nature of certain problems. Students may, for instance, wish to find the number of possible ways to assign a fixed number of vehicles to visit multiple locations and to determine which schedule would be the least costly. Discrete mathematics had its roots in the work of Leonhard Euler in the eighteenth century, but its importance was not fully appreciated until World War II when George Dantzig was assigned the task of effectively allocating the finite number of resources available to the Allied Forces. The ability of computers to perform a finite number of calculations very rapidly continues to be a factor in the development of discrete mathematics.

Math majors will take courses in linear algebra, differential equations, computer science, and symbolic logic. In linear algebra they learn techniques to solve systems of linear equations using matrices and investigate properties of vector spaces, which have many applications in the business world. Differential equations are often applied to the physical sciences.

Some advanced mathematics courses rarely deal with numerical values, but concentrate instead on investigating properties of sets and number systems through more abstract representations.

Math majors are often recruited for positions that emphasize the analytic reasoning developed in math courses. To take best advantage of the many career opportunities, mathematics majors should become skilled in communication and study the humanities as well as the sciences, computer sciences, and economics or accounting. Many math majors learn French, German, or Russian, which are frequently used in mathematical research.

Specializations

Applied mathematics, pure mathematics, discrete mathematics, statistics.

Other majors to consider

Accounting
Actuarial sciences
Applied mathematics
Business administration
Computer science
Economics
Engineering
Information sciences and systems
Management science
Physics
Pure mathematics
Statistics

Careers related to the major

Many new jobs in the twenty-first century will require the ability to use mathematics; yet there is a declining pool of mathematicians to supply the demands of science and technology and to train our next generation of scientists. The opportunities for mathematics majors will be plentiful and diverse. Math majors are sought by medical and law schools as well as by graduate schools and employers in economics, accounting, management sciences, natural sciences, social sciences, computer science, statistics, and communication. The major may lead to careers in business, industry, middle school and high school teaching, government, engineering, statistics, and accounting. With graduate degrees, one can have a career in actuarial science, medicine, law, college teaching, or mathematics research.

For more information

Mathematical Association of America
1529 18th Street NW
Washington, DC 20036
(202)387-5200

Mathematics education

The major in mathematics education prepares students to teach mathematics at the high school or middle school level. Like mathematics majors, students develop skills and knowledge in the field of mathematics; they also take professional education courses.

Interests, skills, and qualities associated with success in the major

Interests. Problem solving, analytic reasoning, games such as chess or computer adventures, working with children, working with computers, leadership, organizing people.

Skills and qualities. Analytic reasoning and logic, oral and written communication, creativity, patience, organizational skills, using computers.

Recommended high school preparation

English 4, algebra 1, geometry 1, precalculus 1, biology 1, chemistry 1, physics 1, social studies 2, history 1, foreign language 2, and computer science 1. A year of Advanced Placement Calculus (if offered) and an additional year of science are recommended.

Typical courses in the major

Calculus
Modern Algebra
Probability and Statistics
Differential Equations
History of Mathematics
Linear Algebra
Classroom Strategies
Curriculum Development

Human Growth and Development
Applied Mathematics
Real Analysis
Foundations of Geometry
Computer Programming
The School in American Society
Methods and Materials

What the major is like

Mathematics education majors must satisfy the requirements of both their college or university and their state's teacher certification program. The preparation of high school, junior high school, or middle school mathematics teachers can vary greatly from state to state and from college to college. The mathematics education major is found in a school, department, or college of education, or in the mathematics department. Some colleges require math education majors first to pursue an undergraduate degree in math before gaining a teacher certificate through a master's or other graduate degree program in education. All programs, however, have two common features: a strong background in mathematics and a sequence of experiences that prepare the student for teaching.

Preparation in mathematics begins with the calculus sequence, which consists of two to four courses that form the foundation for nearly all future mathematics courses and for applying mathematics in engineering, physics, and other sciences. A variety of courses follow the calculus sequence, exposing the student to the specialty areas within mathematics: algebra, analysis, geometry, applied math, and statistics. Students preparing to teach math commonly develop skills in computer programming, using higher-level languages like Pascal, and in the areas of mathematics that relate to computers, such as discrete mathematics. Also, students take courses in subject areas that use mathematics as a tool (economics, physics, chemistry) in order to learn about these applications.

The professional education component includes a core of courses designed to orient the prospective teacher to education: psychology of children and adolescents, role of the school in American society, and research-based strategies for skillful teaching and effective schools. These courses often include field experiences in which students observe or assist teachers within a middle or high school. All mathematics education students take at least one course examining the mathematics curriculum and how to teach it. In this course they receive instruction on how to develop and teach mathematics lessons as well as exposure to the textbooks, calculators, and computer software used in teaching math. Professors often employ a technique called microteaching to allow students to teach brief lessons to fellow math education majors.

Student teaching comes at the end of the program. For approximately 12 weeks, the undergraduate becomes an apprentice teacher under the supervision of a qualified math teacher and a college faculty member. Through a gradual process, the student takes command of the cooperating teacher's classes and develops the skills needed to become a fully certified teacher of mathematics.

Because state laws influence teacher preparation, prospective math education majors should learn the requirements and procedures for obtaining a teaching certificate or license. The requirements often consist of education admission tests, interviews, medical exams, and subject area tests such as the National Teachers' Examination.

Specializations

There are no specializations at the undergraduate level.

Other majors to consider

Chemistry
Computer science
Economics
Engineering
Information sciences and systems
Physics
Psychology
Statistics

Careers related to the major

The mathematics education major can lead to careers as a high school teacher, middle school teacher, training specialist for business or industry, and to other careers in business. With graduate degrees, one can work as a college teacher, education researcher, school principal, or superintendent.

For more information

National Council of Teachers of Mathematics
1906 Association Drive
Reston, VA 22091
(703)620-9840

Statistics

Statistics is the practical science of dealing with data. In the major, students learn to design efficient data-collection systems and to analyze and interpret information derived from the data. A statistician's primary tools are mathematics and computers. Science and logic underlie their thinking.

Interests, skills, and qualities associated with success in the major

Interests. Mathematics, working with numbers, problem solving, quantitative problems.

Skills and qualities. Mathematical, analytic, and numerical competence; practical and technical writing ability; working in groups; computer skills; one-on-one communication.

Recommended high school preparation

English 4, algebra 1, calculus 1, geometry 1, trigonometry 1, biology 1, chemistry 1, physics 1, history or social studies 2, and computer science 1. One year of probability and statistics is recommended if offered.

Typical courses in the major

Applied Statistical Methods
Design of Experiments
Nonparametric Statistics
Statistical Theory
Statistical Computing
Calculus of Several Variables
Computer Programming

Probability
Sample Survey Methods
Regression Analysis
Statistical Quality Control
Calculus
Linear and Matrix Algebra

What the major is like

Statistics is the science of dealing effectively with data. Students majoring in statistics will learn how to design data collection efficiently and to analyze and interpret the resulting data. Statistics is not just a branch of mathematics, but a separate discipline that makes intensive use of mathematics and computers.

Statistics is a relatively young science; its first academic departments were formed in the late 1940s. Although initially a graduate discipline, there are now more than 70 colleges and universities across the country offering undergraduate statistics programs, a number that is slowly growing. Most statistics departments are found within a college of liberal arts and sciences, but several are in business colleges and a few are in colleges of engineering or agriculture. Combined departments of mathematics and statistics are also found, primarily in small to medium-sized institutions.

In the first year of college statistics students concentrate on general education courses and mathematics, including a full year of calculus. Introductory courses in statistics and computer science may be included in the first year, but more typically the statistics course work begins in the second year, after the student has developed sufficient mathematical skills. In the third year, statistics becomes the dominant part of the major. The number of required computer courses varies from program to program and will undoubtedly increase in the future.

Statistics course work varies. Courses in the applied techniques of describing and analyzing data to extract information require strong skills in algebra and computing. Other courses focus on probability and the mathematical theory of statistics, thus demanding abilities in calculus and in logic. Still other courses, which deal with designing experiments and sample surveys, often involve projects in which small groups of students design a study, collect and analyze the data, and present a final report of the results.

Mathematics course work includes matrix algebra and calculus. Students planning graduate studies should study advanced calculus. Computer course work may include an introduction to computer systems and programming languages, such as FORTRAN or Pascal, and instruction in the use of major statistics software.

Courses in the sciences, humanities, and social sciences are very important in statistics. In commerce, business, government, and industry, statisticians routinely advise scientists and researchers in many other fields on how to handle data in a wide variety of projects. This work demands not only the mathematical tools of the statistician, but also skills of communication, teamwork, and technical writing, as well as familiarity with the concepts and terminology of these areas of application.

Specializations

Specialization at the undergraduate level is not common.

Other majors to consider

Actuarial sciences
Applied mathematics
Industrial engineering
Operations research (quantitative methods)

Careers related to the major

The statistics major leads to careers as a statistician with a wide variety of employers in manufacturing, pharmaceuticals, insurance, government statistical agencies, consulting firms, agricultural research, and more. Statistics majors also find careers in actuarial science, statistical programming, operations research, and mathematical analysis. A graduate degree can enhance career possibilities.

For more information

The American Statistical Association
1429 Duke Street
Alexandria, VA 22314-3402
(703)684-1221

Physical Sciences

ALAN LIGHTMAN

Massachusetts Institute of Technology

My serious interest in physics began in my freshman year of college. In the dining hall that year, one of the upperclassmen smugly announced that, on the basis of mechanics alone, he could predict where to strike a billiard ball so that it would roll with no sliding. I was mightily impressed and decided that this was a subject worth looking into.

The physical sciences reflect the wonder and delight and adventure people find in the physical world. Why do birds fly together in a "V" formation? Why is the sky blue at noon and red at sunset? What causes the phases of the moon? Do colored lights mix like colored paints? What shape is the arc of a ball shot from a cannon? How do scientists know that inhaled gas is different from exhaled gas? How do scientists know that the earth is round? How far away is the nearest star? Does outer space go on forever and ever? Does time go on forever? These are all questions in physical science. Many of them we begin asking in childhood, when we first become aware that a world exists outside our own bodies and minds.

The physical sciences reflect also the logic of nature. The flight of birds, the color of the sky, the arc of cannonballs, and a vast array of other phenomena can all be explained by a surprisingly small number of physical laws. From those few basic laws, all else comes as a logical sequence, just as a fantastically large number of chess games can be played from a few simple rules governing the moves of the pieces. For example, from the basic physical law that the total energy of a system cannot change over time, scientists can deduce the speed a bullet needs to escape from the earth, the length of the seesaw needed for a baby to balance an elephant, and the rise in temperature of water after a brick is dropped into it. Why such a law as the conservation of energy exists is not known. Why nature should be logical and orderly at all is the greatest mystery of science. But it is a wonderful mystery.

College courses in physical science include physics, chemistry, astronomy, geology and earth science, atmospheric science and meteorology, and oceanography. These courses usually have more laboratory work and more quantitative detail than do similar courses in high school. In a good college course in a physical science, the principal thing you will learn is how to reason and how to test your ideas. For example, suppose you begin with the belief that the sun is always overhead at noon, as many people believe. By keeping a journal of the sun's position in the sky every hour of the day, throughout the year, you can disprove this belief. Furthermore, by combining this data with knowledge of your city's latitude and some simple geometry, you can *calculate* the tilt of the earth on its axis. You don't have to take anyone's word for it, including your teacher's or your textbook's. You can figure it out yourself. Or suppose you think that the period of a pendulum gets longer, the heavier the weight at its end. The period of a pendulum is the time taken for the pendulum bob to make one complete back-and-forth swing. You can make a pendulum yourself, out of a piece of string with a weight tied to its end, and test your belief with a stopwatch. You will find that the period does *not* depend at all on the weight of the pendulum bob. This miraculous result is closely related to a strange fact about gravity: different objects dropped from the same height hit the floor at the same time (neglecting air resistance). Don't put the pendulum away. Continued experimenting shows that its period does depend on the length of the string. In fact, measuring the period for many different lengths results in a remarkable pattern: the period is proportional to the square root of the length. (Every quadrupling of the length doubles the period.) But don't take my word for it. Go out and make your own pendulum. There is no greater satisfaction than learning something on your own, from scratch. Such learning not only teaches the ways of science; it also teaches self-confidence.

The ability to think and reason, the ability to solve problems, the ability to test ideas and throw out the ones that don't pass muster, increase confidence. These skills are valuable for any career—whether a research geologist, a science teacher, a lawyer, a businessperson, or a homemaker. Physical science prepares you to be a productive and imaginative member of society. And if you do decide to become a professional scientist, perhaps you will find a way to turn photosynthesis into an industrial energy source, figure out how to predict earthquakes, or work out a new "grand unified theory" of the forces of physics.

Physical science majors can expect to take between 10 and 15 science courses and between 2 and 5 mathematics courses, including calculus. A course or two in physics is required of almost all physical science majors. In high school, students should take as much science and math as possible. Even more important, read on your own, do experiments on your own, talk to your friends about science.

In 1989 the American Association for the Advancement of Science, which is the largest organization of professional scientists and science educators in the country, produced a set of recommendations for the final product of a good education in science. Those recommendations include a familiarity with the natural world, an understanding of the key concepts in science, the ability to think scientifically, an understanding of the human side of science, and an ability to use science and the scientific method for the benefit of society. These goals should be kept in mind when selecting your courses. Avoid survey courses, which teach you a little about a lot of topics. A small number of key concepts are far more valuable than a large number of facts, both for the science major and the nonmajor. Introductory courses with no lab work and no experience with the scientific method should be avoided. Without being able to test what you learn, you will never build a firm belief in science on which to build later knowledge. Take courses that concentrate on a few fundamentals, that require problem solving, that relate science to people, that are taught by professors excited about their subject. Take courses that intrigue you.

My neighbor across the street has a 15-year-old daughter who is taking biology. She has been told that the oxygen we breathe is used to burn food in our bodies. Hence, the gas we breathe out should be missing its

oxygen; it should be different from the gas we breathe in. Right? Maybe. One evening, we rummaged through her house and found a jar and a balloon and a candle. She lit the candle and put it under the jar. The candle burned brightly for nearly half a minute and then went out. Then, she painstakingly blew up the ballon with her own exhalations and let that gas into the jar, repeating the experiment. This time, the candle went out in a few seconds. But it was replaced by a broad smile that lit up her face. And the word "awesome."

Astronomy

Students of astronomy seek to understand the entire universe—its constituent parts, such as the stars and planets, and the physical and mathematical laws that govern them.

Interests, skills, and qualities associated with success in the major

Interests. Nature, the night sky, scientific and philosophical issues such as Where do we come from, Why is the universe expanding, and Is there life elsewhere in the universe?

Skills and qualities. Math, science, computers, mechanical ability, physical dexterity.

Recommended high school preparation

English 4, precollege mathematics 3, chemistry 1, physics 1, social studies 2, and computer science 1.

Typical courses in the major

Solar System Astronomy
Galactic Astronomy
Cosmology
Planetary Astronomy
Electricity and Magnetism
Calculus
Computer Science

Stellar Astronomy
Observational Astronomy
Introduction to Astrophysics
Quantum Physics
Optics
Differential Equations

What the major is like

The astronomy major offers instruction to students who are fascinated with and curious about the nature of celestial bodies. In many universities the astronomy program is offered by the department of physics and astronomy. Some institutions offer two tracks in their astronomy programs: one leads to broad, general knowledge of the field and the other, which includes intensive work in physics and mathematics, to preparation for graduate study.

Astronomy programs first provide general introductory courses and then laboratory courses for hands-on observation. In courses in cosmology, students learn the current theories about the origins and future of the universe; courses in planetary astronomy describe current understanding of the surfaces and make-up of the planets and moons in the solar system. Most institutions offer an introduction to astrophysics, the theoretical side of astronomy, which presents the basic physical laws of the formation and evolution of stars, galaxies, and the universe itself. In addition to classroom activities, astronomy students can use telescopes on their campuses or, occasionally, at national observatories. Because the number of majors in most astronomy programs is small, students can expect personal attention from the faculty.

Because students need to combine courses in mathematics and physics with the astronomy curriculum, the major effectively begins in the freshman year. Interested students should therefore contact the astronomy major adviser for help with planning their freshman programs.

An astronomer's activities can range from working at a computer to teaching to observing with a telescope alone on a mountain at night; from running a planetarium to joining a team of scientists on a major research problem to being an astronaut. The profession normally requires a graduate degree; therefore, the undergraduate program should be planned to meet the requirements for admission to the advanced degree program. In addition to courses in astronomy, students must have a strong foundation in mathematics and physics.

Because astronomy is a hobby to so many people, students majoring in the field often have the opportunity to join local astronomy clubs or to work with local school students who are interested in the stars.

Specializations

Optical astronomy, radio astronomy, space astronomy, astrophysics, planetary astronomy, solar astronomy, extragalactic astronomy, cosmology.

Other majors to consider

Computer science
Electrical engineering
Information sciences and systems
Mathematics
Physics

Careers related to the major

Astronomers work in planetariums, science museums, or other public positions. A major in astronomy provides excellent preparation for careers in fields other than the physical sciences. Astronomy majors have become neurosurgeons, high school teachers, trial lawyers, and insurance executives. A graduate degree is required to become a professional astronomer. Most astronomers are affiliated with universities, observatories, or laboratories. About 30 percent work for the federal government.

For more information

American Astronomical Society
Department of Astronomy
University of Texas
Austin, TX 78712-1083
(512)471-1309

Atmospheric sciences and meteorology

Students who major in atmospheric sciences and meteorology study the basic principles of atmospheric physics and dynamics and are concerned with understanding and forecasting our weather.

Interests, skills, and qualities associated with success in the major

Interests. Weather, the behavior of the physical world, the environment, climate, science, mathematics, computer science, geography, serving the public.

Skills and qualities. Analytic reasoning, mechanical reasoning, pattern recognition, logic, computational skills, problem solving, originality.

Recommended high school preparation

English 4, precollege mathematics 4, biology 1, chemistry 1, physics 1, social studies 2, geography 1, foreign language 3, and computer science 1. Literacy in electronics is highly desirable.

Typical courses in the major

Thermodynamics	Atmospheric Radiation
Cloud Physics	Dynamic Meteorology
Weather Analysis/Forecasting	Atmospheric Technology
Local Weather Systems	

What the major is like

The major in atmospheric sciences and meteorology prepares students for careers in weather forecasting and also for graduate study of weather and climate. In many ways the major often called meteorology is a specialization of physics, and advanced mathematics is a basic tool in its study. Before beginning the formal meteorology program, therefore, students take elementary calculus and analytic geometry in the freshman and sophomore years and calculus-based physics in the sophomore year. Later, advanced calculus, linear algebra, or both are required.

Meteorology course work usually begins in the junior year, although some institutions offer introductory courses to sophomores. The formal meteorology program consists of three parts. The first part is physical meteorology: atmospheric thermodynamics (conservation of energy within a mixture of air and water), radiation (light from the sun or infrared radiation emitted by the earth), cloud physics (condensation and freezing of water and precipitation formation), and atmospheric stability (tendencies of warm air to rise and cold air to fall).

The second part is dynamic meteorology (the study of air motions). Here the laws of conservation of energy and momentum are combined to form a complete, generalized mathematical description of the weather. These concepts are then used to explain the weather's structure and behavior.

The third part is synoptic meteorology, which applies basic dynamics and atmospheric physics to the interpretation and prediction of daily weather. Working in the laboratory the student learns to interpret daily weather maps, to analyze data in order to conceptualize the weather system structure, and to prepare forecasts for various locations based on these interpretations. Although a full year of this laboratory is optional for some programs, the U.S. Weather Service and the various branches of the armed forces require the full six semester hours in order for the graduate to be qualified as a forecaster.

Beyond this core in physical, dynamic, and synoptic meteorology, students are encouraged to take one or more electives emphasizing specializations like thunderstorms and weather systems composed of thunderstorms, cloud physics, oceanography, atmospheric chemistry, radiative transfer, tropical meteorology, radar meteorology, satellite meteorology, and climatology. Some institutions offer internship programs.

The degree achieved is generally the Bachelor of Science, although some colleges award the Bachelor of Arts to meteorology majors. As meteorology becomes more complex, education beyond the bachelor's degree will be necessary both for weather forecasting and for scientific research.

Atmospheric science and meteorology may be called by various names, according to what aspect is emphasized in an institution's program. For instance, "atmospheric science" is used widely by programs that emphasize research and play down forecasting. At some institutions meteorology is an optional specialization within an earth sciences or an environmental sciences major. These programs often stress the interdisciplinary aspects of meteorology—combining, for instance, the study of weather with oceanography, biology, or soil sciences. Another specialization, agricultural meteorology, emphasizes the application of meteorology to farming problems.

Specializations

Synoptic meteorology (forecasting and interpretation of daily weather), atmospheric chemistry, theoretical meteorology, observational systems.

Other majors to consider

Applied mathematics
Chemistry
Computer science
Earth sciences
Environmental science
Geography
Information sciences and systems
Mathematics
Oceanography
Physics

Careers related to the major

The major in atmospheric sciences and meteorology can lead to jobs as a weather forecaster, television or radio weather announcer, air quality analyst, agricultural meteorologist, climatologist, or scientific programmer. A graduate degree can lead to careers as a U.S. Weather Service forecaster, research scientist, or college teacher.

For more information

American Meteorological Society
45 Beacon Street
Boston, MA 02108-3693
(617)227-2425

Chemistry

Majors in chemistry study the composition, structure, and properties of matter as well as the reactions that transform one form of matter into another. Because it is an experimental science, students learn to design and perform the experiments that allow a better understanding of the physical world.

Interests, skills, and qualities associated with success in the major

Interests. Problem solving, construction of models or equipment, curiosity about how things work.

Skills and qualities. Taking things apart and putting them back together, visualizing objects in three dimensions, analytic and mathematical skills.

Recommended high school preparation

English 4, precollege mathematics 3, laboratory science 4, history 3, foreign language 2, and computer science 1.

Typical courses in the major	General Chemistry	Instrumental Analysis
	Inorganic Chemistry	Transition Metals
	Organic Chemistry	Chemical Kinetics
	Physical Chemistry	Thermodynamics

What the major is like

Chemistry has traditionally been divided into four areas: organic, inorganic, physical, and analytical chemistry. Organic chemistry is the study of carbon compounds and inorganic chemistry is the study of all other elements. Physical chemists investigate the structure and properties of matter and analytical chemists devise the procedures used to identify and measure individual components of complex mixtures.

Chemistry majors usually take a core curriculum that includes courses in all four areas before concentrating in one area. Their concentration may require advanced courses in methods used to synthesize natural products or active organic compounds; introduction to the instruments and techniques used to identify or analyze unknown compounds; or study of the use of lasers to probe the course of a molecular collision.

All chemistry majors spend considerable time performing experiments in the laboratory. The laboratory experience teaches students to observe the world around them, to draw conclusions from these observations, and to challenge currently accepted beliefs.

Some colleges award a B.A. in chemistry; others award a B.S.. Some offer both degrees. If specified course requirements have been met, the bachelor's degree qualifies the student for professional certification by the American Chemical Society. Many employers look for college graduates with ACS certification because it indicates that a student has been exposed to a thorough preparation that includes practical experience in the laboratory. In the United States approximately 8,000 students major in chemistry each year; most obtain ACS certification. Approximately 30 percent go on to obtain postgraduate degrees in chemistry, business, medicine, or law.

Specializations

Analytical chemistry, inorganic chemistry, organic chemistry, physical chemistry.

Other majors to consider

Biochemistry
Chemical engineering
Environmental science
Genetics, human and animal
Materials/metallurgical engineering
Physical chemistry
Physics
Premedicine

Careers related to the major

The major in chemistry traditionally leads to careers in the chemical, oil, or pharmaceutical industries. Analytic chemists are in demand in almost all process industries and in many government regulatory agencies. Because an understanding of chemistry helps to foster many practical developments (for example, in structural materials, food products, and microelectronic devices), there is a demand in industry for students who have studied chemistry. The following careers require some graduate or professional education: research, medicine, patent law, teaching, and management.

For more information

The American Chemical Society
1155 Sixteenth Street NW
Washington, DC 20036
(202)872-4600

Geology

Geology majors study the evolution, composition, and behavior of the earth. In the field and in the laboratory, students develop skills that are useful for basic research and applied problem solving.

Interests, skills, and qualities associated with success in the major

Interests. The outdoors, remote places, problem solving (qualitative and quantitative), collecting minerals or fossils.

Skills and qualities. Reasoning ability, critical thinking, mathematics and other sciences, oral and written communication.

Recommended high school preparation

English 4, algebra 1–2, calculus 1, geometry 1, trigonometry .5, biology 1, chemistry 1, physics 1, social studies 2, foreign language 3–4, and computer science 1.

Typical courses in the major

Physical Geology	Mineralogy
Petrology	Paleontology
Historical Geology	Structural Geology
Sedimentation	Stratigraphy
Geomorphology	Field Methods

What the major is like

Geology is a diverse and rapidly changing science. Courses within and parallel to the geology program provide essential background and skills. Year-long courses in chemistry, physics, and mathematics (sometimes biology and computer science as well) are often required as part of the geology major and are among the admission requirements of virtually all graduate programs in geoscience.

Students first take introductory courses in physical or historical geology, or both, which establish the foundations: rock, mineral, and fossil identification; landform evolution; plate tectonics; and the geological time scale. Topical courses, such as environmental geology, planetary geology, or oceanography, may also serve as introductions to the major. Most introductory courses and almost all upper-level courses have weekly laboratories of three to four hours or field trips of various lengths.

Upper-level courses are often arranged in sequence, with one course the prerequisite for the next. A semester or a year of mineralogy, for instance, provides the analytic skills (instrumental analysis of the chemical and structural composition of substances, use of the petrographic microscope, etc.) essential in later courses in petrology and structural geology. Paleontology, sedimentation, and stratigraphy commonly constitute a sequence on the origin of sedimentary rocks and the fossil organisms they may contain. Geomorphology and glacial geology courses consider processes that shape the earth's surface. Courses in resources—energy, minerals, and water—examine their origin as well as the process and problems associated with exploring for, recovering, and using these essential commodities.

A unique aspect of geology is its emphasis on the history of the earth, a recurring theme of many courses in the major. Another trademark is its reliance on fieldwork. The field is to the geologist what the library is to a historian; thus, most geology courses include field observations as well as lab investigations. Some undergraduate departments require a semester-long or summer course in field geology for graduation, and most graduate departments require such a course for admission. The summer courses average four to five weeks. Many are based at permanent field-camp facilities in the western states; some are located in other parts of the country and others are traveling programs. These courses offer intensive training in geological mapping and in preparing geological reports. They may also include field trips to localities with classic geological formations in the vicinity of the base camp.

The best-qualified students may be able to find summer jobs as geological field assistants or interns in industry or government after completing their junior year and a field course.

Specializations

Environmental geology, geochemistry, geomorphology, hydrology, mineralogy, mining geology, mining and mineral engineering, petroleum engineering, paleontology, petroleum geology, petrology, stratigraphy, tectonics.

Other majors to consider

Astronomy
Civil engineering
Environmental science
Geological engineering
Geophysics
Oceanography
Soil sciences

Careers related to the major

As natural resources dwindle, geologists are needed in exploration, planning, hazards reduction, and basic research. Although the petroleum and mining industries are still the largest employers of geologists, today an increasing number are hired by engineering and groundwater consulting firms and by local, state, and federal agencies. Graduates can also, with appropriate certification, teach in public schools. A master's degree is usually required for long-term employment and advancement.

For more information

American Geological Institute
4220 King Street
Alexandria, VA 22302
(703)379-2480
(703)379-7963 (fax)

Geophysics

Geophysics is the study of the earth and its atmosphere by physical measurements. Using a combination of mathematics and physics, along with electrical engineering, computer science, and geology and other earth sciences, the geophysicist analyzes measurements taken at the surface to infer properties and processes deep within the earth's complex interior.

Interests, skills, and qualities associated with success in the major

Interests. The outdoors, travel, taking measurements in the field, using quantitative analysis to learn about the earth, computer languages, graphics, and programming.

Skills and qualities. Natural curiosity, quantitative ability, mathematics, physical sciences, computers.

Recommended high school preparation

English 4, algebra 1.5, calculus 1, geometry 1, trigonometry .5, laboratory science 3–4, history 2, foreign language 2, and computer science 1.

Typical courses in the major

Structural Geology	Rocks and Minerals
Field Geology	Advanced Calculus
Differential Equations	Complex Variables
Applied Mathematics	Physics
Mathematical Physics	Linear Signals and Systems
Exploration Methods	Computer Programming

What the major is like

With its use of physics, mathematics, geology and other earth sciences, electrical engineering, and computer science, geophysics can be truly called an applied and interdisciplinary science. It combines these different sciences to study the earth's properties and processes—from the atmosphere and oceans to the shallow subsurface and deep interior down to its central core. Except for boreholes, which penetrate only a small fraction of the outer surface, the earth's interior cannot be directly observed. All that is known about the history, continuing changes, and distribution of resources of the earth's interior must be inferred through detective work based on mastering and applying the sciences and technologies listed above.

Because the earth supplies society's material needs and is the repository of its used products, and home to all its inhabitants, the wide range and importance of this field are apparent. On the applied side, oil companies and mining firms use the exploratory skills of geophysicists to locate deeply hidden resources. Geophysicists assess the strength of the earth's surface when sites are chosen for large engineering and waste-management operations. On the theoretical side, geophysicists try to understand such earth processes as heat distribution and flow; gravitational, magnetic, and other force fields; and vibrations and other disturbances within the earth's interior. Between the pure and the applied is seismology, the branch of geophysics that studies earthquake causes and predictability.

The tools of geophysicists vary. Seismologists extend elastic waves through the earth's highly variable subsurface. Other geophysicists use electrical, magnetic, electromagnetic, and gravitational methods for the analysis of earth properties. Geophysical tools and methods also are increasingly appropriate for studying the moon and the planets.

Geophysics involves four distinct activities: designing field measurement systems, acquiring field measurements, processing field measurements, and interpreting the results. Geophysicists use sophisticated equipment and techniques to acquire data in what are essentially field experiments in the most variable of laboratories—the earth's subsurface. At best these measurements are impure, so sophisticated technologies and skills in physics, mathematics, signal theory, and computer science are required to figure out what they may tell us about earth properties and processes. Such interpretation requires the outlook, understanding, and imagination of a geologist.

Because most undergraduate geophysics majors are found within engineering programs, the first two years of a typical major resemble the beginning of traditional programs in electrical or mechanical engineering.

Students study mathematics, physics (including electricity and magnetism), statics, and chemistry, along with courses in environmental science, geology, and humanities.

The first courses in geophysical exploration are usually taken in the junior year. In the junior and senior years students also take advanced engineering mathematics, modern physics, electronics or semiconductor circuits, more geology, systems analysis, digital circuits, the physics of the earth, field theory, and at least one of the major methods of geophysical exploration. Field camp is generally required in the summer between the junior and senior years.

Geophysical study of the earth, both applied and theoretical, generally extends beyond the bachelor's degree.

Specializations

Students may specialize in exploration (for mineral, water, and energy resources), engineering and geotechnical geophysics (analysis of dam sites, environmental studies such as in waste management), and pure scientific study of the earth and its processes. Within these broad areas, special fields of geophysics include seismology (study and analysis of elastic wave propagation), potential-field methods (earth gravity and magnetism), electrical and electromagnetic methods, and study of the earth's thermal properties.

Other majors to consider

Applied mathematics
Computer science
Electrical engineering
Geology
Mathematics
Physics

Careers related to the major

Exploration geophysicists in industry work for oil, mining, exploration, and well-logging companies acquiring, processing, and interpreting results of large-scale active geophysical experiments. Parallel careers exist in academe and government (with the U.S. Geological Survey). Graduate degrees are needed to teach in college or do advanced research.

For more information

The Society of Exploration Geophysicists
P.O. Box 702740
Tulsa, OK 74170-2740
(918)493-3516

American Geophysical Union
2000 Florida Avenue NW
Washington, DC 20009
(202)462-6903

Oceanography

Majors in oceanography are concerned with the oceans—their movements, composition, and origin; marine plant and animal life; and the wise use of the sea's resources.

Interests, skills, and qualities associated with success in the major	**Interests.** Natural sciences, outdoor activities, the oceans, the marine environment. **Skills and qualities.** Science and mathematics.
Recommended high school preparation	English 4, algebra 1, calculus 1, geometry 1, trigonometry 1, chemistry 1, physics 1, history or social studies 3, and foreign language 2. A half year of music or visual arts is also recommended.

Typical courses in the major

Calculus
Chemistry
Geology
Chemical Oceanography
Physical Oceanography
Field Studies

Physics
Biology
Biological Oceanography
Marine Geology
Marine Geophysics

What the major is like

Oceanography is an interdisciplinary science that integrates principles of biology, chemistry, geology, physics, geophysics, mathematics, botany, zoology, meteorology, and geography. Students begin the major by increasing their basic knowledge of mathematics, physics, biology, geology, and chemistry, which they apply to the study of oceanography at increasingly complex levels. Students engage in fieldwork and collect data which they learn to analyze and interpret. They learn about the specialized methods and instruments of oceanographic research and acquire vital computer skills.

Following introductory course work in all four disciplines of oceanography, students select one of the following for their area of specialization.

Biological oceanography studies the processes that govern the distribution, abundance, and production of plants, animals, and nutrients in the oceanic ecosystem. This specialty emphasizes investigation of bacteria, phytoplankton, zooplankton, and organisms living at the bottom of the sea.

Chemical oceanography investigates the complex chemistry, distribution, and cycling of dissolved substances, nutrients, and gases in sea water, with an emphasis on the mechanisms that control these elements and compounds and on their origins.

Marine geology and geophysics study marine sediments (formation, transport, and deposition); examine the theory of ocean basin formation (plate tectonics); survey processes governing shoreline formation; and consider the origin, structure, and history of the oceanic crust and upper mantle.

Physical oceanography endeavors to understand and predict the sea's motion, ranging in scale from millimeters through tidal and current scales to the great ocean gyres or giant circular currents. The distribution of physical properties (temperature, salinity, sea ice) and air-sea interaction, with its implications for climate, are fertile areas of research.

Specializations

Biological oceanography, chemical or physical oceanography, marine geology, geophysics.

Other majors to consider

Biochemistry
Biology
Chemistry
Environmental science
Marine biology
Zoology

Careers related to the major	A major in oceanography can lead to careers in research, teaching, administration, marine affairs, environmental studies, inspection, computing, instrumentation development, statistical analysis. Many oceanographers are engaged in pure or applied research, and work at sea, on land, in laboratories, and at computers.
For more information	American Geophysical Union 2000 Florida Avenue NW Washington, DC 20009 (202)462-6903 **An Introduction to the World's Oceans.** Alyn C. and Alison Duxbury. Dubuque, Iowa: William C. Brown, 1988. "Careers in Oceanography" is available from the American Geophysical Union.

Physics

Physics majors study a variety of simple systems such as pendulums, violin strings, heat engines, magnets, mirrors, atoms, and galaxies in order to explore how these systems, or particles within them, exchange energy and momentum with their surroundings, exert forces on one another, and move under the influence of these forces.

Interests, skills, and qualities associated with success in the major	**Interests.** Why things behave as they do, quantitative relationships between measurable variables, improving the quality of life. **Skills and qualities.** Computational skills, reasoning logically, using instruments of measurement, solving problems, communicating.
Recommended high school preparation	English 3, algebra 1, calculus 1, geometry 1, trigonometry 1, biology 1, chemistry 1, physics 1, social studies 1, history 1, foreign language 2, and computer science .5.
Typical courses in the major	Classical Mechanics Thermal Physics Thermodynamics Optics Nuclear Physics Quantum Mechanics Electricity and Magnetism Statistical Mechanics Wave Motion Atomic Physics Particle Physics
What the major is like	The physics program is usually designed in a spiral form. Students devote the first year or two to the classical subfields (mechanics, electricity and magnetism, thermal physics, and optics), and are introduced to modern physics and quantum mechanics. Mechanics is the study of motion, forces, energy, and momentum. A course in electricity and magnetism introduces students to the laws governing how charged particles interact and emit

electromagnetic radiation. Thermal physics covers heat transfer and the laws describing how systems exchange energy with their surroundings. Optics is a study of light reflection, refraction, dispersion, and diffraction. In modern physics students examine the behavior of electrons, photons, atoms, molecules, and solids. Quantum mechanics introduces such ideas as the particle nature of electromagnetic waves, the wave nature of particles, energy levels, and the uncertainties that nature imposes on our detailed knowledge of how small particles behave.

The junior and senior years take the student around another turn of the spiral. Whereas the study of the classical subjects is detailed and advanced, analyzing the behavior of atoms, nuclei, and fundamental (elementary) particles is more quantitative and abstract. Laboratory work continues to emphasize experimental design, precision in measurements, analysis of errors, and formulation of valid conclusions from available evidence.

This second turn also provides opportunities for diversions. The student who wants to become a theorist may elect a course in general relativity. Another, who wants to do research at an industrial laboratory, may prefer a course in solid state physics. A prospective secondary school teacher may take a course in teaching methods with a semester of supervised teaching in a local school. A student who intends to attend graduate school begins a third turn of the spiral by electing advanced classical mechanics or quantum mechanics.

While taking these increasingly sophisticated physics courses, students will continue to take mathematics and computer science. The math courses will probably include calculus, linear algebra, differential equations, complex variables, and statistics. The goal of enabling the student to become an independent thinker, a problem solver, and a researcher is greatly accelerated by experience in a research laboratory.

Most physics majors move in one of three directions following the bachelor's degree: They go on to graduate school to study physics or a related field such as engineering or mathematics, they do research in an industrial or a government laboratory, or they teach in junior or senior high school.

Students bound for graduate school should select as much physics and mathematics as possible, in order to prepare for more advanced course work and a research specialty. For industrial or government research, students may substitute courses in solid state physics, experimental methods, and computer science for ones in particle physics, theoretical physics, and abstract algebra. The future teacher would be better off not learning how to solve the Schrodinger equation, but instead aiming for more breadth in chemistry and earth science and a varied teaching experience.

As a rule, these variations can be arranged within the scope of the regular Bachelor of Science requirements. A few colleges have a separate Bachelor of Arts which usually requires fewer credits in physics and mathematics. Some institutions have an engineering physics major, which differs from the regular major by including more courses in design and analysis and fewer in the humanities and social sciences. A few institutions distinguish future teachers from other physics majors, but usually students can prepare for certification by adding about 15 semester hours of professional education courses to the standard physics major.

Specializations

Although specializations exist in physics, a firm commitment to one is usually made only at the graduate level.

Other majors to consider

Astronomy
Astrophysics
Atmospheric sciences and meteorology
Biophysics
Chemistry
Genetics, human and animal
Geology
Geophysics
Mathematics
Molecular and cell biology
Oceanography
Organic chemistry
Physical chemistry

Careers related to the major

The degree in physics can lead to jobs as a researcher or teacher. Graduates will find job opportunities in many types of industry as researchers. With the appropriate teaching credential, students may become middle or high school science teachers. Many physics graduates pursue graduate study in physics. With an advanced degree, they can do research for industrial, government, or nonprofit laboratories, or teach in colleges. Their research may be "pure," extending our knowledge of the universe, or in support of new products.

For more information

The American Association of Physics Teachers
5112 Berwyn Road
College Park, MD 20740
(301)345-4200

The American Institute of Physics
335 East 45th Street
New York, NY 10017
(212)661-9404

Social and Behavioral Sciences

C. PETER BANKART

Wabash College

The range of interests of men and women who study and teach in the social and behavioral sciences is impressive. Within a few doors of my office a psychology professor studies the impact of salt concentrations in infant diets on their food preferences as adults, a feminist psychologist studies the changing role of women in Japanese society, an economist studies decisions consumers make about the extra cost they are willing to pay for organically grown foods, and a political scientist studies the voting patterns from a group of sample precincts in the last election to the United States House of Representatives.

What do all these people have in common? Probably at least the following: a genuine fascination with human beings—their decision-making processes and the way they organize their societies and their lives. Social scientists are concerned with their subjects' inner lives, their values, their prejudices, and their hopes and fears for the future. But beyond this, social scientists are also interested in solving complicated puzzles, in searching for order, and in learning how to predict what people and other animals will do under a wide range of circumstances. Their students are learning how to observe and measure behavior, to apply their observations to theoretical models, and to understand the motives and purposes of complex social organisms.

Social scientists are scholars who learn to think quantitatively as well as qualitatively about behavior. Their task is to use the scientific method to study complex behavioral patterns in a search for the underlying forces that determine when and how that behavior will be manifest. The range of behaviors subject to that scrutiny is unlimited, and the range of methods of inquiry available to today's social scientists is truly comprehensive. The tools of social scientists are as complex as highly powerful computers and the latest methods of carbon 14 dating of fossil remains, and as simple as a pencil, a notebook, and a pair of trained eyes.

One of the most difficult issues facing you if you are interested in a major in the social sciences may be which one to pick. We can think of this as a question of what level of analysis of a problem you find most interesting and meaningful. The social scientist's interest ranges from individual behavior in unique environments (psychology) to collective behavior under certain forms of government (political science) to the influence of culture and society on behavior (sociology and anthropology). Some social scientists are interested in individual behavior and others in the way social organizations function and make decisions. Still others are interested in examining and even influencing the social policy of corporate and government organizations.

Let's imagine, for example, that you are interested in studying the social problem of alcoholism. An anthropologist, a criminologist, an economist, a gerontologist, a political scientist, a public policy specialist, an experimental psychologist, a clinical psychologist, a social worker, and a sociologist would each have special interest in this problem and a characteristic way of defining and studying it. Furthermore, in the end each would make a distinctive contribution to the total understanding of this important social phenomenon. In fact, within each of these separate majors there would probably be several different ways to study alcoholism. A labor economist would look at the problem very differently from a consumer-oriented economist or from an economist whose interest is in health care; a biopsychologist's interest might be very different from that of a developmental psychologist or a health psychologist. The same differences apply in almost all the social sciences.

One of the things that all social scientists would share is a proficiency with numbers, with the statistical raw data associated with the social problem called alcoholism. Probably all of them would use computerized statistical testing procedures to analyze their data, and all the researchers would formulate and test hypotheses about alcoholism that they derived from various theories, from their own previous research, from library research, from talking with their professional colleagues, and from their own special interest in the problem under study.

Another interest shared by social scientists is in communicating with others about their professional concerns. Of course, some work of the social scientist involves the relatively isolated labor of research, but another aspect involves sharing ideas and findings through written reports, oral presentations, group discussions, and even debates. Almost any set of courses in a social science major offers a lively mix of academic activities.

Students majoring in the social and behavioral sciences have few restrictions in the range of their other interests. Many students incorporate several separate interests within the social sciences into hybrid areas, such as political economy, gerontological psychology, criminology and social work, or public administration and criminal justice. But there are no reasons not to combine social science with any other area in any other part of the curriculum. Psychology students, for example, are often drawn to medicine, law, biology, computer science, music and art, or education. Because the social sciences are so broadly defined, they can be combined with almost any other interest, including the possibility of taking some undergraduate courses in an off-campus study program in another country or in another part of this country.

As you look through the descriptions of the various majors presented in this section you will probably be impressed by all the different career paths open to a major in the social sciences. The field prepares students for these careers not so much by teaching specific important facts but by teaching how to approach and analyze important problems effectively and meaningfully. This is vital in the social sciences because the phenomena studied are always changing. Crack cocaine didn't exist 10 years ago, nor did AIDS; a decade ago people were more concerned with inflation and unemployment than with recession and savings and loan failures. But persons trained in social science are able to use the tools they have acquired in their course work to study, explain, and investigate new

social phenomena as the conditions in the society around them change or are redefined.

Graduate school may seem a long way off as you are thinking about an undergraduate major, but it is an option you will want to keep open. Many students entering law school, business school, foreign service school, schools of social work, and schools of education will have majored in one or more of the social and behavioral sciences. So too, of course, will students who decide they want to become professional psychologists or counselors, geographers, anthropologists, or economists.

Unless you are attending an unusual high school, you probably have little concrete knowledge of any of the social sciences, in contrast, say, to your knowledge of mathematics, literature, foreign language, or history. Many students who become geography, political science, anthropology, or social work majors are first introduced to the field when they take a beginning course in college—sometimes even as late as the junior year. It therefore makes sense to think about social science areas of interest and to sample several in the first two years of college. Students may find that economics is fascinating or that gerontology covers intriguing elements of human development or that anthropology evokes special interest. On the other hand, psychology may seem too statistical or the memorization in criminal justice too demanding.

Of course you may already know, right now, that you are interested in one of the social and behavioral science majors. If so, you are in a fine position. By getting an early start in the major, you may be able, by junior or senior year, to study in and about another culture or to participate in exciting original research with a member of the faculty. Perhaps you will find yourself doing anthropological research among native American tribal groups, or working as a student intern in a geriatric or preschool center, or working as a paid research assistant in a professor's laboratory, or helping to create policy on an important social issue as a government intern.

Another advantage to an early start is the opportunity to build connections to other areas of the curriculum and create a personalized, comprehensive four-year plan. An interest in public administration can be combined with a career interest in accounting, criminal justice with urban planning and development. The possibilities are almost limitless. In sum, if you are intrigued by the complexity of the way people behave, the social and behavioral sciences may offer just what you are looking for in a college major.

Anthropology

Anthropology is the study of people—their origins, physical nature, social behavior. Anthropology majors explore human cultural and biological evolution and the way all peoples, from prehistoric times to today, adapt to their environment; form families, clans, tribes, and nations; regulate behavior through laws and government; worship and celebrate; communicate; educate their young; and adapt to change.

Interests, skills, and qualities associated with success in the major

Interests. Curiosity about people and their points of view, travel, reading, cultural diversity, combining library research and direct field observations to come up with new insights.

Skills and qualities. Adaptability, self-motivation, good writing skills, keen observation, learning foreign languages.

Recommended high school preparation

English 4, biology 1, social studies 2–4, history 2–3, foreign language 3–4, and computer science 1. History courses should include world, U.S., and local history if available.

Typical courses in the major

Physical Anthropology
Archaeology
Cultural Anthropology
Primate Behavior
Archaeology Field Methods
Religion and Culture

Music and Culture
Language and Culture
Cultural Change
Human Evolution and Variation
Culture and Personality
Native American Cultures

What the major is like

Anthropology is the study (logia) of humankind (anthropo). Majors in anthropology focus on the similarities and differences between human beings and other primates as well as on the similarities and differences in human populations. Anthropologists are interested in all aspects of what it means to be human.

Students learn how people in different parts of the world live their lives and adapt to their environments. Most institutions require courses in each of the four main subdivisions of anthropology: physical anthropology, cultural anthropology, linguistic anthropology, and archaeology. Elective courses allow students to follow their interests—a specific country or cultural unit, such as Japan or Mexico, or a topic, such as political systems, child-rearing practices, music, or art.

Physical anthropology investigates when and where human beings first appeared; students may even handle stone tools, skeletal materials, and plaster casts of the remains of people who lived many centuries ago. Students may spend time in a local zoo observing chimpanzees and other primates to compare their actions with human behavior.

Cultural anthropology explores specific cultures or concentrates on topics shared by all cultures—religion, politics, law, or ecology. Cultural anthropologists study the cultural diversity found in contemporary societies, from the few remaining peoples who hunt and gather roots and berries to those who shop in supermarkets and live in metropolitan areas such as Tokyo, New York, and London.

Linguistic anthropology examines the relationship of language to other aspects of culture. Students study methods of communication—including body language, dialects, jargon, and slang—and how the language people use reflects the way they perceive and interact with the world around them.

As a rule, instructors will have spent a year or more living and studying among the peoples they are teaching about; the firsthand experience of living for extended periods in other cultures is an important part of graduate anthropological training. This fieldwork in other cultures sets anthropology apart from other social sciences and usually results in engaging lectures.

Most universities have enough faculty to offer courses in the four main subdivisions of anthropology, but few have courses in all the specialized subjects or cover all areas of the world with equal thoroughness. Students interested in a specific society, such as Japan, or a specific topic, such as legal anthropology, should read college catalogs carefully to determine where they will be able to study the topic of interest to them.

In recent years more and more anthropologists have turned to studies of U.S. culture, and this is reflected in course offerings. Special programs at some universities encourage students to apply what they learn to contemporary problems facing the United States and other urban, industrial societies; this is usually called applied or action anthropology.

Specializations

Archaeology, physical anthropology, linguistic anthropology, cultural anthropology, urban anthropology, legal anthropology, culture and personality, applied anthropology.

Other majors to consider

Archaeology
Area studies
Biology
Classics
Ethnic studies
Geography
History
Linguistics
Literature and language majors
Political science and government
Psychology
Religion
Sociology

Careers related to the major

Anthropology provides good preparation for jobs in government, business, social services, news media, museums, and education that require an understanding of cultural and national differences and the ability to work with people from different backgrounds. Archaeologists are employed by local, state, and federal government agencies and small and large consulting and environmental firms to preserve, salvage, and restore archaeological resources. With a graduate degree, one can teach in a college and do research.

For more information

American Anthropological Association
1703 New Hampshire Avenue NW
Washington, DC 20009
(202)232-8800

Criminal justice studies

A criminal justice program teaches students about the dimensions and causes of crime and delinquency; the structure of the American criminal justice system; the operation of criminal courts; and the techniques and theories of law enforcement.

Interests, skills, and qualities associated with success in the major

Interests. Serving others, assisting people who are experiencing difficulties.

Skills and qualities. Working efficiently with others, communicating effectively, making decisions, handling stress.

Recommended high school preparation

English 4, precollege mathematics 3, biology 1, chemistry 1, physics 1, social studies 2, history 2, foreign language 2, music 1, visual arts 1, and computer science 2.

Typical courses in the major

Policing	Community Corrections
Criminal Law	Court Procedures
Theories of Criminal Justice	Institutional Corrections
Private Security	Computer Literacy
Research Methods	

What the major is like

Criminal justice programs give students a perspective on crime, delinquency, and our criminal justice system, usually by combining theoretical courses and practical experience. The purpose of most criminal justice programs is to prepare students for entry-level positions in one of the five main areas of employment: law enforcement, probation, correctional programs, parole supervision, and community rehabilitation services, as well as for further graduate study, such as law school.

Many institutions have started or expanded their criminal justice departments; at some colleges the major is offered within the sociology department. Students frequently study theories about personality development and the causes of juvenile delinquency. They may explore social problems such as discrimination, poverty, age, and unemployment in order to understand some of the causes of crime. The role of the police, correction officers, and the courts at the local, state, and federal levels will be covered. Some programs include related courses on such topics as women and crime, organized and white-collar crime, historical criminology, and crisis intervention. Students may, in addition, learn quantitative methods in order to conduct and communicate the findings of research.

A major emphasis in all programs is effective communication skills. Criminal justice students have to be proficient in verbal skills because there is extensive public contact in the related professions. Writing skills are also emphasized, since written reports constitute an integral part of criminal justice careers. In addition to courses in criminal justice and language skills, students take classes in social work, political science, and sociology.

Specializations

Probation/parole, private security, institutional corrections, law enforcement.

Other majors to consider

Political science and government
Prelaw
Social work
Sociology

Careers related to the major

Thousands of new professionals are needed each year in the areas of law enforcement, court services, and corrections. Criminal justice graduates find employment opportunities in a wide variety of agencies, at local, state, and national levels of government. One of the fastest growing areas of the fields is industrial security and loss prevention for business. Students interested in this area would be well advised to take business and marketing courses. The major may lead to careers as a law enforcement officer, policeman or policewoman, deputy sheriff, probation officer, parole agent, criminal attorney, correctional officer or counselor, industrial security specialist, or loss prevention specialist.

For more information

American Correctional Association
8025 Laurel Lakes Court
Laurel, MD 20705-5075
(301)206-5100

International Association of Chiefs of Police
1110 North Glebe Road, Suite 200
Arlington, VA 22201
(703)243-6500

Economics

The economics major provides a framework for analyzing such issues as inflation, unemployment, monopoly, and economic growth. Students learn how the economic system works to provide goods and services. They study theory, policy, and trends and explore ways to deal with the economic problems of society and the individual.

Interests, skills, and qualities associated with success in the major

Interests. Current issues such as taxes, poverty, the deficit, health discrimination, inflation, the environment, and unemployment; the causes and consequences of economic and social events; human behavior.

Skills and qualities. Solving puzzles, logical reasoning, careful observation, detecting patterns, breaking complex problems into parts, focusing on the heart of an issue, working with numbers, writing clearly.

Recommended high school preparation

English 4, precollege mathematics 4, laboratory science 3, social studies 2, and history 2.

Typical courses in the major

Microeconomic Theory
Macroeconomic Theory
Money and Banking
Business and Government
International Trade
Urban Economics
Environmental Economics
International Finance

Economic Statistics
Labor Economics
Public Finance
Organization of Industry
Economic History
Poverty and Discrimination
Health Economics

What the major is like

Economics is concerned with choices: What are the best ways to make decisions? How do people actually make them? What is sacrificed when someone makes a choice? For in a world of limited resources and unlimited wants, choosing one thing means giving up another. By understanding decision making and the choices people have, economists can predict how people will react to changes. Thus economics can help people understand the causes of economic and social events and devise ways to make the world work better.

Economics is a practical discipline. It plays an important role in the design of tax laws; in the formation of international trade policies; in the design of programs to improve the prospects of poor people; in the regulation of health care, transportation, and the environment; in the control of drug smuggling; and in shaping the monetary and fiscal policies that influence the rate of inflation and availability of jobs. Through study of economics one can gain a better understanding of whether taxes should increase or decrease; whether more or less trade with Japan is desirable; whether an expanded welfare program is needed; whether air bags should be installed on automobiles; how to stop acid rain from destroying forests; and how to make sure there are jobs available for everyone.

Economics also has intellectual appeal, especially for those who like rigorous analysis and problem solving. Economics typically uses simplified models to deal with a complicated, disorderly world. For example, when the interest rate goes up, how does the behavior of the housing industry, of local government, of banks and automobile dealers change? What happens to mortgage rates, to local government services like education and garbage collection, to interest rates paid on savings accounts, and to the cost of a new automobile? Economics applies simple models in order to understand and predict economic behavior.

Economics uses an approach to problem solving that has several distinguishing features. First, it emphasizes insights derived from observed facts. Second, because most problems are complex, it teaches one to isolate the most important facts, and focus on their implications. Third, the basic principles of economics are thought to be universal. A Marxian economist sees class struggle as a consistent, universal behavior that applies to many problems. A market-oriented economist see a different principle at play: balancing of benefits and costs. Both see the world differently, but feel the pattern of behavior they believe is at work exists everywhere.

The college curriculum for an economics major usually begins with principles of microeconomics (the study of individual firms, consumers, and workers) and macroeconomics (the study of aggregate income, employment, and prices). Next, students take two intermediate theory courses and economic statistics. In these intermediate courses issues raised in the introductory courses are reexamined with more powerful analytic tools. Finally, in electives—such as international trade and finance, economic history, public finance, the organization of industry, labor, urban, and regional economics, environmental economics, and comparative economic systems—students learn how basic economic principles apply to a wide range of world problems.

Although the economics department is usually located in a school of liberal arts, sometimes it is part of a business school; there is, however, little difference between the majors offered in each.

Specializations

Specialization within economics is rare at the undergraduate level.

Other majors to consider

Agricultural economics
Business administration
History
Mathematics
Philosophy
Political science and government
Psychology
Sociology
Statistics

Careers related to the major

Economics graduates find jobs in education, government, industry, public policy, and planning. Many become business managers. The field is also excellent preparation for law school or business school.

For more information

Joint Council on Economic Education
432 Park Avenue South
New York, NY 10016
(212)685-5499

Geography

Geography is the study of how people relate to and are shaped by their environment. Students majoring in geography gain a broad perspective on the world's environments and its peoples while gaining a strong background in the physical and social sciences.

Interests, skills, and qualities associated with success in the major

Interests. Analyzing and solving social and environmental problems, doing social and physical scientific research, the relationship of people and their environment.

Skills and qualities. Oral and written communication, field observation, working individually and in groups, collecting data, synthesizing a wide variety of information, thinking creatively, working with computers.

Recommended high school preparation	English 4, precollege mathematics 4, biology 1, chemistry 1, physics 1, social studies 2, history 2, foreign language 3, and computer science 1–2.

Typical courses in the major

Human Geography	Economic Geography
Urban Geography	Political Geography
Computer-assisted Cartography	Remote Sensing
Map Interpretation	World Regional Geography
Climate and Vegetation	Landforms and Soils
Geography of Development	Population Geography
Conservation Practice	Water Resources
Geographic Education	Cultural Geography

What the major is like

Geography is the study of how people in different places relate to their environment, and how their environment shapes their lives. The major in geography provides background for students seeking a broad understanding of the world's environments and how people have adapted to, changed, and organized their physical environment.

The major offers a unique perspective for analyzing issues related to human life and the natural, physical world. This perspective is based on study of spatial patterns (what and where) and processes (how and why). It may be applied at all levels: global, regional, and local. Geography draws knowledge from related fields, such as anthropology, economics, political science, biology, and others.

Students study physical geography—the distribution of various climates, soils, vegetation, and land forms across the earth. They learn about cultural geography—how physical geography affects cultural and economic development. They study populations—how people are distributed, how people move from place to place, the causes of crowding. They examine how political units are created at all levels (local, national, international). During their course work, students gain an understanding of how geographical differences affect events throughout the world.

The geography major begins in the first year with courses that introduce students to the basic knowledge and tools of geography. Students take courses in human geography, physical geography, statistics, and geographic skills such as cartography and remote sensing.

After the introductory courses, students may choose to specialize in an area such as environment-society relations, physical geography, human geography, or geographic information processing. Students should take courses in other departments that relate to their area of specialty. Whether a student specializes or not, geography provides a broad-based education in both the physical and social sciences.

Many institutions offer internships in which students earn academic credit while obtaining important business experience. Students interested in graduate study in geography should take ample course work in computer programming, math, and statistics. Students who plan to work in the field after earning a bachelor's degree should concentrate on application and/or skills courses (cartography, remote sensing). Students taking geography as part of a primary or secondary education program geared to a teaching position should work closely with an adviser in the school of education.

Specializations

Climatology, meteorology, hydrology, biogeography, natural hazards, cartography, political geography, population and economic geography, remote sensing, environmental conservation, urban studies, regional studies, geographic information systems, geomorphology.

Other majors to consider	Biology

Other majors to consider

Biology
City, community, and regional planning
Conservation and regulation
Earth sciences
Economics
Environmental design
Geology
History
International relations
Political science and government
Public administration
Sociology

Careers related to the major

A geographical perspective is a practical tool in almost any field. Careers the major may lead to include: public health specialist, international trade specialist or banker, real estate specialist, cartographer, teacher, urban/regional planner, market research analyst, transportation analyst, policy analyst, water/natural resource analyst, environmental impact analyst, ecologist, community development specialist.

For more information

Association of American Geographers
1710 Sixteenth Street NW
Washington, DC 20009-3198
(202)234-1450

"Careers in Geography" is available from the Association of American Geographers for $2.

Gerontology

Majors in gerontology learn about aging and older persons. Students study physical, emotional, and intellectual changes in the elderly, cultural aspects of aging, and government policies and programs for the aging.

Interests, skills, and qualities associated with success in the major

Interests. Helping people, human development, older people, family relations, improving the quality of life.

Skills and qualities. Oral and written communication, listening, tolerating individual differences, objectivity, relating to others, enthusiasm, determining needs and interests, organizing and managing projects.

Recommended high school preparation

English 4, precollege mathematics 4, laboratory science 3, social studies 2, and history 2. Whenever possible, courses in psychology, sociology, human development, and social problems should also be included.

Typical courses in the major	Biology of Aging	Health and Disease
	Psychology of Aging	Social Aspects of Aging
	Services for Older Adults	Death and Dying
	Counseling Older Adults	Housing Needs of Older Adults
	Food for the Elderly	Physical Activity Programs
	Drugs and the Elderly	

What the major is like

The rapid growth in the number of older persons has increased awareness of their potential and their needs. The major in gerontology generally includes both a liberal arts orientation and preparation for entry-level practice in human services. Courses are interdisciplinary and include content in three areas that help the student understand (1) what it is like to grow old, (2) how an individual typically progresses through the life cycle, and (3) what an aging population means to current and future society.

The first area treats the aging process: the physical and intellectual changes that occur from middle age to the end of life. Courses examine normal aging and disease, effects of the environment and lifestyle choices, intellectual stability, and mental illnesses common to later life, such as Alzheimer's disease.

The second area, courses that look at the life cycle, deals with the influence of family and community on the quality of life of older persons. Studies include the changing role that families play, differences in the way members of minority and various ethnic groups experience aging, and influences of social class on aging.

The third area of study involves the laws, programs, and institutions that help or hinder successful aging in the United States and other countries. Students examine such federal government programs as Social Security, Medicare, and Medicaid; and the ways governments influence private programs through tax incentives and regulation.

Gerontology majors usually spend substantial time in volunteer or internship roles in both profit-making and nonprofit agencies that operate housing, health, mental health, transportation, education, recreation, and social services for the elderly. For example, they may visit senior citizen centers, volunteer in nursing homes, work part time in retirement communities, or have organized field experiences in a government program.

Specializations

Direct services, program planning, administration.

Other majors to consider

Allied health
Business administration
Communications
Health services management
Home economics
Individual and family development
Nursing
Occupational therapy
Psychology
Recreation and community services technologies
Social work
Sociology

Careers related to the major

Employment possibilities for graduates are currently promising and to be found in many areas. They include program development positions in recreation, education, and social services for older people; administration of nursing homes, housing projects, and government programs; and direct service roles in multipurpose senior citizen centers, mental health agencies, and personnel departments of corporations. The development, operation, and coordination of these services form a billion-dollar network of aging services that offers attractive career opportunities for persons with bachelor's and graduate degrees.

For more information

Association for Gerontology in Higher Education
1001 Connecticut Avenue NW
Suite 410
Washington, DC 20036-5504
(202)429-9277

Political science and government

Majors in political science learn about the origins, historical development, and social functions of government. They study how electoral, legislative, judicial, and administrative structures and processes vary from one country and one age to another; how and why governments change, fall, and engage in wars. They also study the behavior of public officials and other citizens involved in politics.

Interests, skills, and qualities associated with success in the major

Interests. Public policy issues such as health care and environmental protection; politicians and public figures; justice, rights, and duties; good and bad government; law, criminal justice, the legal system.

Skills and qualities. Reading critically, writing, thinking analytically, understanding simple tables and graphs.

Recommended high school preparation

English 4, precollege mathematics 4, laboratory science 2, social studies 1, history 3, foreign language 3–4, and computer science 1.

Typical courses in the major

U.S. Government and Politics
The American Presidency
Political Parties
State and Local Government
Bureaucracy
Russian Politics
Third World Politics
American Foreign Policy
American Political Thought
Communism

Judicial Processes
Public Policy Analysis
Minority Politics
Voting Behavior
Governments of Western Europe
African Politics
International Law
Global Issues
Democracy
Political Action Groups

What the major is like

The political science major ("government" at a number of institutions and "politics" at a few) usually leads to the bachelor of arts degree. Political science programs differ widely; it is therefore important to look carefully at the description of the major at a specific institution.

The major usually begins with one or two introductory courses. American government and politics, or a general introduction to politics is frequently required. The program requires courses covering basic topics such as justice, law, and power. After these introductory courses, students take courses in areas of interest to them in topics such as American government, comparative government and politics, international politics, political theory and philosophy, and public (or constitutional) law. Other possibilities are political behavior and area studies, such as African, European, Latin American, Russian, Chinese, Asian, and other governments.

Most programs require students to complete a minor in a related field of study, such as history, sociology, economics, or anthropology. Whether a minor is required or not, in courses outside the political science department students must study principles of human behavior that underlie the actions of citizens, politicians, and public officials; overall social and economic structures and processes; the origins and development of individual political systems; and the geographical aspects of the social and physical environment in which government and politics take place. In some institutions, all students will gain this knowledge through the core curriculum. If there is no core curriculum, students should acquire this basic knowledge through their choice of electives.

Students who have taken civics or government courses in high school are frequently surprised by the differences between high school and college courses in format and class size. They will also discover that college courses take an analytic approach, rather than the historical and current events approach of many high school courses. In large institutions the introductory courses, especially American government, consist of lectures to many students in large auditoriums. But even in large institutions, courses above the introductory level usually have many fewer students and provide opportunities for discussion between students and instructors.

Many programs include senior seminars or other activities to help students tie together the information, knowledge, and skills acquired in their course work and to apply it to investigating problems of particular interest to them. Designing a research project and writing a paper or senior thesis based on that research is a rewarding exercise.

Most programs offer academic and practical experience outside the classroom—for example, internships in public offices, such as those of state legislative committees, public defenders, and county attorneys, or in administrative agencies. Majors may spend a "Washington semester" in such activities combined with related seminars in the nation's capital. Political science departments are often closely involved in their colleges' overseas study programs.

Political science clubs, the national political science honors fraternity (Pi Sigma Alpha), and such campus political organizations as the Young Republicans and the Young Democrats are also part of the intellectual and social life of political science majors.

Specializations

American government and politics, international relations, international politics, comparative politics, political theory, political behavior, politics of a region or continent.

Other majors to consider

American studies
Anthropology
Economics
History
Philosophy

Psychology
Public administration
Sociology

Careers related to the major

The political science major provides a foundation for a variety of careers rather than occupational training for a specific career. Majors traditionally go into the following: business, journalism, government service, law, teaching, foreign service, diplomatic corps.

For more information

American Political Science Association
1527 New Hampshire Avenue NW
Washington, DC 20036

"Careers and the Study of Political Science" is available for $2 from the American Political Science Association.

Psychology

Psychology majors study human and animal behavior and explore the processes involved in normal and abnormal thoughts, feelings, and actions. Students increase their understanding of behavior while learning psychological facts, methods, principles, and generalizations about individuals and groups.

Interests, skills, and qualities associated with success in the major

Interests. Working with people, scientific method, human and animal behavior.

Skills and qualities. Oral and written communication, critical thinking.

Recommended high school preparation

English 4, precollege mathematics 3, biology 2, history or social studies 2, foreign language 3, and computer science 1.

Typical courses in the major

Developmental Psychology
Social Psychology
Learning and Memory
Research Methods
Organizational Psychology
Physiological Psychology

Personality Development
Abnormal Psychology
Perception
Statistics
Cross-cultural Psychology

What the major is like

The major in psychology provides an important perspective on human behavior. Most people are aware of clinical and counseling psychologists who try to help people with problems. But the major emphasizes psychology as a science devoted to the systematic study of human and animal behavior and of the environment in which organisms behave and have experiences. Psychology majors study the methods psychologists use in their research. They learn facts, principles, and generalizations psychologists have discovered in their efforts to understand human beings as individuals and as members of social groups.

Students generally begin the major with a survey course that covers topic areas—biological bases of behavior, sensation and perception, learning, memory, development, personality, abnormal behavior, therapy, and social psychology. At the sophomore level they are likely to take courses treating these same areas in greater depth. At advanced levels students may take courses on more specialized topics, such as industrial and organizational psychology, learning disabilities, health psychology, counseling psychology, and family psychology.

Psychology majors often participate in volunteer activities—for example, working with retarded, disturbed, or physically disabled children or adults. Typically, they also design and conduct at least one research study of their own, using a computer to perform statistical tests on the data they have collected. Through course work, as well as field and research experiences, students learn to think critically about human problems and ways to understand and alleviate them. They also learn the difference between commonsense and scientific approaches to behavior and the advantages of the scientific method.

Depending on the particular sequence of courses, the psychology major prepares students for a career in management, for entry-level work in health and human services, or for graduate study in psychology. Combined with appropriate courses, the major is also background for medicine and law. Psychology is also an important component of a basic liberal arts education.

Specializations

Organizational behavior, health psychology, counseling psychology, biopsychology.

Other majors to consider

Anthropology
Gerontology
Social work
Sociology
Speech pathology/audiology
Sports medicine
Urban studies
Women's studies

Careers related to the major

The undergraduate major in psychology can lead to jobs as a counselor with organizations that counsel young people, the homeless, or drug or alcohol abusers. It can lead to jobs as a mental health or social service worker with state or private institutes dealing with mentally retarded, disturbed, or disabled people. It is also good preparation for further study in business, medicine, social work, law, public administration, or education.

For more information

American Psychological Association
1200 17th Street NW
Washington, DC 20036
(202)955-7600

Public administration

The major in public administration deals with the operations of all forms and levels of government. Students learn about the many skills and challenges associated with implementing public policy in government and in nonprofit organizations.

Interests, skills, and qualities associated with success in the major

Interests. Public and community service, organizing people, teamwork, leadership, working with people from different backgrounds.

Skills and qualities. Leadership, organizational ability, problem solving, bringing people together to work toward a common goal, communication skills.

Recommended high school preparation

English 4, precollege mathematics 3, laboratory science 2, social studies 2–3, history 2–3, foreign language 2, and computer science 1.

Typical courses in the major

Managing the Modern City
The Politics of Bureaucracy
Financial Management
Structure of State Government

Complex Organizations
Public Personnel Administration
Administration of Public Policy

What the major is like

The major in public administration deals with the operations of all forms and levels of government. Students learn about the many skills and challenges associated with implementing public policy in government and also in nonprofit organizations.

Majors in public administration are introduced to the many activities of management professionals who work in local, state, and federal agencies. Public administration courses also frequently cover the activities of nonprofit agencies, such as foundations and charitable agencies.

Introductory courses typically examine the impact of public administration on the daily life of every citizen. Public administrators play a vital role in all aspects—from placing traffic signals to regulating the environment, from protecting the safety of food and drink to providing a wide variety of social services, from determining the content of education to maintaining the peace and security of the nation. Introductory courses also examine the critical role of politics as it influences public administration. In the course of their work, public administrators are in constant touch with citizens, interest groups, and elected officials, thereby creating a lively and exciting interaction. The interplay of federal, state, and local governments, and the business world, also provides an ever-changing environment.

Upper-level courses in this major introduce students to the diverse tasks carried out by public administrators. These include managing human resources (usually in courses dealing with budgets, accounting, and financial management). Other upper-level courses may deal with specific management skills (such as strategic planning) or with personal qualities of an effective public manager (such as leadership and ethical sensitivity).

Public administration majors are strongly encouraged to take a broad range of liberal arts courses such as: English, history, communications, and social sciences, including economics, political science, psychology and sociology.

The undergraduate program in public administration usually has a strong "hands-on" flavor. Courses frequently make use of case studies, simulations, and other activities to provide a sense of what "real life" public administration is all about. Current issues, as recent as what appears in the daily newspaper, often illustrate broader concerns and issues within public administration. Most public administration programs include an internship, in which students gain experience in public or nonprofit agencies. Many institutions offer internships in Washington or state capitals. At some, cooperative programs allow students to alternate semesters (one in the classroom, the next in a governmental workplace), helping them acquire both academic knowledge and practical skills.

Specializations

Local government administration, health services management, public policy, criminal justice administration.

Other majors to consider

American studies
Business administration
Criminal justice studies
Economics
Environmental studies
Health services management
History
Political science and government
Sociology
Urban studies

Careers related to the major

Graduates of public administration programs can find entry-level positions as: assistant city manager, management analyst, budget analyst, personnel specialist, assistant department director, government affairs/government relations specialist. Students who wish to move into upper-management careers, such as that of city manager, may need to complete a graduate degree in public administration.

For more information

American Society for Public Administration
1120 G Street NW
Suite 700
Washington, DC 20005
(202)393-7878

National Assoc. of Schools of Public Affairs and Admin.
1120 G Street NW
Suite 730
Washington, DC 20005
(202)628-8965

Social studies education

A major in social studies education prepares students to teach junior and senior high school courses in history, citizenship, and other social sciences.

Interests, skills, and qualities associated with success in the major

Interests. Serving people, working with people, history, social sciences.

Skills and qualities. Speaking, writing, organizing, working with people in groups.

Recommended high school preparation

English 4, precollege mathematics 3, biology 1, chemistry 1, social studies 2, history 2, and foreign language 2.

Typical courses in the major

Educational Psychology	Social Foundations of Education
Curricula and Methods	Courses in History
Organization of Schools	Courses in Social Sciences

What the major is like

Programs for majors in social studies education have three components: general education, professional education, and history and social sciences. During the first two years of college, students take introductory courses in the arts and sciences, with emphasis on developing their communication skills. The second, or professional, component generally includes courses in the foundations of education, the organization and administration of secondary schools, methods used in teaching social studies, the teaching of exceptional students, classroom management, and educational technology. In addition, most institutions provide for field experiences in social studies classrooms, and all require 10 to 15 weeks of full-time supervised student-teaching in a school.

The history and social sciences component is usually the equivalent of a regular major in history and the social sciences. Most institutions require that most of this work be in history, with some study of each of the social sciences, such as economics and sociology. Other institutions require concentrations of some depth in any subject in which the student wishes to be licensed.

Standards for university programs leading to licenses to teach social studies in secondary schools vary widely from state to state. Most states allow students to complete licensure requirements within a four-year program, typically leading to the bachelor's degree in education. A few states now require a fifth year of study, perhaps capped with a master's degree.

Specializations

Many institutions require that social studies education majors develop one or more concentrations within the broad field of social studies. In a few states, graduates are licensed to teach only their concentrations.

Other majors to consider

Early childhood education
Elementary education
History
Political science and government
Secondary education

Careers related to the major

The social studies education major leads directly to a career as a secondary social studies teacher. With appropriate graduate work, social studies education majors can pursue careers in educational administration, school counseling, or college teaching (either teacher education, history, or a social science).

For more information

National Council for the Social Studies
3501 Newark Street NW
Washington, DC 20016
(202)966-7840

Social work

Social work majors require the knowledge and skills to assist individuals, families, groups, and communities in preventing and alleviating the problems of a modern, rapidly changing society. Students learn to help others and to modify harmful social conditions, promote social and economic well-being, and increase opportunities for all people to live with dignity and freedom.

Interests, skills, and qualities associated with success in the major

Interests. Helping those in need, particularly children, the poor, minorities, the aged, the disabled, and women; enabling others to develop unique, positive responses and solutions to their problems.

Skills and qualities. Empathy, objectivity, perseverance, ability to listen well, analytic ability, imagination, creativity, oral and written communication, tolerance for stress, respect for human diversity.

Recommended high school preparation

English 4, precollege mathematics 2–3, biology 1–2, chemistry 1, social studies 2–4, history 2, foreign language 1–2, and computer science 1. Volunteer work is strongly recommended.

Typical courses in the major

Human Behavior	Community Resources
Social Work Practice	Social Policy and Services
Ethnic/Cultural Variables	Modern Social Problems
Introduction to Psychology	Introduction to Sociology
Social Work Research	Field Practicum/Internship

What the major is like

The social work major provides a sound foundation in the liberal arts with an emphasis on the social sciences. In the first two years of college, social work majors usually complete courses in sociology, political science, economics, psychology, and human biology. In most accredited programs there are no more than one or two required courses in social work during the first two years, although some programs require or recommend volunteer experience in a human service agency at this stage.

In the junior and senior years, students take a substantial number of social work courses. Human behavior and social environment courses integrate the diverse ideas and principles of the social sciences and human biology to provide a strong base for social work practice. Courses in social welfare policy and services describe the range of laws, programs, and benefits that meet human needs. Such courses allow students to analyze how social programs are developed, and how to change them. Research courses teach basic research methods and stress methods of scientifically evaluating social welfare programs. Students learn the methods and techniques needed for general social work practice. The crowning educational experience is a supervised practicum (field internship) in a social service agency. Throughout the program students find an emphasis on understanding and accepting diversity in ethnicity, race, culture, gender, and sexual orientation.

Social work programs may form distinct academic departments in colleges and universities. They may be in joint departments of sociology and social work; they may be offered within a graduate school of social work. Social work licensing and certification requirements in many states require graduation from a program accredited by the Council on Social Work Education; 373 bachelor's-level programs are now accredited by the CSWE. Students should inquire about the accreditation status of the social work programs in the colleges and universities they wish to attend. Individuals graduating from CSWE-accredited bachelor's degree programs are eligible for one year of advanced standing in many two-year master's degree programs.

The sense of calling and commitment in the choice of social work as a profession frequently generates a strong spirit of camaraderie and dedication among social work students. Recently many nontraditional and older students have found social work an attractive choice for a major and career.

Specializations	Not generally available.
Other majors to consider	Art therapy **Criminal justice studies** Education **Individual and family development** **Nursing** **Physical therapy** **Psychology** **Sociology** **Speech pathology/audiology**
Careers related to the major	A bachelor's degree in social work prepares one for general social work in a wide range of settings that include child welfare and public welfare agencies, hospitals and other health care facilities, schools, family services, developmental disabilities services, services for the aged, the juvenile and criminal justice systems, industry, and business. A master's degree is required for jobs involving supervision, administration, or complex research.
For more information	National Association of Social Workers 750 First Street NE Suite 700 Washington, DC 20002-4241 (202)408-8600 (800)638-8799 (202)336-8310 (fax)

Council on Social Work Education
1600 Duke Street
Suite 300
Alexandria, VA 22314-3421
(703)683-8080

Sociology

Sociology examines the effects of social structure on individuals. It involves the study of how social forces affect people's attitudes and behavior. Sociologists uncover patterns in attitudes and behaviors and seek to show how they vary across time, cultures, and social groups.

Interests, skills, and qualities associated with success in the major

Interests. Human behavior, gender, race, research, social structures.

Skills and qualities. Seeing relationships between things such as age and attitudes; seeing that people's attitudes and behaviors are due to more than individual psychological factors; reasoning ability; critical reading; abstract thinking; formulating problems; organizing thoughts; analyzing data.

Recommended high school preparation

English 3, precollege mathematics 2, laboratory science 2, social studies 1, history 1, and computer science .5.

Typical courses in the major

Introductory Sociology
Deviance
Research Methods
Socially Complex Organizations
Minority Groups
Juvenile Delinquency

Social Problems
Gender Roles
Social Psychology
Social Class and Stratification
Sociology of Education
Sociology of the Family

What the major is like

Sociology examines the effects of social structure on individuals. It involves the study of how social forces affect people's attitudes and behavior. Sociologists uncover patterns in attitudes and behaviors and seek to show how they vary across time, cultures, and social groups.

Sociologists study the effects of social structure on individuals. They use scientific methods to gather data from people. Usually they use questionnaires and interviews, but observation and experiments are used as well. They use sample groups of people to draw conclusions about the larger groups from which the samples are taken. Sociologists develop hypotheses about why one thing affects another, such as why women and men differ in church attendance. They gather data to test these hypotheses and construct theories to help make sense of the data and conclusions. They often try to control one or more factors when studying how two factors are related. For example, they might examine how the relationship between parental background and college graduation differs by gender. Their findings often affect social policy. Required courses typically include introductory sociology, research methods, theory and statistics, plus additional courses usually of the student's choosing. Students are sometimes required to select their optional courses from groupings of courses to foster greater diversity in what they study. For example, students may be required to take at least one course on social institutions (e.g., family, education, religion). Many programs offer students the opportunity to serve an internship in a social service organization or agency. Such experiences help students apply what they have learned in the classroom.

Sociology students need to be able to reason and think abstractly. They should have a curiosity about what makes people respond and behave as they do. They will learn basic statistics and how computers help sociologists do research. Many classes involve content with social policy implications. For example, a course on social stratification may involve discussions of how inequality among people might be reduced. The themes and conclusions of the various courses ultimately merge to provide an integrated view of how social structure affects individuals. Students also gain understanding of themselves and their friends in the study of sociology.

Students typically take several related courses in such areas as geography, political science, religion, and economics. Graduates often note that their sociology studies help them think more critically about research reports and question conclusions based on incomplete evidence and faulty reasoning. They also remark on the contribution of the major to their communication skills. They often find that critical thinking skills and exposure to research, statistics, and computers helped them to obtain and succeed in their jobs.

Specializations

Penology (the study of prisons), gerontology, organizational behavior, applied sociology, sociology of law, criminal justice, family life, gender roles, social organization, demography, social psychology.

Other majors to consider

Anthropology
Communications
History
Philosophy
Political science and government
Psychology

Careers related to the major

The sociology major can lead to careers as a human resources manager, teacher, probation officer, market research analyst, social service agency employee, foreign service officer, government official, environmental impact assessment specialist, evaluation research specialist, urban planner, corrections officer, or industrial sociologist. Advanced degrees are required to work as a college teacher, demographer, policy analyst, or research institute manager.

For more information

American Sociological Association
1772 N Street NW
Washington, DC 20036

"Careers in Sociology" is available from the American Sociological Association.

Theology

WATSON E. MILLS
Mercer University

A major in theology, as distinguished from a religion major, generally refers to courses that examine a religion or religious community, including its texts, its belief systems (theology), and its practice (ministry, counseling). The major prepares students for the ministry or for postgraduate study at a seminary or university-related divinity school. In the latter case, an undergraduate majoring in theological studies is similar to a premed or prelaw student taking preparatory courses for further study after college graduation.

The four-year bachelor's degree program consists of general education courses and electives, as well as major field courses.

General education courses, sometimes called core requirements, are the essence of a liberal arts education. Their overall purpose is to help you be better able to think, reason, reach conclusions based upon relevant data, and communicate these conclusions effectively to others. You may select electives from a wide variety of subjects unrelated to your major—computers for example, or a field you learned about while taking core courses.

Your major is specialized training. Courses relating to a specific major provide information, procedures, and techniques that may be used in your career. As a theology major, you might take courses in a variety of aspects of ministry, such as ancient history, philosophy, prison ministry, crisis counseling, and youth ministry. These courses would equip you to do certain tasks, as well as inform you about the theory from which specific procedures have been derived.

But a major is more than just professional training. The major field subjects further your personal and educational development in areas that build upon the general education courses.

As you explore your theology major you will begin to discover that the more specific the course, the more your field of study depends on the work being done in other fields of study. In counseling, for example, sociology and psychology can illuminate the work of those helping people in trouble. If you study the Biblical texts, you will quickly appreciate the usefulness of knowing other languages and having good reading skills as well as the importance of the Greek and Hebrew languages. If your ultimate vocation requires public speaking, you'll need to learn to communicate clearly and effectively and to became skillful in oral argument.

Theological texts

The body of literature that underlies the Judaeo-Christian tradition is extensive. Most students have some familiarity with the Hebrew and

Christian Bibles. But many may not know the other treasures of the Judaeo-Christian tradition, such as the Dead Sea Scrolls, the Apocrypha, and pseudepigrapha. These texts, among many others, make up the literary heritage of the great Western religions, and have been strenuously examined by modern scholars in many fields. Texts are studied using several different methods of inquiry, depending upon the emphases and traditions at various institutions. One method, called literary-historical, assumes that, like all texts, the sacred texts must be considered in relation to culture and history. The student plays the role of a literary detective, examining the various texts and paying attention to : (a) the historical context in which the text was produced (a text written during conflict or war might be more militant than would otherwise be the case); (b) the writer, if known (the identity of the writer may reveal something of his or her own prejudices); (c) the audience to whom the text is addressed (what are their problems and concerns?). When working with books of such antiquity, these puzzles are sometimes very difficult—even impossible—to solve.

Another method of study focuses upon the *type* of literature being studied. For instance, students might study the prophetic works of the Hebrew Bible, or Talmud, comparing them with other similar examples both within and outside the Bible. This critical literary model is very popular with students who like to read widely and make independent judgments.

History

The Judaeo-Christian tradition is often studied in lecture classes. Students do extensive reading in both primary and secondary sources. Some professors structure their courses chronologically; a student might study Judaism from Moses to the fall of Jerusalem, or Christianity from the time of Christ to Alexander the Great.

Others prefer to select a theme, such as monotheism (the belief in one God) and trace its development over time. Historical studies familiarize students with nations, events, persons, and movements of the past. They may also provide a sense of one's heritage as well as an awareness of some present peculiarities and differences within the faith.

Another popular area of study is the history of a particular religion, such as modern American Christianity. These courses offer insight into future directions of a religion.

Theology

Somewhat like history, the study of theology may be pursued in many different ways. Some courses are developed around one or more theological concepts, for example, the nature of God during the period of the Patriarchs or the concept of suffering in the time of Jesus. More common for beginning students is the general survey of theology—sometimes called systematic theology—in which several theological concepts are presented and discussed. These topics might include God, humankind, sin, salvation, last things, etc. Such courses expose students to new ideas and new ways of thinking. In systematic theology, the concepts studied may grow out of the sacred texts mentioned above, but are also shaped over time by the very institutions and traditions that preserve them. Students may also examine theology through the study of the work of great theologians such as Karl Barth, Paul Tillich, and David Tracey.

The practice of the ministry

Some courses focus on the practice of ministry, which includes the actual duties performed by a rabbi, pastor, or priest. These duties require a knowledge of counseling techniques. Psychology and counseling are presented in different ways at various institutions, but there are some similarities. Many colleges and universities, for example, use recent technology: a counseling session may be videotaped so the class can critique the discussion. A college may arrange for students to serve in a parish with a minister, somewhat as a medical intern might join a medical doctor while making rounds. After such experiences students may be asked to describe these opportunities for learning and reflection.

The courses in theology are designed to give you not only specialized knowledge but a sense of how you might put that knowledge to work in the future. Some theology majors will choose the ministry, others literary scholarship, still others may prefer teaching or counseling. The range of possibilities is wide.

Bible studies

The Bible studies major provides a diversified program leading to a bachelor's degree enabling graduates to enter some phase of Christian ministry or to pursue advanced studies in Christian ministry.

Interests, skills, and qualities associated with success in the major

Interests. Serving God by ministering to the spiritual and physical needs of people throughout the world.

Skills and qualities. History, religion, culture of different peoples throughout the world.

Recommended high school preparation

English 3, precollege mathematics 2, laboratory science 2, social studies 2, history 2, foreign language 2–4, music 1, and visual arts 1.

Typical courses in the major

Christian Thought
Later Hebrew History
God, Christ, Holy Spirit
Interpretive Systems
Church and Last Things

Early Hebrew History
New Testament Literature
Man, Sin, Salvation
Missions in Acts

What the major is like

The Bible major is offered in certain Christian educational institutions: Bible institutes, colleges, and universities. In addition to the general education requirements for graduation, a core curriculum centered in and revolving around the study of the Bible and related subjects is the focus of this major.

Broad and diverse in scope, the curriculum studies the entire Bible through the various methods of Biblical interpretation revealed through the history of Christianity. It includes the field of systematic theology, apologetics, church doctrines, Greek and Hebrew languages, as well as exposure to non-Christian religions.

Above all, this major seeks to integrate the Christian faith into all academic disciplines in order to effect spiritual, intellectual, emotional, and social balance in graduates.

Specializations

Students do not generally specialize at the undergraduate level.

Other majors to consider

Anthropology
Communications
Education
History
Philosophy
Psychology
Religion
Sociology

Careers related to the major

The Bible studies major can lead to careers as a pastoral minister, missionary, youth minister, and Christian education minister. Graduate work prepares one for a teaching ministry in Biblical studies and theology.

For more information

Christian College Coalition
329 Eighth Street NE
Washington, DC 20002
(202)546-8713

Theological studies

Theological studies, or theology, is the academic study of the beliefs and practices of a religion or religious community. It is an effort to understand this faith and these practices from a study of its history, literature, and present condition.

Interests, skills, and qualities associated with success in the major

Interests. Exploring the meaning of life, the practice of religion, philosophy.

Skills and qualities. Analytic, logical, and critical thinking.

Recommended high school preparation

English 4, precollege mathematics 2, laboratory science 1, social studies 2, and history 2.

Typical courses in the major

Old Testament	New Testament
History of Philosophy	Introduction to Theology
Church History	Ethics
Systematic Theology	Life and Teachings of Jesus

What the major is like

Theology or theological studies can be a rich and diverse area of study. The major may be found in departments of theology, religion, philosophy and religion, or Biblical studies. Typical introductory courses cover four basic areas: the Bible, systematic theology, church history, and Christian ethics. Theological studies attempts to balance these to provide a broad and solid preparation for the great number of specialties that are available to students who major in theology.

Students examine how the various books of the Bible were united and how they came to be recognized by Jewish and Christian believers as sacred. Students may examine the use of parables and metaphors in non-Biblical literature to see the similarities and differences between the Bible and other literary works. Biblical archaeologists excavate the remains of the Biblical world to bring new light to our study of civilizations and artifacts mentioned in the sacred texts. Biblical sociologists seek to understand better the social settings that may have influenced the lives and thoughts of the Jews and Christians in the Biblical world. Modern Biblical scholars draw on many other disciplines in the course of their study.

Systematic theology reflects the relationship between God and his people and examines questions raised in the Bible. It examines God and the attributes of justice, mercy, knowledge, and power recounted of him, and it asks how these characteristics can be meaningfully attributed to him. It studies the meaning of creation and the fall of man, and it attempts to see how the Bible provides the key to the restoration of humanity and of all creation. It meditates on the problem of evil in a world ruled by God and the meaning of suffering and death. It seeks to understand the Biblical story, in all its depth, as a story about God and about humankind.

Church history examines religious teaching, discipline, spirituality, and worship; the relationship of a religious institution with civil government, other religions, and secular society; and the impact of its believers on the intellectual, cultural, social, and political spheres of society. It examines the attitudes of the religion to contemporary problems, and attempts to determine the effects that social and political environments have on it.

Ethics studies the living faith as exemplified in the religion's personal and social teaching. It examines the importance of the religion's ideals of marriage and family life, attempts to face with reason the challenges of modern medical and economic technology, and tries to judge the best way for believers to be involved in social action and political life.

Each of these four areas of theological studies may lead the student into many allied fields or specialities. Bible study suggests so many other relevant interests that it has, in many colleges and universities, developed into a field of its own. Church history is, in many institutions, part of theological studies, yet in others, it is a subdiscipline within a department of history. In general, systematic theology and ethics remain in theology departments. Yet there is a rich variety of specialties that can be found within these areas. Systematic theology may focus on worship, liturgy, and sacraments. Ethics can lead into specialities such as medical ethics, religious law, political theology, or justice and peace. Students may well begin in one field and, as they pursue their studies, find themselves enticed into another.

In most higher education settings today, theology is studied not just as the preserve of a particular religious community, but in an ecumenical or interdenominational spirit. It studies the theologies of other communities and also the religious practices of the broader non-Christian world. Frequently, this leads to a study of the general characteristics of all religions. This approach to the study of religion, moving away as it does from the beliefs of a particular community, is often the focus of a more recent major in religious studies.

Specializations	Bible studies, Biblical theology, systematic theology, liturgical theology, spirituality, church history, medical ethics, religious education, political theology, history of theology.
Other majors to consider	**Bible studies** **Comparative literature** **English** **History** **Philosophy** **Political science and government** **Religion** **Sociology**
Careers related to the major	The theological studies major prepares students to teach, research, and write within a church context. Like other liberal arts disciplines, it also prepares students for jobs in business, government, public affairs, social

work, and other areas. The degree is excellent preparation for divinity degrees, which enable one to work in lay or clerical pastoral positions. Graduates may also find jobs writing and editing religious publications. A graduate degree is needed to teach in college.

For more information

Council of Societies for the Study of Religion
Mercer University
Macon, GA 31207

Glossary

Academic adviser

An academic adviser is a professor assigned to help students choose appropriate courses each semester. Many students consult their adviser for advice on selecting a major. At some schools, when a student declares a major, or changes majors, he or she is assigned an adviser who teaches in the student's chosen field of study.

Accreditation

A process that ascertains that a college meets acceptable standards in its programs, facilities, and services. Some programs within colleges, such as the journalism or nursing program, may be accredited by professional organizations. The descriptions of majors discuss program accreditation if it is significant in the field.

Applied study

Putting theoretical knowledge to practical use, as in using engineering principles to build new machinery.

Area studies

A program of study that focuses on the history, geography, economics, politics, and culture of a region of the world, for example, Latin America or Eastern Europe.

Bachelor's degree

A degree received after the satisfactory completion of a four- or five-year full-time program of study (or its part-time equivalent) at a college or university. The bachelor of arts (B.A.) and the bachelor of science (B.S.) are the most common bachelor's degrees. In general, a program of study that results in a B.A. requires more liberal arts courses than one resulting in a B.S. College catalogs describe the types of degrees you can earn in each major.

Calendar

See Term.

Capstone course

A senior-year course in which students use information and skills learned in all previous course work in addressing a topic, issue, or set of problems.

Case study

A means of learning by studying a specific example. For instance, students of hotel management might observe the work of an actual hotel to learn how to purchase, conduct a marketing survey, hire and train staff, and advertise.

Clinical study

Clinical study is supervised, hands-on work experience in one or more of the settings in which the student will eventually work. In the health professions, course work is followed by clinical study in a health care facility. This gives students a chance to observe and work with professional health care workers and patients.

College

The generic term for an institution of higher learning; also a term used to designate divisions within a university. A university may consist of various colleges: of arts and sciences, of engineering, of music, of agriculture, of architecture, and more. When a university is divided into colleges, students usually have to apply for admission to a specific college. Colleges within a university will have different requirements: For example, a college of arts and sciences may require two units of a foreign language, and the college of music may require an audition.

Concentration

See Specialization.

Cooperative education

A college program in which students alternate between periods of full-time study and full-time employment in a related field. Students are paid for their work at the prevailing rate. Typically, it takes five years to complete a bachelor's degree under the cooperative plan, but graduates have the advantage of about a year's practical work experience in addition to their studies. Some colleges refer to this sort of program as work-study, but it should not be confused with the federally sponsored College Work-Study Program.

Core curriculum

Many colleges require students to take specific courses in order to gain a foundation in fields that are widely useful, no matter what the student's eventual major. The core may consist of writing, computer literacy, and foreign languages, for example. Some colleges have both core curriculum requirements and general education requirements.

Credit hour
Students earn a number of credit hours, usually 3 or 4, upon completion of a course. Many colleges require students to complete a certain number of credit hours each semester, usually the equivalent of 4 or 5 courses a semester or 3 courses a quarter (see "Term" for an explanation of semesters and quarters). Students will also be required to fulfill certain credit hour requirements within their major. For example, students may be required to earn 124 credits to graduate, of which a minimum of 32 credits must be in the major field of study. College catalogs spell out these requirements, and your adviser can help you plan a course of study that will meet the requirements.

Curriculum
A set or program of courses. Students complete a certain curriculum, consisting of liberal arts courses, electives, and courses in their major, in order to earn their degree.

Department
A group of related programs of study within a college. The Romance languages department, for example, may include programs in French, Italian, and Spanish. Some colleges have only a few departments, and some have a wide variety. Most departments offer several majors. The biology department might offer marine biology, microbiology, and other specific majors.

Discipline
Literature, history, social science, natural science, mathematics, the arts, and foreign language are disciplines; each takes a certain approach to knowledge. For example, literature (and majors within this discipline) examines verbal expression, whereas mathematics seeks to quantify. Students become familiar with the approaches of all disciplines through general education courses.

Double major
At many colleges, students may earn two majors, in related or unrelated fields. It is generally possible to complete two majors in four years. Students who choose to do so usually spend most of their junior and senior year taking courses in the two majors to complete the required number of credits for each.

Elective
Courses of the student's own choosing, in virtually any field or department. Students take three types of courses in order to complete their degree: general education courses, courses within the major, and electives. In general, students can fit an elective course into each semester.

Ethnic studies
A group of courses that focus on an ethnic group such as Afro-Americans, Latin Americans, etc.

Field of study
See Major.

Fieldwork
Study that takes place outside the classroom, and lets students get hands-on experience in their major. Geology majors may spend time in a ravine studying rock formations; dietitians may spend time in a hospital kitchen; anthropologists may explore an excavated site.

General education requirements
Courses that give undergraduates background in all major academic disciplines: natural sciences, social sciences, mathematics, literature and language, and fine arts. Most colleges have general education requirements—students usually take these courses in their freshman and sophomore years, getting the chance to sample a wide range of courses before choosing a major. Students generally choose from a variety of appropriate courses, and take (for example) biology *or* chemistry *or* astronomy. At some colleges, general education courses are referred to as the core curriculum; at others, a few courses within the general education requirements are core courses that all students must take.

Graduate degree
A degree pursued after earning a bachelor's degree. The master's degree, which requires one to three additional years of study, is usually the next degree earned after a bachelor's degree. The doctoral degree requires further study. First professional degrees are also graduate degrees.

Humanities
The branches of learning that explore what it means to be human: to decide what we value, to express our opinions, to interpret what others have expressed, to explore what is meaningful. Courses in language, art, philosophy, and history enable students to explore these issues.

Independent study
Any arrangement that allows students to complete some of their college program by studying independently instead of attending scheduled classes

and completing group assignments. Typically, students plan programs of study in consultation with a faculty adviser or committee to whom they may report periodically and submit a final report for evaluation.

Interdisciplinary major

A major that draws on several disciplines to study a complex subject. For example, environmental studies includes course work in the social sciences, humanities, and sciences to prepare students to deal with environmental problems and issues.

Internship

Any short-term, supervised work, usually related to a student's major, for which academic credit is earned. The work can be full or part time, on or off campus, paid or unpaid. Some majors require the student to complete an internship.

Land-grant university

The federal government established land-grant universities in 1862; these institutions were intended to educate the agricultural work force the country needed. Many are now large universities offering a wide range of subjects, but they still offer a wide range of agriculture-related majors.

Liberal arts

The liberal arts are language and literature, philosophy, history, mathematics, and natural and social sciences. One studies the liberal arts to gain general knowledge and to develop reasoning and thinking skills, rather than to train for a specific profession. Some colleges refer to themselves as "liberal arts" colleges, and encourage their students to gain a well-rounded, general education through study of courses in these areas. No matter what major you pursue, you will probably have to complete a certain number of courses in the liberal arts.

Licensure

To work in some fields, you must earn a license by passing one or several professional examinations. Some of the majors described in this book prepare students to take licensing examinations after earning their bachelor's degree.

Lower-division courses

Courses students are expected to take their freshman and sophomore years. These lay the foundation for further study in a subject area.

Major

The subject area in which students concentrate during their undergraduate study. At most colleges, students take a third to a half of their courses in the major; the rest of their course work is devoted to liberal arts requirements and electives of their choice. In liberal arts majors, students generally take a third of their courses in their chosen field, which they usually must choose by the beginning of their junior year. In career-related programs, such as nursing or engineering, students may take up to half of their courses in their major.

Minor

Course work that is not as extensive as that in a major field, but that gives students specialized knowledge of a second field. Students may choose a minor in the department of their major (for example, a major in comparative literature with a minor in German literature), or in a different department (for example, a biology major with a minor in philosophy). College catalogs describe the requirements for minors.

Multidisciplinary major

A major that uses the perspectives of many disciplines *simultaneously* to examine a problem, event, or situation. For example, women's studies uses history, sociology, literature, and psychology to examine women in various times and cultures.

Postgraduate degree

See Graduate degree.

Practicum

A course, usually in the junior or senior year, in which classroom learning is put to practice in a clinic (for students in medical fields) or the classroom (for education majors). Students are supervised by a working professional during this phase of their education.

Preprofessional program

There is no prescribed course of study required for entrance to the professions of law, medicine, dentistry, or veterinary medicine. However, students preparing for application to professional schools in these areas need to take a rigorous undergraduate program, and premed and predental students must complete certain science courses. The professions accept students from a range of undergraduate majors who can think critically and clearly.

Prerequisite

A course that must be taken as preparation for a more advanced course in the same field. For example, biology would be a prerequisite for insect biology. College catalogs usually indicate whether a course has a prerequisite.

School

A subdivision of a university. The administrative unit that offers nursing courses may be called the "college of nursing" at one institution, and the "school of nursing" at another.

Specialization

A specialization is a branch of study within a major. For example, students majoring in psychology might elect to concentrate on personality and social psychology: to do so, they would fulfill the requirements of the psychology major but select courses (often with the help of their adviser) that would give them a certain depth of knowledge about personality and social psychology. In some programs, a specialization consists of a few courses in the area of specialty; in others, students must choose a specialization and may take 30 to 40 credits in their chosen area. A specialization may help students prepare for graduate study in their area of concentration.

Student teaching

In their senior year, education majors spend time teaching in a local school, under the supervision of a licensed teacher.

Studio

Courses in which students create, under the guidance of an instructor, rather than receive information through lectures. Studio courses are a large component of some fine arts majors.

Term

Colleges divide the school year into shorter periods, called terms. Some colleges are on the semester system, in which students complete two semesters, or terms, each year. Others are on the quarter system, in which they attend three quarters each year. Many colleges offer a summer term of study, enabling students to move more rapidly toward a degree by attending college year-round, or to complete incomplete credits.

Undergraduate

A student in the freshman, sophomore, junior, or senior year of study, as opposed to a graduate student who has earned an undergraduate degree and is pursuing a master's, doctoral, or professional degree.

Upper-division courses

Courses taken during the junior and senior year of study. Often numbered 300, 400, or 500, these build upon the foundation of knowledge gained during the freshman and sophomore years, and provide in-depth knowledge about a topic.

Career Index

Account Executive
  Finance
  Marketing
Accountant
  Accounting
  Business administration
  Mathematics
Actor
  Dramatic arts/theater
Actuary
  Mathematics
  Statistics
Advertising Account Executive
  Advertising
  Marketing
Advertising Media Buyer
  Advertising
Aerospace Engineer
  Aerospace/aeronautical
    engineering
Agricultural Engineer
  Agricultural engineering
Agronomist
  Agronomy
Animal Scientist
  Animal sciences
Animator
  Film arts
Anthropologist
  Anthropology
Archaeologist
  Anthropology
Architect
  Architecture
Archivist
  Art history
  History
Art Administrator
  Arts management
  Dance
  Fine arts
  Music
  Music business
    management
  Studio art
Art Critic
  Art history
  Fine arts
  Studio art
Art Director
  Graphic design

Art Historian
  Art history
  Fine arts
Art Teacher
  Art education
  Fine arts
  Studio art
Artist
  Fine arts
  Studio art
Astronomer
  Astronomy
Athletic Director
  Athletic training
Athletic Trainer
  Athletic training
  Physical education
Audiologist
  Speech pathology/audiology
Auditor
  Business administration

Bank Officer
  Finance
  International business
    management
Biochemist
  Biochemistry
  Molecular and cell biology
Biologist
  Biology
  Biophysics
  Biotechnology
  Botany
  Fisheries and wildlife
  Marine biology
  Microbiology
  Molecular and cell biology
  Zoology
Biotechnician
  Biotechnology
Botanist
  Botany
Budget Analyst
  Accounting
  Economics
  Public administration
Business Manager
  Agribusiness
  Arts management
  Business administration

Classics
  Economics
  Hotel/motel and restaurant
    management
  International relations
  Management
  Music business
    management
  Public administration
Buyer
  Agribusiness
  Fashion merchandising

Cantor
  Jewish studies
  Religious music
Career Counselor
  Arts management
  Management
  Music business
    management
Cartographer
  Geography
Chemical Engineer
  Chemical engineering
Chemist
  Chemistry
Child Care Administrator
  Day care administration
  Individual and family
    development
  Social work
Choir Director
  Music
  Religious music
Choreographer
  Dance
Cinematographer
  Film arts
City Manager
  City, community, and
    regional planning
  Public administration
  Urban studies
City Planner
  Architecture
  City, community, and
    regional planning
  Urban studies
Civil Engineer
  Civil engineering

Film Editor
  Film arts
Film Writer
  Creative writing
  Film arts
Financial Analyst
  Business administration
  Economics
  Finance
  Housing and human
    development
  Management science
  Real estate
Financial Planner
  Family/consumer resource
    management
  Finance
Florist
  Horticultural science
Food Technologist
  Agricultural engineering
  Chemistry
  Food sciences
Foreign Language Teacher
  Asian studies
  Chinese
  Classics
  Comparative literature
  French
  German
  Italian
  Japanese
  Linguistics
  Middle Eastern studies
  Russian
  Secondary education
  Spanish
Foreign Service Officer
  Asian studies
  Chinese
  European studies
  French
  History
  International relations
  Japanese
  Latin American studies
  Middle Eastern studies
  Political science and
    government
  Russian
  Spanish
Forester
  Botany
  Forestry
  Horticultural science

Gardner
  Horticultural science
Geologist
  Geology

Geophysics
Geophysicist
  Geology
  Geophysics
Gerontologist
  Gerontology
  Nursing
  Social work
  Women's studies
Government Official
  African studies
  Animal sciences
  Anthropology
  Asian studies
  Chinese
  City, community, and regional
    planning
  Classics
  Economics
  European studies
  Geology
  German
  History
  Housing and human
    development
  International relations
  Japanese
  Jewish studies
  Latin American studies
  Marine biology
  Middle Eastern studies
  Political science and
    government
  Public administration
  Sociology
  Spanish
  Urban studies
  Women's studies
Graphic Designer
  Graphic design
  Studio art

Health Care Administrator
  Business administration
  Gerontology
  Health services management
  Individual and family
    development
  Medical record administration
  Social work
  Women's studies
High School Teacher
  Agricultural education
  American literature
  Art education
  Art history
  Asian studies
  Classics
  Comparative literature
  English

English education
European studies
German
History
Home economics education
Mathematics education
Music education
Science education
Secondary education
Social studies education
Special education
Technology (industrial arts)
  education
History Teacher
  Afro-American studies
  American studies
  History
  Political science and
    government
  Secondary education
Home Economics Teacher
  Home economics
  Home economics education
Home Economist
  Family/consumer resource
    management
  Home economics
Horticulturist
  Botany
  Horticultural science
Hotel Manager
  Hotel/motel and restaurant
    management
Human Resources Manager
  Agricultural education
  Gerontology
  Human resources
    management
  Labor/industrial relations
  Management
  Public administration
  Social work
  Sociology

Industrial Engineer
  Industrial engineering
Information Systems Designer
  Computer engineering
  Information sciences and
    systems
  Management information
    systems
Instrumentalist
  Music performance
Insurance Broker
  Insurance and risk
    management
Interior Designer
  Architecture
  Interior design

Related Majors

Accounting
  Finance
  Information sciences and
    systems
  Insurance and risk
    management
  Mathematics
  Real estate
Actuarial sciences
  Finance
  Insurance and risk
    management
  Mathematics
  Statistics
Advertising
  Art education
  Communications
  English
  Journalism
  Marketing
  Public relations
  Radio/television
    broadcasting
Aerospace/aeronautical
  engineering
  Computer engineering
  Mechanical engineering
African studies
  Afro-American studies
Afro-American studies
  African studies
  American literature
  Religion
Agribusiness
  Business administration
  Management
Agricultural economics
  Economics
  Finance
Agricultural education
  Agribusiness
  Environmental studies
  Technology (industrial arts)
    education
Agricultural engineering
  Food sciences
Agricultural sciences
  Botany
  Zoology

Agronomy
  Agribusiness
  Biology
  Horticultural science
  Soil sciences
Allied health
  Gerontology
American studies
  American literature
  English
  Fine arts
  History
  Political science and
    government
  Public administration
  Women's studies
Anatomy
  Occupational therapy
Animal sciences
  Agribusiness
  Entomology
  Fisheries and wildlife
  Zoology
Anthropology
  African studies
  Afro-American studies
  American studies
  Art education
  Art history
  Asian studies
  Bible studies
  Chinese
  Classics
  Comparative literature
  International relations
  Japanese
  Jewish studies
  Landscape architecture
  Latin American studies
  Linguistics
  Political science and
    government
  Psychology
  Religion
  Russian
  Sociology
  Spanish
  Women's studies
  Zoology

Applied mathematics
  Atmospheric sciences and
    meteorology
  Geophysics
  Mathematics
  Statistics
Archaeology
  African studies
  Anthropology
  Art education
Architectural engineering
  Civil engineering
Architecture
  Art education
  City, community, and regional
    planning
  Dramatic arts/theater
  Graphic design
  Interior design
  Landscape architecture
  Real estate
Art education
  Dance
  Studio art
Art history
  African studies
  American studies
  Architecture
  Art education
  Asian studies
  Classics
  Creative writing
  Dance
  Dramatic arts/theater
  European studies
  Film arts
  Italian
  Religion
  Studio art
Art therapy
  Art education
  Music therapy
  Occupational therapy
  Social work
  Studio art
Arts management
  Art education
  Communications
  Music business management

Music education
  Photography
Asian studies
  Chinese
  International business
    management
  Japanese
Astronomy
  Geology
  Physics
  Science education
Astrophysics
  Physics
Athletic training
  Physical education
  Physical therapy
Atmospheric sciences and
  meteorology
  Physics

Behavioral sciences
  Occupational therapy
Bible studies
  Theological studies
Biochemistry
  Agricultural engineering
  Agronomy
  Animal sciences
  Biology
  Biophysics
  Biotechnology
  Botany
  Chemical engineering
  Chemistry
  Clinical laboratory science
  Entomology
  Food sciences
  Food sciences and nutrition
  Marine biology
  Microbiology
  Molecular and cell biology
  Oceanography
  Pharmacy
  Zoology
Biology
  Agricultural engineering
  Agronomy
  Animal sciences
  Anthropology
  Biochemistry
  Biophysics
  Biotechnology
  Botany
  Clinical laboratory science
  Environmental studies
  Fisheries and wildlife
  Geography
  Horticultural science
  Marine biology
  Molecular and cell biology

Nuclear medical technology
Occupational therapy
Oceanography
Parks and recreation
  management
Pharmacy
Philosophy
Science education
Soil sciences
Speech pathology/audiology
Zoology
Biomedical equipment technology
  Clinical laboratory science
Biophysics
  Biology
  Physics
Biotechnology
  Biochemistry
  Biotechnology
  Microbiology
  Molecular and cell biology
Botany
  Agronomy
  Biology
  Forestry
  Horticultural science
  Wildlife management
  Zoology
Business administration
  Accounting
  Advertising
  Agribusiness
  Arts management
  City, community, and regional
    planning
  Dramatic arts/theater
  Economics
  Environmental studies
  Family/consumer resource
    management
  Fashion merchandising
  Finance
  Food sciences and nutrition
  Gerontology
  Health services management
  Home economics
  Hotel/motel and restaurant
    management
  Information sciences and
    systems
  Management science
  Mathematics
  Parks and recreation
    management
  Public administration
  Public relations
  Women's studies
Business education
  Technology (industrial arts)
    education

Caribbean studies
  Afro-American studies
Chemical engineering
  Agricultural engineering
  Biotechnology
  Chemistry
  Environmental studies
  Food sciences
  Materials/metallurgical
    engineering
  Mechanical engineering
  Petroleum engineering
Chemistry
  Animal sciences
  Atmospheric sciences and
    meteorology
  Biochemistry
  Biophysics
  Biotechnology
  Chemical engineering
  Clinical laboratory science
  Food sciences
  Food sciences and nutrition
  Home economics
  Marine biology
  Materials/metallurgical
    engineering
  Mathematics education
  Molecular and cell biology
  Oceanography
  Pharmacy
  Philosophy
  Physics
  Science education
  Secondary education
  Soil sciences
Child development, care and
  guidance
  Day care administration
  Early childhood education
City, community, and regional
  planning
  Architecture
  Environmental studies
  Geography
  Landscape architecture
  Urban studies
City/community/regional planning
  Real estate
Civil engineering
  Agricultural engineering
  City, community, and regional
    planning
  Forestry
  Geology
  Housing and human
    development
  Landscape architecture
  Mechanical engineering
  Microbiology

Real estate
    Urban studies
Classics
    Anthropology
    Art history
    European studies
    Fine arts
    History
    Linguistics
    Philosophy
Clinical laboratory
    Nuclear medical technology
Clinical laboratory science
    Nuclear medical technology
Commercial art
    Advertising
Communications
    Advertising
    Bible studies
    City, community, and regional
      planning
    Elementary education
    English education
    Gerontology
    Home economics
    Journalism
    Marketing
    Public relations
    Radio/television
      broadcasting
    Sociology
    Spanish
    Speech
    Women's studies
Comparative literature
    American literature
    American studies
    Art history
    Asian studies
    Chinese
    English
    European studies
    German
    International relations
    Italian
    Japanese
    Linguistics
    Middle Eastern studies
    Russian
    Theological studies
Computer engineering
    Aerospace/aeronautical
      engineering
    Computer science
    Electrical engineering
Computer graphics
    Photography
    Studio art
Computer science
    Astronomy

Atmospheric sciences and
    meteorology
    Biophysics
    Business administration
    Computer engineering
    Entomology
    Geophysics
    Health services management
    Industrial engineering
    Information sciences and
      systems
    Linguistics
    Management
    Management information
      systems
    Mathematics
    Mathematics education
    Music business management
    Music education
    Nuclear medical technology
    Studio art
Conservation and regulation
    Geography
    Horticultural science
Counseling psychology
    Athletic training
Creative writing
    Communications
    Dramatic arts/theater
    English
    Film arts
Criminal justice studies
    Public administration
    Social work

Dance
    Arts management
    Dramatic arts/theater
    Music therapy
    Physical education
Dance therapy
    Music therapy
Dental hygiene
    Nursing
Dramatic arts/theater
    Arts management
    Comparative literature
    Creative writing
    Dance
    English
    English education
    Film arts
    Fine arts

Early childhood education
    Day care administration
    Elementary education
    Home economics education
    Social studies education
    Special education

Earth sciences
    Atmospheric sciences and
      meteorology
    Geography
    Science education
    Soil sciences
East Asian studies
    Japanese
Ecology
    Landscape architecture
    Microbiology
Economics
    Accounting
    City, community, and regional
      planning
    Family/consumer resource
      management
    Finance
    Geography
    History
    Human resources management
    International relations
    Labor/industrial relations
    Marketing
    Mathematics
    Mathematics education
    Music business management
    Political science and
      government
    Public administration
    Real estate
Education
    Agricultural education
    Bible studies
    Communications
    Creative writing
    Dramatic arts/theater
    Individual and family
      development
    Parks and recreation
      management
    Social work
Educational media technology
    Communications
Electrical engineering
    Aerospace/aeronautical
      engineering
    Agricultural engineering
    Astronomy
    Computer science
    Geophysics
    Materials/metallurgical
      engineering
    Mechanical engineering
    Music education
Electrical, electronics and
    communication engineering
    Computer engineering
Elementary education
    Dance

Day care administration
Early childhood education
English education
Social studies education
Special education
Engineering
  Aerospace/aeronautical
    engineering
  Biophysics
  Electrical engineering
  Insurance and risk
    management
  International relations
  Management
  Mathematics
  Mathematics education
  Mechanical engineering
Engineering mechanics
  Mechanical engineering
Engineering physics
  Aerospace/aeronautical
    engineering
  Electrical engineering
Engineering science
  Mechanical engineering
English
  Advertising
  American literature
  Communications
  Comparative literature
  Creative writing
  Fine arts
  French
  German
  History
  Linguistics
  Philosophy
  Public relations
  Secondary education
  Theological studies
English education
  Secondary education
Entomology
  Agribusiness
  Agronomy
  Microbiology
  Zoology
Environmental design
  Architecture
  Geography
  Landscape architecture
Environmental health engineering
  Agricultural engineering
  Chemical engineering
  Civil engineering
  Fisheries and wildlife
Environmental science
  Atmospheric sciences and
    meteorology
  Chemistry

Environmental studies
  Forestry
  Geology
  Oceanography
  Soil sciences
  Wildlife management
  Zoology
Environmental studies
  City, community, and regional
    planning
  International relations
  Landscape architecture
  Public administration
  Urban studies
European studies
  French
  International business
    management
  Italian
  Spanish

Family/consumer resource
  management
  Home economics education
Fashion design
  Art education
  Home economics education
  Textiles and clothing
Fashion merchandising
  Marketing
  Textiles and clothing
Film animation
  Graphic design
Film arts
  Art education
  Arts management
  Communications
  Comparative literature
  Graphic design
  Photography
  Radio/television broadcasting
Finance
  Accounting
  Family/consumer resource
    management
  Insurance and risk
    management
  Real estate
Fine arts
  American studies
  Chinese
  Dance
  Film arts
  Home economics
  Italian
  Russian
  Textiles and clothing
  Women's studies
Fisheries and wildlife
  Agribusiness

Forestry
  Wildlife management
Folklore and mythology
  Classics
Food sciences
  Agribusiness
  Biology
  Home economics education
  Hotel/motel and restaurant
    management
Food sciences and nutrition
  Hotel/motel and restaurant
    management
Foreign languages (multiple
  emphasis)
  Comparative literature
Forestry
  Agribusiness
  Biology
  Botany
  Environmental studies
  Fisheries and wildlife
  Horticultural science
  Wildlife management
French
  Italian

Genetics, human and animal
  Agronomy
  Chemistry
  Physics
Geography
  African studies
  Anthropology
  Atmospheric sciences and
    meteorology
  City, community, and regional
    planning
  History
  International relations
  Zoology
Geological engineering
  Geology
  Petroleum engineering
Geology
  Environmental studies
  Geography
  Geophysics
  Petroleum engineering
  Physics
  Science education
  Soil sciences
Geophysics
  Geology
  Physics
Gerontology
  Nursing
  Psychology
Graphic design
  Advertising

Art education
Interior design
Landscape architecture
Photography
Speech

Health education
   Physical education
Health science
   Athletic training
   Pharmacy
Health services management
   Business administration
   City, community, and regional
      planning
   Family/consumer resource
      management
   Gerontology
   Management
   Medical record administration
   Public administration
   Public relations
   Speech pathology/audiology
   Urban studies
Hispanic American studies
   Afro-American studies
History
   African studies
   Afro-American studies
   American studies
   Anthropology
   Art history
   Asian studies
   Bible studies
   Chinese
   Classics
   Dramatic arts/theater
   Economics
   English
   English education
   European studies
   Fine arts
   French
   Geography
   German
   International relations
   Italian
   Japanese
   Jewish studies
   Latin American studies
   Middle Eastern studies
   Philosophy
   Political science and
      government
   Public administration
   Religion
   Russian
   Secondary education
   Social studies education
   Sociology

   Spanish
   Theological studies
   Women's studies
Home economics
   Gerontology
   Textiles and clothing
Home economics education
   Textiles and clothing
Horticultural science
   Agribusiness
   Agronomy
   Biology
   Botany
Hospitality and recreation
  marketing
   Hotel/motel and restaurant
      management
Hotel/motel and restaurant
  management
   Business administration
   Fashion merchandising
   Food sciences and nutrition
   Home economics education
   Management
   Parks and recreation
      management
Housing and human development
   Family/consumer resource
      management
   Urban studies
Human resources management
   Insurance and risk
      management
   Labor/industrial relations
Humanities
   Art education

Individual and family
  development
   Gerontology
   Home economics education
   Social work
Industrial and organizational
  psychology
   Human resources management
   Industrial engineering
   Labor/industrial relations
   Management
Industrial design
   Graphic design
   Interior design
Industrial engineering
   Management science
   Mechanical engineering
   Statistics
Industrial technology
   Industrial engineering
Information sciences and systems
   Accounting
   Astronomy

Atmospheric sciences and
  meteorology
Computer engineering
Computer science
Management
Mathematics
Mathematics education
Interior design
   Architecture
   Art education
International business
  management
   Accounting
   Asian studies
   Finance
   Japanese
   Latin American studies
   Russian
   Spanish
International relations
   African studies
   Business administration
   Chinese
   Geography
   History
   International business
      management
   Japanese
   Jewish studies
   Latin American studies
   Management
   Middle Eastern studies
   Russian
   Spanish
International studies
   Fine arts
Islamic studies
   Middle Eastern studies

Jewish studies
   Religion
Journalism
   Advertising
   Communications
   Creative writing
   English education
   Fashion merchandising
   Food sciences and nutrition
   Home economics
   Marketing
   Public relations
   Radio/television broadcasting
   Speech
Junior high education
   Elementary education

Labor/industrial relations
   Business administration
   Management
   Urban studies

Landscape architecture
    Architecture
    City, community, and
        regional planning
    Forestry
    Horticultural science
    Real estate
Latin
    Afro-American studies
    International business
        management
    Italian
    Spanish
Latin American studies
    Afro-American studies
    International business
        management
    Spanish
Linguistics
    Anthropology
    Chinese
    Classics
    Comparative literature
    English
    French
    German
    Japanese
    Russian
    Spanish

Management
    Accounting
    Arts management
    Business administration
    City, community, and
        regional planning
    Finance
    Housing and human
        development
    Industrial engineering
    Information sciences and
        systems
    International business
        management
    Management
    Management science
    Mathematics
    Music business
        management
    Real estate
    Urban studies
Management information systems
    Information sciences and
        systems
Management science
    Business administration
    Finance
    Housing and human
        development
    Industrial engineering

Information sciences and
    systems
International business
    management
Management
Mathematics
Music business management
Urban studies
Manufacturing technology
    Industrial engineering
Marine biology
    Biology
    Microbiology
    Oceanography
    Zoology
Marketing
    Accounting
    Advertising
    Family/consumer resource
        management
    Fashion merchandising
    Food sciences
    Food sciences and nutrition
    Home economics education
    Housing and human
        development
    Parks and recreation
        management
    Public relations
    Radio/television
        broadcasting
    Real estate
    Textiles and clothing
Materials/metallurgical
    engineering
    Chemistry
Mathematics
    Accounting
    Aerospace/aeronautical
        engineering
    Astronomy
    Atmospheric sciences and
        meteorology
    Biophysics
    Computer engineering
    Computer science
    Economics
    Geophysics
    Industrial engineering
    Philosophy
    Physics
    Secondary education
Mathematics education
    Secondary education
Mechanical engineering
    Aerospace/aeronautical
        engineering
    Agricultural engineering
    Electrical engineering
    Industrial engineering

Materials/metallurgical
    engineering
    Petroleum engineering
Medical record administration
    Dental hygiene
Microbiology
    Agronomy
    Biochemistry
    Biotechnology
    Chemical engineering
    Entomology
    Food sciences
    Molecular and cell biology
    Zoology
Middle Eastern studies
    International business
        management
Mining and mineral engineering
    Petroleum engineering
Molecular and cell biology
    Biochemistry
    Biophysics
    Biotechnology
    Microbiology
    Physics
Museum studies
    Art education
    Studio art
Music
    Arts management
    Dance
    Dramatic arts/theater
    European studies
    Fine arts
    German
    Italian
    Music
    Music business management
    Music education
    Music performance
    Music therapy
    Occupational therapy
    Philosophy
    Religious music
Music business management
    Arts management
    Music
    Music education
Music education
    Arts management
    Music
    Music business management
    Music performance
    Music therapy
    Religious music
Music history and appreciation
    Music performance
Music performance
    Music
    Music business management

Religious music
Music theory and composition
  Music performance
Music therapy
  Music
  Music education
  Music performance
  Occupational therapy
Musical theater
  Dramatic arts/theater
  Music business management

Native American languages
  American literature
Nuclear engineering
  Chemical engineering
  Mechanical engineering
Nursing
  Athletic training
  Dental hygiene
  Gerontology
  Nuclear medical technology
  Social work
  Zoology
Nutritional education
  Food sciences and nutrition
Nutritional sciences
  Food sciences and nutrition
  Home economics education
  Nursing

Occupational therapy
  Dental hygiene
  Gerontology
  Music therapy
  Nursing
  Physical therapy
  Special education
Ocean engineering
  Civil engineering
Oceanography
  Atmospheric sciences and
    meteorology
  Fisheries and wildlife
  Geology
  Physics
Operations research (quantitative
  methods)
  Business administration
  Information sciences and
    systems
  Management
  Management science
  Statistics
Organic chemistry
  Physics
Ornamental horticulture
  Landscape architecture
Other foreign languages
  Comparative literature

German
Other literature and language
  majors
  Classics
  Comparative literature
  French
  Spanish

Painting
  Graphic design
Parasitology
  Entomology
Parks and recreation management
  Fisheries and wildlife
  Urban studies
Petroleum engineering
  Mechanical engineering
Pharmacy
  Nuclear medical technology
  Nursing
Philosophy
  Art history
  Asian studies
  Bible studies
  Chinese
  Classics
  Comparative literature
  Computer science
  Dramatic arts/theater
  Economics
  English
  English education
  European studies
  Fine arts
  French
  German
  Jewish studies
  Linguistics
  Political science and
    government
  Religion
  Sociology
  Theological studies
  Women's studies
Photography
  Art education
  Film arts
  Graphic design
Physical chemistry
  Chemistry
  Physics
Physical education
  Dance
  Elementary education
  Food sciences and nutrition
  Parks and recreation
    management
Physical therapy
  Athletic training
  Dance

Dental hygiene
Nursing
Occupational therapy
Parks and recreation
  management
Physical education
Social work
Special education
Physician's assistant
  Athletic training
Physics
  Aerospace/aeronautical
    engineering
  Astronomy
  Atmospheric sciences and
    meteorology
  Biophysics
  Chemistry
  Electrical engineering
  Geophysics
  Materials/metallurgical
    engineering
  Mathematics
  Mathematics education
  Nuclear medical technology
  Philosophy
  Science education
  Secondary education
Physiology, human and animal
  Marine biology
Plant pathology
  Agronomy
  Botany
  Entomology
  Horticultural science
Plant sciences
  Animal sciences
  Botany
Political science and government
  Afro-American studies
  American literature
  American studies
  Anthropology
  Asian studies
  City, community, and regional
    planning
  Classics
  Criminal justice studies
  Dramatic arts/theater
  Economics
  European studies
  French
  Geography
  German
  History
  Housing and human
    development
  International relations
  Italian
  Middle Eastern studies

Public administration
Public relations
Russian
Social studies education
Sociology
Spanish
Theological studies
Urban studies
Portuguese
Latin American studies
Predentistry
Clinical laboratory science
Dental hygiene
Pharmacy
Physical therapy
Prelaw
Criminal justice studies
Premedicine
Chemistry
Clinical laboratory science
Pharmacy
Physical therapy
Zoology
Preveterinary
Animal sciences
Clinical laboratory science
Zoology
Printmaking
Graphic design
Psychology
Afro-American studies
Anthropology
Athletic training
Bible studies
Biology
Computer science
Dramatic arts/theater
Early childhood education
Economics
Elementary education
English education
Family/consumer resource
management
Gerontology
Home economics
Housing and human
development
Human resources management
Individual and family
development
Linguistics
Marketing
Mathematics education
Music therapy
Occupational therapy
Parks and recreation
management
Political science and
government
Public relations

Religion
Social work
Sociology
Special education
Speech pathology/audiology
Textiles and clothing
Women's studies
Zoology
Public administration
Business administration
City, community, and regional
planning
Family/consumer resource
management
Finance
Geography
Health services management
Management
Marketing
Political science and
government
Public relations
Real estate
Public relations
Arts management
Journalism
Marketing
Pure mathematics
Mathematics

Radio/television broadcasting
Communications
Film arts
Journalism
Radiograph medical technology
Nuclear medical technology
Range management
Agribusiness
Agronomy
Real estate
Accounting
Finance
Hotel/motel and restaurant
management
Recreation and community
services technologies
Gerontology
Recreation therapy
Occupational therapy
Physical therapy
Rehabilitation counseling/services
Individual and family
development
Occupational therapy
Religion
Anthropology
Bible studies
Chinese
European studies
Jewish studies

Philosophy
Religious music
Theological studies
Religious music
Music
Music education
Russian
International business
management
Russian and Slavic studies
International business
management

Science education
Environmental studies
Secondary education
Technology (industrial arts)
education
Secondary education
Elementary education
Home economics
Science education
Social studies education
Special education
Slavic languages (other than
Russian)
Russian
Social studies education
Secondary education
Social work
Afro-American studies
City, community, and regional
planning
Criminal justice studies
Early childhood education
Family/consumer resource
management
Gerontology
Home economics
Individual and family
development
Music therapy
Nursing
Occupational therapy
Psychology
Urban studies
Sociology
Afro-American studies
American studies
Anthropology
Asian studies
Bible studies
City, community, and regional
planning
Communications
Criminal justice studies
Economics
Family/consumer resource
management
Geography

Gerontology
History
Home economics
Housing and human
    development
Human resources
    management
Individual and family
    development
International relations
Management
Marketing
Parks and recreation
    management
Physical education
Political science and
    government
Psychology
Public administration
Religion
Social work
Speech pathology/audiology
Theological studies
Women's studies
Soil sciences
Agribusiness
Geology
Spanish
Italian
Latin American studies
Special education
Day care administration
Early childhood education
Elementary education
English education
Individual and family
    development
Music therapy
Speech pathology/audiology
Speech
History
Music therapy
Nursing
Psychology
Social work
Special education
Speech correction
Music therapy
Speech pathology/audiology
Nursing
Psychology
Social work
Special education
Sports management
Physical education
Sports medicine
Parks and recreation
    management
Physical education
Psychology

Statistics
Accounting
Business administration
Economics
Finance
Marketing
Mathematics
Mathematics education
Studio art
Art education
Art history
Systems analysis
Information sciences and
    systems
Systems engineering
Aerospace/aeronautical
    engineering
Management science

Telecommunications
Communications
Textile engineering
Textiles and clothing
Textile technology
Home economics education
Textiles and clothing
Theater design
Studio art
Theological studies
Religious music
Tourism
Hotel/motel and restaurant
    management
Trade and industrial education
Agricultural education
Technology (industrial arts)
    education
Transportation and travel
    marketing
Hotel/motel and restaurant
    management

Urban studies
Psychology
Public administration
Real estate

Video
Graphic design
Photography

Wildlife management
Environmental studies
Fisheries and wildlife
Forestry
Parks and recreation
    management
Zoology
Women's studies
Afro-American studies

Comparative literature
English
English education
Psychology
Religion

Zoology
Biology
Botany
Oceanography
Wildlife management

Alphabetical List of Majors

Selected Books and Software from the College Board

Annual college directories

The Scholarship Handbook with *FUND FINDER* **CD-ROM, 1999**. All-new, authoritative listing of scholarships, grants, internships, and loans for undergraduate and graduate students. Detailed information on 3,300 programs in quick, easy-to-use format. 832 pages, paperbound. **Item# 005945** $24.95

The College Handbook with *College Explorer* **CD-ROM, 1999**. "Still the best resource of its kind, the bible of college description guides." — *Randax Education Guide*. Over 2 million copies sold. The only one-volume guide to the nation's 3,300 two- and four-year colleges. 1,700 pages, paperbound. **Item# 005902** $25.95

College Costs and Financial Aid Handbook, 1999. "...an excellent resource" — *Randax Education Guide*. Detailed cost and financial aid information at 3,100 two- and four-year institutions; includes indexed information on college scholarships. 700 pages, paperbound. **Item# 005910** $21.95

Index of Majors and Graduate Degrees, 1999. "A comprehensive, no-nonsense guide" — *The New York Times*. Covers 580 undergraduate majors, 470 master's degree programs, 380 doctoral programs, 10 professional programs, including law, medicine, and dentistry. 682 pages, paperbound. **Item# 005929** $18.95

International Student Handbook of U.S. Colleges, 1999. Provides students outside the U.S. with information they need to apply for study at 3,000 U.S. colleges, including costs, required tests, availability of financial aid, ESL programs. 320 pages, paperbound. **Item# 005937** $21.95

Test prep for College Board programs

10 Real SATs. From the College Board, official source of the SAT: 10 real, complete SATs for student practice, including the one administered in May 1997. With test-taking tips from the test makers themselves. 600 pages, paperbound. **Item# 005678** $17.95

Real SAT® II: Subject Tests. The *only* source of real SAT II practice questions from cover to cover—in a newly revised updated edition. 700 pages paperbound. **Item# 005996** $17.95

AP CD-ROM in U.S. History, 1999. This valuable study tool was designed to complement the written preparation materials provided in the classroom. **Item # 201847** $49.00

AP CD-ROM in English Literature, 1999. This valuable study tool was designed to compliment the written preparation materials provided in the classroom. **Item # 201849** $49.00

One-on-One with the SAT. Invaluable advice and test-taking strategies from the SAT test makers themselves, plus the opportunity to take a real, complete SAT on computer. (Home Version—Windows) **Item# 005139** $29.95

The Official Study Guide for the CLEP Examinations 1999. Learn what CLEP exams are all about and which ones to take to get college credit. Only guide to cover all 34 CLEP exams with sample questions for all tests. 500 pages, paperbound. **Item# 005953** $18.00

General guidance for students and parents

The College Application Essay, Sarah Myers McGinty. Application essay policies of more than 180 institutions, types of questions asked, plus 40 actual questions and analyses of 6 essays. 131 pages, paperbound. **Item# 005759** $12.95

The Internet Guide for College-Bound Students, Kenneth E. Hartman. How to surf the net to get insider opinions as well as official facts about colleges, evaluate college information, find sources of scholarships, much more. 250 pages, paperbound. **Item# 006011** $14.95

Campus Health Guide, Carol L. Otis, M.D., and Roger Goldingay. "...sensible, practical advice based on sound medical science." — Jane E. Brody, *The New York Times*. Stresses the link between a healthy life-style and a productive college experience. Covers birth control, AIDS, alcoholism, suicide, eating disorders, stress, much more. 460 pages, paperbound. **Item# 003179** $14.95

Campus Visits and College Interviews, Zola Dincin Schneider. "...must reading for students and parents." — *The Book Report*. Why they are important, when to visit, what to look for, questions usually asked, much more. 126 pages, paperbound. **Item# 002601** $9.95

Choosing a College: The Student's Step-by-Step Decision-Making Workbook, Gordon Porter Miller. "...an excellent tool..." — *Tri-State YA Book Review Committee, Drexel University*. With exercises, quizzes, and worksheets. 165 pages, paperbound. **Item# 003330** $9.95

The College Board Guide to 150 Popular College Majors. One-of-a-kind reference to majors in 17 fields, with related information on typical courses, high school preparation, much more. 377 pages, paperbound. **Item# 004000** $16.00

The College Board Guide to Jobs and Career Planning, Second Edition, Joyce Slayton Mitchell. Detailed descriptions of more than 100 occupations, with educational requirements, income range, more. 331 pages, paperbound. **Item# 004671** $14.00

The College Guide for Parents, Third Edition, Charles J. Shields. Helps parents guide their teenagers through the entire college admission process, from taking the right courses to applying for financial aid. 187 pages, paperbound. **Item# 004744** $14.00

The Parents' Guide to Paying for College, Gerald Krefetz. Expert advice from a well-known investment analyst and financial consultant on covering college costs, with case studies. 158 pages, paperbound. **Item# 006046** $14.95

Summer on Campus: College Experience for High School Students, Introduction by Shirley Levin. Comprehensive information on more than 450 academic summer programs at over 350 institutions nationwide. 321 pages, paperbound. **Item# 005260** $15.00

Your College Application, Revised and Updated, Scott Gelband, Catherine Kubale, and Eric Schorr. Practical advice from admission professionals on how to document strong points, demonstrate abilities, interests, goals, character, more. 139 pages, paperbound. **Item# 004280** $9.95

Order Form

Mail order form to: College Board Publications, Dept. Y09, Two College Way, Forrester Center, WV 25438 *(payment must accompany all orders)*
or **phone:** (800)323-7155, M–F, 8 am–11 pm Eastern Time *(credit card orders only)*
or **fax 24 hours, 7 days a week to:** (800)525-5562 *(credit card orders only)*
or **online** through the College Board Online Store at *www.collegeboard.org (credit card orders only)*

Item No.	Title	Price	Amount
	Annual college directories		
005945	The Scholarship Handbook with *FUND FINDER* CD-ROM, 1999	$24.95	
005902	The College Handbook with *College Explorer* CD-ROM, 1999	$25.95	
005910	College Costs and Financial Aid Handbook, 1999	$21.95	
005929	Index of Majors and Graduate Degrees, 1999	$18.95	
005937	International Student Handbook of U.S. Colleges, 1999	$21.95	
239414	1999 3-book set: *College Handbook, Scholarship Handbook, College Costs and Financial Aid Handbook*	$45.00	
239413	1999 International 3-book set: *International Student Handbook, College Handbook, Index of Majors*	$45.00	
	Test prep for College Board programs		
201849	AP CD-ROM in English Literature	$49.00	
201847	AP CD-ROM in U.S. History	$49.00	
005678	10 Real SATs	$17.95	
005139	One-on-One with the SAT (Home version, Windows)	$29.95	
005953	The Official Study Guide for the CLEP Examinations, 1999	$18.00	
005996	Real SAT II: Subject Tests	$17.95	
	General guidance for students and parents		
005759	The College Application Essay	$12.95	
006011	Internet Guide for College Bound Students	$14.95	
003179	Campus Health Guide	$14.95	
002601	Campus Visits and College Interviews	$ 9.95	
003330	Choosing a College	$ 9.95	
004000	College Board Guide to 150 Popular College Majors	$16.00	
004671	College Board Guide to Jobs and Career Planning	$14.00	
004744	College Guide for Parents	$14.00	
006046	The Parents' Guide to Paying for College	$14.95	
005260	Summer on Campus	$15.00	
004280	Your College Application	$ 9.95	

Subtotal $ _____

Shipping and Handling
$0 - $20.00 = $4.00
$20.01 - $40.00 = $5.00
$40.01 - $60.00 = $6.00
$60.01+ = 10% of dollar value of order

Shipping and handling $ _____

Total $ _____

Sales Tax: $ _____
(IL,CA,FL,GA,PA,DC,MA,TX,VA,WV, Can.)

Grand Total $ _____

❑ Enclosed is my check or money order made payable to the ***College Board***

❑ Please charge my ❑ MasterCard ❑ Visa ❑ American Express ❑ Discover

| | | | | | exp. date: _____/_____ | |
card number   month   year   cardholder's signature

Allow two weeks from receipt of order for delivery.

SHIP TO:

Name _____ Street Address *(no P. O. Box numbers, please)* _____

City _____ State _____ Zip _____ (_____) _____
Telephone

Now students can practice on real, complete SATs from the College Board—the people who bring you the test!

includes

- ten complete, actual SATs, including the one administered in May 1997, plus information on the PSAT/NMSQT
- tips for improving scores
- pointers for making educated guesses
- hints on pacing
- test-taking advice for both the verbal and math sections

Item # 005678, 670 pages, paperbound, $17.95

One-on-One with the SAT®

The only software that exclusively uses real SAT questions to diagnose strengths and weaknesses to help you get ready for the test

- allows you to take a real SAT on screen
- uses results to build a study plan that helps you focus on weak areas
- provides complete explanations for every answer choice—correct or incorrect, plus on-screen lessons, hints, and hundreds of actual SAT questions for practice

For Windows®
Home Version
Item # 005139 $49.95

Hardware requirements:
386 processor or faster, IBM or 100% compatible PC, with at least 4 MB RAM running under Windows 3.1 or higher, VGA monitor, hard drive with 10 MB of free space, sound card recommended.

The Only Book and CD-ROM with Complete Facts and Figures About All 3,200 U.S. Colleges

The College Handbook 1999

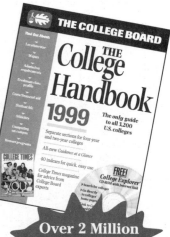

"Still the best resource of its kind, the bible of college description guides."
— Randax Education Guide, 1998 edition

The College Handbook 1999 has been enhanced and redesigned from cover to cover. And now it includes a Windows® version of *College Explorer*® on CD-ROM. This award-winning software lets students quickly pinpoint the colleges that have exactly what they want, then get in-depth information from the *Handbook*. With the click of a button, they can also link to any college's Web site for even more information.

Hardware Requirements: Minimum 486-66 MHz; Windows 3.11 or higher; 8 MB of RAM; 640 × 480 screen resolution, 256 colors; 4X CD-ROM drive.

005902 ISBN: 0-87447-590-2, 1998, 1,754 pages, Windows CD-ROM, $25.95

Over 2 Million Copies Sold

All-New, Expanded Edition Packed with In-Depth Cost and Financial Aid Information

College Costs & Financial Aid Handbook 1999

In addition to authoritative, up-to-date information on tuition, fees, and room and board costs, each college description in new, easy-to-read format, includes:

- average undergraduate financial aid package
- number of freshmen applying for aid and judged to have need
- average percent of estimated need met
- average scholarship amount
- policies to reduce costs
- special payment plans, and more

005910 ISBN: 0-87447-591-0, 1998, 700 pages, $21.95

All-New Book with CD-ROM Helps Students Find Private, State, and Federal Scholarships. Includes Award-Winning FUND FINDER™ Software

The Scholarship Handbook 1999

Students can quickly search nearly 3,300 programs in the College Board's authoritative data base—over 700,000 awards in all—to get a list of the awards for which they're eligible. Then they can go directly to *The Scholarship Handbook* to get detailed facts about each program on their list. They can also use the CD-ROM to link to the Internet to explore other college-funding options.

Also included: expert advice on exploring financial aid opportunities, avoiding scholarship scams, and innovative strategies for planning to pay for college.

Hardware Requirements: Minimum 486-66 MHz; Windows 3.11 or higher; 8 MB of RAM; 640 × 480 screen resolution, 256 colors; 4X CD-ROM drive.

005945 ISBN: 0-87447-594-5, 1998, 620 pages, Windows CD-ROM, $24.95 (available September 1998).

Visit the College Board on the World Wide Web!

College Board online™

educational excellence for all students

what's new

news from College Board

search

STARTING POINTS

STUDENTS & PARENTS

ADMISSION STAFF

FINANCIAL AID STAFF

COUNSELORS

HIGH SCHOOL & COLLEGE FACULTY

COLLEGE BOARD MEMBERS

DIRECTORY OF SERVICES

HIGHLIGHTS

SAT® question of the day

College Board test dates

college search

scholarship search

online SAT® registration

store   library   help   communication

www.collegeboard.org